Starting, Buying, and Owning the Medical Practice

Practice Success Series

Max Reiboldt, CPA

AMERICAN
MEDICAL
ASSOCIATION

Library of Congress Cataloging-in-Publication Data

Reiboldt, J. Max.
  Starting, buying, and owning the medical practice / Coker Group.—
1st ed.
      p. cm.
  Includes bibliographical references and index.
  ISBN 978-1-60359-606-0
1. Medicine—Practice. 2. Physician practice acquisitions. I. Coker
Group II. American Medical Association. III. Title.
  R728.R4453 2012
  610.68—dc23   2011036418

ISBN: 978-1-60359-606-0
BQ13: 11-P-041

CONTENTS

PREFACE

AS COLLABORATION AND ACCOUNTABILITY are reshaping the future of health care organizations, medical practices are responding to the challenges with appropriate adaptations. Providers beginning the journey in medical practice with practice startups and mature practices moving toward more coordinated, accountable care are discovering a variety of partnerships and strategies to deploy to achieve their goals.

Starting, Buying, and Owning the Medical Practice, another vital part of the Practice Success series, is intended to help equip physicians with the know-how to start, buy, and own a practice in a way that suits today's marketplace. Therefore, the book is organized into three parts to reflect the vital and different parts of starting, buying, and owning a medical practice.

Part One, Chapters 1 through 9, presents the fundamentals of practice startup, such as planning and starting the business, selecting a professional path, regulations and licensing, and society memberships and affiliations.

In Part Two, Chapters 10 through 15, the concentration is on practice ownership, encompassing operational policies and procedures; procurement and equipping the practice with information technology; identifying insurance requirements, financial considerations, and assets, followed by guidelines for personnel management, revenue cycle protocols, loss prevention, and establishing policies and procedures for the well-run practice. Marketing and business development are discussed in the final chapter in this section.

For the practice or provider organization that is already established and seeking collaborative relationships, Part Three, Chapters 16 through 20, addresses physician alignment strategies, practice acquisitions, and equity arrangements. Final chapters concentrate on informative topics such as physician diversification and practice mergers.

Regardless of the stage of practice, the status of the provider, or the size of the organization, the information in this book serves as a framework for making the right decisions about medical practice for the present and future.

x

ACKNOWLEDGMENTS

BOOKS WRITTEN BY EMPLOYEES of Coker Group are always touched by many people both inside and outside of our organization. This work is no exception. First, we would like to give a special thanks to the contributions made by our fellow Coker family for their expertise on this project: Justin Chamblee, Karen Chamblee, Cynthia Cox, Aimee Greeter, Sue Hertlein, Deborah Hill, Craig Hunter, Trish Hutcherson, Christine Ingram, Michelle Johnson, Rick Langosch, Crystal Reeves, Mark Reiboldt, Jared Thomas, and Yong Zhang. In addition to our primary author, Max Reiboldt, we thank you for extending your knowledge from your many years of working with medical practices and physician networks.

Kay Stanley, who has contributed to Coker's 50-plus books since Coker's publishing initiative began in the early 1990s, has served as editor. Serving as project manager, Trish Hutcherson has overseen the assignments and kept all contributors on course. Lastly, we appreciate the confidence of Carol Brockman, Continuity Editor at the AMA, in supporting this project and allowing us to expand the *Practice Success* series.

ABOUT THE AUTHOR

MAX REIBOLDT PROVIDES SOUND financial and strategic solutions to hospitals, medical practices, health systems, and other health care entities through keen analysis and problem solving. Working with organizations of all sizes, Reiboldt engages in consulting projects with organizations nationwide. His expertise encompasses employee and physician employment and compensation, physician/hospital affiliation initiatives, business and strategic planning, mergers and acquisitions, practice operational assessments, ancillary services development, PHO/IPA/MSO development, practice appraisals, and negotiations for acquisitions and sales. He also performs financial analyses for health care entities as well as buy/sell agreements and planning arrangements for medical practices.

Reiboldt is President and Chief Executive Officer of Coker Group and has led the firm's growth since the late 1990s to its position today as one of the leading health care consulting firms in the United States and abroad. He is a prolific author and accomplished public speaker on health care management topics.

Reiboldt has authored or contributed to many of Coker Group's 50-plus books. Recent titles include *Selling, Closing, and Valuing the Medical Practice* (AMA, 2012); *Financial Management of the Veterinary Practice* (AAHA, 2010); *RVUs at Work: Relative Value Units in the Medical Practice* (Greenbranch Publishing, 2010); *Physician Entrepreneurs: Strength in Numbers—Consolidation and Collaboration Strategies to Grow Your Practice* (HealthLeaders Media, 2008); *Physician Entrepreneurs: Going Retail—Business Strategies to Grow Beyond Traditional Practice Models* (HealthLeaders Media, 2007); *Financial Management of the Medical Practice,* Third Edition (AMA, 2011); and *Reimbursement Management: Improving the Success and Profitability of Your Practice* (AMA, 2011).

A graduate of Harding University, Reiboldt is a licensed Certified Public Accountant (CPA) in Georgia and Louisiana, and a member of the American Institute of Certified Public Accountants, Healthcare Financial Management Association, and American Society of Appraisers.

CONTRIBUTORS

Justin Chamblee   Justin Chamblee, a Senior Manager at Coker Group, works with clients in a variety of strategic and financial areas, mainly dealing with physician compensation and hospital-physician transactions. This includes the development and redesign of physician compensation plans for private practices and hospital-employed settings, as well as providing guidance to hospitals, physicians, and legal counsel as to the appropriateness of transactions between a hospital and a physician.

Chamblee has been a major contributor to recent Coker publications, including *Selling, Closing, and Valuing the Medical Practice* (AMA, 2012); *Financial Management of the Veterinary Practice* (AAHA, 2010); *RVUs at Work: Relative Value Units in the Medical Practice* (Greenbranch Publishing, 2010); *Physician Entrepreneurs: Strength in Numbers—Consolidation and Collaboration Strategies to Grow Your Practice* (HealthLeaders Media, 2008); *Physician Entrepreneurs: Going Retail—Business Strategies to Grow Beyond Traditional Practice Models* (HealthLeaders Media, 2007); *Financial Management of the Medical Practice,* Third Edition (AMA, 2011); and *Reimbursement Management: Improving the Success and Profitability of Your Practice* (AMA, 2011). Chamblee holds a Bachelor of Business Administration in Accounting and a Master of Accounting from Abilene Christian University. He is licensed as a Certified Public Accountant (CPA) in the State of Texas and is a member of the American Institute of Certified Public Accountants.

Karen Chamblee   Karen Chamblee manages Coker Group's Client Services Program. In this role, Chamblee contacts active clients on a regular basis to ensure they are satisfied with the work being executed on their behalf. In addition, she solicits recommendations for ways Coker can improve services to its clients and works to proactively resolve any concerns that have been identified. New clients receive personal "welcome letters" providing vital information to assist them as they work with Coker Group. Since this initiative began, Coker's client satisfaction ratings have risen from 98% to 99%. Chamblee has been with Coker Group for 6 years and was formerly the Executive Assistant to Coker Group's President/CEO, prior to initiating the customer service/quality control effort. She was an honors graduate from Harding University and an award-winning educator prior to entering the health care arena.

Cynthia Cox   Cindy Cox, a Senior Associate with Coker Group, has more than 15 years' experience in health care and medical practice management, both in primary care and in multispecialty practices gaining knowledge and experience in many areas of health care. Cox draws on her experience and skill in practice management to assist a diverse group of Coker's clients with myriad operational and financial issues, including operations, accounts receivables, revenue cycle analyses, merger assistance, physician education and training in coding compliance issues, coding analyses, medical chart audits, practice assessments, and interim management assignments. Previous positions on the payer side of insurance have given her priceless insight into collections and other insurance issues.

Cox graduated from Clayton College & State University, attaining a Bachelor of Science with a concentration in health care management. She went on to obtain a Master's degree in Science Management with a concentration in health care management from Troy State University. Cox is also a Certified Professional Coder and a Certified Patient Account Representative.

Aimee Greeter   Aimee Greeter, a Manager in the financial services division within Coker Group, works on a variety of consulting projects, including financial consulting, hospital accounts, practice management initiatives, as well as research and writing for various client projects. In a recent engagement, Greeter coordinated post-merger integration efforts for a faith-based hospital system, with a particular focus on human resources and supply chain management.

Greeter earned a Master of Public Health (MPH) in Health Policy and Management from the Rollins School of Public Health at Emory University. In addition, she was an honors graduate of Michigan State University, where she attained a Bachelor of Science (BS) in Human Biology.

Sue Hertlein   Sue Hertlein, a Manager with Coker Group, has more than 25 years of experience in the health care industry, with a strong background in information technology. Hertlein works with clients across the country on numerous technology, strategic planning, and assessment projects. She manages client relations through her keen sense of customer service and ability to anticipate and address needs and deliver results. Her experience includes operational and workflow analysis, PM/EMR assessments and readiness evaluations, vendor analysis/ recommendations, vendor contract negotiations, systems testing, implementation, project management, and community needs assessments.

In addition to her client work, Hertlein also manages research for Coker and assists in obtaining information on new situations that affect the health care industry, such as health care reform, meaningful use/ EHR incentives, accountable care organizations, etc. She has contributed to a number of Coker's publications, including *The Complete EMR Selection Guide*; AMA's *Financial Management of the Medical Practice*, Third Edition; and numerous technology-related articles and white papers.

Deborah Hill   Deborah B. Hill, a Manager in the practice management area, is responsible for managing the delivery of services to physicians, both through client hospitals and to individual practices. Her broad experience encompasses the following areas: billing management, network contract negotiations, referral resource network, coding and consulting services, coding compliance management, negotiation of vendor contracts, EMR implementation, and provider enrollment and credentialing. Hill holds a Master of Business Administration in Healthcare Administration and a Bachelor of Business Administration in Management. In addition, she is a Certified Professional Coder by the American Academy of Professional Coders, and a Certified Medical Practice Executive by the American College of Medical Practice Executives.

Craig Hunter   Craig Hunter, Senior Vice President for the firm's business development, works with health systems, hospital-based networks, multi- and single-specialty groups, and independent practices, facilitating phases of integration and practice development, including mergers, strategic planning, management reviews, and negotiations. Hunter's focus encompasses network development, manpower plans, operational assessments, compensation plans, and medical staff surveys. Hunter provides integrated network services to hospitals and independent practices. He regularly conducts physician need and feasibility analyses for hospitals and private practices, involving staff planning and market analysis. Assignments entail physician contract preparation, analysis, and negotiations. Hunter speaks frequently to health systems and physician executives, administrators, and other health care personnel, and is a published author on such practice management topics as compensation, integration, and physician recruitment and employment.

Trish Hutcherson   Trish Hutcherson, Coker's Marketing Director, manages the firm's publishing division and is responsible for Coker's overall marketing efforts, including projects such as corporate identity, advertising, marketing collateral, direct mail campaigns, Web branding, and Web site design. She has developed marketing and communications expertise throughout her career, providing communication, creative services, event production, and writing in a wide variety of settings, from small organizations to Fortune 500 companies. Hutcherson has a Bachelor of Arts in Communications from Taylor University.

Christine Ingram   Christine Ingram, a Vice President in Coker's Practice Management service line, has more than 20 years of health care experience. She has amassed expertise in all areas of practice management, using her skills and experience to assist Coker's clients with operational and financial issues.

Since joining Coker Group in 2006, Ingram has engaged in many assignments in a variety of settings. Her work encompasses serving as Interim Executive Director of a hospital-owned employed physician network. In addition, she has served as project director to achieve a performance turnaround for a hospital's employed physician network. Other projects include numerous operational assessments and assistance with mergers. Currently, she is an *ex officio* board member and provides ongoing management assistance for an organization in the Southeast. Her work crosses all specialties including multispecialty, cardiology, pain management, and urology. Ingram has a Master of Science in Healthcare Management from Troy State University and is a member of the Medical Group Management Association and the American College of Healthcare Executives.

Michelle Johnson   Michelle Johnson, Director of Human Resources with Coker Group, is a seasoned human resources professional. Prior to joining Coker Group, Michelle worked with large organizations, including American International Group (AIG). Throughout her career, Johnson has been responsible for leading programs, including recruitment, employment, benefits, employee and labor relations, performance management, and training/organizational development. She is adept at assuring compliance with federal and state laws controlling hiring processes (FLSA, EEO), benefits (FMLA, COBRA), and workplace safety (OSHA). Michelle is a member of the Society for Human Resource Management (SHRM).

Rick Langosch   Rick Langosch, a Senior Vice President, works with hospital clients to realize sustainable improvements at the organizational, departmental, and services levels. Coker Group's Hospital Strategies consulting practice provides timely and responsive solutions to its hospital clients in Service Line Analysis, Staffing/Productivity Benchmarking and Analysis, Interim Management, and RAC Audit Readiness. A veteran health care executive, with more than 25 years of experience managing operations and finance in hospitals and physician practices, Langosch has held a wide range of financial, operational, and information technology responsibilities, including multihospital ownership and hospital senior management positions. He uses that experience to assist Coker clients in developing a specific implementation strategy that will produce improved performance and drive profitability for their organizations. Langosch is a graduate of Eastern Illinois University in Charleston, Illinois, and he is a Fellow with the Healthcare Financial Management Association (HFMA). He is active with the Georgia Chapter of HFMA.

Crystal Reeves   Crystal Reeves, Senior Manager at Coker Group, is responsible for managing the delivery of services to physicians, both through client hospitals and to individual practices. She is a recognized leader in medical practice management in areas pertaining to implementing and refining billing and collection services, improving operations, and physician and staff education. Reeves is a sought-after speaker and consultant presenting seminars nationwide on coding and reimbursement, documentation guidelines, front desk operations, and customer service. She is a prolific speaker for associations at the national and state levels, and she has contributed to several of Coker's 50-plus books.

Reeves is certified by the American Academy of Professional Coders (AAPC) and has achieved the status of Certified Medical Practice Executive through the Medical Group Management Association's American College of Medical Practice Executives. In addition, she has attained recognition from the AAPC for coding proficiency in the specialty of oncology.

Mark Reiboldt   Mark Reiboldt, Vice President at Coker Capital Advisors, is also Co-Leader of Coker Group's Financial Advisory Services group. Previously, Reiboldt was with Coker Group, a leading management and strategic consulting firm focused on the health care and life sciences industries. During his tenure, Reiboldt executed numerous strategy, transaction, and strategic financial advisory assignments for the firm's clients. Prior to Coker Group, Reiboldt was with Trammell Crow Company, where he executed transactions for firms in the financial services and communications sectors. Reiboldt has also been a political advisor to numerous elected officials and candidates in Washington DC and throughout the United States. Reiboldt serves on the boards of numerous for-profit and not-for-profit organizations within health care and other sectors. He received a Bachelor of Arts in Political Science from Georgia State University and a Master of Science in Financial Economics from the University of London.

Jared Thomas   Jared Thomas, an experienced attorney and business professional, is the Assistant Prosecuting Attorney in the city of Joplin, Missouri. Thomas provides legal advice and interpretations of federal laws, regulations, statutes, and ordinances, as well as litigates matters for several municipalities in Southwest Missouri. Thomas maintains a private law practice in Neosho, Missouri that focuses primarily on estate and financial planning, health care law, real estate, and small business. His experience includes litigator in contract, tax, real estate, health care, corporate mergers and acquisition, and insurance matters. Thomas holds a Bachelor of Science in Criminal Justice from Missouri Southern State University and is a graduate of the University of Tulsa (Juris Doctor). Thomas is a member of the State of Missouri Bar and licensed as an attorney and counselor at law.

Yong Zhang   Yong Zhang, a Manager with Coker Capital Advisors, previously spent 4 years with Coker Group, a leading management and strategic consulting firm focused on the health care and life sciences industries. During her tenure with Coker Group, Zhang worked for the firm's financial services group where she assisted in mergers and acquisitions, valuations and fairness opinions, and numerous advisory assignments across a wide spectrum of health care subsectors. Zhang earned her Bachelor of Accounting (BAcc) at Fudan University in Shanghai, China, and her Master of Accountancy (MAcc) from the University of Georgia. Prior to her position at Coker Group, Zhang was an accountant at General Motors of China. Zhang is a Certified Public Accountant (CPA) in Georgia and is in the process of completing her Accredited Senior Appraiser (ASA) designation. Zhang is fluent in Mandarin and Chinese dialect, Shanghainese.

REVIEWER

THE AMA AND THE AUTHORS wish to thank Carol Scheele, JD, who has graciously and thoughtfully assisted the AMA and the authors with the peer review. Her significant and valued insights and contribution have made this a better book.

ABOUT COKER GROUP

COKER GROUP, A LEADER in health care consulting, helps providers achieve improved financial and operational results through sound business principles. The consulting team members are proficient, trustworthy professionals with expertise and strengths in various areas. Coker Group represents four service lines: Coker Consulting, Coker Capital Advisors, Coker Technology, and Executive Search. Through these service areas, Coker consultants enable providers to concentrate on patient care.

Coker Group's nationwide client base includes major health systems, hospitals, physician and specialty groups, and solo practitioners in a full spectrum of engagements. Coker Group has gained a reputation since 1987 for thorough, efficient, and cost-conscious work to benefit its clients financially and operationally. The firm prides itself on its client profile of recognized and respected health care professionals through the industry. The firm's exceptional consulting team has health care, technical, financial, and business knowledge and offers comprehensive programs, services, and training to yield long-term solutions and turnarounds. Coker staff members are devoted to helping health care providers face today's challenges for tomorrow's successes.

Service areas include:
- Capital advisory and strategic financial advisory and analysis
- Strategic planning/business planning
- ACO readiness
- Practice operational assessments
- Physician network development
- Disengagements of practices and network unwinds
- Hospital-physician alignment
- Practice management, billing and collections reviews, chart audits
- Compensation
- Post-merger integration and implementation
- Hospital services, medical staff development
- Executive search
- Interim and long-term network management
- Practice appraisals

- Practice start-ups
- Buy/sell and equity analysis
- Group formation and dissolution
- Practice acquisition, mergers, and due diligence
- Compensation reviews, FMV opinion services, and call coverage compensation
- HIPAA assessments and compliance
- MSA development
- Revenue cycle management and procedural coding analysis
- Compliance plans
- Policy and procedure manuals
- Medication and expert witnessing
- Strategic information technology planning and review, including EMR
- HIT software/hardware vendor vetting and procurement
- Contract negotiations
- Project management
- Managed IT services
- Educational programs, workshops, and training

For more information, please contact:

Coker Group
1000 Mansell Exchange West
Suite 310
Alpharetta, GA 30022
800-345-5829
www.cokergroup.com

PART ONE

Practice Start-Up Functions

What does it take to start a new medical practice? It takes planning; establishing a business entity; knowing the professional path to take; adhering to regulations and licensing requirements; belonging to the right organizations; setting up operational policies, procedures, and processes; purchasing information technology; identifying insurance requirements; and obtaining financial backing. Chapters 1 through 9 address the spectrum of knowledge that every physician will need in starting out in medical practice.

Getting Started

The purpose of this chapter is to set forth the processes for establishing your medical practice and recommend the appropriate resources to help you get off to a good start. By strategically mapping out an action plan with a timeline, you will be able to approach this initiative systematically and in accord with your goals and desired results.

Factors Influencing Your Decision

Reaching the decision to start your own practice can evolve from a number of influencing factors depending on your goals, objectives, and, most importantly, your aspirations. The range of starting points will vary depending upon your personality, your unique circumstances, and the current phase of your professional career.

It is important to start organizing your decisions early and to allow plenty of time for adjustments or alternative considerations. Personal networking and professional advice are wonderful ways for you to obtain an inside perspective into what you may be considering and what to expect. At the beginning of this initiative, a number of influencing factors will exist, but none will be more vital than your personal aspirations and desire for success. Table 1-1 is a decision-making tool to help with the process.

TABLE 1-1   Practice Style Decision Maker

Circle the answer that applies.

Questions	Sole Proprietor	Partnership or Group Practice— Part-Owner	Employed
1. Do you prefer to make your own decisions?	Yes	Somewhat	No
2. Are you comfortable with making difficult decisions?	Yes	Somewhat	No
3. Are you organized and detail-oriented?	Yes	Somewhat	No
4. Do you perform well under productivity incentives to see X number of patients?	No	Somewhat	Yes
5. Do you perform well when having your clinical utilization monitored?	No	Somewhat	Yes
6. Do you enjoy marketing and networking?	Yes	Somewhat	No
7. Are you willing to compromise on your objectives or settle on an issue?	No	Somewhat	Yes
8. Are you a competent record keeper?	Yes	Somewhat	No
9. Do you enjoy managing and leadership?	Yes	Somewhat	No
10. Are you good at containing expenses?	Yes	Somewhat	No
11. Do you have the mindset of a business owner who can focus on profits in addition to patient care?	Yes	Somewhat	No
TOTAL:			

How Did You Score?

After answering the questions in Table 1-1, which column contained the highest score?

Sole Proprietor

If you scored the highest in the sole proprietor or solo practitioner column, you will likely be most comfortable as the principal/primary owner of your own medical practice. You may at some point, however, consider employing other physicians or mid-level providers. Furthermore, you may consider allowing a partner to buy into the practice at some point; you will likely always want to maintain for yourself the position of majority shareholder.

The advantages to being a sole proprietor include being able to develop the practice as you would like without having to be concerned with other physicians' wishes. The disadvantages of a sole proprietorship include having to find someone to cover your patients while you are away, overseeing business matters that may take time from patient care, and being able to provide competitive benefits for employees.

Partnership or Group Practice

Always a good starting point to test comfort level with running your own practice, a partnership or group practice will enable you to experience the environment and share the responsibility with your colleagues. New physicians may choose to join an established group practice initially to help them decide whether to form their own partnership or group. Typically, group practice agreements contain a clause that outlines the track to partnership. This agreement will include the organization's expectations of its new physicians and provide a timeline for when a new physician can expect to become a partner. It should also provide information on financial terms of becoming a partner. Many physicians choose this environment to learn from senior physicians and to collaborate in patient care. In order to have a positive experience in joining a group or partnership, it is important that you fully understand the culture, its leadership, its goals, and your personal responsibility within the group. Moreover, take time to fully understand your contract, especially the termination and non-compete provisions. Group practices vary widely in organizational structure, management, and leadership. While some are designed to allow for new physician and non-partners' input and growth, others establish an executive team that makes all major decisions. If your intent is to join a group practice for a short period in order to gain practice management experience, you will want to make sure that the group you choose provides a learning, rather than autocratic, environment. If you join a group practice with the intent of becoming a future partner, you will want to have some guarantee as to when that option would be available to you and the financial requirements to realize that goal.

The advantages to a group practice include shared call coverage, access to other physicians' knowledge and expertise, and shared personnel to handle administrative tasks. The disadvantages include having to gain a consensus in order to make a change.

For those physicians who are interested in starting their own group practice, it will be important to obtain professional assistance in developing the partnership agreement.

Employed

If you scored highest in the employed column, it does not necessarily mean that owning your own practice is not a viable option for you. Many successful solo practitioners started off as employed physicians with full intentions of starting their own practice in a year or two. Starting off as an employed physician provides exposure to how a medical practice operates, and it will give you some time to save money for a sole proprietorship. Employment opportunities exist with established group practices, hospital networks, and locum tenens staffing firms. Working as a locum tenens offers an opportunity to work in and explore different geographical locations before deciding on an area in which to start your own practice.

The advantages of being employed include having a regular paycheck and benefits as well as being relieved of administrative responsibilities. The disadvantages to employment include not having significant input into policies and procedures, reduced control of staff and staffing issues, and typically being held to a productivity standard.

No single approach is better than the others. It is a matter of personal preference, economic considerations, and available opportunities. However, every physician starting out in practice shares the common objective to be successful. The focus of this chapter is to help you consider the decisions that you will need to make when starting your own practice in order to be successful. Various options, such as employment, group practices, partnerships, and practice structures, are addressed in Chapter 2, Choosing an Organizational Structure.

Next we will explore some factors and decisions that will contribute to the success of a medical practice.

Helping Ensure Your Success

Knowing where you are needed and, more importantly, knowing exactly how to position your practice within that community can determine whether or not you will be successful. There are several factors to consider when choosing a practice's location. As could be expected, the majority of physicians prefer to practice in an urban or suburban area that can provide them with many of the benefits we have mentioned:

- Professional growth opportunities for themselves and their partners
- Good schools for their children
- Close proximity to airports and public transportation

Professionals you know can provide valuable information concerning practice opportunities. Professional relationships include those that were formed during medical school and residency and those with practicing physicians who have influenced your career. These contacts can provide you with information on the health care environment where they practice, and they may be able to put you in touch with a contact in an area you have interest in. They may know of groups who are looking to add employed physicians or partnership opportunities. As you begin your practice, professional relationships will also be important for patient referrals, coverage for your patients when you are away, and your own professional growth.

Professional opportunities encompass what an area offers for continuing education, professional stimulation, and the opportunity to practice in a hospital offering the most advanced technology and facilities. If you bring a different specialty or new technique to a community, you may find opportunities that are not offered elsewhere. You may want to review a potential hospital's standings with accreditation and rating organizations, available at websites such as www.qualitycheck.org or www.healthgrades.com (for informal patient opinions).[1] Also, you will want to consider whether the area provides opportunities for professional growth for your spouse or partner.

Where you went to medical school, your residency program location, and your place of birth may all influence your choice of location. Nearly 50% of physicians who practice in towns with populations less than 2,500 grew up in towns of similar size. Studies suggest that there is also a strong relationship between location of postgraduate training and the location of a private practice.

Salary or income potential and cost of living are also strong determinants in the choice of geographical location. Before choosing a location, determine if the area in question is an area of need, in a depressed economy, or in an area of rapid growth. Depending on your specialty, you should learn whether the growth in the area is due to such factors as an influx of young families or a booming retirement community.

Communities that are designated as medically underserved areas (MUAs) or Health Professional Shortage Areas (HRSA) by the US Department of Health and Human Services offer payment incentives (such as Medicare's health scarcity area incentives) and loan repayment to physicians practicing in both urban and rural medically underserved areas.[2] The National Health Service Corps (see nhsc.hrsa.gov) loan repayment program is offered to qualified primary care and some specialty providers (see www.cms.gov/center/rural.asp).[3] Research the demographics of the location for the per capita income, age, payer and gender mix and inquire at the hospital whether the area needs additional physicians in the specialty or if the area is considered a Health Professional Shortage Area

Your personality and your specialty will influence whether you would be content to establish your practice in a rural area. Although 20% of the US population lives in rural areas, only 9% of physicians practice there, and only 3% of recent medical school graduates plan to do so. Most rural physicians are primary care physicians, while family physicians belong to the only specialty group that distributes itself proportionally to the population in rural and urban areas.[4]

The quality and availability of housing, cultural opportunities, and the educational system should all be considered when selecting a location. Proximity to a major airport, public transportation, and recreational opportunities may also influence your decision. Finally, climate and even quality of the environment may be factors to consider.

Hospital proximity, physician back-up and on-call arrangements, religious affiliations, group practice opportunities, the willingness of other physicians to refer patients, and professional support are important.

The new physician entering solo practice will also want to check availability and average cost per square foot for office space and the availability of qualified professional and support staff.

Take the time to write down your objectives, constraints, and goals for success. Use that information to help you in the decision-making process. Many sources are available for obtaining information about practice opportunities in geographic locations that best suit your needs.

Where to Look for Employment Opportunities

The following is a brief list of places to look for employment opportunities:

- Residency program directors
- American Medical Association's placement service
- Specialty society placement service
- State and county medical societies
- Classified ads in journals (eg, *Journal of the American Medical Association, New England Journal of Medicine,* and specialty journals)
- Physician recruitment companies
- Advertisements on hospital and academic medical center Web sites

The Effect of Malpractice Premiums on Practice Location

Malpractice insurance costs also represent an economic factor to consider. Malpractice costs and environment vary widely from state to state and between specialties, so these costs should be factored in early in the decision-making process. Information is available at Web sites like www.mymedicalmalpracticeinsurance.com to compare malpractice costs by state.[5] A recent AMA trends study showed that more physicians were seeking hospital employment as a relief from rising malpractice insurance costs and reduced payer reimbursement.[6]

Where to Find Information Concerning a Geographic Location

When in need of specific geographic location information, the following are great sources:

- Census Bureau For more information go to census.gov/regions
- The individual state's Department of Tourism and official state government site that can provide links to licensing requirements, labor laws, and tax information.
- Area Chamber of Commerce
- Local and state medical societies
- American Medical Association (particularly their Competition in Health Insurance publication)
- The Kaiser Family Foundation also provides a wealth of information by state on patient demographics, percentage uninsured, poverty rate, malpractice claims and number of hospital and availability of nursing and non-physician providers.[7]

How to Determine the Area's Need for a Physician

When searching for a practice location, the following will help in determining an area in need:

- County or state medical society
- Chief of Medical Staff at the area hospital(s)
- Other physicians
- Pharmacists
- Benchmarks are available from a number of resources, such as the Medical Group Management Association and Practice Support Resources, that provide information on the number of physicians by specialty generally needed to serve a patient population base.[8] Benchmarks further provide an estimated number of new patients per year that a specialty will need to attract in order to grow the practice.
- Newspapers from the areas under consideration.

Once the options have been narrowed to two or three locations, visit these areas to help you arrive at your final decision. Visit the local hospitals and talk with the Chiefs of Medical Staff. Determine how long it will take to obtain hospital privileges. Inquire as to whether the hospital is legally and financially able to assist new physicians coming into the area, and confirm that the hospital is not closed to new staff members. Also inquire as to the hospital's expectations of its staff physicians for call schedules.

Once You Have Decided on a Location

Once you have decided on a location, you can begin preparations for entering practice. The next step is to apply for a state medical license and apply to the Drug Enforcement Administration in the state for a DEA number for writing prescriptions. You may choose to complete these applications personally or engage an organization experienced in this application process to assist you. The time it takes to receive your license and DEA number will vary by your unique circumstances and the state in which you will be practicing.

It will also be necessary to complete applications to obtain staff privileges at the hospital. Contact the medical staff office to inquire about credentialing applications. This process usually takes several months for completion, so it is beneficial to begin the process as soon as possible.

Once the practice address has been finalized, you can begin applying for a National Provider Identification number (NPI), as well as Medicare, Medicaid, and other payer provider numbers. Obtaining provider numbers from third-party payers can be a long process. Since physicians that do not have provider numbers are not able to bill for services, it is very important to begin this credentialing process early.

For physicians who are joining a group practice, there may be administrative assistance available for obtaining licenses and assisting with the credentialing process.

If you are planning to open a practice of your own, you will need at least 12 months lead time to do your research, select a location, and complete other necessary arrangements. Because so many details are involved, a time line is provided to help you stay on track (Table 1-2). The professional, economic, and residential characteristics of potential practice sites are key factors to consider in your location decision. Using this tool will ensure awareness of everything that must be accomplished before joining a group or opening your own practice.

You can delegate some objectives on the timetable to individuals that you trust. These designees will need to be experienced, persistent, and pay attention to detail. You, the physician, should take the responsibility of seeing that all the requirements are completed on time.

During the start-up process, you will be asked to provide copies of all your licenses, identifier numbers, reference letters, and other credentialing documents numerous times. To prepare, begin now to build a file that includes the original and several copies of this information.

TABLE 1-2 Time Line for Starting to Practice Medicine

Photocopy or print this time line and keep it as a reference. Work on completing these steps whenever possible. Not all requirements will apply to all practice options. Each line is coded: E = employed physician, GP = physicians joining a group practice, and SP = physician starting a solo private practice.

One Year Before Starting Practice	Check as Completed	Responsible Party
1. Make final decision on practice location. (E, GP, SP)	❏	
2. Check on membership for: (E, GP, SP)		
County medical society	❏	
State medical society	❏	
American Medical Association	❏	
3. For comparison purposes, get copies of contracts from groups or corporations that are being considered (GP, E). (See group practice questionnaire in Chapter 3, Selecting Your Professional Path.)	❏	
4. Begin to examine net worth in terms of capital available for start-up costs. (SP) (See Chapter 9, Financial Considerations and Capitalization of the Medical Practice.)	❏	
5. If possible, reserve office telephone number (or answering service number). (SP)	❏	
6. Find out the date when telephone books are printed. Have the practice name listed in both the white and yellow pages. (SP)	❏	
7. Visit banks and begin shopping for a loan. Pick up loan applications and meet loan officers. Determine what information the bank will need to evaluate the loan application. (SP) (See Chapter 9, Financial Considerations and Capitalization of the Medical Practice.)	❏	
8. Open:		
Checking account, personal (E, GP, SP)	❏	
Checking account, business (SP)	❏	
Savings account, personal (E, GP, SP)	❏	
Savings account, business (SP)	❏	
9. Draw up an income/expenditure projection for first year of practice. Talk with several bankers regarding borrowing money; submit applications. (SP) (See Chapter 9, Financial Considerations and Capitalization of the Medical Practice.)	❏	

(continued)

TABLE 1-2 Time Line for Starting to Practice Medicine (*continued*)

Nine Months Before Starting Practice	Check as Completed	Responsible Party
1. Check sites for leasing/buying medical office space. (SP)	❑	
2. Check zoning ordinances with local city hall and/or zoning board regarding signage, type of businesses allowed in the area; ask about any anticipated changes. (SP)	❑	
3. Check on utility requirements for the office. (SP)	❑	
4. If leasing, see if any leasehold improvements are needed and when these improvements can be made. (SP) (See Chapter 10, Financial Asset Considerations.)	❑	
5. Determine office layout and design. (SP)	❑	
6. Determine office and medical equipment needed. If installing X-ray equipment, check with the state health department, radiological health section, to see if they require special registration or certification. Make the same checks for laboratory or outpatient surgery facilities. (SP) (For laboratory license information, see Chapter 4, Regulations and Licensing Requirements.) For Certificate of Need (CON) for surgery center, check your state's requirements.[10]	❑	
7. Choose advisors (as appropriate). (See Chapter 1, Getting Started.)		
Accountant (E, GP, SP)	❑	
Attorney (E, GP, SP)	❑	
Banker (E, GP, SP)	❑	
Insurance broker(s) (E, GP, SP)	❑	
Management consultant (SP)	❑	
Real estate broker (E, GP, SP)	❑	
Other (eg, computer consultant) (E, GP, SP)	❑	
8. Evaluate office lease and/or partnership agreement contracts with an attorney before signing them. (See Chapters 3, Selecting a Professional Path, and 10, Financial Asset Considerations.) (SP)	❑	
9. Obtain bids on major office equipment that will be needed; compare leasing versus purchasing. Be sure to get a written guarantee of delivery date and in-transit insurance. (See equipment list and budget in Chapter 10, Financial Asset Considerations.) Select a practice management system/EHR system. (SP) Stand-alone system, application service provider.	❑	

(*continued*)

TABLE 1-2   Time Line for Starting to Practice Medicine (*continued*)

Nine Months Before Starting Practice	Check as Completed	Responsible Party
Consider electronic medical records. (SP)	❏	
Consider billing options (eg, in-house, outsource). If outsource, begin looking at options. (SP)	❏	
Dictation equipment (SP) (N/A with EHR)	❏	
Intercom system (ie, determine whether it will be separate from telephones) (SP)	❏	
Exam rooms/medical equipment (SP)	❏	
Photocopy/fax/scanners (SP)	❏	
Computer terminals for staff members with needed software (SP)	❏	
Telephone equipment and switchboard (SP)	❏	
Calculators (SP)	❏	
Light signaling system (SP)	❏	
Reception room/office furniture and decorations (SP)	❏	
Tool kit/flashlight/crash cart if necessary (SP)	❏	
10. If in a partnership, complete the details of the partnership agreement; have it drawn up and signed by each partner.	❏	
11. If new to the state or newly graduated, obtain medical licensure application and license.	❏	
12. Obtain DEA application and registration: (E, GP, SP)	❏	
Federal: Application for registration available through the Department of Justice, Drug Enforcement Administration, local or state office. If necessary, contact the national office: Drug Enforcement Administration, P.O. Box 28083, Central Station, Washington, DC 20005, (202) 724-1013.	❏	
State: Check local medical licensing board to see who issues prescribing licenses in the state. The state pharmacy board or the Department of Registration and Education usually does this.	❏	
13. Inform the state medical licensing board of the new address. (E, GP, SP)	❏	
Six Months Before Starting Practice	**Check as Completed**	**Responsible Party**
1. Obtain the services of an answering service: (SP)		
Physicians' exchange (eg, hospital or medical society) (E, SP, GP)	❏	
Personal (office) (SP)	❏	

(*continued*)

TABLE 1-2   Time Line for Starting to Practice Medicine (*continued*)

Six Months Before Starting Practice	Check as Completed	Responsible Party
Page/cell phone service (SP)	❏	
Call forwarding (SP)	❏	
2. Elect a pension plan or individual retirement account.	❏	
3. Check with the medical society regarding their position and guidelines on advertising in the local newspaper, and other forms of announcements. Many will provide mailing labels and assist with printing. (SP)	❏	
4. Contact health plans to obtain credentialing applications and standard agreements.	❏	
Contact Medicare to obtain PECOS application and associated documents. Apply for provider number(s), Medicare, Medicaid. (SP, E, GP, check with employer)	❏	
Obtain a Medicare fee schedule. (SP)	❏	
5. Obtain a Current Procedural Terminology coding book (CPT 2012). (SP)	❏	
6. Obtain an International Classification of Diseases Book (ICD-9/10-CM). (SP)	❏	
7. Apply for hospital staff privileges. (SP, E, GP)	❏	
8. Start to develop Web site. (SP)	❏	
9. Order medical record system. (SP) (N/A with EHR)	❏	
10. Order signage for office. (SP)	❏	
11. Notify pharmaceutical representatives and other appropriate salespersons of the new practice.	❏	
12. Obtain county and city occupational licenses available from the county/city clerk's office or city hall. (See Chapter 4, Regulations and Licensing Requirements.)	❏	
13. If outsourcing billing, contract with 3rd party billing company.	❏	
14. Inquire at hospital about group purchasing services.	❏	
15. Outline medication and vaccine needs for start up.	❏	
16. Develop practice encounter form.	❏	

(*continued*)

TABLE 1-2 Time Line for Starting to Practice Medicine (*continued*)

Three Months Before Starting Practice	Check as Completed	Responsible Party
1. Arrange for professional malpractice insurance. (SP, GP, E; check with employer)	❏	
2. Arrange for office insurance. (Call 800 458-5736 for information on AMA-sponsored insurance plan.) (SP) (See Chapter 8, Identifying Insurance Requirements.)	❏	
Office overhead (SP)	❏	
Office liability (SP)	❏	
Business interruption (SP)	❏	
Employee fidelity bond (SP)	❏	
Office contents (SP)	❏	
Umbrella: Provides comprehensive catastrophic liability coverage for liability claims beyond the limits of regular liability programs. (SP)	❏	
Workers' Compensation: This is often required by law and is determined on a state-by-state basis. Check with the state's workers' compensation board or industrial commission. (SP)	❏	
Health: Major medical for self, dependents, and employees. (SP)	❏	
Disability (SP, E, GP; check with employer)	❏	
Life (SP, E, GP)	❏	
Automobile (SP, E, GP)	❏	
3. Arrange for telephone service installation. Consider purchasing telephone equipment. (SP)	❏	
4. Consider arranging for acceptance of credit cards (eg, VISA, MasterCard American Express) at the new office through a local bank. (Call 800-366-6968 for information on AMA-sponsored VISA program.) (SP)	❏	
5. Talk with the local newspaper regarding practice announcement ads.	❏	
6. Order office-opening announcements.	❏	
7. Arrange to give talks to community groups on health topics. (SP, GP) (See Chapter 15, Marketing and Business Development Considerations.)	❏	
8. Negotiate final health plan contracts and fee schedules.	❏	

(*continued*)

TABLE 1-2 Time Line for Starting to Practice Medicine (*continued*)

Three Months Before Starting Practice	Check as Completed	Responsible Party
9. Meet physicians who are potential referral sources. Send letters, arrange appointments. (SP, GP)	❏	
10. Find out if a patient referral service is available through the local medical society. Send them essential information. (SP, GP)	❏	
11. Check on memberships in civic and church organizations. (SP, E, GP)	❏	
12. Arrange for movers, if necessary. (SP, E, GP)	❏	
13. Contact the State Department of Labor for state employment regulations and wage and hour information. (SP)	❏	
14. Write preliminary job descriptions for employees. (SP)	❏	
15. Write policy manual for office employees. (SP)	❏	
16. Check local resources for personnel. (SP)	❏	
17. Start interviewing for office/clinical personnel. (SP)	❏	
18. Apply for Federal Employer Identification Number through the local Internal Revenue Service Office (SS-4 Form). (SP)	❏	
19. Apply for State Employer Identification Number through the state employment office/labor department. (SP)	❏	
20. Obtain "Small Business Tax Guide" and Federal Estimated Income Tax Form through the local IRS office, or attend small business tax seminar at the local IRS office. (SP)	❏	
21. Obtain State Estimated Income Tax Form through state department/labor department. (SP)	❏	
22. Obtain payroll-withholding booklets (ie, federal, state, city) through local IRS office. (SP)	❏	
23. Review tax requirements with accountant. (SP)	❏	
24. As needed, arrange for:		
Janitorial service	❏	
Snow removal	❏	
Laundry service	❏	
Grounds maintenance	❏	
25. Order clinical supplies and set-up inventory control system. (SP) (See Chapter 10, Financial Asset Considerations.)	❏	

(*continued*)

TABLE 1-2   Time Line for Starting to Practice Medicine (*continued*)

Three Months Before Starting Practice	Check as Completed	Responsible Party
26. Order business supplies: (SP)		
Appointment cards	❑	
Business cards	❑	
Patient recall system	❑	
Petty cash vouchers	❑	
Letterhead stationery and envelopes	❑	
Deposit stamp for checks	❑	
Prescription pads	❑	
Purchase order forms	❑	
Preprinted telephone message pads	❑	
27. Determine likely office hours based on community need. (SP)	❑	
28. Determine fee schedule. (SP)	❑	
29. Select and order magazines: (SP)		
For reception room	❑	
Medical journals for self	❑	
30. Purchase office equipment and furniture; arrange delivery date. (SP)	❑	
31. Arrange for: (SP)		
Laboratory services for patients	❑	
X-ray services for patients	❑	
32. Notify area pharmacies of new practice. (GP, SP)	❑	
33. Write patient information booklet and have it printed. (SP)	❑	
34. Order insurance forms (HCFA 1500 Claim Form from the AMA: 800 621-8335).	❑	
35. Check on status of all payer applications.	❑	
36. Check on status of clearinghouse/billing company.	❑	
37. Order practice encounter forms—numbered.	❑	
One Month Before Starting Practice	**Check as Completed**	**Responsible Party**
1. Start setting up office. (SP)	❑	
2. Have utilities turned on: (SP)		
Telephone	❑	
Electricity	❑	
Gas	❑	

(*continued*)

TABLE 1-2 Time Line for Starting to Practice Medicine (*continued*)

One Month Before Starting Practice	Check as Completed	Responsible Party
Water	❏	
Internet	❏	
3. Hire and train office personnel regarding: (SP)		
Telephone techniques	❏	
Collections	❏	
Appointments	❏	
Office policies	❏	
4. Decide on collection/insurance policy. (SP)	❏	
5. Hang out shingle (post sign). (SP)	❏	
6. Establish a petty cash fund. (SP)	❏	
7. Establish a charge fund. (SP)	❏	
8. Place announcement in community paper and medical society bulletin: (SP, GP)		
Advertisement	❏	
News release	❏	
9. Mail announcements to physicians, pharmacists, hospitals, and health groups. (SP, GP)	❏	
10. Plan office open house. (SP)	❏	
11. Start accepting appointments. (SP)	❏	
Opening Day of Practice	**Check as Completed**	**Responsible Party**
1. See first patient.	❏	
2. Congratulate self. The practice is open!	❏	

Selecting Professional Assistance

Because of the complexity of business in general, and medical practice management in particular, you cannot discount the need for professional advice and consultation. New physicians should seek guidance from expert advisors, specifically professionals experienced in health care management. To help you through the complex maze of professional advisors, the following are summaries of their services and the roles they are expected to play. It may be wise to seek recommendations from other physicians concerning these advisors.

Legal Assistance

An attorney will help set up the legal structure of your practice or assist with reviewing your contract of employment or partnership. Only use attorneys who understand and have experience in health care law. Many business arrangements have been constructed that did not pass the requirements particular to health care law. Consider using an attorney to review your lease, purchase agreements, and other contracts, especially those involving long-term commitments, such as a billing services agreement or practice management support contracts.

Accounting Assistance

To ensure that the practice provides the best tax advantages and flexibility, you will need to engage an experienced accountant. Along with the attorney, an accountant should be consulted before setting up your legal structure because the legal structure can affect tax liabilities. The accountant will also assist with setting up accounting processes as well as establishing the internal controls for tracking cash flow, profit and loss statements, payroll withholdings, quarterly taxes, and operating budget. The person providing accounting advice does not necessarily have to be a certified public accountant (CPA). Nonetheless, selecting the right accountant should be considered on the basis of technical knowledge and experience in health care and the ability to meet your needs. The following descriptions will help differentiate between the various types of accounting services.

- **Certified Public Accountant.** A CPA will typically have the highest level of expertise in the field of accounting due to their certification requirements. In addition, like other certified professionals, CPAs must comply with licensure and continuing education requirements. A CPA will generally charge by the hour and is typically more expensive than other accounting professionals. Finding a CPA that is experienced in operations of medical practices will be well worth the extra investment.

- **Accounting and Bookkeeping Services.** Accounting and bookkeeping services are widely available and can generally provide the same types of services as that of a CPA, but they may be limited in how much tax planning and/or business advice they can provide. Carefully check references and the reputation of firms that are being considered and, more significantly, verify that they are experienced in operations of medical practices.

- **Payroll Services.** Payroll services offer online timekeeping and payroll administration, payroll tax and worker's compensation administration, 401(k) administration, and often offer a group health insurance and other benefit plans for smaller organizations at a reasonable cost.

■ **Practice Management Services.** These companies generally assist with the full spectrum of operations. They can perform such services as hiring employees, maintaining the books, payroll, purchasing, billing and collections, managed care contracting, and other services related to operations. Their fees can be based on a percentage of net collections or a flat monthly fee. Typically the most common arrangement is to base fees on a percentage of net profits after expenses, so there is an incentive for both maximizing revenues and minimizing expenses. It is important to verify references and their success in managing operations of a medical practice.

■ **Management Service Organizations (MSO).** An MSO is typically formed by hospitals that will allow its members to collectively share in benefits and services that are difficult to obtain on an individual basis. Such services include group purchasing, contracting with managed care, billing services, practice management systems, and staffing. Some offer electronic health record (EHR) systems also. The basic concept of an MSO is having strength in numbers. Because of Stark laws,[9] an MSO owned by a hospital will rarely have any financial interest in a practice, and therefore they typically do not provide the accounting services or services related to the financial performance of the practice, as described in the other types of management services.

■ **Independent Physician Organizations (IPO), Independent Physician Associations (IPA), and Physician Hospital Organizations (PHO).** These organizations can be similar to an MSO. However, they are generally seen in areas with a heavy concentration of managed care in the marketplace. Their primary focus is on obtaining market shares for its members as well as acceptable reimbursement from the payers.

Regardless of whether you choose an accountant, bookkeeper, practice management services, or combine these services with an MSO, IPO, IPA or PHO, be sure the service meets your needs. The following list contains services that could be considered for outsourcing:

■ Budgets and financial forecasting

■ Periodic reviews of the financial performance of the practice. This should include monthly preparation of financial statements.

■ Routine audits, and checks and balances

■ Consultative reviews of IRS and other regulatory laws and penalties

■ Consultative advice for 401(k) contributions, real estate, investing, and financial planning

■ Payroll and payroll taxes

■ Leadership and advice at meetings to discuss the performance of the practice and to recommend improvements where needed.

During the initial start-up phase of the practice, advisors, such as brokers, real estate agents, and lenders, will be utilized. A local bank can also be a resource for options on establishing a line of credit. Most lenders will require a business plan or pro-forma of the business. This will be discussed later in Chapter 9, Financial Considerations and Capitalization of the Medical Practice.

Other Advisors to Consider

The following are other advisors to consider for the practice:

1. **Insurance Agent or Broker.** There are several types of insurance that must be selected for the new practice. Following are the types of insurance that will need to be considered:

   ■ Malpractice

   ■ General liability and property insurance

   ■ Employee health insurance

   ■ Disability insurance

   ■ Workers' compensation insurance

   ■ Life insurance

   Choosing an agent or broker is critical. There are a number of considerations to ensure that the practice is properly insured. For example, will the insurance plan cover the cost to recreate medical records if they are destroyed? Is the practice protected if the information system becomes damaged and the practice is unable to recover critical information to be used for collecting payment for services? Who is responsible if other tenants in the building flood the office space? Who is responsible if a patient falls in the parking lot or just outside the office? Is the practice protected from breaching a patient's privacy as mandated under the Health Insurance Portability and Accountability Act (HIPAA).

2. **Practice Management Consultant.** Many physicians and physician groups go through the entire practice cycle without ever seeking the assistance of an experienced practice management consultant. Unfortunately, these physicians probably spend many hours of their own valuable time and effort on projects that a consultant could handle in a fraction of the time. In particular, a physician new to practice or in a practice transition will benefit greatly by using an experienced consultant. Besides offering operational

advice and organizing the practice set up, the seasoned consultant can develop policies and procedure and compliance manuals, fee schedules, employee handbooks, and job descriptions for the practice. For established or existing practices, engaging a consulting firm to complete an operational assessment can uncover areas where practice efficiencies can improve and where revenue can be enhanced for improvements in billing and collections procedures.

When selecting the practice consultant, ask candidates for the names of other physicians whom the consultant has helped. Talking with these references provides a feel for the consultant's knowledge, the nature of the assignments, and the success of the project in which the physician received assistance.

Use a written agreement (between the physician and the consulting firm) listing, as specifically as possible, what you expect to be achieved. Corresponding to this list, the consulting firm should state exactly the work they will provide, including a time line for completing the work and costs.

Conclusion

The more you know about yourself and the better prepared you are to start out in medical practice, the more likely and sooner you will achieve success. By understanding the scope of the start up and by working through a methodical timetable, you will be able to check off the tasks as you accomplish them and be fully equipped on opening day to see your first patients.

Begin the start-up process by establishing your relationships with trusted advisors and maintain them throughout the years. While professional advisors may appear to be expensive, the knowledge and expertise of a consultant who is experienced in setting up a medical practice will more than offset the cost. In addition, it will save you valuable time and provide the security of knowing the consultant is working from experience and proven techniques gained from years of establishing successful medical practices.

The next chapter will explore the various options that are available for structuring and positioning your practice as a viable entity.

References

1. Joint Commission Accreditation Hospital Organizations (JCAHO), www.qualitycheck.org and www.healthgrades.com. Accessed June 19, 2011.

2. Medically Underserved Areas/Populations are areas or populations designated by the Health Resources and Services Administration (HRSA) as having: too few primary care providers, high infant mortality, high poverty and/or high elderly population. Health Professional Shortage Areas (HPSAs) are designated by HRSA as having shortages of primary medical care, dental, or mental health providers and may be geographic (a county or service area), demographic (low income population), or institutional (comprehensive health center, federally qualified health center, or other public facility).

3. Rural Health Clinics Center, Centers for Medicare and Medicaid Services, www.cms.gov/center/rural.asp. Accessed June 19, 2011.

4. Krupa, C. 2011. "Unequal distribution of doctors hurts children's medical care." *American Medical News,* February 1. www.ama-assn.org/amednews/2011/01/31/hlsb0201.htm. Accessed June 19, 2011.

5. To review malpractice rates by state, go to www.mymedicalmalpractice insurance.com/medical-malpractice-insurance-rates.php. Accessed August 29, 2011.

6. American Medical Association Council on Long Range Planning and Development. 2008. *An Environmental Analysis Report: Healthcare Trends 2008.* American Medical Association, p.19. www.ama-assn.org/resources/doc/clrpd/2008-trends.pdf. Accessed June 19, 2011.

7. Kaiser Family Foundation. www.statehealthfacts.org/. Accessed June 19, 2011.

8. Medical Group Management Association. www.mgma.com/. Practice Support Resources. www.practicesupport.com/. Accessed June 19, 2011.

9. Stark Law Information on penalties, legal practices, latest news and advice. www.starklaw.org/. Accessed June 19, 2011.

2 Choosing an Organizational Structure

In starting a medical practice, one of the first and most important questions to ask is "What form of legal entity should be used?" or "How should I organize my business?" Also, as the practice grows and adapts to constant challenges, it is essential to revisit the issue of whether the chosen entity is still the best form of organization for the business. Simply, regulatory and market variables necessitate careful ongoing consideration.

The purpose of this chapter is to give an overview of various business structures and models that may be chosen when establishing a medical practice. Each business structure has steps to be taken and procedures to follow. They also have advantages and disadvantages to consider that may have long-term effects on the operations. The important point is to be informed so that the right choices can be made to fit your style and personality and to ensure the formation of a legal and viable business.

Types of Medical Practices

When considering starting your own practice, carefully consider the sort of entity it will be to ensure the greatest success. Under the existing laws, there are four major types of medical practices that can be established. Following is a brief overview.

- **Sole Proprietorship (one physician).** This type of business has one owner who makes all decisions. Fewer corporate legal formalities are required for a sole proprietorship than the other types of medical practices. All income or losses, which include deductions for business expenses, belong to you. Moreover, the sole proprietor is personally liable for all debts, loans, and liabilities.

- **Partnership (group practice).** A general partnership is an association of two or more persons as co-owners who contribute money or property to form a business. The partnership must file an annual tax return (ie, Form 1065), but the business itself is not taxed. Instead, its net income (or loss) is attributed (although not necessarily distributed) to the partners in proportion to the investment; individually, they report the profit or loss on their own tax return (ie, Schedule E, Form 1040).

- **C or S Corporation (solo or group practice).** A corporation is a legal entity that is authorized by a state to operate under the rules of the entity's charter. The most complex business organization, a professional corporation, is formed by a group of investors and has the rights and liabilities separate from the individuals involved.

- **Limited Liability Company (LLC) (group practice).** Shareholders of limited liability corporations are not personally liable for debts of the company.

Group practices can have several variations, including nonprofit practices, foundations, and associations, in addition to the more typical partnerships and corporate practices. Your legal and tax advisors can help determine which structure meets your specific needs. The way in which you structure your practice will depend upon your personality, comfort level, and personal preferences. The following is a basic description of each structure.

Sole Proprietorship

A sole proprietorship is an unincorporated business that is owned by one individual. Its primary advantage is its ease of formation—it is the simplest form of business organization to start and maintain. The business has no legal existence apart from you, the owner. Its primary disadvantages are that it can have only one owner, which could limit opportunities for adding partners in the future. However, the business and legal structure can be changed at that time, if needed. Its liabilities are your personal liabilities, and you undertake the risks of the business for all assets owned, whether used in the business or personally owned. You include the income and expenses of the business on your own tax return.[1]

With autonomy as the major advantage, a solo practice allows the physician to be in control and to establish practice guidelines, office hours, policies and procedures within ethical and medical constraints. Good candidates for a solo practice tend to be independent and entrepreneurial and enjoy the business side of operating a practice. This would be a good time to refer back to the self-assessment tool in Chapter 1, Table 1-1, Practice Style Decision Maker, to see how you scored. You

TABLE 2-1 Sole Proprietorship: Advantages and Disadvantages

Advantages	Disadvantages
Control A sole proprietor controls the money and makes the decisions.	**Funding** Obtaining capital can be a challenge due to fewer assets.
Easy to Set Up Few legal restrictions. Simple to start and maintain.	**Threats** If the owner becomes injured or incapacitated, the business will suffer.
Flexibility The sole proprietor owns the business.	**Liability** The owner is 100% responsible and takes all the risks.
Easier Taxes No separate tax form required.	**Responsibilities** One hundred percent of the decisions will rest with the owner.

may even want to reconsider some of your answers now that you know more about what is involved.

In a sole proprietorship, the physician is personally liable for all the debt and legal technicalities of the practice. The tax status is simplified in that the physician uses the Internal Revenue Service (IRS) Form 1040, Schedule C (ie, Profit and Loss from Business) to file practice earnings and expenses.

There are a number of disadvantages to a solo practice. In addition to financial exposure, you will not have others to share responsibilities, both for delivering medical care and running an office. This also means that covering or obtaining coverage for the practice during the evening or during vacations will also be your responsibility. It can initially mean less personal time for your family and yourself. As the practice grows, you will likely employ another physician or add mid-level providers to offset the obligations for call coverage and to cover your time off. Another disadvantage is the potential lack of negotiating leverage with managed care plans.

Table 2-1 specifies the advantages and disadvantages of a sole proprietorship. More pros and cons are covered later in this chapter.

Getting Started

To start a sole proprietorship, simply begin conducting business after the items discussed in Chapter 1 have been considered and completed. Open a separate bank account to keep track of the practice's finances, and keep records of all of the expenses and revenues connected with running the practice.

A sole proprietorship is usually operated under the name of the individual owner, although other names can be used. If the individual owner's name is not used, a fictitious name, trade name, or DBA (doing business as) certificate will need to be filed in the town, city, or county where the practice is located. Take care to select a name that is not the same or similar to another practice and avoid using *incorporated* or *company* unless the business is actually a corporation.

Call local government offices for information and application forms that are required in your state and locality (eg, business licenses, zoning occupancy permits, tax registrations, etc).

Control

As owner of all assets of the business, the sole proprietor controls the business. Employees may help manage the practice, but the owner has legal responsibility for the employees' decisions and ultimate control over the business.

Liability

The sole proprietor has unlimited personal responsibility if the practice fails or has losses and can be sued individually by creditors for non-payment. The business creditors can go against both the business' assets and the owner's personal assets, including bank account, car, or house. Likewise, personal creditors can make claims against the sole proprietor's practice assets.

Insurance may be purchased to cover many of the risks of a sole proprietorship. However, the owner is personally liable for operating losses.

Continuity and Transferability

As long as its owner is alive and desires to continue the practice, the sole proprietorship can exist. The sole proprietorship ceases to exist when the owner dies. At that point, the assets and liabilities become part of the owner's estate. All or a portion of the practice's assets can be freely transferred to another person.

Taxes

All income from the practice is taxed at applicable individual tax rates, with income and allowable business expenses reflected on the individual tax return. No separate federal income tax return is required of the sole proprietor, although the proprietor must pay self-employment tax on the business income.

Pros and Cons

Following are the pros involved with establishing a sole proprietorship:

- Inexpensive to start
- Simple to run

The cons of owning a sole proprietorship are as follows:

- Owner has unlimited personal liability for business
- Business has unlimited liability for owner's personal liabilities
- Ownership is limited to one person

Partnership

A partnership is the relationship that exists between two or more persons who jointly operate a trade or business. Each person contributes money, property, labor, or skill, and expects to share in the profits and losses of the business.[2] A partnership is not a taxable entity. In a partnership, the partners include their share of the income or loss on their individual tax returns. Partners are not employees and should not be issued an IRS Form W-2 in lieu of Form 1065, Schedule K-1, for distributions or guaranteed payments from the partnership.

Partners invest in their business to make a profit and are equally responsible for the success or failure of it. It is always a good idea to go into a partnership with someone you can trust and count on to make the commitments and sacrifices that are needed to have a successful medical practice.

It is advisable to have a written agreement signed by all partners, which addresses major issues relating to the practice, including:

- How much time and/or money the partners will contribute to the practice
- How business decisions will be made
- How profits and losses will be shared
- What will happen to the practice and to a partner's share of the business if that partner dies, becomes disabled, or stops working/contributing to the practice
- How long the partnership will exist
- When the partnership will make distributions (ie, payments of income earned based upon partnership share) to its partners

Other issues the partnership agreement may address are:

- Business name
- Types of partners (eg, general, limited, active, silent)

TABLE 2-2   Partnership: Advantages and Disadvantages

Advantages	Disadvantages
Equal Rights Each partner has equal rights in management and conduct of partnership.	**Liable for Acts of the Partnership** Each partner is liable for acts of commission or omission assumed by the partnership as a whole.
Shared Decision Making All partners must give consent when bringing in new partners.	**Liability for Partner's Acts** The partnership can neither sue nor be sued. However, each partner is liable for any suit against a partner if the suit concerns the principal nature of the business—in this case medicine.
Shared Rights Partners have the right to a formal accounting of partnership affairs.	**Equal Benefits** A partner who does not contribute equally to the practice will still expect equal benefits.
Shared Responsibilities Each partner has the responsibility to sustain a fiduciary relationship with the other partners.	**Shared Failure** Compensation is based on group performance. If a partner fails to achieve financial success, the group income will suffer.
Less Risk Partnership profits must be divided equally among the partners or based on a prearranged schedule.	**Goodwill Not Portable** Upon leaving a partnership, rarely will the physician recoup an investment, especially the goodwill that may now be associated with the practice as a result of all efforts.
Responsibilities Financial responsibilities are shared.	**Exposure to Loss** If a partner leaves, the group will be affected as a result of bearing the overhead to which the departing physician contributed.

- Draws and salaries
- Dispute resolution
- Arbitration
- Lines and limits of authority

Partnerships in medical practice can be formed by two or more established physicians coming together to do business, or when an existing solo practitioner or established practice is seeking to replace retiring members or to grow or expand. One advantage of a partnership is that there is usually a period of employment prior to the "buy in," which would allow the physician time to evaluate the job. Table 2-2 addresses some of the advantages and disadvantages of a partnership.

Partnerships

Partnerships are either general partnerships or limited partnerships. A general partnership is created when two or more individuals agree to create a business and jointly own the assets, profits, and losses. Creating a limited partnership requires following certain steps established by each state's statues. Partnerships offer the advantage of more than one owner. A disadvantage is that general partners are personally responsible for losses and other obligations of the business.

Getting Started

To start a general partnership, agree—first orally and then in writing—with one or more individuals to jointly own and share the profits of a business.

A limited partnership consists of one or more general partners (ie, those who are generally liable for the business) and one or more limited partners (ie, those who have limited liability). It must follow the statutory requirements of the state or it will be treated as a general partnership. (See more about limited partnerships and limited corporations later in this chapter.)

Partnerships often use the name of the partners as the name of the business. If all the partners' names are not used, or if none of the partners' names are used, a fictitious name certificate may need to be filed.

Many states require partnerships to file certificates either with the local government or in the office of the secretary of state or its equivalent. Check with the local government office to determine the state's requirements.

The partnership should keep separate bank accounts and financial records for the practice so that the partners know of the entity's profits and losses.

Control

The partnership agreement should state what percentage of the practice and profits each partner owns. Otherwise, each partner will own an equal portion of the business and profits and liabilities of the practice.

The agreement should also specify who would control and manage the business of the partnership. Otherwise, all general partners have equal control and management rights and must consent and agree to partnership decisions. Any partner can bind the partnership and the individual partners to contracts or legal obligations, even without the approval of the other partners.

In a limited partnership, the general partners handle the management and control of the business. State law restricts the types of control and management the limited partners can undertake without jeopardizing the limited partnership's existence.

Liability

A general partnership has characteristics of both a separate legal entity and a group of individuals. The partnership can own property and conduct business as a separate legal entity. The general partners are jointly and severally liable for the partnership (ie, all of the partners are liable together and each general partner is individually liable for all of the obligations of the partnership). This means that a creditor of the partnership could require you individually to pay all the money the creditor is owed. Your partners would then reimburse you for their share of the debt or loss.

Before joining a general partnership, determine whether your partners can financially afford to share the losses of the partnership. If you are the only partner with any assets or money, the creditors of the partnership can require you to pay them in the event of failure, and you may be unable to get reimbursement from your partners.

Limited partners do not have personal liability for the business of the partnership. Limited partners are at risk only to the extent of their previously agreed-upon contributions to the partnership. This may be seen as less risky for the limited partners.

Continuity and Transferability

A partnership exists as long as the partners agree it will and as long as all of the general partners remain in the partnership. If a general partner departs, the partnership dissolves and the assets of the partnership must be sold or distributed to pay first the creditors and then the partners. The partnership agreement may provide for the continuation of the business by the remaining partners, in which case it may not have to be sold upon the withdrawal of a general partner. The departing general partner is entitled to an accounting to determine his or her shares of the assets and profits of the partnership. The partnership agreement should also cover how partners will be paid for their shares of the partnership upon departure or death.

The partnership agreement should state whether a partner could sell his or her partnership shares. In many states, the sale or transference of a partnership share requires the consent of all the other partners. Even if a partner does transfer a share of the partnership, he or she will remain personally liable for the business losses incurred prior to the sale of that interest.

Taxes

Although a partnership tax return is filed (for informational purposes only), each partner individually pays taxes on his or her share of the practice income. In certain cases, a partner may be required to pay tax on income from the partnership, even without having received any of the income. Partners must also be required to pay self-employment tax on their partnership income.

Pros and Cons

The following are a few of the pros involved with partnerships:

- Very flexible form of business
- Permits ownership by more than one individual
- Avoids double taxation
- Has few legal formalities for its maintenance

The cons of becoming part of a partnership include:

- Partners have unlimited personal liability for business losses
- Partnership is legally responsible for the business acts of each partner
- General partnership interest may not be sold or transferred without consent of all partners (again, inquiry should be made concerning each state's requirements as this component does vary from state to state)
- Partnership dissolves upon death of a general partner

Corporate Practice

A stock corporation has certain advantages that make it worth considering as a business form. A corporation is considered a separate legal entity; the owners of the corporation (eg, shareholders, stockholders) are not personally responsible for the losses of the business. Although usually owned by more than one individual, it is possible for only one individual to create and own 100% of a corporation.

A stock corporation may elect Subchapter S status for tax purposes, if it meets the following requirements:

1. Corporation has no more than 35 shareholders
2. Corporation has only one class of stock

TABLE 2-3   Corporate Practice: Advantages and Disadvantages

Advantages	Disadvantages
Protection There is limited liability to the individual physician.	**Limitations** Only physicians can be shareholders.
Benefits The corporation pays benefits (ie, medical insurance, life insurance, disability), making it an expense that is tax deductible.	**Double Taxation** Physician salaries and profits of the corporation are taxed. Assuring that the corporation has small, if any, profit can offset this.
Centralized Management Authority and responsibilities are assigned to the appropriate parties, leaving physicians to concentrate on patients.	**High Cost** It is quite costly to establish a corporation. Legal fees are high (eg, attorneys' fees are approximately $250 or more per hour), and Social Security payments are higher for the physicians.
Continuity of Life/Transferable Ownership The corporation will last beyond the careers of the present physicians. Ownership interest can be transferred easily through the sale of stock representing the value of the corporation's assets.	**Highly Structured** Managing a corporation requires extensive organization (eg, board meetings with accurate minutes, formal notices of annual and quarterly meetings, election of officers, proper revision of bylaws and articles of incorporation, as required). A bi-annual registration fee of $150 or more to medical licensing board is typically required.

3. All shareholders are United States residents, either citizens or resident aliens

4. All shareholders are individuals

5. The corporation operates on a calendar year financial basis (due to taxation requirements)

Corporate practice reduces the personal and financial risk to the individual physician, while providing opportunities to shelter income through a qualified retirement program. However, incorporating can be a complicated undertaking because the corporation is considered a distinct legal entity with no ties to any individuals. Table 2-3 lists the advantages and disadvantages of the corporate practice.

Getting Started

Doing business as a corporate entity calls for compliance with your state's requirements for creating the corporation. Physicians may be required to do business as a professional corporation. The shareholders or stockholders must agree on the following to create a corporation:

- The name of the business
- The total number of shares of stock the corporation can sell or issue (ie, authorized shares)
- The number of shares of stock each of the owners will buy
- The amount of money or other property each owner will contribute to buy his or her shares of stock
- The business in which the corporation will engage (ie, medical practice)
- Who will manage the corporation (ie, directors, officers)

Once these issues are settled, shareholders must prepare and file articles of incorporation or a certificate of incorporation with the corporate office of the state. Most states charge an initial fee for filing the corporate documents and an annual fee for allowing the corporation to continue. States vary on rules and fees; to determine what fees will apply, call your state's corporate commission or Secretary of State.

The corporation will also need *bylaws*—a set of rules of procedure by which the corporation is run. Bylaws include rules regarding stockholder meetings, director meetings, the number of officers in the corporation, and the responsibilities of each officer.

As a legal entity separate from its owners, the corporation will need a separate bank account and separate records. The money and property that the shareholders pay to buy their stock, and the assets and money that are earned by the corporation, are owned by the corporation and not by the shareholders.

Corporate documents sent to the state must include the name of the corporation. The state will reject the name that is chosen if it is already in use by another company. Most states can tell the caller by telephone if the selected name is available. If possible, avoid using a name that is similar to existing practices.

Control

Shareholders elect, by a majority of the outstanding shares, a group of individuals to act as the board of directors, with ultimate control belonging to those who hold a majority of the shares. Directors' terms of service often are for more than one year and are usually staggered to provide continuity. Shareholders can elect themselves to be on the board of directors. Major decisions must be approved by the shareholders, such as amendments to the articles of incorporation, merger with another practice, and dissolving the corporation. States vary on their requirements for voting, decision making, and other provisions. Seek professional advice for options that are permissible in your state.

The board of directors makes major decisions for the corporation. The board is required to meet at least once a year. Each director is given one vote; usually the vote of a majority of the directors is sufficient to approve a decision. Directors may be paid, although this is not required. The board elects the officers of the corporation, usually a president, vice president, secretary, and treasurer. In some states, one person may hold any or all of these offices.

Officers of the corporation are responsible for running the day-to-day business of the corporation. Although they often are employees of the corporation and receive a salary, they can be non-employees and/or serve without pay. The shareholders can be elected as officers.

Stockholder-employees may be paid with wages or a salary for work performed and may receive a dividend or distribution of stock. Dividends typically are paid pro rata, usually as an amount per share, but always according to bylaws and any shareholder agreements. The board of directors makes decisions about payment and timing of dividends. A decision may also be made by the board to forgo a dividend payment because of cash flow or business uncertainties. Shareholders have no rights to any of the money of the corporation other than salary or wages if dividends are not distributed. As a separate legal entity, the money it makes belongs to the corporation.

Liability

As a legal entity apart from its owners, creditors of the corporation may look only to the corporation and the business assets for payment. Individual shareholders are not personally liable for the losses of the business if the corporation is properly established and operated. The shareholders' risk is limited to their investment in the corporation, provided that the shareholders comply with the statutory requirements for the corporation, which includes keeping the money, accounts, and assets separate from their personal accounts. However, if the shareholders personally underwrite (ie, guarantee the obligations of the corporation in order to borrow money or to rent space), then they are legally responsible for the obligations they have personally guaranteed. Shareholders' loans to the corporation are subordinated to other loans of the corporation if the business fails.

Continuity and Transferability

Corporate existence lasts as long as its shareholders agree that it serves its purpose. Stockholders can transfer ownership, or corporations can add owners by sale of all or a portion of the stock, either by selling stock directly from the corporation or by having the current owners sell some of their stock. (Before selling shares of stock to outsiders, check to see whether federal or state securities laws permit the sale.)

Medical practices that are corporations are often owned by a small group of shareholders who all work in the practice. Often they formally agree to certain restrictions on the sale of their shares, so that they can control who owns the practice.

Taxes

The corporation must file its own income tax returns and pay taxes on its profits. It must report all income it has received from its business and may deduct certain expenses it has paid in conducting its business.

Dividends paid to shareholders by the corporation are taxed to each shareholder individually, which is in effect a double taxation. The corporation pays taxes on its profits, and the shareholders must pay income taxes on the dividends paid to them from the profits. Taxes are based on personal salary and corporate profits, and they require separate tax returns.

Generally, a Subchapter S corporation does not pay taxes on the income generated by the business. Income or losses are passed on to the individual shareholders and reported on their tax returns, divided among the shareholders based on the percentage of stock they own. Shareholders may be required to pay taxes on the income of a Subchapter S corporation even if they are not paid any dividends or distributions from the corporation.

Pros and Cons

The following are the pros related to forming a corporate practice:

- Provides limited liability to owners
- Is easy to transfer ownership
- Is easy to add additional owners/investors

The cons of establishing a corporate practice include:

- Is more costly to set up and maintain
- Requires separate tax returns
- Is subject to double taxation

Other Business Models and Alternatives

Sole proprietors can enjoy some of the advantages of a partnership through alternative arrangements. Similar to limited partnerships are limited liability corporations (LLCs); however, some guidance and caution are warranted in these models, as explained in the following section.

Limited Liability Corporation

Although not applicable in every state, the IRS does permit a fourth option, the limited liability corporation, as an approved corporate structure. It provides the owners with the best aspects of both the corporation and the partnership. Check with your attorney or Secretary of State or Department of Corporations to verify whether your state recognizes the LLC as a legal corporation. While the LLC structure is appropriate for most forms of business, state law in some states set up a parallel structure for doctors, lawyers, accountants, and other professionals called professional LLC (PLLC).

Under PLLC provisions, members are not liable for the overall obligations of the LLC. However, each member is liable for any negligence, wrongful act, or misconduct committed by the member or by any person under his or her direct supervision while rendering services on behalf of the LLC.

Membership in the PLLC may only be transferred to other professionals who are eligible. At least one of the professionals forming an LLC must be authorized (licensed) to render professional services in the state where the LLC is formed. In the case of a medical PLLC, all members must be licensed in that state.

The following are the advantages of forming an LLC:

- The personal liability of each member of an LLC is limited to his or her personal investment in the LLC. This means that no member of the LLC is personally liable for the debts of the entire organization.

- The LLC offers pass-through tax benefits (ie, there is no entity level tax on the entity's income, but only a tax on the individual's share of the entity's income).

Other notable features about an LLC are:

- **Ownership.** Partners and shareholders (members) are owners of an LLC. To ensure pass-through tax benefits, membership in the LLC may not be transferred without consent of a majority of the members of the LLC. Anyone can be an LLC member.

- **Management.** The LLC may be managed by its members or by one or more managers appointed by the members.

- **Rights and Responsibilities.** LLC members generally vote in proportion to their ownership interests, and all matters require the approval of a majority of the members. As with any other type of business, the LLC must obtain a certificate of authority to conduct business in another state. However, the other state must recognize the LLC structure and its qualification requirements.

Getting Started

For information on how to start an LLC, see the Getting Started section under Partnerships and Corporate Practice earlier in this chapter.

Control

For information on the issues of control with regard to an LLC, see the Control sections under Partnerships and Corporate Practice earlier in this chapter.

Liability

For more information on LLC liability issues, see the Liability sections under Partnerships and Corporate Practice earlier in this chapter.

Continuity and Transferability

For more information on continuity and transferability of an LLC, see the Continuity and Transferability sections under Partnerships and Corporate Practice earlier in this chapter.

Taxes

An LLC may be a sole proprietorship, a corporation, or a partnership. (A minimum of two members is required for federal tax purposes to operate an LLC as a partnership.) Consequently, the applicable tax forms, estimated tax payment requirements, and related tax publications depend upon whether the LLC operates as a sole proprietorship, corporation, or partnership. The default entity for federal tax treatment of an LLC with two or more members is a partnership. The default entity of a limited liability partnership (LLP) is a partnership and the partnership tax forms, estimated payment requirements, and partnership publications apply. An LLC and/or LLP is allowed to make an entity election with Form 8832, Entity Classification Election.[3]

Office-Sharing Arrangements

While this is not a legal structure, some physicians choose to share offices in order to share the cost of operations with another physician. The two (or more) parties should maintain a written agreement concerning their arrangement.

Patients should be informed that the physicians have separate legal entities. If there is no written agreement, and if patients assume that the physicians are partners, any and all physicians may be implicated in a malpractice litigation. The parties also need to be mindful of any Stark anti-kickback regulations, such as allowing another physician to share office space, supplies, staff, or other resources in exchange for their referrals. Allowing such activity would be a direct violation of the law. For a complete listing of the Stark Law regulations go to oig.hhs.gov/. These scenarios underscore the importance of establishing a written agreement.

The written agreement should include the following:

- A statement of purpose (eg, "This agreement is solely for the purpose of sharing office space for the practice of medicine and is not an agreement creating a partnership between the two parties.")
- Names of the parties involved, the location of the office, whether the parties enter into the lease, or one physician sublets or leases a part of his or her owned space to another physician; the term of the lease agreement
- How the office space will be allocated
- How expenses will be allocated (ie, equally, based on allocated space, by a predetermined formula, borne separately)
- Allocation of personnel. (Sharing staff members carries some risks for the physicians. It is recommended that each physician employ his or her own employees.)
- Provisions for purchase of equipment and furniture
- General liability insurance/health insurance coverage. (This may be purchased as one policy at considerable savings to all physicians. Check with your insurance agent.)
- Provisions in case of the death or disability of one of the physicians
- Provisions for a physician to end the agreement (eg, assignment of telephone number, division of furniture and equipment, substitution of another tenant)

Comparing Legal Entities

In summary, Table 2-4, Comparison of Legal Entities, compares aspects of these business models to be considered when setting up your medical practice.

For more information, refer to the Small Business Administration's *Selecting the Legal Structure for Your Business* at www.sba.gov/library/pubs. Because state laws vary, consult with an attorney to obtain the legal advice necessary for establishing your practice.

TABLE 2-4 Comparison of Legal Entities[4]

	Difficulty and Cost to Form	Difficulty and Cost to Maintain	Risk of Owner Liability	Difficulty of Tax Preparation	Flexibility of Ownership; Bringing in New Owners	Cost of Terminating Business
Sole Proprietorship	Low	Low	High	Low	Low	Low
Partnership	Low to moderate	Low	High	Moderate	Moderate	High
Corporation	High	High	Low	High	High	High
Sub S Corporation	High	High	Low	High	Low	High

Conclusion

The best way to make a good decision about choosing the organizational structure for your practice is to have a broad base of knowledge of the advantages and disadvantages of each business entity. Then you will be able to make an informed decision based upon your personality and preferences. Regardless of which type of organizational structure you select, you will need to adhere to the tax requirements and comply with the regulations that apply to that legal entity.

References

1. Internal Revenue Service. Choosing a Business Structure. www.irs.gov/newsroom/article/0,,id=183918,00.html. Accessed June 18, 2011.

2. Internal Revenue Service. Partnerships, Small Business/Self-Employed. www.irs.gov/businesses/small/article/0,,id=98214,00.html. Accessed June 18, 2011.

3. Internal Revenue Service. Small Business/Self-Employed. www.irs.gov/businesses/small/article/0,,id=98277,00.html. Accessed June 18, 2011.

4. US Small Business Administration. *Selecting the Legal Structure for Your Business.* http://archive.sba.gov/idc/groups/public/documents/sba_homepage/pub_mp25.pdf. Accessed August 29, 2011.

3

Selecting Your Professional Path

Chapter 1, Getting Started, and Chapter 2, Choosing an Organizational Structure, present the various options for going into practice, weighing the pros and cons of each option. Although the business model of the entity may vary, the three primary options to consider are the following:

- **Option One:** Solo Practice
- **Option Two:** Group Practice (includes partnerships)
- **Option Three:** Hospital Employment

The third option that physicians need to consider in the current health care market is employment by hospitals. Because of the dynamics of the current health care industry, including increasing costs, higher numbers of uninsured patients, and overall decreasing levels of reimbursement, physicians are often choosing to bypass private practice and work directly for a hospital as an employed physician. As this option for physicians has very little to do with starting, buying, and owning a medical practice, it is outside the scope of this text. (Note: The relevance of high numbers of uninsured patients is dependent upon whether the Affordable Health Care Act of 2010 is found to be constitutional—a matter which is before the courts at this writing.)

Employment Contract

When considering opportunities to join a group practice, most physicians will first join as an employed physician, with opportunities for shareholder status in future years. With this being the case, the physician must first enter into an employment relationship, which entails the

TABLE 3-1   Practice Option Grid

	Positives	Negatives
Solo Practice	• Independence • Clinical and operational autonomy • Immediate rewards for efficiency	• Total risk for practice and clinical management • Must develop own patient base • No financial cushion • Costly due to full funding of start-up costs
Small Group Practice	• Greater role in governance than in larger group • Shared risk and overhead	• Responsible for colleagues' performance • Less independence than solo practice • Shared financial losses
Large Group Practice	• Overhead costs and financial risk spread among more physicians • Clinical synergies • Referral opportunities • Strength in negotiating with third party payers	• Reduced independence • Reduced governance role • Liability for group financial and clinical performance
Employee Status	• Low financial risk • Guaranteed paychecks • Relief from practice administration	• Limited income growth potential • Little independence or control • Future tied to organization's success

signing of an employment agreement. Understandably, almost every employment contract is written to favor the employer. Nevertheless, it is important for physicians to protect their rights by ensuring that the contract is fairly written.

Before signing any type of employment agreement, it is important for physicians to know what key terms to look for and how to interpret the contract language. In many cases it is good to consult a qualified health care attorney to assist in navigating this process. It is also important to understand that there is always room for negotiation. Very rarely are the terms initially presented considered to be final terms. In general, it is a good start to thoroughly read the contract and first get clarification on any areas where there is a lack of understanding. Once this has been completed, any points that are a cause for concern should be highlighted so that they can be further discussed with the practice. These should then be ranked in order of importance. Once the physician has a solid foundation for negotiations, he or she should present these key concerns to the practice and negotiate firmly on the highest ranked items and be willing to concede in areas of less concern.

Employment contracts generally include the following clauses. We have outlined some key questions of consideration for each.

1. **Terms of the Contract**
    a. Does the contract become effective on the date it is signed or on the day you start to work?
    b. What is the length of the contract?
    c. Does it have an automatic renewal? Is it subject to renegotiation at the time of renewal?

2. **Duties**
    a. What is the expectation for baseline clinical hours?
    b. What specific call duties will the employee be expected to handle relative to practice patients and the emergency department?
    b. Is the employee restricted in entering into other contracts outside of the employment relationship? For example, moonlighting, clinical research, expert witness testimony, etc. If so, how will the revenue associated with such be treated?
    c. Will the physician have the ability to limit the number of uninsured or underinsured patients seen?
    d. Will there be any restrictions on treatment protocols?
    e. What penalties, if any, are incurred if the employee voluntarily terminates employment before the contract expires?
    f. What provisions will apply if the employee is called to jury duty or military duty?

3. **Compensation**
    a. What salary will the employee receive? Is this guaranteed or simply a draw on actual profits?
    b. Is there a productivity expectation associated with base salary?
    c. What opportunities are there for the base salary to increase?
    d. What opportunities exist for incentive compensation, and how are they calculated?

4. **Benefits**
    a. Are pension and/or profit sharing plans available? What is the vesting schedule?
    b. Will the employer pay the employee's malpractice insurance premiums?
    c. Who pays for tail insurance? (See Chapter 8, Identifying Insurance Requirements, for discussion of tail insurance.)
    d. Will the physician employees participate in the group life, disability, or other insurance plans?

e. What additional fringe benefits will the employee receive?

    (1) Vacation

    (2) Sick leave/discretionary days

    (3) CME/conventions/postgraduate work

    (4) Professional books and periodicals

    (5) Professional dues

    (6) Medical equipment

    (7) Office space

    (8) Clerical help

    (9) Automobile allowance

    (10) Moving allowance

5. Buy-In Agreement

a. What triggers will exist for the physician to obtain shareholder status in the practice? Will they be based on time, profitability, productivity, etc?

b. What percentage of the practice will the employee be able to purchase at buy in?

c. How will the buy-in amount be calculated and what will be the resultant cost?

d. How will the buy in be treated? Lump-sum payment, reallocation of profits to effectuate a pre-tax buy in, structured payment plan?

6. Covenant Not to Compete (Restrictive Covenant)

a. Will the employee be asked to sign a covenant not to compete? What are the specific terms of such a covenant?

b. How enforceable is a covenant not to compete in the state where the contract is signed?

c. How reasonable is the time limit associated with the covenant not to compete?

d. Are there any other clauses in this contract that impose certain obligations or restrictions on the employee?

e. Will there be a liquidated damage clause allowing a physician to buy out of the noncompete clause?

7. Termination

a. Will there be a termination without cause provision? If so, what is the length of the notice period required? 30 days, 90 days, 180 days? Can either the physician or employer implement this provision?

b. Does the contract terminate on disability or death of the employee, or will the employee's family or estate be subject to contractual obligations?

   c. Upon termination, can the employer hold the employee accountable for under-performance losses?

   d. Under which, if any, of the following conditions will the contract automatically be terminated?

     (1) Loss of hospital privileges

     (2) Suspension, revocation, or cancellation of employee's right to practice medicine

     (3) Employee refuses to follow practice policies or procedures

     (4) Employee commits an act of gross negligence

     (5) Employee is convicted of a crime (felony)

     (6) Employee becomes impaired due to alcohol or drug abuse

     (7) Breach of contract terms

     (8) Employee becomes disabled (eg, after how many days?)

Understanding Restrictive Covenants

A restrictive covenant, or a covenant not to compete, may be described as an express provision of an employment contract or a partnership agreement that restricts the right of the employee or associate, after the conclusion of his or her term of employment, to engage in a business similar to or competitive with that of the employer, partner, or seller of the practice.

Such restrictions are usually limited to a specified scope, time, and geographical area. In jurisdictions where there are no statutory limitations on restrictive covenants, the general rule is that the courts will enforce such covenants if they are reasonable in view of all of the circumstances of a particular case. In assessing the reasonableness of a particular restrictive covenant, a court may consider three major tests of reasonableness, as follows:

- It is no greater than necessary to protect the employer in some legitimate interest

- It is not unduly harsh and oppressive on the employee

- It is not injurious to the public interest

Each case is decided individually; differing time limits and geographical restrictions could be judged as reasonable in a particular case. Courts tend to enforce restrictive covenants in contracts more often for the sale of a practice or business than in employment or partnership contracts.

It is important for physicians contemplating employment to understand the effect that a restrictive covenant will have on the physician's ability to continue practicing in the service area should he choose to leave the practice. Further, it is often beneficial to obtain legal advice on the restrictive covenant provisions to understand how market-based and enforceable they are. If the employer insists on a covenant, the physician may wish to negotiate the following:

- A trial period before the restrictive covenant becomes operative
- An eventual time frame after which the covenant is no longer in force
- A provision that states that the restrictive covenant is null and void if the employee is terminated without cause or if the employee terminates the agreement for cause

Income Distribution and Expense Allocation

Some groups pay each physician a salary and a portion of net revenue, if any, that remains after paying expenses and physician salaries. This excess may be paid to each physician equally or distributed according to a formula. If you will be receiving a base salary and participating in the distribution of net revenue, it is important to understand the income distribution formula.

Income Distribution

Following are various examples of income distribution that you may encounter in practice options:

- **Equal Distribution.** Each member receives an equal share of the practice profits.
- **Productivity.** The profits availability for distribution are allocated based on each physician's individual productivity contribution, which can be measured using cash collections, work Relative Value Units (wRVUs), or gross charges.
- **Hybrid:** This is simply a mix between an equal and productivity-based distribution, wherein parts of the profits are allocated equally, with the remaining based on productivity.
- **Formulas.** While not always applicable, there are a number of factors that can impact the income distribution plan of a practice. Some of these factors are as follows:
  - Goodwill/Longevity
  - Stock ownership
  - Productivity
  - Board certification
  - Administrative roles (eg, managing partner, etc)
  - New patients
  - Referral sources
  - Teaching/Faculty position

In most instances, because of the focus on profitability within private practice, the main component of an income distribution plan is the productivity of the physicians, coupled with the practice's overhead. The other factors rarely play a significant role.

Note: Stark regulations prevent practices from directly allocating the revenues/profits from certain ancillary services directly to the referring physician, at least for governmental payers (Medicare and Medicaid). While there are various means of allocating these ancillaries in a compliant manner, the most common method is an equal allocation among participating physicians.

Methods of Expense Allocation

The following are four methods used to allocate expenses:

- **Equal Allocation.** This is the easiest method in that the expenses of the practice are simply allocated equally among the members of the practice. Thus, each physician shares equally in the cost of operating the practice, regardless of who consumed the resources.

- **Direct Costs.** Any costs incurred that can be attributed directly to a physician are charged directly to that physician. This allows each physician to practice in a style he or she prefers without negatively impacting other physicians who choose to practice in a different manner.

- **Indirect Costs.** Costs such as rent, utilities, and maintenance are charged to each physician based on some method of allocation. The allocation can vary based on the type of expense considered. For example, rent and other facility costs can be allocated as a per-square-foot charge, whereas drug costs can be allocated as a percentage of revenue. The intent with this model is to allocate costs consistent with consumption. Thus, physicians who consume more resources incur a greater charge.

- **Expenses as a Percentage of Productivity**. Each physician is charged for expenses at the same rate he or she generates income for the practice. If the physician generates 40% of the income, he or she has a commensurate share of the expense (ie, 40%). In a multispecialty group, the surgical specialists may object to this type of allocation, because primary care physicians typically use much more space than other physicians.

Compensation

The following are types of physician compensation:

- **Guarantees.** A form of base compensation that is not at risk based on the level of productivity.

- **Draw.** A form of base compensation that is paid as an advance on future earnings. Thus, the profits allocated to the physician will take into account the draw or advance payment. That is, the draw will be subtracted from the amount paid to the physician from the profits.

- **Productivity Incentives.** Additional compensation paid to the physician for exceeding certain goals. These goals may include cost containment, utilization, patient satisfaction, or revenue. In most instances revenue (productivity) and cost containment are the key factors.

- **Benefits.** The benefit package will come at a cost to the employer and therefore is often considered part of the total compensation. In some cases, benefits may be compensated by agreeing to less base pay.

As a gauge of the compensation being provided, it is beneficial to compare to industry benchmarking sources, such as those provided by the Medical Group Management Association, Sullivan, Cotter and Associates, and American Medical Group Association. Conversely, it is important to note that these benchmarks also include statistics on productivity that must be met to achieve the salary benchmarks. A new physician may have lower productivity, which must be kept in mind before making any demands to be paid at these benchmark levels.

Group Practice Questionnaire

Use the questionnaire in Figure 3-1 to gather information about each practice you consider. By gathering the same information on each type of practice, a fair comparison using the same criteria can be generated.

Conclusion

If starting your medical practice means joining a group or affiliating with an existing organization, you will need to know a great deal about employment agreements and compensation arrangements. Gather all the facts and assess the conditions of employment before signing on with an existing practice to make sure that the organization is a good fit for your practice style and goals.

General Information

Date:

Name of group:

Office address:

Telephone:

Addresses of satellite offices:

Name of person to contact for future information:

Home telephone number:

Group Structure

What is the legal structure of the group?

❑ Partnership

❑ Professional Corporation

❑ Limited Liability Corporation

❑ Individuals sharing space

Single or multi-specialty?

Who are the group's partners and/or principal stockholders?

Name: Age: Gender: Specialty: (for each physician)

Who are the employed physicians?

Name: Age: Gender: Specialty: (for each physician)

Are there physicians planning to retire? If so, what is the expected date(s) of retirement?

Are there plans to increase the size of the group?

What is the ultimate goal regarding size?

What makes up the group's geographic market area (eg, counties, miles)?

What is the population of the group's market area?

How many physicians in my specialty, not associated with this group's market area?

Area Hospitals

List hospitals where group members have staff privileges.

Name: # of beds: (for each)

Are there other hospitals in the area?

Does the group place restriction on having privileges at other hospitals?

Buy-In Opportunities

Does the group offer partnership to all physician employees?

What are the criteria for partnership?

What are the number of years of employment required?

FIGURE 3-1   Group Practice Questionnaire

Is buy in required?

Are the buy-in requirements written into the original employment contract?

Practice Styles

What is the ethical orientation of the group (ie, abortions, birth control, euthanasia)?

Is there a feeling of compatibility and cooperation among group physicians?

Are all group members board certified?

Do any group members have a particular skill or certification that sets them apart from other specialists in the same field? If so, what are these skills?

Are academic appointments encouraged?

Are there constraints placed on time spent in teaching activities?

Do any of the physicians have personal or practice problems or limitations of which associates should be aware?

How many physicians have left the group in the last three years?

Were they employees or partner physicians?

What were their reasons for leaving?

Will the other physicians in the group be introduced before making a decision?

Social Interactions

Do the physicians seem to have a good relationship with each other?

Is socializing expected or discouraged among physicians?

Do spouses socialize with each other?

Have the spouses of the group's physicians been introduced?

How does the physician's spouse feel about the other spouses that have been introduced?

Do any of the physicians have personal/social problems?

Income Distribution

How is practice income distributed?

❑ Equally

❑ Based on productivity

❑ Based on formula. If formula, what factors are used to determine income?

What method is used to allocate expenses?

❑ Income and expenses shared equally

❑ Income and expenses based on productivity

❑ Income based on productivity, expenses shared equally

(Read Income Distribution and Expense Allocation on page 48 to interpret the answers to these questions.)

FIGURE 3-1   Group Practice Questionnaire (*continued*)

Office Facilities

What was the first impression of the office appearance?

How long has the group practiced at this address?

How many square feet are there in the facility?

What ancillary services are provided in the office?

How accessible is the practice location to patients?

Are parking facilities adequate? If not, what plans exist to improve this?

Will a personal consulting office be available?

How many exam rooms does each physician have?

If there are satellite locations, are the physicians rotated through each location?

What is the rotation schedule?

Is the office clean? Well organized? Well equipped?

Are there plans for future expansion?

Is the size of the reception area adequate?

Is there adequate seating in the exam rooms (eg, three seats per exam room is average)?

Is special equipment available if a specialty requires it?

Is the facility owned by the group, by the physicians personally, or leased from another
   entity?

What is the distance to hospital(s)?

Is the practice in a high growth area or in a declining neighborhood?

What days and hours are the offices open?

Group Governance

How are decisions made within the group?

❑ Majority vote?

❑ Governing board?

❑ Senior physicians?

❑ Informal clique?

❑ Consensus?

Who makes day-to-day decisions versus long-term decisions or changes?

Is there an office manager/administrator?

To whom does this person report?

Are there regular business meetings?

How often are they held?

Are all physicians required to attend?

FIGURE 3-1   Group Practice Questionnaire (*continued*)

Office Personnel

How many employees in the practice? Clinical? Administrative?

What is the staff-to-physician ratio?

Are physician extenders used? How many Physician Assistants? Nurse Practitioners?

Does each physician have a personal clinical assistant?

Does the office appear over- or understaffed?

How are patients treated by the staff?

Does the staff seem efficient, courteous, and professional?

How many staff members have left voluntarily within the last year?

What were the reasons they left? (ask staff members)

How many staff members have been terminated?

Have they been replaced?

Is there good communication between staff and physicians?

Financial Overview

What were the total charges last year?

What were the adjusted charges last year (eg, after contractual write-offs, such as Medicare and managed care)?

What were the total collections for the same period?

What were the total expenses?

What is the breakdown of expenses?

What are the total accounts receivable?

What are the total dollars of A/R over 90 days? Percentage of total A/R?

Does the practice have an operational budget?

How does it compare with actual figures?

Does the group review financials together every month?

What reports will be routinely provided?

What is the fee schedule, and how it is established?

Are billing and collections done in-house?

If not, how is it handled?

Is the practice computerized?

What software is used for practice management and EHR?

Who handles the payables (eg, office manager, accountant, other)?

Who signs the checks?

FIGURE 3-1   Group Practice Questionnaire (*continued*)

Payer Mix/Contracting

Are all physicians participating in Medicare/Medicaid?

What percentage of practice is Medicare/Medicaid?

What requirements are there in participating in various insurance plans, including governmental payers?

What is the overall payer mix of the practice?

Does the group have any capitated contracts?

Any incentive contracts (Accountable Care Organization (ACO) participation, other payer
incentive plans)?

Patient Distribution

How are new patients distributed if no preference is given?

How is the patient load distributed?

Who sees nursing home patients?

What is the current call schedule rotation?

Malpractice Issues

What has been the group's malpractice experience?

Are any malpractice suits pending?

Are any considered to have merit?

Are any liabilities retroactive?

FIGURE 3-1   Group Practice Questionnaire (*continued*)

Regulations and Licensing Requirements

Health care is one of the most highly regulated industries in the nation, with many exposures to liabilities and bureaucracies. An initial challenge in starting a medical practice is learning the plethora of rules and regulations that govern health care. It is important to know the state requirements for starting and continuing a medical practice while keeping in mind the scores of federal regulations and procedures. Especially daunting is that the rules are constantly changing, which requires continuous education for the practitioner and practice staff. However, with the proper resources, you can maneuver your way through the minefield successfully.

The purpose of this chapter is to provide a resource directory for local, state, and federal regulations and licenses required for starting a practice and beyond. To have one source available with the requirements of every regulation would require a huge volume, with information of immeasurable proportions. Bear in mind that in some cases the regulation may not be entirely applicable and/or some may not be available in this book. For example, Joint Commission on Accreditation of Healthcare Organizations (JCAHO) regulations apply only if your practice is owned by a JCAHO-approved hospital. In any case, we want to provide you with a comprehensive listing of necessary resources for these regulations for starting your practice and ongoing compliance.

Regulations can be overwhelming. Our advice is to become familiar with the basics, know where to find additional answers when you need them, and, if in doubt, contact the proper resource for information.

License Resources and Requirements

The resource and information that follow are license requirements and regulatory resources for setting up a medical practice, followed by resources for regulations related to continuing practice.

Employer Identification Number

As an employer, you will need an Employer Identification Number (EIN). All correspondence with the IRS and all tax payments must reference this EIN. You can apply for an EIN several ways, but regardless of how it is obtained, a Form SS-4 will need to be completed, which may be obtained at any IRS or Social Security Administration Office or online at www.irs.gov. The telephone number and address for the local IRS Service Center are available in the telephone book under state and/or federal government listings (blue pages) or at www.irs.gov/localcontacts/index.html. Once the application form has been completed and mailed, it takes approximately five weeks to receive the EIN.

The most expeditious way to apply is online, and once all validation is done, you will get your EIN immediately upon completion. You can then download, save, and print the EIN confirmation notice. The EIN can also be applied for by telephone. Likewise, telephone applicants immediately receive their EIN. However, you will need to complete the Form SS-4 before calling your state's IRS Service Center. When the EIN is obtained by telephone, the completed form must be mailed or faxed within 24 hours.

State Tax Identification Number

A state tax number may also be needed from the Director of Revenue in your state. Check with your accountant to be certain that all required identifying numbers for establishing a medical practice in your state have been received. It is always prudent to have a knowledgeable accountant to converse with on initial tax issues that arise when starting a medical practice, as well as to answer any questions or problems that may arise in the future.

State Medical License

Call the State Board of Medical Examiners to obtain the necessary application forms and a list of any back-up documents that may be needed to apply for your state license. For a complete Internet listing of contact information for the Board of Medical Examiners in your state, go to www.ama-assn.org/ or go to the Federation of State Medical Boards at www.fsmb.org/.

Medical Staff Privileges

Before hospital medical staff privileges are awarded, you must be licensed to practice medicine in your state. In order to obtain privileges from each hospital, it is a good idea to visit each hospital in the area where you need to obtain staff privileges. Complete the necessary credentialing forms and collect any other documents that may be needed for obtaining admitting privileges. If you are joining a group practice that already has staff privileges and need to be on call immediately, temporary privileges may be awarded until a license is received.

Federal Narcotics License/Drug Enforcement Administration Registration Number

Under the Controlled Substances Act of 1970, if you have never had a Drug Enforcement Administration (DEA) number, you will need to contact the Department of Justice at the following address to obtain a license to dispense narcotics. New applicants will use DEA Form 224, Application for Registration. This form is for the retail pharmacy, hospital/clinic, practitioner, teaching institution, or mid-level practitioner categories only. The current fee is $210 for three years.

United States Department of Justice
Drug Enforcement Administration
Central Station
P.O. Box 28083
Washington, DC 20038-8083
(202) 307-7725
(800) 882-9539
www.deadiversion.usdoj.gov/drugreg/reg_apps/index.html

All registrants must report any changes of professional or business address to the DEA. Notification of address changes must be made in writing to the DEA office that has jurisdiction for your registered location. For a list of DEA offices go to the DEA website noted above. Direct requests to the address that is listed for your state for the following actions:

- Request a modification to your DEA registration (address change)
- Request order form books
- Status of pending application

DEA Form 224A, Renewal Application for Retail Pharmacy, Hospital/Clinic, Practitioner, Teaching Institution, or Mid-Level Practitioner, is also available at the DEA website.

State Narcotics License

Some states will also require you to have a state-issued narcotics license and/or a drug license through the state pharmacy board. Check with your state Medical Board to see if the state requires a state DEA license in addition to the federal license. If you are practicing in more than one state, you will need a federal DEA number for each state.

Center for Medicare and Medicaid Services

It is essential to become familiar with the ongoing issues and developments from the Centers for Medicare and Medicaid Services (CMS). CMS is a federal agency within the US Department of Health and Human Services that administers the Medicare program and works with state governments to administer Medicaid and the Child Health Insurance Program (CHIP), and develop insurance portability standards. CMS has also developed Administrative Standards from the Health Insurance Portability and Accountability Act of 1996 (HIPAA), quality standards in long-term care facilities, and clinical laboratory quality standards under the Clinical Laboratory Improvement Amendments (CLIA).

National Provider Identifier

Obtaining a National Provider Identifier (NPI) is mandatory when starting a medical practice. NPI is a distinctive identification number for covered health care providers. Covered health care providers, all health plans, and health care clearinghouses must use the NPIs in the administrative and financial transactions adopted under HIPAA. The NPI is a ten-digit number that is intelligence-free. This means that the numbers do not carry other information about health care providers, such as the state in which they live or their medical specialty. The NPI is simply a HIPAA Administrative Simplification Standard that must be used in lieu of legacy provider identifiers in the HIPAA standards transactions.

CMS has developed the National Plan and Provider Enumeration System (NPPES) to assign these unique identifiers. Health care providers can apply for NPIs in one of three ways:

- For the most efficient application processing and the fastest receipt of NPI, use the web-based application process. Simply log onto the National Plan and Provider Enumeration System (NPPES) and apply on line (see nppes.cms.hhs.gov).

- Health care providers can agree to have an electronic file interchange organization (EFIO) submit application data on their behalf (ie, through a bulk enumeration process) if an EFIO requests their permission to do so.

- Health care providers may wish to obtain a copy of the paper NPI Application/Update Form (CMS-10114) and mail the completed, signed application to the NPI Enumerator located in Fargo, ND, whereby staff at the NPI Enumerator will enter the application

data into NPPES. This form is now available for download from
the CMS website or by request from the NPI Enumerator. Health
care providers who wish to obtain a copy of this form from the
NPI Enumerator may do so in any of these ways:

- Phone: 1-800-465-3203 or TTY 1-800-692-2326
- E-mail: customerservice@npienumerator.com
- Mail: NPI Enumerator
            PO Box 6059
            Fargo, ND 58108-6059

Medicare Provider Number

If you will be providing medical services to Medicare recipients, you will
need to apply for a Medicare Provider Number. CMS has this information on their website at www.cms.gov/. The NPI is required to be submitted when you apply for a Medicare Provider Number. You can apply for
the number in one of two ways.

First you can fill out the PDF fillable format online and mail it. This
means that you can fill out the information required by typing into the
open fields while the form is displayed on your computer monitor. Fill-
ing out the forms this way before printing, signing, and mailing means
more easily readable information, which also means fewer mistakes,
questions, and delays when your application is processed. Be sure to
make a copy of the signed form for your records before mailing.

Secondly and the most efficient method for submitting your enrollment application, is to use the Internet-based Provider Enrollment,
Chain and Ownership System (PECOS). PECOS guides you through
the enrollment application so you only supply information relevant to
your application. PECOS also reduces the need for follow-up because
of incomplete applications. Using Internet-based PECOS results in a
more accurate application and saves you time and administrative
costs. Mail your completed application and all supporting documentation to the Medicare fee-for-service contractor (also referred to as a
carrier, fiscal intermediary, Medicare Administrative Contractor, or
the National Supplier Clearinghouse) serving your state or geographic
location.

Routinely submitted with the Medicare enrollment application is the
Electronic Funds Transfer (EFT) Authorization Agreement (Form CMS
588) and the Medicare Participating Physician or Supplier Agreement
(Form CMS 460).

The Medicare application fee is $505 as of 2011; however, based
upon provisions of Section 6401(a) of the Affordable Care Act (ACA)
this fee will vary from year-to-year based on adjustments made pursuant to the Consumer Price Index for Urban Areas. The application
fee is to be imposed on institutional providers that are newly enrolling,

re-enrolling, revalidating, or adding a new practice location when applications are received on and after March 25, 2011.

Medicaid Provider Number

Medicaid is a health insurance program in the United States for low-income people. If you want to be paid for services rendered to Medicaid patients, you must become a Medicaid provider. As a participating Medicaid provider, you can see Medicaid patients and get reimbursed for medical and medical-related services by the government. Medicaid is a state-administered program, and each state sets its own guidelines regarding eligibility and services. Therefore, it is necessary to contact your local department of health services. The following website will direct you to the correct state agency: www.cms.gov/apps/contacts/.

Business License

In addition to registration with the Secretary of State, a city and/or county business license may be necessary. If the practice is within the city limits, go to city hall to purchase your license. If the practice is outside the city limits, most likely the license can be obtained by applying at the county courthouse. In rare instances, both a city and a county license may be needed.

Laboratory License

In October 1988, the federal government passed the Clinical Laboratories Improvement Amendments (CLIA), which became effective in September 1992. This program requires all entities that perform even one test, including the test granted waived status under CLIA on ". . . materials derived from the human body for the purpose of providing information for the diagnosis, prevention or treatment of any disease or impairment of, or the assessment of the health of, human beings" to meet certain federal requirements. If an entity performs tests for these purposes, it is considered under CLIA to be a laboratory and must register with the CLIA program.

The CMS has made available the CLIA Application for Certification Form (CMS-116) at www.cms.gov/clia/. This website provides not only the form that needs to be used in your circumstance, but also instructions on completing the form, guidelines for counting tests for CLIA, the tests commonly performed, and their corresponding laboratory specialties and/or subspecialties. This form should be completed and mailed to the address of the local state agency for the state in which your laboratory resides and not to CMS.

Costs are involved in having an in-office laboratory. Each level has a registration fee and an annual inspection fee. Other costs are in proportion to the level of the laboratory and the annual test volume.

Other Regulatory Agencies, Programs, and Issues

The physician must be cognizant of ongoing issues and policies of agencies that regulate the practice of medicine. Particular attention must be paid to decisions and actions by the Center for Medicare and Medicaid Services (CMS) and the many programs initiated and created by CMS; the Health Insurance Portability and Accountability Act of 1996 (HIPAA) regulations; accreditation standards of the Joint Commission on Accreditation of Healthcare Organizations (JCAHO) that may affect your practice; and activities of the Office of the Inspector General (OIG) and the Department of Justice (DOJ). As an employer, other important agencies should be considered, such as the Occupational Safety and Health Administration (OSHA), the US Department of Labor (USDOL), and the Equal Employment Opportunity Commission (EEOC). Some of these initiatives are described in this section.

Health Insurance Portability and Accountability Act

The Administrative Simplification provisions of the Health Insurance Portability and Accountability Act of 1996 (HIPAA, Title II) required the Department of Health and Human Services (HHS) to adopt national standards for electronic health care transactions and national identifiers for providers, health plans, and employers. To date, the implementation of HIPAA standards has increased the use of electronic data interchange, and provisions under the Affordable Care Act of 2010 will further these increases. This will include requirements for operating rules for each of the HIPAA covered transactions, a unique, standard Health Plan Identifier (HPID), a standard and operating rules for electronic funds transfer (EFT), and electronic remittance advice (RA) and claims attachments.

In addition, health plans will be required to certify their compliance. The Act provides for substantial penalties for failures to certify or comply with the new standards and operating rules. For more information regarding HIPAA, including additional provisions under the Patient Protections and Affordable Care Act (Affordable Care Act or ACA) of 2010, go to www.cms.gov/HIPAA/.

Office of Inspector General

The Office of Inspector General (OIG) protects the integrity of the Department of Health and Human Services (HHS) programs, as well as the health and welfare of the beneficiaries of those programs. The OIG's responsibility is to report all program and management problems and to offer recommendations to correct them to the Secretary of the Department and Congress. The OIG's duties are carried out through a nationwide network of audits, investigations, inspections, and other mission-related functions performed by the OIG components. For more information on activities of the OIG and its effect on the medical practice, visit oig.hhs.gov/.

Department of Justice

The Department of Justice (DOJ) enforces the law and defends the interests of the United States by providing federal leadership in preventing and controlling crime, seeking just punishment for those who are guilty of unlawful behavior, and ensuring fair and impartial administration of justice for all Americans. For more information, visit www/usdoj.gov. The DOJ works with HHS to prevent Medicare fraud and abuse and to bring charges against those who violate the Medicare and Medicaid programs.

Recovery Audit Contractors

In an effort to prevent waste, fraud, and abuse in Medicare, CMS launched the national recovery audit contractor (RAC) program. RACs are independent contract auditors who detect and correct improper payments in the Medicare program. If the RACs find that any Medicare claim was paid improperly, they will then request repayment from the provider if an overpayment was found or request that the provider is paid in full if the claim was underpaid.

Section 302 of the Tax Relief and Health Care Act of 2006 made the Recovery Audit Program permanent and required the Secretary to expand the program to all 50 states by no later than 2010. The newest list of national RACs is available at www.cms.hhs.gov/RAC.

Zone Program Integrity Contractors

Zone program integrity contractors (ZPICs) are organizations hired indirectly, or in connection with other CMS affiliated contractors, by CMS to perform a wide range of medical review, data analysis, and Medicare audits. While ZPIC audits are similar in many ways to other Medicare audits currently performed nationwide, they differ in one very important aspect—potential Medicare fraud implications. Of all the current CMS audit initiatives, such as RAC and MIC audits, it is vital that providers facing ZPIC audits immediately and effectively address targeted audit issues.

Medicaid Integrity Contractors

Medicaid integrity contractors (MICs) are similar to RACs but for the purpose of fighting Medicaid fraud, waste, and abuse. They are independent auditors contracted by CMS to review and audit health care provider's claims as well as provide education. Although MICs are not utilized in every jurisdiction at the present time, it is important to be aware of them and the goal to expand their use throughout the nation.

Quality Improvement Organizations

CMS contracts with one organization in each state, as well as the District of Columbia, Puerto Rico, and the US Virgin Islands to serve as that state or jurisdiction's quality improvement organization (QIO) contractor. QIOs are private, mostly not-for-profit organizations, which are staffed by professionals—mostly doctors and other health care professionals—who are trained to review medical care, help beneficiaries with complaints about the quality of care, and to implement improvements in the quality of care available throughout the spectrum of care.

By law, the mission of the QIO program is to improve the effectiveness, efficiency, economy, and quality of services delivered to Medicare beneficiaries. Based on this statutory charge, and CMS program experience, CMS identifies the core functions of the QIO program as:

- Improving quality of care for beneficiaries
- Protecting the integrity of the Medicare Trust Fund by ensuring that Medicare pays only for services and goods that are reasonable and necessary and that are provided in the most appropriate setting
- Protecting beneficiaries by expeditiously addressing individual complaints, such as beneficiary complaints; provider-based notice appeals; violations of the Emergency Medical Treatment and Labor Act (EMTALA); and other related responsibilities as articulated in QIO-related law.

Program Safeguard Contractors

CMS awards some integrity task orders to program safeguard contractors (PSCs) to perform the work of detecting and deterring fraud and abuse in Medicare. Similar to RACs and ZPICs, a part of their duties is to investigate and determine the facts and magnitude of alleged fraud and abuse. Upon completing investigations, PSCs determine whether to refer the investigations as cases to law enforcement.

However, CMS typically limits the contract with the PSC to one specific task at a time and expects PSCs to be more innovative and effective in data analysis, moving beyond the capabilities of carrier and fiscal intermediary fraud units. This was one of the reasons for awarding contracts to PSCs. CMS expects a significant part of PSC data analysis to be proactive by allowing more self-initiated exploratory analysis that seeks previously unidentified patterns or instances of fraud and abuse.

Federal Employee Program

As a health care provider it would be useful to familiarize yourself with the Blue Cross and Blue Shield Association (BCBSA) Government-wide Service Benefit Plan, also known as the federal employee program (FEP). FEP has been part of the Federal Employees Health Benefits Program (FEHBP) since its inception in 1960 and covers roughly 4.5 million federal employees, retirees and their families out of the nearly 8 million people (contract holders as well as their dependents) or about 57% of those receiving benefits through FEHBP. BCBSA works with the Office of Personnel Management to administer the Service Benefit Plan on behalf of the 39 independent Blue Cross and Blue Shield companies. Visit www.fepblue.org to find out more information regarding this program.

Children's Health Insurance Program

The Children's Health Insurance Program (CHIP) is jointly financed by the federal and state governments, is administered by the states, and is designed to expand health care coverage to more than 5 million of the nation's uninsured children. Within the broad federal guidelines, each state determines the design of its program, eligibility groups, benefit packages, payment levels for coverage, and administrative and operating procedures. CHIP provides a capped amount of funds to states on a matching basis. Federal payments under Title XXI to states are based on state expenditures under approved plans effective on or after October 1, 1997.

Joint Commission on Accreditation of Healthcare Organizations

The Joint Commission on Accreditation of Healthcare Organizations (JCAHO) evaluates and accredits nearly 18,000 health care organizations and programs in the United States. JCAHO is an independent, not-for-profit organization and is the nation's predominant standard-setting and accrediting body in health care. Its mission is to improve the safety and quality of care provided to the public through the provision of health care accreditation and related services that support performance improvement in health care organizations. For more information on JCAHO and its effect on the medical practice, visit www.jcaho.org.

Occupational Safety and Health Administration

The Occupational Safety and Health Administration's (OSHA) mission is to save lives, prevent injuries, and protect the health of America's workers. OSHA and its state partners have approximately 2,100 inspectors, plus complaint discrimination investigators, engineers, physicians, educators, standards writers, and other technical and support personnel spread over more than 200 offices throughout the country. This staff establishes protective standards, enforces those standards, and reaches out to employers and employees through technical assistance and consultation programs. Medical practices are subject to OSHA Guidelines for Bloodborne Pathogens and adherence to OSHA's hazard communication standards. For more information, visit www.osha.gov.

US Department of Labor

The US Department of Labor (USDOL) fosters and promotes the welfare of job seekers, wage earners, and retirees in the United States by improving their working conditions, advancing their opportunities for profitable employment, protecting their retirement and health care benefits, helping employers find workers, strengthening free collective bargaining, and tracking changes in employment, prices, and other national economic measurements. In carrying out this mission, the USDOL administers a variety of federal labor laws, including those that guarantee workers' rights to safe and healthful working conditions; a minimum hourly wage and overtime pay; freedom from employment discrimination; unemployment insurance; and other income support. The USDOL also administers ERISA plans for self-insured employers. For more information, visit www.dol.gov/ on the Internet, and for poster information, see www.dol.gov/elaws/posters.hth/.

Equal Employment Opportunity Commission

The Equal Employment Opportunity Commission (EEOC) protects the civil rights of those in the workforce through enforcement of various employment laws. For example, employers may not discriminate against employees based on race, sex, religion, national origin, physical disability, or age. For more information on the EEOC's application to small businesses such as medical practices, go to www.eeoc.gov/small/overview. The EEOC and employment laws are addressed in *Personnel Management of the Medical Practice,* Second Edition, part of AMA's Practice Success Series.

Conclusion

Starting a medical practice requires adherence to an overabundance of rules and regulations. If the necessary steps are not taken in complying with both the state and federal licensing and regulatory requirements, the practitioner could find him or herself swimming in a nightmare of penalties and legal consequences. This chapter will help you start out on the right foot, stay abreast of the ever-changing requirements, and assist you in staying on track. Only you are responsible for keeping informed of the issues and noting changes as they occur through announcements and bulletins released by the state you practice in and by different regulatory agencies.

5

Society Memberships/ Practice Affiliations

A medical practice is an enterprise that requires collaboration and coordination with other people and entities. Physicians need to be involved with other members of their profession and health care entities on a daily basis. These interactions include call coverage, sharing services, referrals, tenancy in professional office buildings, and more.

Managed-care initiatives sometimes compel physicians to enter affiliations with providers in other organizations and relationships, such as independent practice associations (IPAs), individual practice organizations (IPOs), and management services organizations (MSOs.

Furthermore, many physicians are involved in civic organizations as a way to contribute to their communities, to have a voice in local affairs, and to network. This chapter examines the benefits of memberships and affiliations.

Medical Society Membership

Memberships in professional associations can benefit physicians throughout their careers, both individually and corporately, through the exchange of information and networking. While not required, membership in various medical societies benefits the physician through networking opportunities and the receipt of vital information. Moreover, your practice will thrive by leveraging the resources of these affiliations. Your practice will also benefit from your staff members' participation in key professional affiliations and memberships.

Because of the numerous choices available and the considerable expense of dues, you should carefully consider what each organization has to offer and what its function will be for your practice. Annual membership fees, in general, range from $100 to $1,000, or more. You will want to choose the affiliations that will be most beneficial to you and the practice. If you are in group practice or an employee, check to see if payment of dues is a benefit your organization provides.

The following associations are worth consideration.

American Medical Association

The American Medical Association (AMA) provides the physician a source of help and information about every aspect of the practice of medicine no matter where your practice is located. The AMA speaks out on issues that are important to patients, physicians, and the nation's health. AMA policy on national health issues is decided through its democratic policy-making process at biannual meetings of the AMA House of Delegates. The House is comprised of physician delegates from every state; nearly 100 national medical specialty societies; federal service agencies, including the Surgeon General of the United States; and six sections that represent hospital and clinic staffs, resident physicians, medical students, young physicians, medical schools, and international medical graduates.

You do not need be a member of the AMA to receive information or attend AMA-sponsored seminars. However, as a member, you will receive a discount on seminars, publications, and other services offered through the AMA. The AMA is also an excellent source for continuing medical education (CME) and educational material.

National and State Specialty Societies

National and state specialty associations provide educational opportunities and information about particular specialties and allow you to interact with other physicians who share the same specialty-specific concerns. Table 5-1 lists these organizations. To learn about membership benefits, contact the organization of interest.

Specialty medical societies and state and county medical societies belonging to the AMA House of Delegates are known as the Federation of Medicine. To link to the Federation of Medicine, go to www.ama-assn .org/ama/pub/about-ama/our-people/the-federation-medicine.page.

A list of names and addresses of professional associations are available in Appendix A, Professional Associations.

State and Regional Medical Organizations

Table 5-2 lists state and regional medical organizations that are in the House of Delegates of the AMA. Because of their roles in lobbying with respect to state legislation, providing information on state and regional issues, and networking and leadership opportunities, membership in

TABLE 5-1   The Federation of Medicine

Aerospace Medical Association

American Academy of Allergy Asthma & Immunology

American Academy of Child & Adolescent Psychiatry

American Academy of Cosmetic Surgery

American Academy of Dermatology

American Academy of Facial Plastic and Reconstructive Surgery

American Academy of Family Physicians

American Academy of Insurance Medicine

American Academy of Neurology

American Academy of Ophthalmology

American Academy of Orthopaedic Surgeons

American Academy of Otolaryngology-Head and Neck Surgery

American Academy of Otolaryngic Allergy

American Academy of Pain Medicine

American Academy of Pediatrics

American Academy of Physical Medicine & Rehabilitation

American Academy of Sleep Medicine

American Association for Thoracic Surgery

American Association for Vascular Surgery

American Association of Clinical Endocrinologists

American Association of Electrodiagnostic Medicine

American Association of Gynecological Laparoscopists

American Association of Hip & Knee Surgeons

American Association of Public Health Physicians

American Clinical Neurophysiology Society

American College of Allergy, Asthma, & Immunology

American College of Cardiology

American College of Chest Physicians

American College of Emergency Physicians

American College of Gastroenterology

American College of Medical Genetics

American College of Medical Quality

American College of Nuclear Medicine

American College of Nuclear Physicians

American College of Obstetricians and Gynecologists

American College of Occupational and Environmental Medicine

American College of Physician Executives

(*continued*)

TABLE 5-1   The Federation of Medicine (*continued*)

American College of Physicians–American Society of Internal Medicine
American College of Preventive Medicine
American College of Radiation Oncology
American College of Radiology
American College of Rheumatology
American College of Surgeons
American Gastroenterological Association
American Geriatrics Society
American Medical Group Association
American Orthopaedic Foot and Ankle Society
American Psychiatric Association
American Roentgen Ray Society
American Society for Clinical Pathology
American Society for Dermatologic Surgery
American Society for Gastrointestinal Endoscopy
American Society for Reproductive Medicine
American Society for Surgery of the Hand
American Society for Therapeutic Radiology and Oncology
American Society of Abdominal Surgeons
American Society of Addiction Medicine
American Society of Bariatric Physicians
American Society of Cataract and Refractive Surgery
American Society of Clinical Oncology
American Society of Colon and Rectal Surgeons
American Society of Hematology
American Society of Plastic Surgeons
American Thoracic Society
College of American Pathologists
The Endocrine Society
National Medical Association
North American Spine Society
Radiological Society of North America
Society of American Gastrointestinal Endoscopic Surgeons
Society of Cardiovascular & Interventional Radiology
Society of Critical Care Medicine
Society of Nuclear Medicine
Society of Thoracic Surgeons

TABLE 5-2 House of Delegates of the AMA	

Alabama	**Massachusetts**
Medical Association of the State of Alabama	Massachusetts Medical Society
Arizona	**Michigan**
Arizona Medical Association	Michigan State Medical Society
California	**Minnesota**
California Medical Association	Minnesota Medical Association
Colorado	**Mississippi**
Colorado Medical Society	Mississippi State Medical Association
Connecticut	**Missouri**
Connecticut State Medical Society	Missouri State Medical Association
District of Columbia	**Montana**
Medical Society of the District of Columbia	Montana Medical Association
Delaware	**Nebraska**
Medical Society of Delaware	Nebraska Medical Association
Florida	**New Hampshire**
Florida Medical Association	New Hampshire Medical Society
Georgia	**New Jersey**
Medical Association of Georgia	Medical Society of New Jersey
Hawaii	**New Mexico**
Hawaii Medical Association	New Mexico Medical Society
Illinois	**New York**
Illinois State Medical Society	Medical Society of the State of New York
Chicago Medical Society	**North Carolina**
Indiana	North Carolina Medical Society
Indiana State Medical Association	**North Dakota**
Iowa	North Dakota Medical Association
Iowa Medical Society	**Ohio**
Kansas	Ohio State Medical Association
Kansas Medical Society	**Oklahoma**
Kentucky	Oklahoma State Medical Association
Kentucky Medical Association	**Oregon**
Louisiana	Oregon Medical Association
Louisiana State Medical Society	**Pennsylvania**
Maine	Pennsylvania Medical Society
Maine Medical Association	**Rhode Island**
Maryland	Medicine & Health Rhode Island
Med Chi: Maryland State Medical Society	

(*continued*)

TABLE 5-2 House of Delegates of the AMA (*continued*)

South Dakota	**West Virginia**
South Dakota State Medical Association	West Virginia State Medical Association
Tennessee	**Wisconsin**
Tennessee Medical Association	Wisconsin Medical Society
Texas	**Regional Medical Organizations**
Texas Medical Association	Southern Medical Association
Utah	**National**
Utah Medical Association	American Medical Association
Virginia	American Osteopathic Association
Medical Society of Virginia	National Medical Association
Washington	
Washington State Medical Association	

these associations can be beneficial. For more information, go to www.ama-assn.org.

Local Medical Societies

Local medical societies (ie, city and/or county) provide insight into the local concerns of medical practitioners and allow physicians to share ideas and information with other physicians who are practicing in the area.

Civic Groups

Becoming involved in local civic groups, schools, and other local organizations can benefit your practice indirectly and you personally, providing an opportunity to contribute to the community. Physicians often grow their practices by being known in the community in addition to establishing themselves based on their professional accomplishments. The more positive name recognition you can achieve, the more likely patients will be comfortable in seeking health care from you.

Other Practice Affiliations

Managed Care Organizations

In today's market, whether you are a participating in managed care may determine whether you are seeing patients. Therefore, considering affiliations with managed care organizations (MCOs) is essential.

Once the address for the practice has been chosen, begin completing credentialing applications for participation in various managed care plans. The credentialing process is often lengthy and can take 60 to 90 days to process, so start early. It will be beneficial to see managed care patients as soon as you open your office.

Before attempting to participate in every plan available, do some investigative work. For example, if you are a specialist, ask primary care physicians in the area what plans they belong to and which ones have the best reputation and the most patients. To receive referrals, participation in the same plans as the primary care providers is necessary.

If you are joining a group practice, discuss managed care participation with the medical director or practice manager. If you are joining a group practice, applications will most likely be completed for you, but you will be required to sign and attest to the accuracy of the information. The required information for the applications will include, but is not limited to your medical license, board certification, drug enforcement agency (DEA) number, hospital participation, and malpractice insurance.

Be sure to read the section on managed care in Chapter 13, Loss Prevention and Risk Management, before entering the managed care arena. You will also want to include your managed care affiliations in your marketing efforts so that patients and referring providers will know which plans you participate in.

Call Group Affiliation

A major hurdle in solo practice is finding other physicians in your specialty with whom to share call. Check with other physicians to see if there is an opportunity to join an existing call group. It may be necessary to take the initiative and start a new group. As a solo physician, look for every opportunity to share call with other physicians. Also, call coverage may be a requirement for hospital staff privileges. Without call coverage, there will be little opportunity for leisure or family time.

Physician Referral Service

Many hospitals have a physician referral service. Contact the local hospital(s) to see if such a service exists. Request to be added to the referral list for your specialty. These referral services often limit the number of physicians in each specialty. For this reason, it is best to sign up immediately or be put on a waiting list, if necessary. Ask whether they handle the referrals on a rotating basis or whether they give each patient a list of available physicians.

Emergency Room Coverage

Although the local hospital may have full-time emergency room coverage, opportunities may be available for you to work extra hours. If you are interested in doing that, contact the emergency room director at each hospital to see if such opportunities exist. If you are joining a group practice, check your contract to be sure there are no restrictions concerning employment outside the group.

Conclusion

Belonging to organizations that help you professionally is a wise move. Such organizations provide valuable resources and associations. From interpretation of rules and regulations, to continuing education opportunities and meeting local colleagues, you will most likely benefit from joining—and participating in—professional organizations at the local, state, and national levels.

CHAPTER 6

Operational Policies, Procedures, and Processes

Medical practices today are facing an environment of ever-increasing complexity in patient management and third-party payment administration. To offset those complexities and reduce overhead costs, more practices are choosing to automate their processes through integrated billing, accounting, medical record keeping, and appointment scheduling. Computerized practices are generally more efficient and have better internal controls.

The arrival of managed care and increased overhead has made using computers in the medical practice not only helpful but essential. The volume of reports and other statistical data requested by managed-care organizations can be handled efficiently only by a computerized practice management system. Developing a technology infrastructure and selecting systems will be discussed in more detail in Chapter 7, Equipping Your Practice with Information Technology. The purpose of this chapter is to discuss the operational procedures and processes necessary in your new practice, particularly establishing a fee schedule, purchasing supplies, and managing accounts payable.

Establishing a Fee Schedule

There are various methods for establishing and reviewing fees in a medical office. The following are a few of the issues and methods to consider:

- Your fees should be comparable to other practices in your geographic area.

- Make use of fee analyzer products. These products can be ordered in printed and on-line format, and they provide ZIP-code specific information about usual and customary fees charged in your local billing area.

- Use the Resource-Based Relative Value Scale (RBRVS) compiled by the Centers for Medicare and Medicaid Services (CMS) as a baseline for setting and updating fees regularly. (For additional information, go to www.cms.gov/physicianfeesched/.)

The Medicare fee schedule has been based on the RBRVS system since 1992. Most indemnity insurers and managed-care organizations base their reimbursement on this standardized national system. Additionally, most managed care fee schedules are negotiated using multipliers (usually several multipliers for various code ranges) of this standardized schedule. Using this system also allows you to compare your payer reimbursements in a more uniform manner.

The Resource-Based Relative Value Scale in a Nutshell

The Resource-Based Relative Value Scale (RBRVS) is used to determine allowable reimbursement amounts and global days for surgery for Medicare Part B physician services. In the development of the RBRVS system, CMS (then Health Care Financing Administration) assigned a Relative Value Unit (RVU) to more than 7,000 Current Procedural Terminology (CPT) codes. Today, there are approximately 7,800 CPT codes. For the complete and comprehensive history of RBRVS, visit www.ama-assn.org/ama/pub/physician-resources/solutions-managing-your-practice/coding-billing-insurance/medicare/the-resource-based-relative-value-scale/overview-of-rbrvs.page. The Medicare Payment Advisory Commission (MedPAC) is another excellent resource concerning RBRVS (www.medpac.gov/index.cfm).

Each RVU has three components:

- **Physician Work RVU**—estimated to be 52% of the total RVU. The physician work RVU is based on the amount of time typically required to perform the service, the technical skill and mental effort required, and the psychological stress of caring for the patient.

- **Practice Expense RVU**—estimated to be 44% of the total RVU. This consists of all non-physician expenses needed to perform the service.

- **Malpractice RVU**—estimated to be 4% of the total RVU.

When added together, these equal the total RVU.

> (Work RVU × Work GPCI) + (Overhead RVU × Overhead GPCI)
> + (Malpractice RVU × Malpractice GPCI) × Conversion Factor
> = Total Allowable

FIGURE 6-1   The Complete RBRVS Formula

Prior to 1997, the total RVUs were multiplied by a standard conversion factor to arrive at the allowable payment amount. Prior to 1997, Medicare established a conversion factor for surgery, another for primary care services, and a third for nonsurgical services. Now there is one conversion factor for all 3 services, which is set at 33.9674 for 2001. See Figure 6-1 for the complete RBRVS formula.

Recognizing that the cost of practicing medicine (cost of living, practice expense, and malpractice insurance) varies in different parts of the country, CMS assigned a Geographic Practice Cost Index (GPCI) to each component of the RVU for each CPT code. There is also a differential depending on the location (facility or non-facility) where the service is performed. This results in all physicians in a given geographical area being reimbursed the same amount for a CPT code regardless of specialty. (Note: The Relative Value Units are reviewed annually.)

Establishing fees based on the RBRVS system is the method of choice. Because CMS has already established the RVUs for each CPT code, using the Medicare fee schedule to establish your fees is very simple. Additionally, depending on the standard fees offered by large payers and the success of your contract negotiations, fees should be greater than the highest allowable paid on your submitted claims.

For example, if a competitor charges $115 for CPT code 99213 (Level 3 Established Patient Office Visit) and the 2011 Medicare Allowable for Code 99213 in your area is $69.11, the Medicare fee can be increased by 50% (approximately $105), and setting the standard fee at $105, will still be competitive in the area.

Cost of Providing a Service Versus Practice Fees

However the fees are set, the practice cannot afford to deliver a service for a fee that is less than the cost of providing the service.

It is a fact that CMS took the cost of providing a service into account when it established the practice expense RVU for each service. However, the CMS may not consider all the expenses in managing a medical practice. To maintain a practice that affords a reasonable profit/salary margin after the bills are paid, it is essential to keep in mind the cost of supplies and other operating expenses. With time, expenses should be somewhat predictable. These predictable expenses are referred to

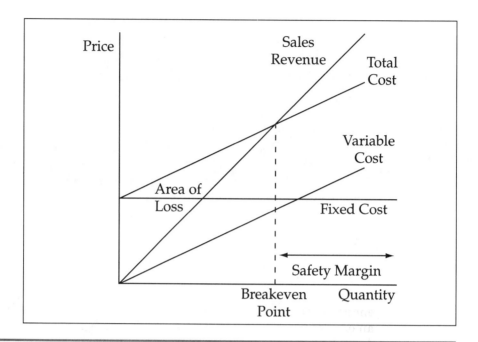

FIGURE 6-2   An Example of a Breakeven Chart

as fixed costs. The secret to making a profit in business is knowing the fixed and variable costs. The fixed cost will not vary by adding additional output, but the variable cost may go up slightly. Figure 6-2 is an example of a breakeven chart that can be used to determine exactly what needs to be produced to exceed the breakeven point.

For example, rent will stay the same whether the practice sees 10 patients a month or 100 patients per month, but supply costs will go up some with patient volume. With that said, profits will start the moment cost is exceeded, which is why it is important to know how much output (ie, productivity) must be achieved each day to exceed operating cost.

Understanding the costs of providing special services in the practice will help identify those service lines that are less profitable and that may need to be deleted from the practice menu. Without a clear understanding of the actual time and resources required to provide a service, profit calculations are only approximations. The specific factors included in the calculation include physician time, support staff time, supplies, fixed overhead, and variable overhead consumed to provide the service. The calculations can be completed in several ways, but unit cost analysis is the most common method.

Case Study

A physician opens her office at 8:00 am. The daily fixed cost (eg, rent, staff, utilities) is $500 per day. The variable cost (eg, supply, repairs, overtime) has been calculated to be $150 per day. The total daily cost is $650 per day. Based on collections throughout, it is calculated that her average reimbursement per patient is $62 per patient. Based on this information, she needs to see 10.48 patients during the day to cover her operating cost before she can start paying herself. How many additional patients she sees beyond the breakeven point will determine her compensation. Based on this study, if the provider wants to pay herself $150,000 per year, she will need to see an average of 20.48 patients per day and contain her cost to its current levels.

Purchasing Supplies

One of the routines that must be put into place in a medical practice start up is purchasing supplies. How supplies are purchased can influence whether the practice is profitable. The first step in developing an organized purchasing system is to centralize the ordering process. Assign one person to be responsible for ordering supplies. In a new office, the office manager/office assistant should order supplies. Having one person in charge eliminates duplicate orders, adds consistency and objectivity, and prevents having sales representatives talk to more than one person. The employee in charge of purchasing becomes familiar with necessary supplies and can shop around for the best prices.

Centralized ordering will also allow the purchaser to determine the quantity of each supply used over a given time (eg, monthly). Establishing usage guidelines based on this information allows development of an inventory process that will reduce unnecessary inventory and minimize the tendency to place rush orders that increase expenses.

Today most supply ordering is done online and the purchaser may be able to develop a "favorites" list for easy ordering. Setting up a par level inventory system will also help prevent unexpected delays because items/supplies have been exhausted. Many vendors will also affix their own inventory item number stickers to the supplies. As an item is used, simply peeling off the sticker and adding it to the patient encounter form for data entry will allow your practice management system to create a supply order list of billable items through a simple report.

It is important to get the best price possible for medical and office supplies. Initiate a request for proposal (RFP) to several vendors for those most commonly ordered items to compare prices and service guarantees. This should be done every couple of years to ensure that you are getting the best price possible.

The tips in Figure 6-3 will help minimize the cost of supplies.

1. Create vendor files by company name and file all invoices and statements in chronological order. File the folders in alphabetical order.

2. Be familiar with price breaks for regularly used items so that they can be ordered in quantities that provide the best price.

3. Purchase office supplies from vendors that provide delivery within 24 hours. This allows constant inventory and minimizes storage space onsite.

4. Every 12 to 24 months, check the prices on standard items and compare vendor prices. Ask for competitive bids from three different vendors.

5. Verify the payment terms and any opportunities for prompt payment discounts.

6. Be aware of items being put on back order, especially if the supplies are required to provide a service to a patient. Seek a vendor that can reliably provide these items.

7. Log all chemical orders on the Material Safety Data Sheet (MSDS) log.

8. Negotiate for better prices!

FIGURE 6-3   Tips for Purchasing Supplies

Accounts Payable

Practice operations must include the accounts payable function, which encompasses writing checks, paying bills, and accounting for money spent. To set up a system for accounts payable, you may choose to purchase an off-the-shelf accounting package. Such packages are generally reasonably priced, will produce a general ledger, keep track of income, provide expense statements, and write checks. This is a viable option, particularly if the Office Manager already has experience with accounting software.

Practice management systems may also offer modules to handle the accounts payable (AP) function—usually at a higher price than off-the-shelf AP. With the availability of reasonably priced AP software in the marketplace, however, it is unnecessary to forfeit any vital features of an accounts receivable (AR) package merely because it is offered. For example, you may see that it costs $2,000 to purchase an AP package with your practice management system, although you may think the AP and AR need to be interconnected. If spending this extra money for the AP module would cause you to forfeit a more important feature of the practice management software, such as online insurance verification, it is wiser to purchase the off-the-shelf AP software.

Most practices engage outside accounting firms to generate financial statements using output from the accounts payable and the accounts receivable information.

Chart of Accounts

The chart of accounts is simply a list of numbers that identify each category of expense in your practice. The practice's accountant will help establish a chart of accounts. Make sure the list is not too cumbersome. This information is necessary for the accountant to properly allocate expenses for tax purposes and cost accounting.

As an example, assume that the account number established for medical supplies is 105. A check is written to XYZ Supply Company for hypodermic needles. The check should be made out to XYZ Company in the proper amount, and the account number 105 should be noted on the check stub. This number tells the accountant that the check to XYZ was for medical supplies. For internal use, the invoice numbers that are paid should also be listed on the stub.

Correctly allocating expenses is essential to efficient practice operations. For accuracy, the person writing the checks—not the accountant—should be responsible for determining the account number to put on the check stub. Keep a copy of the chart of accounts available for ready reference.

Paying Bills

The accounts payment process works best if bills are paid only once each month. Unless a substantial discount is offered for early payment, never pay bills in less than 30 days from the date of purchase. Keep the money in the bank working for you as long as possible, not in the vendor's bank earning interest.

Pay bills from invoices, not from vendor statements. Vendors seldom have the same billing cycle you have. If payments are made from a statement, an invoice may mistakenly be paid twice. Most vendors will allow you to determine your invoice date.

At the same time each month, follow this routine outlined in Figure 6-4 for paying bills.

Establishing a workable accounts payable system at the start of your practice is critical. Accurate tracking of supply costs reduces overspending and panic buying, provides information needed for budgeting and forecasting, and gives the accountant the information necessary to prepare financial statements and tax returns.

1. Collect all the invoices that have been received from a vendor in the last 30 days. Make sure that the person receiving the goods has initialed the invoice to show that all goods ordered were received and in the proper quantities. Total the invoices and write a check for this amount.

2. Write every invoice number that is being paid and the amount on the check stub. Do not forget to put the chart of accounts number on the check and the check stub.

3. Staple the invoices together, mark them *paid,* and write the date and check number on them. Buy a rubber stamp for this purpose.

4. File the paid invoices in the vendor folder for that company. Keep only the invoices for the current year in the folder. At the end of each year, the invoices should be filed with other accounting papers for that year.

FIGURE 6-4   Payment Process

Conclusion

A medical practice is a business operation that requires the institution of certain policies and procedures. Establishing the fee schedule is one of the first steps in this process. Once that is in place, an accounting program and purchasing protocols can be set up. Consult with your accountant to ensure that you get off to a good start.

7

Equipping Your Practice with Information Technology

Many facets are involved in selecting a computer system, and comparing vendors and products can be daunting. With all the options available today, few can avoid being confused when equipping a medical practice with information technology. Moreover, new government regulations require information technology (IT) systems to meet certain standards and comply with guidelines to be eligible for financial performance incentives and to avoid reductions in Medicare reimbursement. All of these factors make selecting an IT system one of the more critical phases of the process of starting, buying, and owning a practice.

New systems today are also much more complex—no longer are they merely basic accounting software. Most vendors offer fully integrated systems that include accounting, patient information, scheduling and registration, inventory management, prescribing retail medications, purchasing solutions, and electronic health records (EHR) systems built on a single platform. Consequently, the IT decision is now much more mission-critical and lasting. The economic ramifications of a poor decision are also much higher because the system will affect virtually all components of the medical practice.

The purpose of this chapter is to present the fundamental options so that good decisions can be made about what system or systems will meet the needs of the medical practice. While discussed in more detail throughout the chapter, below are the most critical fundamentals.

- **Starting**—A new practice just starting out must undertake selection and procurement of a new system. It is always easier to start a practice using EHRs rather than converting paper charts to EHRs. It is also wise to consider only fully integrated solutions so that practice management and EHR are one and the same, thus eliminating the need to undergo expensive interfacing. It is also important that the system conforms to the Meaningful Use (MU) standards under the Medicare and Medicaid EHR Incentive Programs and that the EHR vendor is certified under the program to prevent being penalized by reimbursement reductions. You will also need to make the decision either to install the system on site or purchase a hosted solution, also known as *cloud computing* or *software as a service* (SAAS). Cloud computing is becoming a popular trend for start-up practices because it requires little capital outlay and the practice does not have to rely on expensive hardware and IT expertise.

- **Buying**—Buying into a practice will have some variance on the approach depending on what solutions already exist. A critical requirement is to confirm that the seller can transfer the software license and contracts to the new owner. Some vendors prohibit the transfer of a system to a new owner. It would be devastating to purchase a new practice and learn after the sale that the system in use is nontransferable. You also need to verify that the practice has paid for all the maintenance, that the software is still under a support agreement, and that the version in use is still under warranty. The practice may have an installed EHR, but the product could be discontinued and without support.

- **Owning**—A practice will benefit by maintaining all documentation with all IT vendor contracts, support agreements, software and licenses, etc. This will make it easier to ensure that the system is being kept up to date and that a support agreement is in place. All information on what is necessary to legally transfer the software licenses, maintenance contracts, hardware agreements, etc, should be maintained in one location. Furthermore, the cost of maintaining, replacing, or upgrading technology is a critical aspect of owning a practice.

Defining Your Requirements

The process of defining your needs will require an objective evaluation of your current processes. This will obviously require a different perspective if you are buying a practice with existing technology in use. In this case, you will have to determine if you can accept the existing system or will need to replace it. In the case of a start-up, you have the opportunity to explore several IT options.

Based on our experience, the following is a good checklist for gathering information about a practice that is necessary for defining needs and objectives for an IT system.

1. **If possible, establish a small workgroup:** This should consist of stakeholders forming the new practice or staff acquired from the acquisition. This will encourage group participation, and it will provide a broad range of viewpoints.

2. **Examine your current or projected workflow:** Have each member of the selection committee review his or her own department, and encourage all employees to contribute information about workflow and operations. This will serve two critical objectives. The first is to develop a global understanding of current process. The second, and most important, is to flush out any operational threats or points of failure.

3. **Technical assessment:** Technical assessments should be completed by someone who is qualified and knowledgeable in computers, security, and networking. The following items should be assessed:

   i. Equipment locations, especially servers and networking equipment

      a. Servers are in a low-traffic area.

      b. Servers are in an area that has environmental controls 24 hours a day, seven days a week.

      c. Dimensions of equipment—current and future

      d. Space required to support the equipment

      e. Equipment space accessible and there is room to work on the equipment

   ii. Electrical requirements

      a. A dedicated outlet is available for each server. Failure to supply a dedicated outlet could result in voiding the warranty with the server manufacturer. Install the type of outlet required by the manufacturer (for example, within four feet of each server).

      b. All peripheral devices have 110-volt outlets. A surge protector is recommended for all computer/printer equipment. Two receptacles are required for all workstation locations and network printers that do not have a built in network interface.

   iii. Phone lines and connectivity

      a. What is the current bandwidth and is it adequate?

      b. Who is going to support and set up connectivity?

      c. Is there adequate space to install networking equipment?

   iv. Cabling requirements

      a. Minimum CAT 5 cabling provided with each end labeled properly

b. Will the current patch panel support all the additional new computers? (Note: Patch panels are collections of cables and plugs designed for easy access by technicians. They appear as front-opening surfaces with numerous connections leading to different devices.)

v. Itemize existing equipment and software

vi. Data conversions (only if an existing system already exists)

vii. Develop an infrastructure diagram of both the network and hardware.

4. **Scheduling:** Scheduling is a major factor in workflow and should be well understood and documented. The scheduling process is what sends all other activities into motion and triggers several events to occur. Knowing what works well and what does not work well will help you select a system best suited for your practice:

i. How is scheduling currently handled or projected to be handled?

ii. Are there other resources that need to be scheduled (ie, procedure room, surgeries)?

iii. How are walk-ins handled?

iv. What information is gathered and collected at the time of registration?

v. How are appointments confirmed?

vi. Consider the need for scheduling reports.

5. **Registration:** This function should also be included in the assessment for an integrated financial/EHR system. The following areas need to be analyzed:

i. What information is needed for new patient registration?

ii. How are demographic updates handled?

iii. How does the practice management system assign account numbers that are needed for interfacing?

iv. Are fee tickets up to date, or will changes be necessary?

6. **Existing practice: methods for chart pulling and filing:** Examining the current methods will produce a lot of helpful information about processes and how they will be converted to an electronic record keeping system.

7. **Phone calls:** Documenting phone calls will require extensive revamping with an EHR. Knowing how your processes are handled today will allow the practice to select a vendor based on its ability to make the most significant improvements in routing, responding, and documenting calls. The practice should also consider how after-hours calls are handled.

8. **Numbering prescriptions, labs, and orders:** These are all significant components of the current workflow that will be affected by the EHR. Consider these areas:

   i. Who is responsible for handling prescription refills, and how is the process communicated?

   ii. What are the policies for the following items?

      a. After-hours prescription refills

      b. Calling in prescriptions

      c. Samples

   iii. How are labs and radiology orders handled?

   iv. How are labs and radiology results reviewed and documented?

   v. How are labs and radiology results communicated to the patient?

After defining requirements, the next steps will be to contact vendors and request a product demonstration. A demonstration can be done over the Internet, but we recommend having the vendor do the demonstration in person to allow for some direct interaction. We recommend the following demonstration tips:

- Allow plenty of time for each vendor to demonstrate the product. Generally it takes 1 to 2 hours per module. So if you are looking at practice management and EHR, allow 2 to 4 hours per vendor.

- Include staff members from various departments to act as subject matter experts for examining functionality that affects their areas of operations.

- Demonstrations can be time consuming and overwhelming. Limit formal product demonstrations to only the top 2 to 3 most preferred vendors.

- Consider using product evaluations tools such as a scorecard or checklist to compare each vendor. Your scorecard should include requirements that are important to the practice, and you should have each vendor specifically address the areas being scored. This will help with making a side-by-side comparison. Here are a few suggestions to include on your scorecard:

  - Ease of use

  - Physician friendly

  - Easy to modify and customize

  - Ability to improve revenue

  - Improve coding

  - Interfacing

After the demonstrations, consider asking the vendor to provide access to a trial version of the system or remote access to the software to give you some hands-on time to interact with the system before making a formal commitment.

After the software demonstrations are completed, identify a vendor of choice. Then complete reference checks using open-ended questions to get the most descriptive answers. The following checklist is helpful when obtaining information from vendor references.

Topic	Notes
1. Why did the practice select the software vendor?	
2. How has the system performed?	
3. Did the vendor meet expectations of the practice?	
4. Did training meet expectations? Was the trainer knowledgeable and helpful?	
5. What was the performance of the entire implementation team, such as technical, interfacing, setup, etc?	
6. Did the vendor meet all project deadlines? If not, what caused the delays?	
7. What problems arose during implementation and how were they resolved?	
8. How did the vendor react to issues and problems?	
9. How were defects handled, if any?	
10. How were new releases/upgrades handled?	
11. Describe unexpected circumstances, both good and bad.	
12. What do you like most about the system?	
13. What do you like least about the system?	
14. Did the vendor stay on budget?	
15. How easy was it to customize the system?	
16. Did the vendor try to blame others for problems or take responsibility themselves?	

The final question: "If you had it to do all over again, would you still choose the same vendor?"

In many cases, a customer who is unhappy with the vendor may not have been prepared to undergo an EHR transformation, so it is not always the vendor's fault. Sometimes customers who complained throughout the entire reference call would still choose the current vendor. It is best to talk to several references to see if there is an emerging trend. If most of the references are positive, then chances are good the vendor will live up to expectations. Mostly negative responses would give reason to be concerned and possibly to avoid this vendor option. The key is to look for trends. It would also be good to have the vendor explain or provide a rebuttal about complaints to get both sides of the story. Now that you have defined needs and completed demonstrations and reference checks, the final stage is to negotiate a contract and the terms and conditions of the financial arrangement for procurement of the new system. To ensure successful negotiations, we recommend the following next steps:

1. Identify vendor costs for all functions: fixed, ongoing, present, and future. Here are a few areas to look at:

   a. Initial costs

   b. Hardware cost

   c. Software cost

   d. Communications cost

   e. Installation cost

   f. Ongoing support cost

   g. Implementation cost

   h. Support cost

   i. Technical support cost

   j. Integration costs

   k. Interface cost

   l. Entitlement to new releases/bug fixes

   m. The cost of tailoring

   n. Future upgrades and releases. (These should always be at no additional cost.)

2. Recognize various software features and how they affect cost. For example, a web portal may be supplied by a third-party vendor who will also expect payment. Vendors will frequently utilize third-party databases for life art, dictionaries, and formularies. These databases typically require an annual renewal fee.

3. Address software customizations, especially integration requirements.

4. Gather competitive data, and always have a viable second choice. Let both vendors know they are under consideration.

5. Develop a quote comparison spreadsheet.

Reviewing the Proposed Contract and Negotiating the Terms and Conditions

To prepare for contract negotiations, develop a list of all issues that need to be negotiated. Define the issues and the desired outcome. Prioritize the list and identify non-negotiable criteria. Sort your priorities by deal-breaker items, neutral items, and "wish list" items.

The following are some key points to include in your contract review:

- Implementation plan
- Software customizations
- Criteria for acceptance
- Terms of payment
- Software and hardware maintenance fees
- Price protection on maintenance fees
- Cost of EHR or PM system
- Addition of future providers/users
- Future recurring fees
- How problems are handled
- How to terminate and exit the relationship

In addition, having a simple problem-resolution clause in the contract will allow you and your vendor to work through difficulties.

Also, you will want to negotiate the terms and conditions in the contract language. The easiest way to negotiate payment terms is to establish a fee schedule tied to deployment success, such as the following:

1. 25% due at signing of the contract
2. 25% due after successful and tested installation of the hardware
3. 25% due after successful and tested installation of the software
4. 25% due after successful "go-live"

Your terms should also state that maintenance will be paid for after the system is implemented. Most vendors try to collect the annual maintenance at the time of signing the contract.

Modifying the Contract Language

It should come as no surprise that vendor contracts are not designed with the client's best interest in mind. This is not to say the vendor is trying to beat you out of a good deal; it is just that vendors also have a lot at risk, and they can be easy targets for lawsuits. To some extent, you want your vendor partner to be protected from clients who bring unwarranted lawsuits against the vendor, putting it and the clients it supports in jeopardy. It is never, under any circumstances, in a vendor's best interest to have an unsatisfied client. Most vendors are serious about staying in business and will exhaust all reasonable efforts to keep their clients happy because their future sales depend on it.

It is also important to be very respectful and professional during the negotiations. It is never wise to push your vendor to the point of being unreasonable. Remember, you will be relying on the vendor for several years. Therefore, mutually acceptable terms and conditions should be the end goal. That being said, the following is a list of suggested contract modifications to request from the vendor.

1. **Acceptance period hardware:** Acceptance will be 90 days after the software is installed, and all hardware is working in accordance with performance expectations. Hardware not properly installed by the vendor will be corrected at the vendor's expense, including travel expenses for on-site work.

2. **Acceptance period software:** Acceptance will be 90 days after the go-live of each module. Software not properly installed by the vendor (including third-party software) will be corrected at the vendor's expense, including travel expenses for on-site work.

3. **Implementation:** All vendor personnel serving on the implementation team and trainers must have a minimum of one year of employment in their current role with the vendor. The client does not agree to accept anyone with less than one year of implementation experience. The client may also request substitute staff.

4. **Support fees:** Support cost should be based on what is actually installed and in use. For example, if you purchase an EHR system with an integrated patient portal, the cost associated with the portal should be due upon activation, not at time of contracting. The support fee does not start until 90 days after the go-live stage. If the practice is installing multiple modules, the vendor will charge support fees for only the portion installed, with a starting point of 90 days after the system goes live.

5. **Deal Breaker—Assignment:** The vendor will allow assignment under the following conditions: a merger, an acquisition, a buy out, a name change, a corporate reorganization, or a successor organization. Assignment to a parent, subsidiary, and another entity within the organization is acceptable.

6. **Application Service Provider (ASP):** The client may become an ASP or data center of the software to other health care providers in the area. The client will be required to pay the vendor the license fees for additional users. The vendor may be

contracted at its applicable rates to provide training and support services to the practices hosting from the client.

7. **Future upgrades, new releases, version changes, mandated modifications:** The vendor will provide continuous/unlimited upgrades/new releases and patches to the client under the service agreement at no additional cost. Training and installation to support the new releases/upgrades/patches will be covered under the standard maintenance agreement.

8. **Third-party software:** The client expects the third-party software recommended by the vendor to perform as required and to be compatible with the application. The client will purchase the recommended software in accordance to the vendor's requirements. The vendor will pay the replacement cost or cost to purchase alternative third-party software if the recommended software does not meet the requirements or if it compromises the performance of the application.

9. **Warranties:** The vendor guarantees to correct any error, malfunctions, or performance defects in its software within 90 days of the reported problem. If the error cannot be corrected within 90 days or reasonable substitution cannot be established, the client will be given a 100% refund of all expenses paid to the vendor, including hardware and expenses paid for professional services and travel expenses.

10. **Termination:** The client can terminate the contract for any reason with a 90-day notice. Upon termination, the vendor will provide a de-conversion file in an ASCII rich text format. The vendor will agree to provide one test tape and one live-data tape in the format noted above. At no time can the vendor shut down the software under any circumstances without the client's prior approval. The client will be allowed an indefinite amount of time to transition from the software.

11. **Increases to support fees:** The vendor can only increase its support fees at the rate of 1% less than the Consumer Price Index. Additionally, the vendor cannot look back retroactively for more than a one year if the fee is not increased.

12. **Additional support fees:** Unforeseen customization and other services outside of the scope of the agreement will be mutually agreed to.

Methods for Acquiring and Deploying Technology

Generally, there are three primary ways to acquire and maintain a technology infrastructure: (1) Standalone Systems, (2) Application Service Providers (ASPs), and (3) Web-based Systems/Cloud Computing.

Standalone Systems

Standalone systems, also known as the Client Server Approach, call for installing a central processing unit (CPU), or server, that will run the software application. Servers, which can be local or remote, are connected to other computers in the office by networking the workstations together.

As an overview, the term *standalone system* simply implies that the application will reside on a dedicated server installed onsite at the practice. This approach will require the purchase of a software license and the necessary hardware to run the application.

The standalone approach is the most traditional and widely used approach. However, through the innovation of the Internet and virtual private networks (VPN), companies around the world are now offering alternative methods for delivering their information system (IS) solutions (discussed later in this chapter). The standalone approach is still a viable option, nonetheless, with its own advantages. Standalone systems are recommended to many practices, even after evaluating the alternatives, including ASPs. (See Figure 7-1, Client/Server Model, for a technical illustration of the standalone approach.)

The standalone system approach encompasses the following:

1. Select the vendors that will be needed to achieve the desired results. For example, the team of vendors compiled will consist of one with a practice management (PM) system, one with an electronic health records (EHR) application, one with an appointment reminder application, and one for claims scrubbing. Choosing a vendor for each application is called *best-of-breed selection,* which allows the building of the "perfect" system. However, this method is more costly compared to fully integrated solutions in which the entire system operates on a single database and is contracted through a single vendor.

2. Agree on terms, maintenance cost, customization and consulting fees, support fees, future upgrade charges, and new software release expenses. In addition, consider recurring fees that include, but are not limited to, electronic data interchange (EDI) fees, electronic eligibility fees, statement fees, electronic payment posting, and supply costs.

3. Purchase the hardware that is needed to run the applications. If the PM, EHR, and e-mail systems are purchased, it is likely there will need to be three servers plus an interface server to tie all the applications together. (Smaller practices generally require 1 to 2 servers.) The software vendor will generally include in the quote professional services to assist with the installation of the hardware. You could contract with a local technical expert if the vendor does not provide this service. Also, consider contacting an IS consultant for an explanation of hardware requirements.

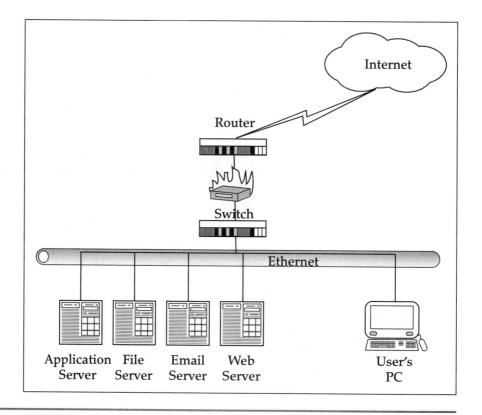

FIGURE 7-1   Client/Server Model

Source: The iLIANT Corporation

4. After installing the hardware, the applications will be ready for installation.

5. Once the applications are installed, the databases and file queries need to be built. This allows the system to be defined with resources and information specific to payers, referring providers, and charges. It will also be necessary to build payer profiles (formats) and to configure the EDI for electronic claims submission. Generally the vendor providing the software will take responsibility for setting up these configurations and may also recommend preferred EDI partners.

6. With a new system, allow for some testing and time to work out the bugs. Almost always, a new system will have some initial problems. (Caution: If applications combine by taking the best-of-breed approach, all the vendors will need to collaborate to resolve issues. This is often problematic with the installation of stand-alone systems that integrate multiple applications.)

7. After inspection and testing, begin the training process, which will require 2 to 5 days.

8. Go-live. (Begin using the system applications.) The average implementation time for a standalone system is 60 to 120 days from start to go-live stage, with the majority of the installations being completed within 90 days. For a comparison, this is an average of about 30 to 60 days longer than implementing an ASP. Therefore, if rapid deployment is necessary, the ASP approach would be more accommodating (discussed below).

The advantages and disadvantages of an on-premise client/server approach are:

Advantages	Disadvantages
Practice owns the system	Ongoing maintenance, including upkeep cost and upgrading cost is paid by the practice
More control over functionality and interfaces	Performance updates required
Ability to customize as needed. (Most vendors charge $130 to $200 per hour for customization.)	Hardware upgrades
	Software upgrades
	Recurring fees
	Support fees
	System administration responsibilities
	HIPAA responsibilities, including keeping up with business associate agreements with suppliers/vendors
	Disaster protection and recovery responsibilities
	Detecting and preventing intrusions

The Application Service Provider (ASP) Approach

Using an ASP is a lot like outsourcing transcription. Instead of hiring a full-time employee with benefits to transcribe dictation, the service is outsourced and the practice pays for the service by the line or word. With an ASP, a practice generally pays a fixed monthly hosting fee and outsources the system and all the maintenance and upkeep to the ASP.

An ASP is a company that will allow the use of its software applications on a subscription-based payment arrangement and deliver it in real time over an Internet connection or through a dedicated data communications line. Also known as *application hosting,* this approach allows practices to take advantage of powerful applications without having to purchase, install, and maintain them. Moreover, no substantial cash outlay is required, and deployment can be rapid because the system is already developed and running.

The ASP approach includes the following:

1. Select an ASP that offers the software applications and services that are desired.
2. Determine if any data conversion or migration is required. If so, establish the parameters and timeline for conversion/migration.
3. Agree on terms. (The fee is fixed and there is nothing to buy, thus the process is straightforward.)
4. Establish connectivity. (This can take 30 days or more and varies by location.)
5. Determine the number of workstations and users that need to access the system.
6. Connect a dedicated data communications line or virtual private network (VPN) to the ASP's data center. (The ASP will handle this for you.)
7. Application is turned on and training started 1 to 5 days after connectivity.
8. Two to 5 days of training.
9. Go-live with new ASP.

Implementation time for an ASP, from start to the go-live stage, will average from 30 to 60 days, with the majority of the installations being completed within 40 days after the line is installed. If necessary, the system could go live within 1 day of installing the line, but users will need training and the database will require some customization.

Because the telephone service provider is responsible for installing the line, installations can be delayed due to scheduling issues.

Advantages and disadvantages of the ASP approach can be summarized as follows:

Advantages	Disadvantages
Software is never outdated (always on the most current version)	Connectivity required (additional expense)
All upgrades and new releases included	Optimal performance contingent on bandwidth speeds
All support included	Customization and interfacing subject to the ASP's approval
System maintenance and upkeep provided	Control imposed by the ASP; may limit some functionality
Interfacing provided and supported	Data stored off site
Access to industry experts (IT experts)	Loss of control
No major hardware required (low capital investment)	The stability (ie, instability) of the ASP partner/data center
No unexpected fees (monthly fixed amount)	
Minimum cash outlay	
Disaster protection	
Data redundancy and data mirrors	
HIPAA compliant	
Future IS compliance standards handled by the ASP	
Access to information anywhere in the world through a secure Internet connection	
Avoid capital expenses, maintenance fees, supporting, and upgrading fees	
Transfers the responsibilities of managing the application so practice can focus on patients	
System is already developed and ready for rapid deployment	
Assures customer an ongoing return on investment. Because the system is rented, the customer can cancel the subscription when it is no longer a benefit to the practice (subject to contractual terms and conditions)	
An array of applications from which to choose	

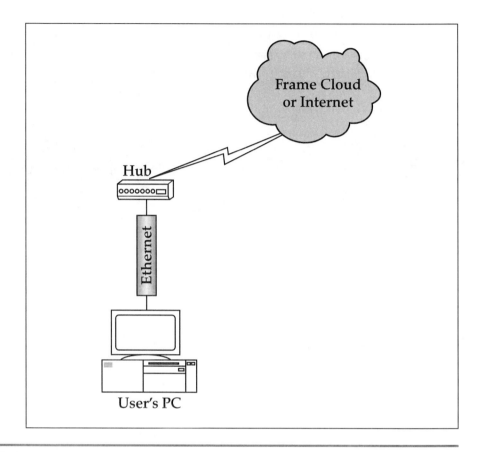

FIGURE 7-2 ASP Client Model

Source: The iLIANT Corporation

The cost for a single ASP can range from $1,500 for basic billing application with limited functionality to $100,000 for a fully integrated EHR system on a wireless network with interfaces to outside entities, such as the hospital, lab, and radiology. However, the average price for a good practice management system for a single provider with four users will range from $25,000 to $60,000 (hardware included).

ASPs are usually less expensive when analyzed over a five-year period. For example, an ASP will charge a monthly hosting fee that generally ranges from $200 to $800 per month per provider and includes the following services:

- Complete practice management system
- Continuous upgrades at no additional cost
- Internet access
- Routine system back-ups
- Disaster recovery

- 24-hour security protection
- 24-hour data protection
- Technical and user support
- Training
- Ongoing system maintenance

Figure 7-2 is an illustration of the ASP Client Model.

Internet/Web-based Application

Practice management applications delivered over the Internet are similar to the ASP approach, except they are considered by some experts to be less secure, and connectivity can be less reliable. Applications delivered over the Internet offer providers an economical opportunity to get started without a major investment.

Other considerations before investing are the history of the application and the vendor's stability. Products and vendors are in and out of the marketplace without regard to their customers who sometimes are left without solutions and recourse. In current-day vernacular, if a vendor *sunsets* (ie, discontinues) an application or goes out of business, you will have what is referred to as an *orphan* application. Over time the application will become outdated, and the resources to support it will be unavailable. Spend time researching each vendor, their financial stability, and their references. Request a site inspection, but be cautious to avoid the vendor's showroom sites. Vendors will often offer inducements to their showroom sites that refer them business.

If you are considering an EHR, it is recommended that you shadow a physician in a live clinical setting to experience the tool firsthand while it is in use.

The remainder of this chapter will discuss strategies for leveraging and securing technology for the medical practice, whether it is in the context of first-time purchase or in replacement of an existing system to achieve greater outcomes as well as meet requirements for meaningful use (MU).

Using Technology in Your Practice

The health care industry is often considered inefficient and laced with labor-intensive processes to accomplish even the simplest functions. As practices continue to face these challenges, and with added pressure on their bottom lines, processes will need to improve for a practice to survive. Technology has revolutionized the world, yet most physicians still

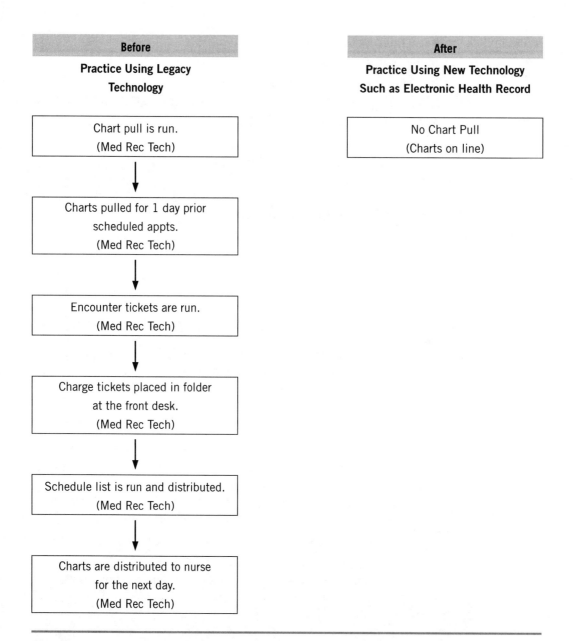

FIGURE 7-3   Workflow Comparison for Paper Chart Versus Electronic Health Record

Source: Cerner Corporation.

work in environments that rely on labor-intensive processes to perform their jobs. Even practices that have instituted technology improvements do not get to realize the benefits because they fail to match the processes around the technology.

As it has been stated so well by H. James Harrington in *Business Process Improvement:*

Automating a bad process not only ensures that we can do a bad job every time, but that we can do it faster and with less effort than before.

To illustrate, Figure 7-3 looks at the typical workflow processes for pulling a single chart in comparison to working with electronic medical records. It shows that having data readily accessible without the hassles of manually searching has its benefits.

Case Study

It is 2:00 am and the emergency room calls because a patient had an adverse reaction to the medication prescribed, and the patient does not recall the name of the drug. Will you remember? This is when a central database that stores all of your patients' medical records, accessible from home, would really come in handy. From the database you could fax or e-mail the entire chart to the emergency room if necessary.

The Paperless Office

The previous case study may not sound achievable for the medical practice, but it is. Many practices are achieving automated benefits through technology, including a totally paperless office and offices with fully integrated data repositories.

Although the benefits and possibilities are endless, costs are a consideration for any practice—especially at start-up when investment precedes revenue. For this reason building the technology infrastructure should be planned well when you are starting a practice. The objective is to avoid decisions that result in forced changes and revisions, requiring the practice to rebuild at a later date to meet its needs and objectives.

In the beginning you will need to decide how you want to use technology in your practice. In today's market, it is easy to get distracted by the endless number of gadgets and vendors. Moreover, some vendors will distract you with bells and whistles through dynamic presentations without revealing the true functionality of the application. Never take a vendor's word about how the application will work. Require them to show you a medical practice that is using their technology and accomplishing what you desire. Also, be sure to avoid the showroom sites.

The goal of this chapter is to keep you from making the single most common mistake that many physicians make when purchasing technology—making a decision with very little information! This results in buying the wrong technology or purchasing too much technology because you think it would benefit the practice.

Just because you read an article or see a flashy demonstration of a vendor's product, or hear about a colleague's system, do not be quick to commit. Remember, the practice will be around for a long time. Be mindful of your investment and bear in mind all long-term goals and the economic ramifications of these decisions. Many of the solutions provided in today's market include hidden fees and recurring expenses that are often overlooked at the time of purchase. Consequently, you must do your research.

When building the technology infrastructure, consider the following factors:

1. **Cost.** While money drives many decisions, higher costs must be weighed against increased revenue and benefits. Select technology based on its ability to save you money and time. For example, should the practice spend thousands of dollars every year ordering encounter forms or superbills, or purchase a practice management system that will allow the practice to design and print its own forms at no cost? Can the process be taken a step further and all charges captured electronically on a personal digital assistant (PDA) [1] or Windows CE® device,[2] and synchronized back into the billing module[3]?By taking this extra step or investing in a tool to eliminate the paper superbill and the charge entry process, operating cost is reduced. As a result, this approach would eliminate the encounter form altogether and the labor cost to enter the charges. Moreover, the system would likely scrub the claim (ie, remove any errors or mistakes before it is sent to the insurance company to prevent costly denials) against your documentation to ensure that you remain in compliance, which is an immeasurable benefit, plus you will likely realize a higher level of reimbursement.

   As noted, be mindful of hidden and/or recurring expenses, such as transaction fees, support fees, or future upgrades that can increase the cost of the solution.

   The following are hidden expenses are often overlooked:

   - Ongoing maintenance and support for hardware and software
   - Electronic transactions, such as electronic claims, insurance eligibility, remittance, and statements. Avoid arrangements that require a per-transaction fee unless the cost is justifiable.
   - Future upgrades and new releases. Be advised that most medical software vendors will develop a new version every 12 to 18 months, necessitating ongoing upgrades. Some vendors require their clients to pay for each new release. Other vendors include all continuous upgrades at no additional cost.
   - Customization is almost always charged at an hourly rate of $100 to $200 per hour, depending on the requirements.
   - Data conversions. Most vendors will charge from $2,000 to $5,000 to convert data from another system. (Vendors will

almost always agree to negotiate on this fee to get the new business.)

Be aware of all recurring expenses—not just the initial sale price of the technology solution.

2. **Functionality.** While most functions are possible, in theory, one must be realistic. For example, some practice management systems incorporate rules into their processes, which are known as *rules-based systems*. A great tool, the rules alert the end user before a mistake is made. However, the rules must first be put into place and kept up to date before the benefits can be realized. Some systems allow the practice to link directly with the payers to obtain eligibility and payer-specific rules. Do not assume the rules come with the system.

   Another functionality that can often be misleading is voice recognition. While this technology continues to improve, it generally requires months to train the application to become familiar with the user's voice. Even then, achieving 100% accuracy with this system is unlikely. When involved in a demonstration of voice recognition software, be mindful that presenters spend considerable time training their systems. Ask for permission to speak into the system yourself, and you will instantly see a difference.

3. **Integrated versus Interface.** Integrated systems generally run on a single database with all of the functionality and workflow converging through a single application. Integrated systems, which usually have lower licensing costs and do not require costly interfaces, are usually less expensive. However, if the integrated system cannot perform all the desired functions, it will require an interface to another application to provide those functions.

   Interfacing or combining applications (ie, known as the best-of-breed approach) will allow buyers to build their perfect system. This approach is often used when specialized features are required or in the case of enhancing a legacy system, instead of replacing it altogether. The disadvantage of interfacing is having to deal with multiple vendors. This requires them to communicate with one another and, at times, share their technical expertise.

Conclusion

Become an informed purchaser. Resist the temptation to buy too much too soon before knowing the practice's objectives. Consider various options, research vendors thoroughly, and tap into the resources of trustworthy consultants before you over- or under-invest in technology solutions. The same holds true for upgrading information technology for the existing practice. Let the buyer beware!

References

1. A personal digital assistant (PDA) is a handheld computer that serves as an organizer for personal information. It generally includes at least a name and address database, to-do list, and note taker. PDAs are pen-based and use a stylus to tap selections on menus and to enter printed characters.

2. Microsoft CE® is Microsoft's personal assistant product. Data is synchronized between the PDA and desktop computer via cable or wireless transmission. msdn.microsoft.com/en-us/sync/bb887608. Accessed July 15, 2011.

3. For more information, contact Med3000 (formerly the iLIANT Corporation) at www.med3000.com.

8

Identifying Insurance Requirements

Among the most crucial decisions to make for the practice includes the consideration and subsequent purchase of various types of insurance coverage. Due to the many liabilities inherent in the practice of medicine, protecting yourself through insurance will be of vital importance to your practice. Most states require the physician to carry certain types of insurance such as malpractice insurance. Hospitals and managed care plans often require malpractice and/or liability insurance coverage, as do banks, leasing companies, and a number of other external entities. Additionally, you will need to decide what level of risk you are willing to take and what protections are financially feasible. For example, will you insure small losses that you might incur, or do you accept the risk and absorb replacement cost—and at what level?

Knowing what to protect is another concern. As an example, consider a patient who trips on loose carpet and falls in your office. The patient may sue both you and the owner of the building, even if you lease office space in a medical building. (See Chapter 13, Loss Prevention and Risk Management, for information on developing a risk management plan.) If the fall occurs within your suite, both you and the landlord may potentially be liable, thus business insurance coverage is essential.

Every medical employer carries insurance policies in addition to professional liability coverage (ie, malpractice insurance). This might include property insurance, commercial general liability insurance (CGL), life insurance, overhead disability insurance, workers' compensation insurance, group health insurance, and fidelity bond insurance that protects the practice if there is embezzlement. The purpose of this chapter is to address the many questions about insurance that arise in a practice start up and direct you to the appropriate resources to address your needs.

Professional Liability Insurance

Professional liability insurance, or medical malpractice insurance, is available through various sources, including traditional insurance companies, physician-owned companies, self-insured companies, group purchasing programs, and risk retention groups. What is available to you depends largely upon how much coverage you plan to purchase and the insurers in your area. Not all insurers operate in every state.

Depending upon your specialty, professional liability insurance may be your single highest expense, and it will be one of the most important insurance policies you can buy. According to Kaiser State Health Facts, a source for state health data, there were 9,894 medical malpractice claims paid in 2010 totaling over $3.3 billion.

Choosing a Professional Liability Insurer

Aspects to consider when choosing an insurer for medical malpractice insurance include the following:

- **Company's Financial Condition.** Because litigation may take as much as 3 to 5 years, seek coverage from a company with financial stability that is apt to be around and has sufficient resources to defend you. This financial data is often available on state department of insurance websites, or you may want to check with your state medical society for their recommendations. Be aware that a number of large insurers have exited the malpractice insurance business in the last decade. It is important that the state where you are practicing also have a strong guaranty fund to back up insurers in the event of insolvency.

- **Risk Management/Loss Prevention Assistance and Advice.** In addition to conducting risk assessments of your practice, your professional liability carrier should be a resource for training, education, and guidance for your staff to implement loss prevention measures that strengthen the practice.

- **A Comprehensive Policy.** Make sure you know what your policy covers and does not cover. Review a copy of the policy, paying particular attention to the exclusions.

- **Experienced Claim Professionals and a Strong Legal Network.** Just as you would research any professional you hired, research and scrutinize prospective malpractice insurers by checking references and evaluating credentials. Ask questions about how defense will be handled in the event of a claim, to what extent you will be required to participate in your own defense, and be aware that the insurer may have off-loaded some of the risk to a reinsurer.

Purchasing Coverage for Malpractice Claims

Consider the following points when purchasing medical malpractice coverage:

- **Purchase adequate limits.** Many physicians purchase coverage based on the minimum requirements of the hospital(s) in which they practice, usually $1 million per occurrence and $3 million aggregate, or similar limitations mandated by health plans. However, a single occurrence can exhaust the coverage under an existing policy. The aggregate should be two to three times the occurrence limit.

- **Understand the difference between occurrence coverage and claims-made coverage.** An occurrence policy provides coverage during the time period it is in place when an incident that leads to a lawsuit occurs, regardless of when a lawsuit is filed. It should only be purchased from companies that have strong financial strength ratings, with strong underlying state guaranty funds. However, occurrence coverage is not always available in every location and for every specialty. Therefore, it may be necessary to obtain claims-made coverage, which covers only the time period when the claim occurred. Thus, claims-made policies provide coverage if the claim is made during the policy period (after the retroactive date, and before the termination date). When a claims-made policy terminates, so does the underlying coverage, unless extended reporting coverage, also known as a *tail* is purchased. Tail coverage can be expensive, and some physicians forgo it. An alternative to purchasing a tail is to change carriers and ask the new carrier to cover all of the exposure back to the original retroactive date—known as *picking up prior acts*. In this scenario, physicians must appreciate which carrier is responsible for which acts and report all adverse incidents accordingly.

- **There is an advantage with continuous coverage.** Some insurers deny the renewal of existing policies or refuse to set the cost or offer tail coverage for future claims based on incidents that have occurred during the policy period. Thus, if there is no continuous coverage and the policy term is one year (for example), then the insurer is free to modify the policy at the end of that one-year term. If the policy is continuous in nature, the insurer cannot unilaterally modify its terms; thus, the importance of consideration of continuous coverage as a coverage option. The policy period is shown on the declarations page of the policy.

- **Higher limits of liability are more expensive.** Consider whether they may be cost effective for you or not.

- **Name your professional corporation on your policy.** Because most legal actions will name both you and your corporation, be sure to name your professional corporation on the policy.

- **Consider insuring the corporation separately.** By doing so, available coverage may be increased for a fraction of the cost of increasing your individual limits.
- **Make sure all professionals in your practice are properly covered.** Office professionals, such as nurses, professional assistants, nurse practitioners or midwives, under your employment should be properly covered through their own coverage.
- **Check with the insurer about discounts.** Ask if they give a discount for using an EHR system or having certain risk policies and procedures already in place, for example.

If you are joining a medical group, most likely the group's policy will cover you. The premiums may be a part of your compensation package. If you already have malpractice coverage that you will terminate when you join the group, you will need to purchase tail coverage to cover any potential litigation stemming from actions prior to the new group coverage taking effect. Be sure you check with the new group/employer to find out who is responsible for payment of premiums for tail coverage. Leave nothing to chance.

Business Insurance

Certain aspects of office management and equipment must be covered by insurance to provide financial protection. One way to purchase the protection that is needed for your practice is to buy a professional office package (POP). Insurance for a medical practice should include general liability, business contents, property (if you own the building the practice occupies), umbrella liability, business auto, computer, employee dishonesty, business interruption insurance, and equipment breakdown coverage.

Commercial General Liability Coverage

The commercial general liability policy is a comprehensive form of coverage that provides protection from lawsuits brought against you by third parties. A third-party person is any individual other than the policyholder, the insurance company, or persons specifically exempted from coverage under the policy. The policy typically includes personal injury, product liability, advertising liability, and contractual liability. Look for policy limits of $1 million to $5 million. The additional cost for the higher limits is often minimal, and thus should be considered.

You will also want to consider non-owned and hired automobile liability coverage for damages to a third party by an employee's vehicle used for the business of the practice, such as going to the bank or post office. This coverage would also include damages to a third party incurred by an employee using rented automobiles while working on behalf of the practice.

Property Insurance

A considerable amount of money has been spent to purchase the furniture and equipment necessary to start your practice. Evaluate the cost to replace the tangible assets owned by the practice to determine the proper amount of insurance to purchase. Purchase an adequate amount of property insurance to replace fixed assets in the event they are destroyed by fire or another disaster. In addition, include office supplies, medical supplies, medical books and journals, artwork, files, and file contents.

You may purchase many options through your property insurance. Depending on locale, you may want to consider earthquake or flood coverage, which are usually excluded from property policies. Always request special perils or all risk coverage. Consider higher deductibles to reduce costs.

Computer Coverage

Your property insurance will likely cover the computer hardware; however, you may wish to purchase additional coverage that includes loss due to power surges or loss of data or theft. Consult a software vendor to see how much software insurance is needed for the practice's licensed software.

Business Interruption Insurance

Business interruption coverage, which is important and typically inexpensive, is coverage for when your office becomes inaccessible due to a covered property loss (eg, fire, hurricane, etc). This coverage is such that you could be reimbursed for lost revenue, continuous expenses, and/or lost profits associated with certain catastrophic losses. Be sure that the coverage includes funds for a temporary office, necessary operating expenses, advertising the new location to your patients, and the expenditures to move back into your office once the damages are repaired.

Employee Dishonesty Insurance or Fidelity Bond

This coverage protects your practice from losses due to employee theft or embezzlement of funds. It will be necessary for you to specify which employees are covered under the insurance policy and who may be subject to individual scrutiny by the insurer. Other types of coverage, such as theft of money and securities while on the premises or in transit, forgery, funds transfer fraud, computer fraud, money order and counterfeit currency fraud, credit card fraud, and coverage for investigative costs for covered losses, may also be available. Be careful about provisions that cause the policy to terminate if the employer hires a known embezzler or discovers the embezzlement and takes no action.

Equipment Breakdown Coverage

This insurance covers the cost to repair or replace equipment that may be a means of generating significant revenue to your practice. Coverage also includes lost revenue for the period that the equipment is unusable. Discuss this option and coverage with your insurance broker.

Umbrella Policy

In addition to the standard office package, you may want to consider an umbrella policy, which provides comprehensive catastrophic coverage for claims beyond the normal limits of the regular policies. These policies generally start at a $1 million coverage and go up from there and can be relatively inexpensive.

Workers' Compensation Insurance

Workers' compensation insurance is mandatory in most states if you have a certain number of employees. This coverage pays for and/or reimburses employees (and officers as appropriate) for injuries, losses, and accidents associated with the workplace. Each state regulates benefits and costs so most policies in a given state have identical coverage. Many insurance companies provide a separate plan specifically for workers' compensation coverage. Make sure the policy you purchase is covered by your state's insurance insolvency fund.

Premiums are based on payroll estimates for a 12-month policy term, subject to a final audit to adjust for changes. All wages should be included in the payroll estimates, including bonuses. Overtime, however, may be adjusted to its regular time equivalent, rather than the time-and-a-half wage rate. This adjustment could be helpful as premiums are based on total wage dollars expended.

Inquire about the following when purchasing workers' compensation insurance:

- Insurer's provider network (if any)
- Safety program discounts

- Caps for officers (which can offer big savings). Some states do not require owners or principles of a business to cover themselves under workers' compensation plans. Because premiums are based on wages paid by the practice, a substantial sum can usually be saved by not covering yourself. This is only advisable, however, if you already have a good disability policy and health insurance plan in place.

Employee Insurances

Although not addressed in this chapter, numerous options are available for employee insurance coverage (if elected by the physician or practice). This will typically include medical, dental, vision, long-term and short-term disability, and life insurance. Ideally, one broker qualified in employee insurance offerings would be most beneficial as the physician is contemplating what and how much coverage to include in offering benefits to employees.

Purchasing Insurance Policies

Following are guidelines for purchasing insurance products:

- Higher deductibles usually mean lower premiums.
- Avoid overbuying. Expensive add-ons are unnecessary if you have good coverage on your basic policy.
- Select appropriate policy limits and buy larger amounts of protection when it is economical. Increasing your limits under a liability policy is usually cheaper than adding coverage under a second policy.
- Consider self-payment on smaller claims, adhering to legal parameters as some policies do not permit direct payments because they want all transactions to flow through their processing. Even though this is atypical and seldom the case, we encourage the practice to verify this restriction if applicable. Consult with your insurance advisor or plan on this option.
- Give prompt attention to any third-party claim.
- Pay premiums annually (or semiannually) instead of monthly. Typically, an annual payment is less expensive than monthly installments.

Insurance coverage is no substitute for risk management. Work with your insurance agent to develop a sound loss-prevention program for all forms of practice liability. Conducting a regular loss prevention in-service education program will keep your employees aware of the importance of loss prevention and on-the-job safety.

Review your insurance program regularly. Read your policies and confer with your insurance agent or consultant (and with legal counsel, as appropriate) regarding your insurance program. Policies, state law, and individual needs differ and costs vary. A sound insurance program to achieve adequate protection of corporate and personal assets requires careful and continuous review.

Conclusion

Buy the insurance that is needed—whatever the practice scenario—to protect both the practice and yourself from exposure to liabilities and to meet legal requirements. Get help from a trustworthy advisor and work closely with a reputable insurance agent or broker to make good decisions to limit your exposure to loss.

Reference

1. Anderson RE. Billions for defense: The pervasive nature of defensive medicine. www.thedoctors.com/TDC/PressRoom/IntheMedia/CON_ID_000694. Accessed June 18, 2011.

9

Financial Considerations and Capitalization of the Medical Practice

On average, a physician coming out of residency will have likely accrued debt in excess of $139,517, according to 2007 data. Now consider that most new start-up practices can operate for as long as 3 to 4 months without any substantial cash flow to support operations. Even practices once owned by hospital networks or physician practice management companies (PPMCs)—with a track record of profitability—that are considering venturing into private practice are apt to experience cash flow lag time.

Many practice start-up situations will require some kind of financing or infusion of start-up capital. This is nothing out of the ordinary; many businesses borrow cash every day for new ventures that cannot be sustained without some kind of outside help. Not only will cash be needed until the practice can support itself, but some kind of initial investment will be necessary to purchase tangible items and equipment required to launch and build the entity going forward.

Without personal wealth or other sources of funding, the capital needed to start and sustain a medical practice will likely have to be obtained from an outside source. At some point in the start-up stage, financing or a line of credit will have to be established.

The purpose of this chapter is to discuss the process of obtaining adequate financing for starting a medical practice.

Financing Options

Paradoxically, there was a time when it took very little to secure a reasonable amount of money for purchasing a car or even a house; however, the money to start a small business, especially a medical practice, typically requires an extensive application process, which can often be a daunting task for physicians as new business owners.

First, when physicians try to procure capital to start a practice, they face two common problems: (1) usually, they are leveraged extensively and carrying a high debt load as result of approximately 12 years of post-graduate education, and, (2) medical practices have very little tangible assets—or collateral—to secure this debt. The physician's greatest asset is knowledge, and as significant as this may be, a bank cannot repossess knowledge in the event of default on a loan. Further, although there is a reasonable likelihood that the new practice venture will be a success—or at least will be able to sufficiently service debt—a new business always carries a higher degree of risk than an established business. Commercial lenders must take this into consideration as they evaluate the appropriate structure, terms, and risk profile of a particular applicant.

Not all banks are reluctant to lend money. Plenty of lenders will actively seek out opportunities to loan money to physicians; however, raising this critical capital will likely still require some additional effort beyond what would typically be involved with financing a house or a car. Often times—especially in relatively smaller markets—lending money to a new physician is a great public relations tool, as health care services are often perceived by the public as a community benefit. In other cities, banks have organized special small business or physician lending programs, which again, are great public relations tools for banks. Physicians pursuing capital should take advantage of those opportunities.

The Small Business Administration (SBA) is another resource. This federally funded program does not actually lend money, but it does guarantee the lender that the loan will be repaid in full. This enables many more small businesses to gain access to capital without having an extensive and/or quality credit history. However, borrowers will have to work with institutions that participate in these SBA programs (most larger banks do); and as a government program, the administrative process and paperwork can be burdensome.

Private lenders that specialize in one specific field, such as health care, are another option for financing a start up. While these boutique lenders are viable options to traditional sources of capital, using them can be expensive. Finance charges and services received from boutique lenders are typically at a premium, since they do have a more narrow focus than general lenders and will typically offer a greater degree of knowledge within the borrower's specific industry. Thus, turn to them only after all other options have been exhausted.

Conversely, specialized lenders in health care are likely to be more understanding of a physician's needs; therefore, they should not be overlooked. Keep in mind that when a traditional institution, such as a bank, is reluctant to lend you money because you are asking for a large amount of unsecured credit, the boutique lender may be more willing to listen.

Most boutique lenders have more leeway to work with physicians that do not have a perfect credit history. Further, a boutique lender may offer the perfect opportunity to a physician who is highly leveraged with their original lender, but needs additional cash flow in order to maintain short-term viability.

Hospitals may provide certain types of funds for physicians as long as they comply with Stark regulations. In addition, physicians in health professional shortage areas are able to obtain loan forgiveness and other assistance under the federal program established for that purpose.

Types of Credit

There are numerous types of loan structures that a borrower can pursue, and each type of credit facility will typically have unique terms, including interest rate, maturity (ie, term), and prepayment provisions. The term "credit facility" broadly refers to a specific loan between a borrower and a lender. More specifically, a credit facility often includes the typical lending structures involved with traditional business loans, such as lines of credit, revolving credit ("revolvers") and term loans. The two most common types of credit that a medical group will procure are a line of credit and revolving credit, discussed further below.

A line of credit (LOC) refers to an arrangement between a lender and borrower involving a maximum loan balance that the customer can borrow from the bank. The borrower can draw (ie, pull capital from) on the LOC at any time within the life of the LOC until they reach the ceiling amount. The terms of the capital borrowed under the LOC remain the same throughout the life of the LOC, unless the facility involves specific terms or changes in terms upon reaching certain thresholds of capital drawn under the LOC.[1] The most significant benefit of an LOC—and the key reason why LOCs typically make the most sense for medical groups—is that the borrower only pays interest on the capital that they have actually drawn under the LOC, as opposed to the full amount allowed under the facility. Another key benefit is that the capital is available to the borrower at any time during the life of the LOC. Conversely, a key item that borrowers will need to consider when establishing an LOC with a commercial lender is the long-term viability of the bank providing the capital. Throughout the 2007 economic downturn, many small businesses ran into significant trouble as their banks went out of business, leaving the company without access to capital that was critical to the business cash flow. Further, the overall crisis resulted in significant declines in access to capital as lenders reduced their lending volume and enhanced risk requirements, ultimately resulting in banks imposing tighter reigns on lending volume and terms of credit.

Somewhat similar to a line of credit, a revolving credit facility involves the borrower paying a commitment fee in order to gain access to capital in a designated facility as needed. The amount of capital sourced under a revolver will typically fluctuate even on a monthly basis, depending on the borrower's cash flow needs.[2]

Revolvers are typically used for operational cash flow and liquidity purposes; however, many companies, particularly larger corporations, will often use revolvers when they are entering a growth mode and seeking acquisition opportunities, thus allowing them to have access to critical debt financing when it comes time to close the deal. In these cases, the company can typically justify paying the commitment fee in return for not having to facilitate capital when a deal is already lined up, which can sometimes result in a transaction failing. However, the borrower will always have to designate in their "sources and uses" (described further in subsequent sections) that they intend to use the revolver for the purpose of making acquisitions, as opposed to using it for general operating capital.

Another form of debt that is common with many health care facilities is bond debt. A bond is a security issued by a company to an investor acting as the lender and involves a defined time frame (ie, maturity) and interest rate structure (ie, variable, fixed, synthetic, etc). Bonds are typically issued by larger entities, such as health systems, hospitals, and large medical groups with extensive ancillaries and outpatient facilities; however, as the health care industry evolves more toward clinical integration where hospitals are integrating with physicians practices, bond debt is becoming more common for health care entities of all sizes. Bonds are also becoming more common as physician groups seek growth opportunities and look to different types of public financing solutions, such as Build America Bonds and different HUD programs, for launching new ventures and/or facilities. Capital raised via the sale of bonds can be used for a wide range of activities, including the financing of a specific project such as building a new facility, as well as to make acquisitions. For instance, one trend that has recently become more prominent within a number of markets is that of multi-specialty groups purchasing regional medical centers or critical access hospitals that are older or have ceased operations. The groups will then transition the facilities into specialty surgical hospitals or other types of outpatient services entities.

The Pro Forma

An extravagant business plan is not typically necessary for a new medical practice, which will most often have a relatively straightforward business model. However, before you can even think about walking into a bank or some other lender and asking for a line of credit, you must have financial projections. If professional help was obtained to develop a business plan for the practice, the work will likely encompass pro forma financial projections. In most cases a full business plan is unnecessary at this stage, and the pro forma alone will suffice.

A pro forma is a projection. It is a compilation of data based on reasonable assumptions as to the performance of an entity. A very useful tool, a pro forma is used to forecast the operating results of a practice (or any other entity). A pro forma is more than just a budget, in that a budget is typically used for revenue and expense targets for the purpose of short-term operational management, while the pro forma is typically used for longer-term projections that incorporate broader and more in-depth assumptions that can ultimately be utilized to derive a value for the particular going concern in question.

Any lending institution that a physician approaches to start a line of credit will require the physician to have a projection of how the business will perform. In addition, the institution will almost always insist that an independent third party develop (or at least verify) the financial projection (ie, someone with no interest in how the business performs).

A pro forma is no different from the financial statements of any other company. It usually contains a detailed profit and loss statement (ie, income statement) and a statement of cash flow. What makes this document unique, however, is the fact that all of the information contained in these statements is prediction, not fact. This is why, in addition to these statements, the pro forma must contain detailed information concerning the assumptions used to create the statements. Without this data, the profit and loss statement and statement of cash flow are meaningless.

This is why it is integral to this process to have someone knowledgeable in the operations of the entity be involved in the creation of such a document. Remember, you are asking lenders to disperse a sizable amount of money, so they will need to be fully aware and knowledgeable of all relevant details to ultimately incorporate that information into their risk assessment. How and when do you plan on making money? How and when do you plan on spending the capital? And, most importantly, how and when do you plan on paying back their money? The answers to these key questions are typically referred to broadly as "sources and uses," which as one might imagine, allude to an entity's sources of capital, sources of revenue, and uses of the borrowed capital. However, while a borrower can likely clarify the sources and uses in a very general sense, the more capital you are trying to procure, the more detailed planning and projections will be necessary for the lender to adequately evaluate the risk and likely returns on a specific credit facility.

The pro forma consists of two main categories: revenues and expenses. Certainly, anyone can write down a revenue number and an expense number, but the acid test is whether they are realistic figures based on rational and justifiable assumptions, and whether there is sufficient documentation to support the assumptions. If not, the pro forma is meaningless.

While the pro forma should be accurate and realistic, it is still a projection, and projections can—and will—vary from the actual results. The best tool in developing a pro forma is common sense. If it does not look right, then it probably is not.

As previously mentioned, a pro forma can be divided into two categories: expenses and revenues. With some detailed analysis as to the type of practice, the services that will be offered, and a myriad of other issues, these two can be accurately hypothesized.

For instance, the staff that will be needed is fairly predictable. Typical salary ranges for employees in the area are generally attainable. Add a percentage for benefits (ie, retirement plan contribution, health insurance, etc), and you will be able to obtain a reasonable idea of what the total employee salary expense will be. You can also form projections using a reasonable growth percentage applied to the previous year's expense figure for the other fixed expenses incurred in the practice, and nearly half of the projections for expenses will be completed. The next expense category that you will need to consider is variable expense, which refers to the expenses that fluctuate with revenue. For certain items, such as medical supplies, equipment, and drugs, for instance, one can project these expenses to fluctuate based on the same percentage that revenue will fluctuate in each year of the pro forma.

Next, consider revenues, which are typically more challenging to project, because they will involve more unique assumptions and will ultimately drive the overall value derived from the pro forma model. The revenue assumptions will ultimately be determined by the volume and pricing that the physicians plan and/or anticipate producing at different points in the new venture's growth horizon. One method of projecting volume in certain types of practices would be to research the average collections per visit, procedure, or service for the specialty of the practice. Then you would review the practice's historical patient volume and procedure utilization to ultimately project a reasonable metric for patients per day. Multiplying these two metrics could then generate the average revenue per day.

Another method for projecting revenue is to break down the "unit volume" that an individual physician performs and project the volume going forward. When you apply the unit volume figure to a wRVU figure, you can then apply that metric to collections per wRVU ratio. This will generate the total collections that the physician can expect to receive based on doing a certain volume of procedures at an estimated level of wRVUs. When you total this collections figure for each physician in the practice, this could be the practice's projected revenue from professional collections. This method can often be more difficult to apply, because there is a significant amount of analysis that you will have to do in order to determine the physician's historical wRVU rates and to ensure that the projected rates are consistent with a reasonable volume projection. However, if the data is available to use this method, it can often be more accurate on an individual physician basis because it eliminates the financial impact of different procedures, patients' insurance, and collections rates.

These are only a couple methods for projecting revenue and are very simplistic examples at that, which most likely will not apply to every practice or situation. Regardless of the method being applied, the valuator must consider the results of a calculation or projection and determine whether the results are realistic or are they just numbers on a piece of paper. Just because the math works on paper does not necessarily mean a model represents a realistic scenario for the subject being valued. This is where the knowledge, experience, and research on the part of the valuator must come into the equation, evaluating the merits of a model or set of projections.

If it were this easy, of course, anyone could build a pro forma, but unfortunately it is not this easy. In fact, a great deal more analysis is involved before even the first statement can be produced.

For instance, to be as accurate as possible, the physician(s) will want to know or at least have a good idea what equipment will be needed. For the most part—depending on the specialty—most of the tangible items will be similar from practice to practice. Every practice needs items such as exam tables and secretarial chairs and waiting room chairs, and knowing this is very important to the preparation of the pro forma. This equipment will likely be the biggest single cash outlay by the practice. This is why it is best to determine exactly what each physician wants and does not want before the pro forma is developed. A sample list of items is included in Figure 9-1. This encompasses a list of the most general medical and office equipment that a practice will need to operate.

Further, when one is projecting revenue, he or she may have to consider multiple sources of revenue if the practice involves diversified service lines or perhaps incorporates ancillaries, which are often billed separately. It may be that the revenue projections will need to incorporate more detailed and technical assumptions, often getting down to specific procedural (using CPT codes) and RVU projections for each individual physician involved in a group.

Once the foundation of expenses and revenues has been established, they can be used to construct the profit and loss (ie, income) statement and the statement of cash flows. If these statements are going to be used to procure financing or a line of credit, the committee that reviews this information will not only look at the basis from which it was formed—the assumptions—but it will also look at the manner in which it has been presented. This is why the profit and loss (ie, income) statement and statement of cash flows should be prepared in accordance with generally accepted accounting principles (GAAP). This will ensure that while the person reviewing the pro forma will have never seen it before, they will be familiar with the manner in which it has been created.

Medical Equipment	
Quantity	Description
	Adult scale
	Anesthesia machine
	Aspirator
	Audiometer
	Autoclave
	Biohazard trash hamper
	Blanket warmer
	Bronchoscope
	Cautery unit
	Chlestech LDX Lipid Profile System
	Colposcope
	Defibrillator
	Digital thermometer
	Doppler
	Double-lock narcotics cabinet
	EKG machine
	EKG stand
	Electrosurgical generator
	Endoscopy
	ENT wall unit
	Exam stool
	Exam table
	Eye chart
	Handheld cobalt blue light
	Handheld pulse oximeter
	Hematology analyzer
	Infant scale
	IV poles
	Laparoscopic video system
	Liquid nitrogen tank w/ladle
	Mayo stand
	Medical lighting
	Microdermabrasion system
	Microscope
	Midmark spin stool

Medical Equipment	
Quantity	Description
	Ophthalmoscope
	Otoscope
	Outpatient exam light
	Pelvic light
	Procedure table
	Pulmonary function unit
	Pulse oximeter
	QuickVue influenza test
	Scale
	Sphygmomanometer
	Spirometer
	Sterilizer
	Stethoscope
	Thermometer
	Two-section X-ray viewbox
	Tycos stethoscope
	Tympanometer
	Vision screener
	Vital signs monitor
	Wall unit sphygmomanometer
	Wheelchair
	X-ray machine and processor

Office Furniture/Equipment	
Quantity	Description
	Bookcase
	Break room chair
	Break table
	Waiting room chair
	Coat rack
	Coffee table
	Copy machine
	Couch
	Credenza
	Credit card machine
	End table

FIGURE 9-1   Pro Forma Initial Questionnaire

Office Furniture/Equipment	
Quantity	**Description**
	Executive chair
	Executive desk
	Fax machine
	Filing cabinet
	Floor lamp
	Large refrigerator
	Manager's desk
	Medical record cabinet
	Parsons table
	Point side chairs w/o arms
	Printers
	Reception desk
	Safes
	Secretarial chair
	Step stool w/handle
	Table lamp

Appliances/Equipment	
Quantity	**Description**
	Bottled water machine
	Coffee maker
	Extension cords/surge protectors
	Flashlight
	Mail meter
	Microwave
	Outdoor combo ashtray
	Refrigerator (large)
	Refrigerator (small)
	Soda machine
	Telephone system
	Microwave oven
	Toolbox
	Trash cans
	Typewriter
	Video player and monitor

FIGURE 9-1   Pro Forma Initial Questionnaire (*continued*)

Other Financing Considerations

A key consideration that many medical business owners should be aware of is the risk that they are taking when obtaining debt to finance their businesses. Today's lending environment is very different from what it was 5 or 10 years ago. Banks generally have much more stringent requirements imposed on them by shareholders and regulatory authorities, which translate into more extensive requirements for borrowers. In many cases and indeed with many of the health care businesses, both large and small, lenders will require the owners of the business to make a personal guarantee to ensure the strength of a specific loan. This means that in the event something happens to the solvency of the business entity, the borrower is still personally obligated to repay the debt to the creditor. In the event of insolvency of the business where a personal guarantee is involved, this can often result in the guarantor having to declare bankruptcy due to their inability to repay the debt.

If at all possible, borrowers should avoid at all costs putting a personal guarantee on their debt; however, in some cases, this will be unavoidable. Further, if you were in a position previously where a personal guarantee was required, but have since been able to sufficiently service the debt and meet all covenants and obligations under a specific credit facility, you may be able to refinance the remainder of the debt and/or even undergo a full recapitalization, which involves completely changing the financial and capital structure of an entity. While the refinancing and recapitalization processes can be arduous, they are often more than justified in order to obtain better terms and reduced risk. This will often involve removing any personal guarantees that a business owner had to make previously.

Another key consideration that borrowers should be aware of in regards to managing their debt is interest rate risk management. Interest rate risk refers to the risk a borrower incurs as a result of changing interest rates, which can increase or decrease the cost associated with a particular credit facility. In an increasing interest rate environment, borrowers will have to pay more to service their debt, which will have a direct effect on operational cash flow, as well as their longer-term pro forma and strategic plans. One strategy for managing interest rate risk is a swap or, more specifically, an interest rate swap. While most people will often assume that swaps—which are technical derivative securities—are something that only large, publicly traded corporations and Wall Street investment banks do, swaps are actually done every single day by medical practices of all sizes and structure.

A swap is essentially an agreement between two counterparties where "one stream of future interest payments is exchanged for another based on a specified principal amount." Interest rate swaps often involve borrowers exchanging a fixed payment debt structure with a floating payment structure, which is linked to a defined interest rate mechanism, often London Interbank Offering Rate (LIBOR), thus allowing the borrower to take advantage of better interest rates.[3] When a business is able to gain a lower interest rate on their debt, this will have a direct positive benefit on the entity's profitability and overall long-term value. As such, swaps can be very advantageous tools for all kinds of businesses to pursue. Further, as swaps become more common within the health care industry and among health care business owners, a number of financial advisory firms and lenders have emerged that specifically work with medical practices and other health care entities to facilitate swap transactions that facilitate more optimal interest rates for borrowers.

Conclusion

Procuring a line of working capital or financing for the start up of your medical practice should not be harder than your board exams! Gaining access to credit may not be quite as easy as it once was because of the lagging economy and the growing list of requirements lenders are imposing on borrowers in today's marketplace, but there will always be people who are willing to lend capital for a reasonable business venture. Even if your credit is less than stellar, there will be some lender willing to provide the necessary financing.

Preparation is the most critical component. Most lenders are not going to lend an individual or business entity hundreds of thousands or millions of dollars just on their good name and a guarantee that the proposed venture should be successful. Banks are in their business to make money, and they need some proof that time and effort has been invested and the proper amount of research done to make the venture successful. Further, lenders have their own risk management protocols and credit requirements with which they must comply, including obligations to their shareholders, as well as to the federal and state authorities that govern lending practices. As such, a high quality and well-presented pro forma is a must when applying for a line of credit.

References

1. Interest Rate Swap, www.investopedia.com/terms/i/interestrateswap. asp. Accessed April 12, 2011.

2. Line of Credit, www.investopedia.com/terms/l/lineofcredit.asp. Accessed April 12, 2011.

3. Revolving Credit, www.investopedia.com/terms/r/revolvingcredit.asp. Accessed April 12, 2011.

PART TWO

Practice Purchasing and Ownership Considerations

Buying a medical practice is a monumental embarkation that calls for serious considerations in areas of financial assets, personnel, revenue cycle protocols, loss prevention and risk management, internal controls, policies and procedures, and marketing and business development. Chapters 10 through 15 deal with the challenges that every practice buyer will face.

10 Financial Asset Considerations

Among the many decisions involved in starting a medical practice is choosing a location for the office and how to furnish and equip it. Your specialty, practice style, and locale will impact your choice of office space. Access to capital will be a major factor in the choice of furnishings and fixtures as well as office equipment. The purpose of this chapter is to review the variables that need to be considered in order to make decisions that are beneficial to the growth and function of your practice.

Selecting an Office Location

The type of practice you will be establishing is one of the key considerations relative to the office site you select. Choosing a geographic area that is in line with your specialty is critical to the success of the practice. For example, an obstetrician will need to have easy access to a hospital in order to admit patients and deliver babies, while a pediatrician may need to be located in the suburbs where he or she is accessible to families with children.

In addition to geographic location, it is important to know exactly what you want or do not want in a lease before you start looking. For example, how much space will be needed initially, and how much space will be needed to sustain the growth of the practice? Several Internet websites offer the ability to calculate square footage requirements for office space by inputting information about your business. One such site is www.officefinder.com. OfficeFinder is a national organization that provides assistance to tenants. In addition, the considerations listed in Table 10-1 should be reviewed prior to beginning the office location decision process.

TABLE 10-1   Office Space Planning Checklist

Item	Notes
Features	
• Best three features of current space	
• Worst three features of current space	
• Most important features	
Timing	
• Occupancy date	
• Timeline for process	
Location	
• Geographic location	
• Access	
Budget/Cost	
• Budget and cost	
Site Accessibility	
• Freeway access	
• Public transportation	
Layout Type	
• Offices versus open work areas	
Employees	
• Number	
• Sizes of offices and work areas	
• Windows	
• Special needs	
Lease Options	
• Expansion	
• Extension	
• Termination	
• Contraction	
• First right of refusal on adjoining space	
Reception Area	
• Seating	
• Upgrades	

(*continued*)

TABLE 10-1   Office Space Planning Checklist (*continued*)

Item	Notes
Work Areas	
• Types	
• Sizes	
• Equipment	
• Special electrical needs	
Lease Length	
• Lease length	
• Extension options	
Growth Projections	
• 3 year	
• 5 year	
• 10 year	
General Feel	
• Spacious or efficient	
• Lighting	
• Quality	
Conference Rooms	
• Seating capacity	
• Number	
• Image	
• Public/Private	
Security	
• Building	
• Neighborhood	
Amenities	
• Lunch rooms	
• Coffee bars	
• Lounge	
• Rest rooms	

(*continued*)

TABLE 10-1   Office Space Planning Checklist (*continued*)

Parking	
• Number on site	
• Total required	
• Cost	
Mechanical Systems	
• Elevators	
• HVAC	
• Off-hours operation	
Identity	
• Signage	
• Visibility	
Image	
• Type of building	
• Location in building	
• Location on floor	
• View	
• Building and floor size	
• Quality of improvements	

Source: *Office Space Planning Checklist.* www.officefinder.com/checklist.html. Accessed June 22, 2011.

Negotiating a Favorable Lease

Location, not cost, should be the determining factor in an office lease. Remember that a lease is a binding agreement and you may be locked in for several years. Also, leasehold improvements and other concessions can often be negotiated up front.

How much you are able to negotiate on the lease rate varies with supply and demand. For example, if ample office space is available, negotiating an excellent deal is highly possible. Conversely, if only limited office space is available, the landlord will be much less willing to negotiate. Go into lease negotiations only after completing research regarding the rental environment in the geographic area under consideration. This should include determining the current lease rates for similar properties in the area. Having this knowledge will create a more even "playing field" during the negotiation process. If possible, present a competing lease agreement to further reinforce the desired lease terms and rate.

Set priorities for the items that are important to you in the contract and seek advice from an attorney before you sign. Obtain all terms of the leasing arrangements in writing. Make no agreements based simply on a verbal assent regardless of who the landlord will be. A well-written lease protects both the lessor and the lessee.

What to Look for in an Office Lease

Below is a list of some considerations in office leasing that are most important to physicians:

- **Know Your Timeline.** Making a decision on the right space and location can take weeks or even months.

- **Know the Description of Your Space.** Be sure to understand how the space is being measured; then personally measure it. Hallway space is sometimes included in the square footage. Do not pay for space that cannot be used, especially common areas such as a lobby or foyer that is shared with other tenants. Check to see if the rental agreement includes parking spaces. Find out how many and where they are located, and if there is a fee related to the parking areas. If patients have no place to park, the office space is useless. A good rule of thumb is one parking space for every chair in the reception area.

- **Know Your Terms.** We recommend that you sign an initial lease for no more than three years. This will allow enough time to test the suitability of the locale for your practice. A viable practice should begin to show strong profits by the third year. While a 10-year lease may feature an attractively low rent, terminating it may be hard if you decide to move to another location.

- **Know Your Renewal Options.** As an alternative to a long-term lease, consider signing a 3-year lease with two 3-year options to renew. These options should include any future rental increases in writing.

- **Know Your Rental Terms.** Know to whom the rent is payable. A landlord who lives far away is not likely to be as responsive to your requests for repairs and improvements as one who lives in the same town.

- **Know Your Escalation Clause.** Even a 3-year lease may have rental increases every year. These increases are usually based on the landlord's taxes and cost of operations, such as maintenance and utilities. Rent in commercial space is quoted as cost-per-square-foot annually.

- **Know Your Damage Deposit.** Find out the amount of the damage deposit and if your deposit will earn interest. Be sure that all repairs are made before move in or that an appropriate clause noting the needed repairs is included in the lease. Most leases have some wording concerning the condition of the space after the lease has expired. Some will state that "all leasehold improvements become the property of the landlord," or "the premises must be returned to their original condition." In either case, the tenant loses. You will either give up items you have installed, such as sinks, cabinets, wallpaper, and even window treatments; if not, you will have to resurface and repaint the walls. This can be expensive if you decide to move.

- **Know Your Escape Clause.** Be sure that the office lease contains an escape clause releasing you from your obligations should you lose your medical license, hospital privileges, or become disabled. An escape clause should also be included to protect your estate in the event of your death.

- **Know the Items and Services Furnished.** Maintenance, security, repairs, lawn mowing, and snow removal all fall into this category. Make no assumptions about anything. Any services furnished and costs covered must be itemized in the lease. Check out the credentials of the building maintenance service and be sure they are bonded. If you plan to see patients at nontraditional hours, be sure you know the hours of operation for the air conditioning, elevators, and security. Be clear about the kind of signage that is allowed or provided.

- **Know What Type of Insurance Is Provided by the Landlord.** Learn what kind of coverage the landlord has for accidents that may occur in the foyer, parking lot, and other shared spaces. Determine, with the assistance of an insurance agent, the level of supplemental policy coverage needed for any gaps that may exist.

- **Know the Terms for Remodeling and Redecorating.** Does the lease agreement state how often your office will be repainted or the carpet replaced? How often does the landlord repaint or redecorate the common areas? Who pays for these improvements?

- **Know the Terms for Subleasing.** If you choose to move before your lease expires, will you be allowed to sublet your space? Does the lease restrict the sublet clause to certain kinds of businesses? While you want the sublet clause to be reasonable, you also want to assure that another tenant does not sublease space to an undesirable tenant.

- **Know Your Unfit-for-Occupancy Clause.** This clause usually covers storm damage and other acts of nature. However, you will want to ensure that the lease covers other disruptions, such as loss of heat or air conditioning. You may not be able to see patients for several days, and you want to be sure you do not have to pay rent for those days the space is uninhabitable.

- **Know Your Rights of First Refusal.** This clause should state that you will be offered the first opportunity to lease any additional space that becomes available in your building. If your practice grows rapidly, you will want this option to expand rather than relocate.

Chapter 9, Financial Considerations and Capitalization of the Medical Practice, lists the basic pieces of furniture and equipment necessary to start a medical practice. In the following pages are discussions about leasing office equipment, medical devices, and furniture.

Acquiring Equipment

To successfully operate a new medical practice, the appropriate tools and equipment are necessary. This includes appropriate and accessible space (as discussed above) as well as both medically related and other operating supplies. Acquiring these supplies and equipment calls for a knowledge base that many physicians may not possess. However, the following information may help you make these decisions. Consider the advice of an accountant and a trustworthy health care consultant to prevent overbuying or overspending.

Leasing Versus Purchasing

Before acquiring equipment items, discuss with your accountant the advantages of leasing versus purchasing equipment. Leasing entails higher interest rates, but requires lower down payments. Generally, because of limited access to capital in a practice start up, highly technical equipment should be leased rather than purchased. Most vendors will offer the option to lease equipment, and most leasing companies will offer several leasing options. After the purchase price is established, your accountant will calculate the alternatives and advise you on the best way to obtain the item, based on the capital that is available, current interest rates, the technology of the equipment, and total cash investment requirements of the practice start up. Leasing also allows you to diversify your debts and does not tie up your working capital.

Another option for obtaining a lease is to utilize a leasing consultant/ broker who will conduct research to determine the best available rate. Leasing consultants have helped many physicians acquire all of their purchases through a single lease, instead of obtaining a separate lease for each item. Along with the convenience of making one payment, consolidating financing arrangements into a single lease will likely achieve a lower overall finance rate.

For certain types of equipment, leasing may be a viable option when considering what the equipment will be worth in five years. For example, a computer selling for $2,000 today will be outdated in five years and worth $150. With a lease, you would just turn the equipment back to the leasing company at the end of the term, replace it with a new computer, and continue with the lease. Following are some examples of equipment that is often leased.

Telephone System

When it comes to buying equipment, vendors will often emphasize bells and whistles, when all that is really needed is functional equipment—often the case when it comes to telephone systems. For example, some vendors will attempt to sell you the top-of-the-line system with features that will rarely be used. *Selling short* is another method vendors will use to take advantage of consumers. Vendors will sell you equipment without informing you that additional apparatuses may be required or that the system will be outgrown in a year, ensuring you as a repeat customer for equipment upgrades. For these reasons and because outgrowing equipment is common for new businesses, leasing is often a good option. Leasing offers the convenience of not having to own equipment that routinely requires replacing.

Because the telephone system will be a vital link between you and your patients, knowing and buying the right system will be critical. *Key systems* are mostly common for small businesses because they do not need a lot of features. Key systems are also inexpensive—much less expensive than a private branch exchange (PBX), an in-house telephone switching system that interconnects telephone extensions to each other as well as the outside telephone network. Another leading-edge consideration is PC-based telephones (telephone software that resides on the personal computer). These systems can offer all the features of the large systems at the price of a key system. A good resource for telecommunications and buying tips for telephone systems and PC-based systems is available at www.commweb.com, which offers product reviews, buying guides, and case studies.

In recent years, as mobile phones and softphones (ie, phone capabilities serviced through a computer rather than a standard desk phone) have grown in popularity, the costs associated with telephone systems have declined. Therefore, it is important to leverage this knowledge when negotiating the lease terms for your desired system.

Medical Devices

You will likely be adding expensive medical devices that, like telephone systems, can become obsolete as newer, more efficient technology and equipment are developed. Some companies offer a comprehensive line of medical devices for the convenience of not having to contact a separate vendor for each device. To enhance their attractiveness and convenience, these vendors may also offer financing or leasing arrangements. Be extremely cautious, however, before adding any medical devices to the practice before knowing if third-party payers will reimburse for services performed using these devices.

Another option for obtaining equipment is to consider purchasing or leasing pre-owned or refurbished devices still under a manufacturer's warranty. Inquire about close-out or demonstration models, which are often sold at a discount. It is important to maintain a low overhead when starting out by not adding a great deal of expensive equipment until you establish the patient volume necessary to support the added expense. Doing so will allow you to justify the purchase before going into debt over a piece of equipment that will likely be outdated before its revenue generating potential is optimized.

Copy Machines

Leasing a copy machine with a solid service contract is a wise decision. Copiers are relied upon extensively and will be needed on a daily basis within the practice. They are complex machines with hundreds of moving parts and require ongoing maintenance; a practice cannot be without a functional copier for extended periods of time. Owning one can be expensive, especially when considering the cost of ownership over the life of the copier. Therefore, leasing a copy machine is a popular solution. There are many leasing programs to be considered, but be cautious of the commitments that are made. For example, some agreements may offer attractive terms, but the agreement may obligate the lessee to purchase copier supplies exclusively through one vendor. In many instances, supplies from such vendors are two and three times more expensive than prices offered at local office supply stores.

Also, know the performance level of the copier that is being considered. Copiers will almost always have a three- or four-digit model number. The last two digits indicate the number of copies per minute (CPM) that the machine will generate. While so many copies per minute may seem insignificant, consider the amount of unproductive time the staff will spend standing at the copier. Also compare the warm-up speed, the reset speed, and the initial copy speed. Then compare performance to cost.

Finally, scanning is typically a capability seen in newer copiers, and the value of this technology should also be considered in your copier purchase. The ability to scan using the copier will also help reduce strain on the fax machines and printers in your office.

Fax Machines and Printers

Unless you are using high-end printers and fax machines, you may discover that purchasing is more economical than leasing this equipment since cost of ownership is somewhat less expensive and the equipment is low maintenance. For example, a business fax machine will retail for approximately $150 to $200. If it ever needs to be replaced, it is more economical to purchase outright rather than paying a monthly lease payment for several years.

Computers

In Chapter 7, Equipping Your Practice with Information Technology, the options are discussed for deploying and acquiring technology, which entails the purchase of computer hardware to run the system. Regardless of what method is selected for delivering technology, you will need to purchase some type of computer hardware. The application service provider (ASP) approach and other web-based options will require the least amount of hardware to be purchased because there will be no need for an on-premise server. However, some hardware such as workstations, printers, and mobile devices will still need to be purchased and installed at the practice. Many physicians who are just starting their practice see the purchase of a computer as a key step in the right direction. However, it is recommended that, before rushing out to buy an expensive computer, you determine the overall hardware requirements within the practice's global information system strategies. Otherwise, a computer may be purchased that is not compatible with the long-range plan. When it comes to leasing computer hardware, more physicians are opting to purchase their system because computers have become much more affordable, especially pre-owned units that are sold for $100 to $300.

Be cautious of any software vendor that discourages you from buying your own hardware. In many cases the software vendor will buy the equipment from the same places you could buy it, but mark it up 10 to 20% before reselling it to you. Some vendors will require you to use their preferred equipment because of their software and support requirements, but you should still be allowed the option of buying your own hardware.

Furniture

Leasing furniture is also an option, but for a practice starting out, buying used furniture may be a better choice. The market is flooded with used furniture, and it is fairly common to find matching pieces. Moreover, furniture in the waiting room will receive its share of abuse; therefore, new furniture will look old after a few months of heavy use. Artwork and other decorative items can be added without excessive expense if you know where to look, such as furniture close-out stores or "big box" home goods stores.

When it comes to buying or leasing assets, there are plenty of options to consider. Regardless of the direction chosen, it is extremely important to stay within your budget, especially during the initial months of starting the business. Keep in mind that it can take up to

90 days before any revenue is generated and up to 1 to 2 years before the revenue stream is fully realized. For this reason, your overhead, including your investment in supplies and equipment, must be considered before adding layers of expense.

Conclusion

Selecting an office space and engaging in a lease arrangement and negotiations are some of the most confusing aspects of a start up. Purchasing equipment, furniture, and fixtures for your practice can be difficult as well. Most of these decisions are long lived and expensive. Seek help from your attorney, accountant, your practice manager, or health care consultant who has the practice's best interest in mind and experience in working with others in similar circumstances.

CHAPTER 11

Personnel Considerations

An overview of the essentials of personnel management is presented in this chapter. As an employer, the physician starting a medical practice must know quite a bit about labor and employment laws that govern all businesses in addition to knowing about customary compensation and benefits. Further, employers have responsibilities and standards that are a part of management.

Even as an employee, a physician is viewed as an authority figure in a medical practice. The clinical assistants and administrative staff expect the physicians to understand and follow the rules. If you plan to become an employee of a group practice, hospital, or other entity, you should have a working knowledge of the laws and statutes regulating the medical practice, and a thorough understanding of the internal personnel guidelines that pertain to managing the employees. Your practice manager should also be skilled and have experience and expertise in this area.

Employment Laws

Employment laws are the rules and regulations that form the basis for managing personnel. They are designed to protect the rights of the workforce and should govern your relationships with your employees.

Employment discrimination laws seek to prevent discrimination by employers based on age, disability, equal pay/compensation, genetic information, national origin, pregnancy, race/color, religion, and sex. Discriminatory practices include bias in job application procedures, hiring, firing, advancement, job assignment, compensation, various types of harassment, and other conditions and privileges of employment. Employment discrimination laws are embodied in federal and state statutes.

Resources are furnished at the end of this chapter that will give extensive information concerning employment laws.

Equal Employment Opportunity Commission

The Equal Employment Opportunity Commission (EEOC), established by Title VII of the Civil Rights Act of 1964, interprets and enforces the Equal Pay Act of 1963, Age Discrimination in Employment Act of 1967, Title VII, and Title I of the Americans with Disabilities Act.

Title VII of the Civil Rights Act of 1964

Title VII of the Civil Rights Act of 1964 applies to most employers with 15 or more employees on the payroll for each working day of 20 or more weeks in the current or prior year. It prohibits discrimination against an employee on the basis of race, color, religion, national origin, or sex in all terms and conditions of employment including equal opportunity to participate in training programs and equal opportunity for advancement. In some states and local jurisdictions these protected classes have been expanded to include sexual orientation and marital status.

Title VII was amended by the Pregnancy Discrimination Act of 1978, which forbids employers from discriminating against workers on the basis of pregnancy, childbirth, or related medical conditions. Employers are required to treat pregnancy the same as any other temporary disability.

Both Title VII and the Pregnancy Discrimination Act of 1978 are enforced by the EEOC. There are also state employment discrimination agencies responsible for enforcement of state laws and regulations. For detailed EEOC information see www.eeoc.gov/.

Title VII of the Civil Rights Act also prohibits sexual harassment and harassment based on any other protected category. Sexual harassment is unwelcome sexual advances, requests for sexual favors, and any other verbal or physical conduct of a sexual nature that results in a tangible employment action, or that is severe or pervasive enough that it unreasonably interferes with an individual's work performance, or creates an intimidating, coercive, hostile, or offensive environment.

Harassment occurs when an individual is treated less favorably with regard to the terms and conditions of his/her employment and/or has been subjected to unwelcome severe or pervasive conduct that effects his/her working conditions based on race/color, national origin, sex, religion, age, or any other protected status. The most common form of harassment is sexual harassment. Title VII prohibits gender-based discrimination in compensation practices. Employers should base compensation practices on performance and seniority or systems that measure the quality and/or quantity of work. Jobs with similar functions and working conditions that require equal skill and responsibility should compensate equally.

Age Discrimination in Employment Act

Both Title VII and the federal Age Discrimination in Employment Act (ADEA) prohibit employers to discipline or discharge an employee who is more than 40 years of age because of age and applies to both employees and job applicants. The ADEA contains explicit guidelines for benefit, pension, and retirement plans. The ADEA does not regulate job-related discipline.

The ADEA covers all private and public employers with 20 or more employees, labor organizations, and training programs.

Americans with Disabilities Act of 1990 (ADA) and ADA Amendments Act of 2008

The ADA protects persons with disabilities from discrimination in employment, public services, public accommodations, and telecommunications. For employers with 15 or more employees, the ADA established many responsibilities relating to this class of individuals. The statute has two components that affect the medical practice. The first one pertains to discrimination in hiring or employment and requires an employer to make reasonable accommodations for an employee with a disability if he or she can perform the essential functions of the job. The second component pertains to accommodations that must be provided for persons with disabilities to access your facility or services. These accommodations, for example, would include having a wheelchair ramp or a restroom that is large enough to accommodate a wheelchair. Employers are not required to take actions that involve undue hardship to the business.

Genetic Information Nondiscrimination Act of 2008

This act protects the privacy of personal genetic information by prohibiting health insurance companies and employers from collecting and using genetic information in the course of hiring, firing, or terms or privileges of employment. Final regulations were published in January 2011.

Fair Labor Standards Act of 1938

Administered by the Department of Labor, the Fair Labor Standards Act (FLSA), commonly referred to as the Wage and Hour Law, regulates workers' time and money. This law defines the 40-hour workweek, sets minimum wage (eg, currently $7.25 per hour), restricts child labor, and sets requirements for overtime pay. The FLSA applies to all employers with at least two employees and whose annual sales total $500,000 or more or who are engaged in interstate commerce—a legal requirement so broad that it includes those who make telephone calls and send mail from one state to another.

Most FLSA violations occur because employers misunderstand the rules stipulating which workers are covered and must be paid minimum wages and overtime for any hours over 40 hours that they work each week.[1] (Employment classifications are defined later in this chapter.)

Equal Pay Act of 1963

The Equal Pay Act, which amended the Fair Labor Standards Act, prohibits paying wages based on gender. It provides that where workers perform equal work in jobs requiring "equal skill, effort, and responsibility and performed under similar working conditions" they should be provided equal pay.

Rights of Military Personnel

The Uniformed Services Employment and Reemployment Rights Act of 1994 (USERRA) prohibits employment discrimination on the basis of an individual's membership, application for service, performance of service, or obligation for service in the uniformed services. USERRA covers all employees who perform military service, either voluntarily or involuntarily, including active duty, training for active or inactive duty, and full-time National Guard duty. Employers may not take any of the following actions on the basis of military service or obligations:

- Deny initial employment
- Deny reemployment
- Terminate the employee
- Fail to promote the employee
- Fail to provide the employee any benefit of employment

If military service was a factor in the decision to take any of these actions, the employer must prove that the action would have occurred despite the military service to avoid charges of discrimination. USERRA applies to virtually all employers regardless of size.

Discrimination for Sexual Orientation

Though not a part of federal law pertaining to civil rights, there is a growing body of law preventing or occasionally justifying employment discrimination based on sexual orientation. Employers should check with their state Department of Labor to see if there is legislation against discrimination based on sexual orientation.

Workplace Privacy

Privacy is a person's right to keep personal information away from the world at large—the right to be left alone. However, an employee's desire for personal privacy may conflict with an organization's need to collect employment-related information and act upon it. Increasingly, employers are being held responsible for workers' conduct during the employment relationship and sometimes for prehire conduct an employer should have discovered. For protection, employers are searching workspaces and electronic documents, running credit checks on potential hires, and requesting detailed medical information. The Fair Credit Reporting Act allows employers to use information obtained in a credit and background check for employment purposes, but requires employers to inform applicants, within 3 days of the request, that an investigation report has been requested.

The US Constitution does not grant a right to privacy for workers in private companies, but other provisions give some workers such rights. Basically, the ADA and the Family and Medical Leave Act (FMLA) protect a worker's health status (ie, employee medical records). More importantly, HIPAA established an entirely new standard for employee privacy and has extensive regulations on the subject. The worker's health records must remain confidential and separate from the employee's personnel file.

Other relevant legislation to protect the privacy of the applicant or employee includes the Fair Credit Reporting Act (FCRA) and the Electronic Communications Privacy Act (ECPA).

Employment Classifications

Part of the practice's responsibility when hiring the practice staff encompasses obtaining a working knowledge of the Fair Labor Standards Act (FLSA). This complex law determines whether an employer is subject to federal minimum wage and overtime requirements. Most medical employees are covered. For compliance, first ascertain the status of your practice. Then, determine the exempt or nonexempt status of each employee using the descriptions below.

Exempt Status

The following employment categories defined by the FLSA have been adapted for application to the medical practice for defining employees who are exempt from overtime pay requirements. Additional information is available at www.dol.gov/compliance/laws/comp-flsa.htm# factsheets.

These categories include:

- **Executive Employee.** Employees must meet all of the following definitions to be exempt (eg, practice administrators are typically considered exempt):
  - Minimum salary: $455 per week, paid on a salary basis
  - Primary duty: manages enterprise, department, or department subdivision
  - Other job characteristics
    —Directs the work of two or more full-time employees
    —Exercises discretionary powers
    —Authorized to hire and fire or to recommend those actions
  - Must spend no more than 20% of working hours in nonexempt duties
- **Administrative Employee.** Employees must meet the following definitions to be exempt:
  - Minimum salary: $455 per week
  - Primary duties:
    —Office or nonmanual work
    —Work directly related to the management or general business operations (eg, functional areas; accounting; quality control; marketing; human resources; and computer network, Internet, and database administration)
    —Works directly in academic instruction or training
  - Other job characteristics:
    —Uses discretion and independent judgment regularly with respect to matters of significance
  - Must spend no more than 20% of time in nonexempt duties
- **Professional Employee.** Employees must meet all the following requirements to be exempt (eg, physicians, registered nurses, registered or certified technologists, dental hygienists, physician assistants, speech pathologists, and physical therapists are typically considered exempt):
  - Minimum salary: $455 per week
  - Primary duties: work requires advanced knowledge acquired through specialized study of an advanced type in a field of science or learning
  - Other job characteristics
    —Must consistently exercise discretion and judgment
    —Intellectual in nature
  - Must spend no more than 20% of workweek on activities unrelated to professional duties

Nonexempt Status

Common medical practice positions that typically are considered
nonexempt are:

- Licensed practical nurses
- Nurses' aides
- Laboratory technicians or assistants
- Clerical workers
- Orderlies
- Food service employees
- Janitorial employees

Wage Records Requirements

The FLSA requires that employers keep certain records on wages
and hours worked each day as well as total hours worked each week.
Wage records should include the following basic information for each
employee:

- Employee's full name and Social Security number
- Address, including ZIP code
- Birth date, if younger than 19
- Gender and occupation
- Time and day of week when employee's workweek begins
- Hours worked each day
- Total hours worked each workweek
- Basis on which employee's wages are paid
- Regular hourly rate of pay
- Total daily or weekly straight-time earnings
- Total overtime earnings for the workweek
- All additions to or deductions from the employee's wages
- Total wages paid each pay period
- Date of payment and the pay period covered by the payment

Unless the employee is exempt from overtime pay, the employer
must pay one-and-one-half times the employee's regular rate of pay for
all time worked over 40 hours in one workweek. Even if an employer
pays every two weeks, there can be no averaging of hours in the pay

period. For example, if the employee works 30 hours the first week of the pay period and 50 hours the next week, he or she is entitled to 10 hours of overtime pay for the second week. Overtime is based on hours worked over 40, not including vacation and sick leave taken during the same pay period.

Employment Contracts

The most common type of employment agreement in the health care industry is the oral, *at-will* agreement. The concept is that an employee can quit at any time, or the employer can terminate the employee at any time, with or without reason.

At-will does not apply to a job in which a contract is in effect and that states a specific period of employment. The right of the employer to apply the at-will doctrine does not override the restrictions placed on the employer, such as the discriminations defined in Title VII of the Civil Rights Act of 1964. Violations of this and other laws will likely result in wrongful termination lawsuits.

By using the term *at-will* versus *just cause,* an employee serves at the discretion of the medical practice and therefore may be dismissed with or without cause. Using the term *just cause* sets a prerequisite that justifiable cause must be shown in order to discharge an employee. The practice's employee handbook (discussed later in this chapter) should use specific language indicating that employees of your practice are employees at-will and specify termination procedures and any appeal rights.

Posting Requirements

Federal and state laws often require employers to post a notice about a particular law. Usually provided as posters or permits, these notices should be in a conspicuous place easily accessible to all employees (eg, typically, the breakroom). Listed below are the posters that employers are required to display under federal law.

Age Discrimination, Disability Discrimination, Equal Employment

- Poster titled Equal Employment Opportunity Is the Law
- Available from national or regional EEOC offices or at www.dol.gov/ofccp/regs/compliance/posters/pdf/eeopost.pdf.

Child Labor, Minimum Wage, and Overtime

- Wage-hour poster 1088 (Federal Minimum Wage)
- Available from the US Department of Labor poster office and regional offices or at www.dol.gov/whd/regs/compliance/posters/flsa.htm.

Family and Medical Leave

- Poster required by Family and Medical Leave Act of 1993
- Available from the US Department of Labor poster office and regional offices or at www.dol.gov/whd/regs/compliance/posters/fmlaen.pdf.

Polygraph Testing

- Wage-hour poster 1462 (Employee Polygraph Protection Act)
- Available from the US Department of Labor poster office and regional offices or at www.dol.gov/ofccp/regs/compliance/posters/pdf/eppac.pdf.

Safety

- Occupational Safety and Health Act (OSHA) poster 3165 (Job Safety & Health It's the Law!)
- Available from the US Department of Labor poster office and regional offices or at www.osha.gov/Publications/poster.html.
- OSHA also requires posting an annual summary of on-the-job injuries (OSHA Form 300A—Summary of Work-related Illnesses and Injuries)

Military Personnel

- Uniformed Services Employment and Reemployment Rights Act (USERRA) poster
- Available from the U.S. Department of Labor at www.dol.gov/vets/programs/userra/poster.htm

Posters may be obtained from the government agency charged with enforcing a particular law. Most agencies have developed a single poster that satisfies the requirements of several different laws administered by that agency. Also, private companies publish posters that employers are required to post. Contact the following agencies to obtain these posters:

Equal Employment Opportunity Commission Clearinghouse
PO Box 541
Annapolis Junction, MD 20701
800-669-3362

US Department of Labor 866-4-USA-DOL (866-487-2365)

Workers' Compensation

Physicians may think of workers' compensation in regard to the medical care it provides to other employers' workers. However, the physician-employer must cover his or her own employees with workers' compensation insurance.

Information that outlines your responsibilities can be obtained by contacting the workers' compensation board in your state. An insurance agent is also a good resource for information about workers' compensation requirements.

OSHA Workplace Requirements

The Occupational Safety and Health Act (OSHA) was enacted in 1970 to assure safe, healthful working conditions for employees. Employers are required to furnish employees with a place of employment that is safe from recognized hazards. In the medical office, bloodborne pathogens are the hazard of greatest concern.

It is the responsibility of every medical employer to obtain complete information for compliance with OSHA regulations. The *OSHA Handbook for Small Businesses,* which includes self-inspection checklists, is available on OSHA's website or at www.osha.gov/Publications/small business/small-business.pdf.

Hiring Employees

All employees need guidelines and rules to understand what is expected of them. A well-written job description is the best way of communicating a description of the duties for which an employee is responsible.

Your first priority should be to hire an experienced practice manager. Expect to pay a higher wage to an experienced person, but by doing so you will recoup this extra expenditure in efficiency and dollars collected. Once the practice manager has been hired, he or she can develop job descriptions and screen applicants for the clinical assistant and other staff as needed.

Give a great deal of thought to the duties of the practice manager and prepare a job description before beginning the advertising or hiring process. The Medical Group Management Association (MGMA) has a certification process through its American College of Medical Executives

program, which may be one criterion for employment. Extensive information regarding hiring staff is available on the MGMA Career Center
website.

A job description usually includes the following elements:

Job Title	Name of the Job
Job Summary	A one- or two-sentence summary that defines the overall function of the job.
Job Qualifications	A brief listing of educational and experience qualifications.
Duties and Responsibilities	A list of the major job tasks describing what is to be accomplished.

Sample job descriptions for a practice manager and a clinical assistant are provided at the end of this chapter.

Setting a Salary Range

Personnel salaries and benefits will be your largest single expense. You
will want to hire the person with the best skills at the most affordable
pay. Developing a salary range for each job title is the recommended
way to set salaries. Staff salaries should be predicated on the following:

- How much the practice can afford to pay now and what you can
  probably pay next year
- The average salary for the same job within the community for
  staff with the same level of experience and education

Sources for Developing a Pool of Candidates

The following are sources for developing a pool of candidates for a position at the practice:

- State and local MGMAs (which generally have a job listing and
  recruitment service)
- Community colleges
- Private vocational schools
- State and local chapters of the American Association for Medical
  Assistants
- Pharmaceutical and equipment representatives
- Hospital personnel department
- Employment agencies

Placing an Effective Classified Advertisement

The Civil Rights Act of 1964 applies to the advertising, application, and hiring process. Ads must be carefully written to avoid any appearance of discrimination based on gender, age, race, religion, national origin, or disability. Use the basic components of the job description to write the ad, focusing on what the job requires rather than the type of person that is preferred. For screening purposes, when posting an open position online, have candidates send their resumes to a dedicated website link or a general mailbox rather than listing a telephone number, your office address, or your personal e-mail address. Using the Internet is faster and cheaper than other methods. Following are some things to consider:

- Post jobs on career sites
- Subscribe to databases that allow you access posted resumes
- Create a careers page on your company's website

Preparing for the Interview

Review the written resumes that were received and choose at least five candidates with the required qualifications. Give each of these resumes a priority rating. Screen the top five applicants by telephone first. It may be preferable to have all five candidates come in for a face-to-face interview, or the choices can be narrowed down to two or three candidates.

Be organized in the face-to-face interviews, having a prepared list of questions to ask each candidate. This will allow you to compare the candidates on the same basis. Give each interviewee a copy of the job description and have him or her complete an EEOC-approved employment application form. Using an EEOC form will assure that you are not violating any of the Title IV statutes. These forms are available through the American Medical Association.

Every employer develops a unique interviewing style. You may want to begin your interviews by telling the candidate a little about yourself or your specialty. Share with the candidate why that particular geographic area was chosen, where you went to school, and what your philosophy is about the practice of medicine. Next, the following topics could be addressed:

- Ask if the candidate has reviewed the job description and whether there are questions about the essential functions of the job.
- Ask about the applicant's experience with each task listed on the job description. Ask how he or she performs these tasks in current position or a previous job. Write the answers on a separate piece of paper. Do not write on the job description, application form, or resume, avoiding any comments that may be perceived as discriminatory.

- Ask open-ended questions that require the applicant to provide information. Avoid questions that can be answered yes or no.
- Remain neutral in your responses. Do not show approval or disapproval.
- Watch for nonverbal clues that indicate tension or anxiety.
- Zero in on topics of interest to you and investigate further.
- Quickly review your objectives.
- Document key points.
- Let the candidate know what happens next.

Interviewing Questions

Use the following list of questions with each candidate, making notes on a separate piece of paper, not on the resume or application.

- What did you like best about your last (current) position? What did you like least about it?
- Which of your past positions did you find most satisfying? Why?
- How would your last (current) supervisor describe you? In what area would he or she say you need the most improvement?
- What is one of your most significant on-the-job accomplishments?
- What academic areas of study interest you the most? What, if any, helped prepare you for your field?
- What did you like best about your last supervisor? What did you like least?
- What change would you (or did you) make in the last office you worked in?
- Describe your experiences in collecting money for medical bills.

Checking References

Reference checking is vitally important to medical employers, especially since they are increasingly being held responsible for negligent hiring decisions. Unfortunately, previous employers are generally reluctant to convey information about employees. One physician will usually be willing to tell another about the performance or abilities of an employee due to the significance of the decision. Be sure to thank the person for their cooperation. The following are steps that can be taken to ensure a smooth hiring process:

- Request that each applicant provide two or three references, preferably a former employer or supervisor.
- Call the references instead of accepting letters of reference at face value.

- Ask to speak to the applicant's immediate supervisor.
- Ask if the applicant is eligible for rehiring.
- Listen for what they do not say.

Orientation or Trial Period

When hiring, inform the new employee that he or she will be subject to a 90-day temporary or trial period to be used for orientation and training. During this period, monitor the employee's attitude, work habits, and capabilities, and assure that he or she is receiving the proper instructions.

The employee or employer may end the at-will employment relationship at any time during this initial period, with or without cause, and without advance notice. Employees will assume regular permanent status upon satisfactory completion of the orientation period.

During the start up of a medical practice, all policies are not yet likely to be in a handbook or manual. Developing written policies should be a matter of priority when opening a practice. There are numerous standard policies and procedures manuals available from the MGMA, AMA, and state medical societies that can be purchased and modified to address the needs of the individual practice. If these policies are in place on the first day, present the employee with a copy of the policies and take time to explain the basic work rules and regulations, including:

- Compensation and benefits
- Payroll deductions
- Vacation schedules and sick leaves
- Safety and health

Ask the employee to read the policies and offer to answer any questions. Address any other issues, such as dress codes, overtime, etc. After reviewing the policies, the employee should sign an acknowledgment form, which should be placed in the personnel file.

Personnel Files

Every employee, including the physicians, should have a well maintained personnel file for the documents listed below. The typical file should contain all government-mandated forms and employee benefit enrollment forms, as applicable:

- Resume
- Employment Application
- Reference Checklist

- W-4 Form: Employees Withholding Allowance Certificate
- State Income Tax Withholding Form, if applicable
- Payroll Set-Up Information
- Health Insurance Enrollment Form
- Long-Term Disability Enrollment Form (if offered)
- 401(k) Enrollment Form (if offered)
- Flex Benefits Form (if offered)
- Personnel Policies Acknowledgment Form (Disclaimer)
- Department of Homeland Security, US Citizenship and Immigration Services Form I-9: Employment Eligibility Verification Form
- Attendance Records
- Employment Letter
- Salary Change Information
- Performance Reviews
- Warning or Disciplinary Letters
- New Employee Checklist
- Training Checklist
- Confidentiality Pledge
- Contact List in Case of an Emergency

Personnel files should be kept in a locked cabinet or hard copies can be scanned and filed electronically (as with most personnel documents, an electronic format is generally acceptable), and they should be accessible only to the designated employee responsible for maintenance. Employees have the right to access their files at any time in the presence of a designated employee.

Personnel files should be retained for at least 3 years following termination. Applications of persons not hired should be maintained for a year.

Performance Appraisals and Salary Reviews

Each employee should have a performance appraisal every year, either at a designated time for annual reviews or on the anniversary of the employee's hire date. Following are pointers on conducting a successful performance review:

- **Use a preprinted form.** Give the employee a copy a week or two in advance and ask for a self-evaluation on performance.

■ **Conduct performance reviews separately.** Do not conduct a salary review during performance reviews. By combining the two, employees may concentrate on compensation rather than performance.

■ **Allow adequate time.** Give the review process enough time to address the necessary topics; avoid rushing.

■ **Choose a quiet location.** Conduct the appraisal in a confidential atmosphere.

■ **Highlight needed improvements.** Set specific goals and time lines for improvement.

■ **Get a signature.** Ask the employee to sign off on the form acknowledging that the review was conducted.

■ **End review on a good note.** Close the discussion with a compliment.

Salary Reviews

As a matter of necessity, salary increases must be based on practice profits. When funds are available, salary increases should be based on merit. Based on an employee's performance, merit raises can be motivators to recognize special effort or provide an incentive to improve. Know who is contributing, what they add to the practice, and how much. Do not be afraid to make a distinction; this is the point of merit increases.

Make sure all employees understand how salary increases are calculated and how they are given. Explain the process in the employee handbook or manual.

Counseling, Discipline, and Termination

Managing a staff requires counseling, discipline, and some eventual terminations. Make every effort to work with your employees so that they may give their best to their duties. Note and file in the personnel file any disciplinary discussions held with the employee, documenting what was said and the subsequent response. These records will substantiate the reasons for termination if this action becomes necessary. Having proper documentation reduces your exposure to loss from claims brought by a disgruntled staff member.

Before beginning the termination process, keep the following points in mind:

■ Employees must understand the terms of any temporary employment period. It is important that they know the grounds for dismissal; that no advance notice will be given; and that severance pay and unemployment benefits may not be extended. (Check your state statutes.)

- All policies governing grounds for dismissal, disciplinary procedures, grievance procedures, and so on must be clearly outlined in the employee handbook or manual. Be sure that all standards are equally and impartially applied to all employees.

- Any decision to terminate should be the final step in a clearly documented and well-defined process. Make sure all alternatives have been exhausted first.

You may have a host of reasons for beginning the disciplinary process for an employee. The employee must be made aware of unsatisfactory performance or behavior and be given a chance to improve; after giving ample opportunity to no avail, the employee should be terminated without delay.

The Employee Handbook

A key part of an employer's communication program is the employee handbook. It provides information on basic rules and policies that affect job conditions and should be issued to each employee upon employment. The following general information will help in determining what to include in an employee handbook.

Your staff needs to understand:

- What is expected of them and what they can expect of you
- Your policies on wages, working conditions, and benefits
- What services the practice provides to patients

The employee handbook should reflect the mission and philosophy of the physician. Handbooks protect the employer. Guesswork can be eliminated when either the employer or employee can refer to a written policy.

Handbooks give employees a sense of security. With all the rules and policies in one place, each person knows what is expected. When benefits are listed and explained, each person knows what is provided. Handbooks can also help motivate employees.

Employee Handbook Format

A simpler and more economical method is to provide employee handbooks in an electronic format and then distribute the handbooks by posting your handbook online via the Internet, company intranet, or web-based human resource software. With an electronic handbook, it is easier to make modifications, and you can quickly redistribute revised versions. However, if you choose to print and distribute hard copies, some employers use two formats: a small bound hand-book for employees, and a loose-leaf policy and procedures manual for managers. Both books should include an employee acknowledgment form.

Make the booklet attractive; put it together in such a way that employees will want to read it. Consider these suggestions for making the contents easy to read:

- Limit the use of words with three or more syllables
- Keep each sentence 20 words or less
- Limit discussion of subjects to one page
- Use drawings, charts, and illustrations where applicable
- Leave at least one-quarter of each page blank
- Limit the number of pages

Choose a writing style and be consistent throughout. Use gender-neutral terminology. A handbook should cover what employees need to know to get along on the job—the policies and procedures that employees will encounter almost every day. Avoid subjects that change frequently or that are incorporated in other documents, such as a lengthy and detailed description of benefit plans.

Table 11-1 provides a sample table of contents that can be used as a checklist for deciding what to include in a handbook.

Employee handbooks vary considerably because of individual needs and circumstances; therefore, the amount of information provided varies. A medical practice may also consider publishing Occupational Safety and Health Act, Clinical Laboratories Improvement Act (CLIA), and other government regulated guidelines in its handbook. For the overall purpose of a handbook, however, referencing these rules is appropriate, while covering them more extensively in other documentation (ie, the policy manual). Regardless, be sure the practice's acknowledgment form covers all handbook materials and policies. The most important aspect is to actually adhere to all rules in the employee handbook and the policies and procedures manual.

Policies and Procedures Manual

A policies and procedures manual differs from an employee handbook as it is comprehensive. It details every aspect of company policy and the procedures for following those policies. A manual is a complete reference tool for managers and supervisors providing them the reasoning for the policies, which enables them to better enforce the policies.

TABLE 11-1   Sample Table of Contents for Employee Handbook

Welcome Letter and Introduction

- Letter of Appreciation to Current Employees
- Letter of Welcome to New Employees
- Purpose of Handbook
- Background of Practice
  —Organization Chart
  —Physician(s) Biographical Information
- Equal Employment Opportunity Statement
- Suggestion and Complaint Procedures

Employment Policies and Procedures

- Nature of Employment
- Introductory Period
- Employment Relations
- Supervisor's Responsibilities
- Employee's Role and Responsibilities
- Work Schedules
- Rest and Meal Periods
- Overtime Policy
- Attendance and Punctuality
- Time Records
- Personnel Records
- Payday
- Payroll Deductions
- Performance and Salary Reviews
- Resignation/Termination
- Telephone, Computer and Internet Use

Benefits

- Holidays
- Vacations
- Hospital and Medical Insurance
- Life Insurance
- Pension and Profit-Sharing
- Training
- Educational Assistance Program
- Service Awards
- Workers' Compensation
- Sick Leave
- Disability Leave
- Personal Leave
- Bereavement Leave
- Jury Duty

Safety

- Safety Rules
- Emergency Procedures
- Personal Protective Equipment
- Reporting Accidents

Employee Conduct and Disciplinary Action

- Standards of Conduct
- Confidentiality Policy
- Smoking Policy
- Drug, Alcohol, and Substance Abuse Policy (including testing, if applicable)
- Sexual and Other Forms of Impermissible Harassment
- Security Inspections
- Solicitation
- Personal Appearance and Dress Code
- Corrective Discipline Procedures

Summary and Acknowledgment

- Disclaimer Statement

Sample Job Descriptions

Figures 11-1 and 11-2 are sample job descriptions for positions that can be found in a medical practice. These job descriptions can be used to prepare specific descriptions for jobs in a practice. They can also be used for performance appraisals and employee counseling. As responsibilities change, revise the descriptions accordingly.

Position: Practice Manager

Reports to: Physician(s)

Job Summary: Responsible for medical office activities, including accounting and financial procedures. Supervise non-medical staff.

Specific Requirements:
—Furnish physician, accountant with account aging each month
—Conduct regular staff meetings
—Responsible for accounts payable system
—Supervise, train all front office personnel
—Assist in creating, updating business administration policies
—Update office personnel policy manual as needed
—Maintain controls on accounts receivable system
—Prepare financial reports at end of month for physician, accountant
—Approve all Medicaid, Medicare, and other write-offs in consultation with physician
—Approve credits, refunds to patient accounts
—Arrange personnel schedules and vacations
—Responsible for all hiring, training and terminating of office personnel
—Conduct performance, salary reviews for office personnel

Job Qualifications:
—BA or AA degree in Business or Health Administration required. Previous medical office experience also required. CMPE certification desirable.
—Supervisory experience preferred. Knowledge of medicolegal principles and medical ethics is necessary.

FIGURE 11-1   Job Description: Practice Manager

Conclusion

Starting a medical practice involves becoming an employer as well as functioning as a supervisor of staff members. The physician in a medical practice or the practice manager has to be knowledgeable about a number of employment laws and skillful in hiring and managing staff members.

Position: Medical Assistant, Clinical

Reports to: Office Manager

Job Summary: Assist physician with patient examination and treatment. Also responsible for patient histories, routine lab procedures, collection, and preparation of specimens for transport to lab.

Specific Requirements:
—Maintain general appearance, cleanliness of exam rooms
—Sterilize instruments, maintain diagnostic equipment
—Prepare, replenish supplies; maintain inventory
—Prepare, drape patients for examination
—Take patient histories, height, weight, temperature
—Give certain medications, injections under physician supervision
—Assist in collection of specimens; instruct patients regarding preparation for tests
—Record laboratory, X-ray, EKG data on patient charts
—Receive and organize the handling of medication samples
—Dispose of contaminated and disposable items
—Perform other tasks as requested by office manager or physician

Job Qualifications:
Graduate of medical assistant training course or nursing program. Previous clinical experience and knowledge of anatomy, physiology, and terminology required. Medical office experience helpful.

FIGURE 11-2   Job Description: Medical Assistant, Clinical

Reference

1. Repa, BK. The FLSA: The Law of Time and Money @2000 HR One. library.lp.findlaw.com/scripts/getfile.pl?FILD-legpub/hr/ hr000002&TITLE=Subject&T. 08/10/2001.

12

Revenue Cycle Protocols

When you are starting out in medical practice, getting paid for services that are rendered consumes most of your time—and it's harder than you think. When you are starting out, it may be hard to believe that collecting payments from patients and third-party payers could be the bane of your existence. The purpose of this chapter is to help you establish a sound protocol for billing and reimbursement processes that will enable you to collect and to expedite payment to fund your practice. The difference in whether payment is collected or not boils down to setting up a financial policy for payment and collections and implementing a course of action for filing claims with insurance carriers. Essential to the process is having well-trained practice staff who can relate to the patients and work with the payers to get the job done.

Collecting from Patients

Collection begins at the time the patient calls for the appointment and the scheduler explains the practice's financial policy. A simple request for an address so that the patient can be sent a practice brochure that includes the payment policy or informing the patient that copayments and deductibles are due at the time of service will establish expectations of payment. This is especially true for patients who may be incurring large bills for in-office services or have large deductibles or copayments. Make sure you have a designated person assigned the responsibility of requesting payment for services or a financial counselor who can help patients develop a payment plan. Having the right person in this role is critical to the collections process. This individual must be pleasant and well-trained. Following these simple and practical guidelines will increase the probability of collecting payment at the time of service.

Use collection etiquette or good manners when collecting from a patient by remembering these pointers:

- Respect the patient's privacy
- Use eye contact
- Address the patient by name
- Ask how, not if, the patient would like to pay
- Be prepared to explain the services and charges
- Be prepared to offer payment options if the patient is unable to pay in full
- Do not confront the patient
- Do not humiliate or embarrass the patient
- Smile and say, "Thank you!"

At the initial or return visit, routinely follow these same steps.

You should always include in your financial policy a set minimum payment expected at the time of service for self-pay patients. For more information on collecting from the patient, including preparation of your practice's financial policy, see the Billing the Patient section later in this chapter.

Collecting at the Time of Service

The best opportunity you have to collect your fee is to ask patients to pay while still in the office. Collect copayments, deductibles, and open balances during the registration process if possible, and confirm payment during the check-out process by asking courteously, "How would you like to pay today? By cash, check, or credit card?" Speak matter-of-factly, using the patient's name. Be willing to explain the charges or answer any questions. Remember, reimbursement for services begins with front office operations. This includes the initial information collected at the time the visit was scheduled to the collection of copayments, deductibles, and prior balances once the patient is in the office. Collecting and entering accurate patient insurance information at the time the appointment is made enables staff to calculate the appropriate balance due from the patient. Then the focus can be made on in-office collections once the patient is in the office. Developing front office policies around collecting copayments and past due balances is appropriate and necessary to ensure maximum revenue. This means the practice should calculate the expected in-office collection rate and develop policies to ensure staff understand the importance of collecting copayments and past due balances. Based on the specific payer mix of the practice, the estimated amount of in-house collections can be determined and goals and expectations set around collections.

Collecting from Payers

Much more challenging than collecting from your patients is the complexity of obtaining reimbursement from insurers. The marketplace consists of a variety of plans and payers that include indemnity plans, managed care plans, and government-funded programs, such as Medicare, Medicaid, and workers' compensation programs. Some insurers have many policies and procedures that you will be obligated to adhere to if you are a participating provider. Whatever your specialty, you are likely to face many obstacles and much resistance to reimbursement for services rendered.

From 80 to 90 percent of your patients are covered by some form of insurance. This may include a state or federally funded government program. An efficient practice management system will facilitate claims processing, yet there are still obstacles to overcome in order to collect payment. The more you know about how insurance companies and government payers work, the more successful you will be in collecting. Following is basic information on various plans and an overview of how they will affect your ability to collect your charges.

Let's first take a closer look at the different types of payers to better understand the complexity of obtaining reimbursement.

Indemnity Plans

Indemnity plans pay for services based on a percentage of the charge or through a predetermined fixed rate. This type of plan offers increased flexibility for patients when deciding who and when they will see a physician.

Example

You charge a patient $1,000 for repair of an inguinal hernia. The indemnity insurance plan says the usual and customary fee is $800, so they pay 80 percent of $800, not 80 percent of $1,000. The patient then is responsible for paying $360 to the physician instead of the $200 (or 20 percent of $1,000) they expected to pay. Often, the patient receives an explanation of benefits (EOB) that includes a statement similar to this: "Your physician's fee is higher than the usual and customary fee for this service/procedure. The usual and customary fee for this procedure is $800, so we are reimbursing 80 percent of $800."

Managed Care Plans

Managed care plans are contractual arrangements between the insurance company and the physician or group of physicians, hospital, and ancillary providers providing outpatient or inpatient services. There are three different types of managed care plans available which include:

- Point of Service Plans (POS)
- Health Maintenance Organizations (HMO)
- Preferred Provider Organizations (PPO)

Each type of plan listed above contracts with physicians and other providers to reimburse for services provided to a network of patients. This helps insurance companies better control the cost of care and utilization of services. Generally, HMO plans are the most restrictive and only pay for services obtained within the contracted network, whereas PPOs and POS plans pay for services both in and out of network. However, the cost to the patient is often higher when services are obtained out of network.

Example

In your practice you charge $150 for a standard new patient visit. The managed care plan will pay the visit at the contractual rate. This rate was established during the negotiation process and is usually a percentage of the current or past Medicare allowed amount. These rates are different for each plan. In this example the contractual rate is $100 for the visit. The patient will be responsible for any co-payment due at the time of the visit, and the remaining balance must be adjusted from the patient's account. Patients cannot be billed for this adjustment rate.

Without an understanding of how the insurance company pays for a particular procedure or how this fee is calculated, the patient is apt to be annoyed with the physician practice. Therefore, it is wise to inform the patient of expectations before performing a service or surgical procedure. This is usually done by the financial counselor for the practice or customer service representative. Explain to the patient that the fee for the service may not be the same as the insurance company's reimbursement. Also explain that your fees are set so that you can provide a high quality service, pay your expenses, and remain competitive in the marketplace. Open communications keep patients happy and set successful physicians apart from their peers.

New physicians entering the marketplace have an advantage in that they grew up with the managed care concept. Physicians that have been in private practice for many years have had to learn a new payment process and modify the way they view patient care. As mentioned above, several types of plans are offered in most areas, and most insurers sell some type of managed care plans that generally pay the provider on a discounted fee for service or a capitated basis.

Discounted Fee-for-Service Plans

In a discounted fee-for-service plan, the payer/insurance plan negotiates with the physician for a discount off the physician's regular fee schedule for a particular service in exchange for the promise of a potential increase in patients. Generally, the physician receives no guarantee in the number of patients he or she will receive from the plan. These managed care products are typically called Preferred Provider Organizations (PPO), Point of Service Plans (POS), or Health Maintenance Organizations (HMO).

Capitated Plans

In a capitated arrangement, the physician agrees to provide a specified list of services to each patient assigned to the practice for a set dollar amount each month (ie, per member per month). The insurer pays the physician this specified amount whether or not the physician sees the patient in the office. The amount may vary depending on the specialty and the services that the physician is required to provide within the capitated amount. This is often termed a risk-sharing arrangement.

Example

The physician has 100 patients assigned to her practice for which the insurer pays a capitated fee of $15 per member/per month (pm/pm), or a total of $1,500. If the physician sees 20 of these patients in a month and these patients require a total of $1,800 worth of services, she has lost $300. However, if the physician sees only 5 of the 100 patients in a month and their services total $200, she has made a gross profit of $1,300. Thus, the physician assumes the risk that the number of patients accessing the practice will exceed her cost of doing business.

This example is an oversimplification of how reimbursement works in a managed care market. It is intended to explain the various types of insurance plans that you will encounter in a private practice. Before accepting and/or signing any kind of agreement with a managed care organization, the practice should understand the complexities of the system. Also, have an attorney or experienced health care consultant review any contract before signing it. The practice administrator or accountant should periodically review the practice's expenses to reimbursement for each payer to ensure the costs for providing care are managed appropriately. Payer contracts should be renegotiated each time the term period is complete. Having an outside consultant or company to help with these negotiations is well worth the cost in the long run. These contracts, if not managed and negotiated properly, can cause a practice to risk viability in today's marketplace.

Workers' Compensation Insurance

All employers must provide workers' compensation insurance to cover the medical and disability expenses incurred by the worker from a job-related injury. Many states administer workers' compensation insurance billing directly. In these states, the physician sends the claims directly to the state's agency. Other states require employers to contract with an insurance company for payment of work-related claims. In either case, benefits and payments are predetermined by legislation, based upon the state and the company. Request a packet of information from your State Workers' Compensation Board or Industrial Commission in preparation for accepting patients with work-related injuries and before processing claims.

When accepting a patient for a work-related injury, the practice should follow the guidelines specific to workers' compensation reimbursement within the state you provide the services. Below are some examples of typical guidelines used for workers' compensation; however, there will be some variations depending on the state in which your practice resides.

- Before seeing the patient, get authorization for treatment from the employer.
- Try to get a written request for treatment from the employer.
- If a written request is not possible, call the employer for authorization. Use a simple telephone consent form to record the authorization.
- The employer must notify the insurance company of the injury. Without a first report of injury, reimbursement may be delayed.
- Treat workers' compensation claims as any insurance claim, file in the unpaid claim file, and follow up routinely.
- The first claim form should reach the insurance company within 10 days of first treatment even if treatment is completed.
- Physicians cannot bill patients for treatment of work-related injuries.

Insurance Filing and Follow-Up

Insurance claims processing consumes a large portion of administrative time. Setting up workable policies and systems initially will help assure that insurance reimbursement provides a steady flow of cash into the practice. After the patient leaves the practice and the charge is captured, claims are submitted to the appropriate carrier. This process involves many steps including editing and claim scrubbing, sending claims to your clearinghouse, resubmitting corrected claims, and following up to ensure payers pay claims correctly and timely. Medical practice management software can file an electronic version of an insurance claim with Medicare and Medicaid. This electronic format is required with indemnity insurance carriers and managed care plans as well. Before these claims are submitted to the payers, there is a claims scrubbing process. These claims are usually batched and scrubbed with various edits to ensure a clean claim is submitted; this means that claims are put through an electronic process to check for proper procedure codes and diagnosis codes. Once claims are clean and have passed through the edits developed by the payer, they are submitted to the electronic clearinghouse. These claims are sorted or batched by payer and submitted. Once the payer accepts the claims, a report is sent back to the practice verifying the number of claims accepted and rejected. Automation simplifies the filing process and allows the practice to submit claims daily, which is recommended. However, the claim filing process is only one small part of the reimbursement process. Monitoring the filed claims and assuring that insurers are paying them quickly requires much more effort.

Develop a claim filing protocol similar to the following example to streamline this process:

- File claims at least twice weekly; daily is preferable.

- Check all claims for accuracy and complete information and process them through your claims scrubbing software before sending them.

- Most insurance companies promise a 30-day turnaround time for payments if they receive a clean claim. Some states have enacted legislation requiring payers to pay claims within a certain time frame. Be aware of the laws in your state and report any violations to the proper authorities.

- Print out a claims pending report daily; call the insurance carrier on all claims that they have not paid within 30 days of the filing date. If your computer cannot generate this report, enter filed claims on an insurance log. Enter the date, the patient name, the insurance company, and the amount filed on the log sheet. Check the log sheets every day to determine which claims have not been paid in 30 days and follow up by telephone.

- Call the insurance companies to ask about unpaid claims. Calling is more effective than simply resubmitting the claim. If the insurance company says it has not received the claim, then it must be resubmitted. Many insurance companies now allow providers to access their claims on line so denied claims can be viewed, corrected, and resubmitted without delay. This is a very efficient way to monitor claims and reduce denials.

- Print out an aged accounts analysis by payer each month to learn which companies pay on time and which ones habitually exceed a

30-day turnaround time. (This is not a standard report on every system. It is worthwhile to request that the system be set up to provide this report.)

■ Call the plan administrator and request an explanation of the plan's poor payment history. Most managed care contracts guarantee 30-day reimbursement if the claims are submitted in order. If you do not receive your payments as agreed, a letter should be submitted to the plan and a complaint filed with the state Department of Insurance.

■ Make contractual adjustments at the time they make the payment so the claim will be adjudicated.

■ Conduct a periodic review of Explanation of Benefits (EOBs). Contractual payments should be compared to the negotiated amount to ensure correct payment.

Consistent follow-up is the key to satisfactory reimbursement. If insurance claims are filed and forgotten, you may find yourself with a cash flow shortfall. Give employees a copy of the written policy. Make them accountable for following these routines.

Billing the Patient

Patient follow-up on unpaid claims is also necessary to collect outstanding balances. The practice should have established policies on collecting unpaid balances from patients. This should include the number of statements to be sent to patients and the financial policies the practice has developed to assist patients with unpaid balances if necessary. Any staff member of the practice who interacts with patients regarding past due balances needs to be aware of the practice policies and the applicable laws regarding collections. This includes an understanding of the Fair Debt Collections Practices Act. This act applies to first-party attempts to collect for most medical practices and includes specific restrictions such as:

■ Patient collection calls cannot be made before 8 am or after 9 pm

■ Being aware of not disclosing reason for call to a third party

■ Scripting messages left on a voicemail for a patient to return a call

Again, establish a written financial policy that you can present to your patients before they receive treatment. This financial policy should explain payment expectations and your policy on filing insurance claims.

The following is a list of important points to include in the written financial policy:

- A statement that payment for services is expected at the time of service unless arrangements are made prior to treatment or unless the patient is covered under a managed care plan or government program.

- The office will file insurance claims for services rendered, but the patients are not relieved of responsibility for payment because they have insurance.

- Patients must pay copayments due at the time services are rendered.

- Statements are mailed every 30 days. Any balance left unpaid after 90 days should be considered for further collection methods. This may include collection letters and/or turning the claim over to a collection agency.

- Financial arrangements can be made for payment of bills that are more than a specified amount (you choose your limit). This may include setting up automatic payments from the patient's checking account and/or charge account.

Statements sent to patients should itemize the procedures and include the entire amount due, even if an insurance company will pay most of it. Many practice management software programs will produce statements that show both the amount presumed covered by insurance and the portion for which the patient is responsible.

Patients should receive statements regularly for any outstanding amount. Your billing cycle can be set up in several ways. The traditional method is to send all statements at the end of each month. Other methods include sending statements twice monthly, one half on the 15th and one half on the 30th. The third method is to send some statements out each week according to letters of the alphabet. These last two billing methods spread the cash flow and the associated payment posting work more evenly throughout the month.

The following are a few billing tips for the practice:

- Send each patient a billing statement within 30 days after the date of service.

- Call each patient who has an unpaid bill 45 days after the date of treatment. Ask if a problem has prevented payment of the bill. Make note of any comments made by the patient.

- If the patient says that he or she cannot pay the full amount of the bill, offer to set up a payment schedule.

- Remind the patient of a previous balance.

- If the patient makes a partial payment, set up (and record) a payment agreement.

TABLE 12-1   Patient Billing and Follow-up Schedule

Action	Time Frame
Send 1st statement	Within 30 days of date of service
Send 2nd statement	30 days after date of service
Call patient with unpaid bill; if patient says he/she is unable to pay, set up payment schedule	45th day after treatment date
Call patient; record comments	75th day after date of service
Send 3rd statement	90th day after date of service
Send letter stating that payment is due within 20 days or account will be turned over for collection	100th day

- Offer the patient a payment envelope.
- Remember to say "Thank you."

Officially terminating the patient/physician relationship is important when a patient does not meet financial obligations. The physician cannot refuse to treat an established patient who owes the practice money unless the relationship has been formally terminated. See Chapter 13, Loss Prevention and Risk Management, for more information on patient termination.

As with insurance filing and billing, a structured process for patient billing and follow-up is the most important factor in achieving reimbursement. Table 12-1 offers a sample of a patient billing and follow-up schedule.

Using a Collection Agency

Not all patients pay their medical bills. After you have exhausted all your in-house collection techniques, it may be best to turn some accounts over to a collection agency.

Choose a collection agency carefully, being mindful that the agency's collection methods reflect on your practice. Talk with other physicians or office managers to see which agency they use. Ask if they are satisfied with the services they receive and what percentage of accounts turned over for collection are paid. Use the checklist in Figure 12-1 for selecting a credible collection agency.

Question	Answer
1. Is the agency a member of the American Collectors Association?	
2. Is the agency in total compliance with the Fair Debt Collection Practices Act and HIPAA?	
3. What percentage of their business is medical?	
4. How are the accounts broken down per collector?	
5. How many accounts per collector?	
6. Does the agency have a training program?	
7. Does the monthly collection summary show when they listed the account and how much was paid?	
8. What are the agency's hours?	
9. Will they work accounts between 6:00 pm and 9:00 pm when most patients are available?	
10. How quickly does the account get on the desk of a collector?	
11. What reports do they provide?	
12. Does the agency report non-payers to the credit bureau?	
13. How long will the agency work on an account before they deem it noncollectible?	
14. How much commission do they charge?	

FIGURE 12-1   Checklist for Selecting a Collection Agency

Besides the items listed above, the following points should be considered:

- Get copies of all the letters the agency will send to your patients.
- Do not turn over accounts of less than $50.
- Record that the patient's account has been moved to a collection agency.
- Never pay commission up front.
- Make sure accounts can be recalled any time.
- Have a written agreement. Read the fine print. (A HIPAA Business Associate Agreement will also be required.)
- Do not allow the agency to litigate an account without your permission.
- Report changes in the collection status of an account to the agency.
- Use two agencies simultaneously on separate accounts so their efficiency can be evaluated.

■ Establish a time limit on how long an agency is entitled to a percentage of amounts collected after an account is withdrawn.

Using Credit Cards to Enhance Collections

Acceptance of credit cards for payment of medical bills is routine in most offices. This offers an excellent option for physicians because it brings funds into the practice immediately and transfers the risk of nonpayment to the credit card companies.

Almost every bank offers vendor/merchant accounts that will allow you to deposit credit card payments into the bank for processing. Some credit card companies will transfer the funds to your bank electronically so that you have access to the money immediately.

Each bank sets its own service charge for processing credit card transactions that are generally based on a percentage of your overall deposits and range from 2 to 8 percent. The service charge is often negotiable. If you have no deposit history with the bank, your negotiating clout may not be very strong. If the bank accepts electronic transfers of your funds from the credit card companies, the service charge should be lower.

Your credit card merchant account does not have to be in the same bank as your checking account. However, you will find that it is more convenient, and you will generally receive favorable service charge rates from your own bank.

Also, many practices have payments mailed to a lockbox at their bank. Many banks now offer a wide variety of services to help streamline the process of payment posting. Payments are deposited immediately, and often patient checks can be scanned to a drive for payment posting into the practice management system. Other lockbox services include reformatting electronic payments to ensure direct posting into your practice management system is easy and consistent.

Controlling the accounts receivable process will assure that your practice is financially successful. Collecting monies due is not a process that runs on its own. The physician should take an interest in this process. Establish measurable goals and make employees accountable for responsibilities in the process.

Even though physician practices have been exempted from the federal Red Flag Rules, it is important to have an internal process for protecting patient credit card numbers and other financial information. (Note: The Red Flags Rule requires covered entities to develop a written plan to prevent, detect, and mitigate instances of identity theft and fraud. On December 18, 2010, President Obama signed into law the Red Flag Program Clarification Act of 2010, which clarifies the type of creditor that must comply with the Red Flags Rule. This law supports AMA's long-standing argument to the Federal Trade Commission that the Red Flags Rule should not be applied to physicians generally.)

Writing a Collections Policy for Your Practice

During the early stages of a practice start up—before bad habits have a chance to develop—institute a collections policy. Table 12-2 is an example of policies and procedures that have been set up for handling collections at a practice.

TABLE 12-2   Policies and Procedures for Handling Collections

COLLECTIONS POLICY

Policy

Practice staff charged with collection of receivables will operate within established legal guidelines and protocols during the pursuit of payment on outstanding patient account balances.

Purpose

To define guidelines for collection of patient account balances.

Procedure

- Practice staff members DO NOT engage in any conduct that may be construed as harassment, oppression, or abuse of anyone in connection with collection of debt. Conduct disallowed includes, but is not limited to:
  —verbal abuse
  —threats to inform debtor's employer of debt
  —disclosure of debt to any third party
  —invasion of individual's privacy.
- Telephone collections may occur Monday through Friday, 8:00 am to 9:00 pm, Saturday, 8:00 am to 5:00 pm, unless instructed otherwise by the patient.
- Patients may be contacted at their place of employment, unless otherwise instructed by the patient.
- All accounts must be approved by the physician or practice administrator before referral to a collection agency.
- Threats of legal action may not be used UNLESS such action is likely.

(continued)

TABLE 12-2 Policies and Procedures for Handling Collections (*continued*)

ACCOUNT RESPONSIBILITIES/STANDARDS

Policy

The office staff must pursue collection of outstanding patient account balances and perform all subsequent write-offs without delay.

Purpose

To expedite reimbursements on patient accounts and to reduce outstanding accounts receivable.

Procedure

- Maintain the standard or better.
- Review Explanation of Benefits (EOBs) daily and pursue unpaid services.
- Report trends regarding changes or delays in reimbursement from payers to the manager.
- Prepare timely write-offs, taking adjustments at the time of posting.
- Take bad debt write-offs as soon as an account is determined to be noncollectible.

Recommendations

Use the collection feature on the practice management system to facilitate timely follow-up, or use a tickler system to remind you.

ACCOUNT FOLLOW-UP WITH PAYERS

Policy

Manager assigns accounts to the appropriate practice staff for timely follow-up and account maintenance.

Purpose

To ensure all patient accounts receive timely follow-up and subsequent account maintenance.

Procedure

- All accounts over 30 days old are reviewed and pursued for prompt payment, which is accomplished by following up with the insurance companies.
- The tickler system or the practice management system should be used to systematically follow up on accounts. (NOTE: A manual tickler system can simply consist of writing the patient's account number on a designated calendar date to make the return status call.)
- All follow-up calls with the payer should be documented in the practice management system, noting the following information:
  —Name and telephone number of the insurance company that was contacted
  —Name of contact person at the insurance company
  —Brief summary of discussion
  —Date payment is expected

(*continued*)

TABLE 12-2 Policies and Procedures for Handling Collections (*continued*)

PROBLEM PAYERS

Policy

Accounts receivable issues should be identified and resolved in a timely manner. Problematic issues are documented and should be followed up by management.

Purpose

To ensure all contracted payers are compliant with specific contract terms and that all noncontract payers remit appropriate reimbursement in a timely manner.

Procedure

- Notify physician or manager of any problems involving payers.
- Attempt to quantify the scope of the problem (ie, total claims outstanding, the dollar and aging associated with those claims).
- Once the information is quantified, contact the payer's provider representative to discuss resolution of the issue within 15 days. The conversation should be documented and a letter sent to the provider representative confirming the conversation and the expected outcome.
- If no resolution is reached by the 16th business day, contact the provider representative to inform of the intent to send a certified letter to the medical director requesting resolution within 15 days.
- A copy of this letter should also be sent to the patient's employer group, to the attention of the benefits manager. This information is useful for the benefits manager when negotiating for benefit plans for employees.
- If resolution has not been received within the stipulated 15 days, the next option will be to consider engaging legal representation or a health care consultant to resolve the issue.

Recommendations

Thoroughly review the payer contracts for all restrictions and stipulations. Before entering into any contract with a payer, have a legal representative or consultant review the agreement.

Conclusion

In addition to delivering high-quality patient care and service, do a good job collecting from patients and third-party payers and your practice will be on the road to success. Have good billing and collection protocols in place and a well-trained staff to carry them out.

CHAPTER 13
Loss Prevention and Risk Management

Risk management is the core of successful practice management. The practice must prioritize its risk plan and create operational consistency. Without a good risk management program, you may pay some grave consequences, such as being removed from the Medicare program, being hit with fraud and abuse charges, or facing noncompliance with other government regulations.

Risk management has evolved beyond reducing exposure to professional liability actions to more complex issues. Now, risk management has grown to protecting the practice's financial and physical assets through insurance and proper management techniques and behaviors. A good risk management program will reduce practice expenses and limit exposure.

Risk management is more than a program to prevent lawsuits: it is how a medical practice provides care for patients and improves the quality of life for physicians and their staff. Successful risk management requires close attention to building strong physician-patient relationships and capable physician-administrator teams.

Your malpractice insurer is likely to have risk management materials and programs and will be a helpful resource to your practice. Both the malpractice insurer and the state medical licensure board will have guidelines and interventions to assist in the development of the program.

Critical Tasks in Risk Management

Following are the critical tasks involved in risk management:

1. **Maintain legal compliance with corporate structure.**
   As presented in Chapter 2, Selecting a Business/Legal Entity,
   business entities (ie, sole proprietorships, partnerships, corporations, Sub S corporations) have specific requirements for
   governance and tax reporting. Once the business entity is established, make sure that you maintain compliance with the legal
   and tax guidelines applicable to your organization. Seek professional advice and assistance from your attorney and accountant.

2. **Develop record-keeping procedures.** Maintain records for
   your practice in relationship to your organizational structure.
   If yours is a corporation or partnership, you must live by your
   bylaws and articles of incorporation or by the decisions of the
   partners. Your attorney and accountant can advise you on
   record-keeping requirements.

3. **Develop conflict resolution and grievance procedures.**
   Managing risk encompasses personnel management, operational policies and procedures, OSHA compliance, and labor laws.
   The ability to resolve internal and external conflicts is important. Set up the necessary processes to anticipate, address, and
   resolve problems before they become issues that put your practice at risk of a lawsuit, fines, or penalties.

4. **Obtain liability insurance.** Liability protection includes professional malpractice, directors' and officers' (for corporations),
   errors and omissions, medical, disability, and property insurance for your employees, business, and property. Before purchasing such insurance, assess the level of risk. Seek the advice
   of a reputable and trustworthy insurance agent or broker.

5. **Establish personnel and property security plans.**
   Establish a policy for unauthorized or inappropriate use of the
   Internet and electronic equipment and resources, such as computers, telephones, and other technology that are available to
   practice staff. These policies and protections should be a part of
   your employee handbook and administered consistently.

6. **Develop and implement quality assurance and patient
   satisfaction programs.** Following are examples of a loss prevention program to promote quality and satisfaction:
   a. Identify existing or potential patient care problems
   b. Establish criteria for patient care responsibility
   c. Measure and monitor the actual performance of the staff
   d. Investigate and resolve problems or complaints
   e. Monitor the corrective action

    f. Educate employees about government regulatory programs and the record-keeping requirements for each program

    g. Provide continuing education for both employees and patients

7. **Establish confidentiality policies.** Protect your practice by having employees sign confidentiality agreements stating that violations of practice confidentiality and breaching patient confidentiality will be cause for termination. Medical records must also be protected as a part of the practice's policies and procedures. The policy must address federal, state, and local regulations surrounding privacy and confidentiality, medical records policy and distribution, and organizational information flow.

8. **Negotiate and comply with contractual arrangements.** The practice is responsible for negotiating contracts, performing due diligence on them, and understanding them. If you are unable to get enough information on the company or understand the contract language or its implications, seek outside assistance from a third party, such as a reputable consulting firm.

9. **Maintain compliance with government mandates.** Many laws result in somewhat confusing policies and procedures, such as self-referrals and safe harbors. Thorough knowledge of federal, state, and local laws and regulations regarding human resources, OSHA, self-referral, fraud and abuse, Medicare fraud and abuse, ADA, anti-trust, and research is mandatory—regardless of the vagueness of their interpretations.

10. **Develop a network of advisors.** Seek advice and assistance from trusted professionals (eg, accountants, lawyers, insurance companies, coding experts, local Medicare office, consultants) for knowledge about the rules and changes that continually occur.

Addressing Areas of Risk Through Operational Improvements

The following sections individually address each area of practice operation and provide suggestions for developing a loss prevention protocol in these areas.

Scheduling

A common source of patient dissatisfaction and subsequent increase in the risk of a professional liability claim is the length of time the patient must wait for an appointment with the physician. The busy practice staff may not realize that when a patient endures long waits, they perceive a lack of concern. Consider these details when scheduling patients:

- The length of time it takes to get an appointment
- The receptionist's demeanor
- Whether the receptionist asks patients who call for an appointment permission before putting them on hold
- The average length of time a patient is left on hold on the telephone

Patients become annoyed if the wait time for an appointment exceeds 15 minutes. The maximum time a patient should wait in the reception area is 30 minutes. To decrease the patient's wait time, follow these recommendations:

- Schedule extra time for new patients or special procedures.
- Allow enough time before and after seeing patients. Avoid overbooking patients.
- Inform patients of any delays in the appointment schedule and the cause for the delay.
- Call patients at home or at work to advise of any expected delays.
- Block time each day for walk-ins and emergencies. Fill these times no earlier than the evening before.

Additional pointers on scheduling are introduced in Chapter 15, Developing Policies and Procedures.

Documentation of appointment information is almost as critical as the progress note itself in relation to managing risk. Always track all appointment questions and concerns using the following guidelines:

- Record missed or canceled appointments in the patient's chart.
- Do not erase, white out, or otherwise obliterate any appointment in the appointment book or computer schedule.
- Document any attempts to reach the patient to reschedule a missed appointment. If the patient's condition warrants, send a certified letter. (See also Chapter 15, Marketing and Business Development Considerations.)

Billing and Collections

Many malpractice claims are a response to collection efforts that are offensive. A written collection policy assures that all practice staff members know what the policy is and how to handle each billing and collection situation (see Table 12-2, Policies and Procedures for Handling Collections, in Chapter 12, Revenue Cycle Protocols). In addition, also consider addressing the following issues in the policy as a measure of risk management:

- Patient education—letting the patient know before the first appointment about fees and payment requirements.

- A review process and procedure for circumstances that require special action.

- The quality of care standards

- The patient's satisfaction. If the patient balks at paying a bill, discuss it to reach an agreeable payment arrangement, if possible.

- Determine at what the point the cost of taking legal action versus how much the patient owes is economically reasonable and what is an acceptable small balance write-off.

- Understanding patients' rights concerning privacy and the physician-patient relationship. (Do not send any medical information to a collection agency.)

- Awareness of Fair Debt Collection Practices Act. Periodically evaluate the collection agency's practices. (See also Chapter 12, Revenue Cycle Protocols.)

Environment

The patient develops a first impression of the kind of medical care that will be provided from the practice environment. If the surroundings are pleasant, clean, and convenient, patients will more likely view you as competent and providing quality care. Consider the following suggestions as a part of your risk management plan:

- To prevent patient injury, evaluate the facility to ensure easy access. Check all patient care areas, including the parking lot, to identify potential safety hazards.

- Provide comfortable office furnishings to allow the patient to feel at ease. Check furnishings periodically to assure that they are in good condition. Take steps to ensure cleanliness and good housekeeping. Messy or dirty offices create a negative impression and significantly affect the patient's perception of quality of care.

- Have furnishings that meet the needs of various patients. Soft and/or low seating is problematic for women who are pregnant, senior citizens, and persons with disabilities. Remove obstacles that could cause tripping or falls. Breakable and small objects can be hazardous to children.

- Keep the room at a comfortable temperature and provide plenty of lighting.

- Under the Americans with Disabilities Act, state and local governments are required to follow specific architectural standards in the new construction and alteration of buildings. Public entities such as medical practices are not required to take actions that would result in undue financial and administrative burdens. However, they are required to make reasonable modifications to policies, practices, and procedures where necessary to avoid discrimination, unless they can demonstrate that doing so would fundamentally alter the nature of the service, program, or activity being provided. The practice must comply with basic nondiscrimination requirements that prohibit exclusion, segregation, and unequal treatment. There are specific requirements related to architectural standards for new and altered buildings; reasonable modifications to policies, practices, and procedures; effective communication with people with hearing, vision, or speech disabilities; and other access requirements. For more information, go to www.ada.gov.

Medical Equipment

Patients may be injured because of faulty or improper use of equipment. The practice administrator should institute a policy of regular maintenance and use of all equipment, in addition to the following training practices:

- Train all employees on the proper use of equipment.
- Document the training, time, and place in each employee's personnel file.
- Calibrate all equipment as recommended by the manufacturer.
- Maintain a log of all equipment maintenance and service.
- Report to the malpractice insurance carrier or business insurance carrier any patient injury associated with a piece of equipment. Remove the equipment and all its collateral equipment from service if it is injurious.
- Avoid tampering with the equipment or sending it to the manufacturer for repair until the insurance company has been notified and they offer instructions.
- Do not document any assumptions about an equipment malfunction or improper usage in the medical record.

Emergencies

Your risk management plan should also include a written protocol for handling a medical emergency, such as the following:

- Post emergency numbers, such as ambulances, hospitals, poison control, etc next to all telephones.

- Require all staff to stay current on cardiopulmonary resuscitation (CPR).

- If the office has emergency equipment and/or medications, train all staff to use such equipment and drugs. Not having this equipment on hand is better than to have untrained employees using it. There is often less liability in doing nothing than in doing something incorrectly.

- Conduct periodic emergency drills to role play various emergency scenarios.

Privacy and Confidentiality

Communication between the patient and physician is confidential and critical to the patient-physician relationship. The patient's right to confidentiality and privacy extends to all members of the practice staff. Many suits are filed based on breach of confidential information. Only the patient has the right to decide what information may be revealed to others.

The US Department of Health and Human Services (HHS) issued the Privacy Rule to implement the requirement of the Health Insurance Portability and Accountability Act of 1996 (HIPAA). The purpose of the Privacy Rule is to assure that patients' health information is protected while allowing the health information needed to provide and improve health care to be shared and to protect the public's health and well being. The key elements of the Privacy Rule include:

- Protected health information, which is defined as individually identifiable health information held or transmitted by covered entity or its business associate, in any form or media, whether electronic, paper, or verbal. This includes:

  - The patient's past, present, or future physical or mental condition

  - The provisions of health care to the patient

  - The past, present, or future payment for the provisions of health care to the patient

  - Common identifiers include:

    —Name

    —Address

    —Birth Date

    —Social Security Number

- The key purpose to the Privacy Rule is to define and limit the circumstances in which a patient's protected health information may be used or disclosed.

- Permitted uses and disclosures
  - Release information to the patient who is the subject of the information
  - For treatment purposes
    —The provision, coordination, or management of health care and related services
  - Payment
    —This encompasses activities of a health plan to obtain premiums and determine or fulfill responsibilities for coverage and provision of benefits.
    —Additionally, to obtain reimbursement for health care delivered to a patient and to obtain payment or be reimbursed for provision of health care
  - Health care operations
    —Quality assessment and improvement activities, including case management and care coordination
    —Competency assurance activities, including provider or health plan performance evaluation, credentialing, and accreditation
    —Conducting or arranging for medical review audits or legal services including fraud and abuse detection and compliance programs
    —Specified insurance functions such as underwriting, risk rating, and reinsuring risk
    —Business planning, development, management, and administration
    —Business management and general administrative activities of the practice
  - Other permitted disclosures with limitations include (for more details refer to www.hhs.gov/ocr/hipaa)
    —Uses and disclosures with opportunity to agree or object
    —Required by law
    —Incidental use and disclosures
    —Public interest and benefit activities
    —Public health activities
    —Victims of abuse, neglect, or domestic violence
    —Health oversight activities
    —Judicial and administrative proceedings
    —Law enforcement purposes
    —Descendents

—Cadaveric organ, eye, or tissue donation

—Research

—Serious threat to health or safety

—Essential government functions

—Workers' compensation

- Authorization must be written in specific terms and must be in plain language and contain specific instructions regarding the information to be disclosed or used, the person(s) disclosing and receiving the information, expiration, right to revoke in writing, and other data.

- Limiting uses and disclosures to the minimum necessary protected health information needed to accomplish the intended purpose of the use, disclosure, or request.

- Privacy practices notice must be provided to all patients that describe how protected health information may be used or disclosed.

  - The notice must state the practice's duties to protect privacy, provide notice of privacy practices, and abide by terms of the current notice.

    —The notice must describe patient's rights including the right to complain to HHS and to the practice if they believe their privacy right have been violated.

  - Patients should sign an acknowledgment of receiving the notice.

Refer to www.hhs.gov/ocr/hipaa for more details.

Handling Patient Complaints

A patient often shows dissatisfaction and intentions to sue long before the legal papers are served. A staff member may be the first to be aware of a patient complaint. All complaints must be brought to the physician or practice manager's attention, no matter how minor the incident may seem. No complaint should be ignored. The risk management plan should include the following guidelines:

- Institute a formal complaint policy in the office. Use an incident report form and a complaint log to track the occurrence and disposition of all patient complaints. Do not enter this information in the patient's medical record.

- Notify the physician or practice manager of the complaint on the day it is received.

- Respond to the complaint quickly and follow up with the patient.

Termination of the Patient-Physician Relationship

The inferred contract between a patient and physician begins not when they make an appointment, but when examination or treatment begins. Once a patient-physician relationship has been established, the physician is not free to terminate the relationship without formal, written notification. This process is often regulated by the state medical board. The patient-physician relationship continues until it is ended by one of the following circumstances:

- The patient terminates the relationship.
- The physician formally terminates the relationship.

Failure to terminate may constitute patient abandonment and bring about fines or legal action if the patient is harmed by the abandonment.

There may be circumstances in which it is deemed necessary to terminate the patient-physician relationship. For example, perhaps the patient is noncompliant, and it is believed that continued treatment would increase the chances of a complication or poor outcome. Maybe the patient is rude or abusive, or maybe the physician and the patient just do not get along. Or, perhaps the patient routinely fails to pay his or her bills. Any of these reasons and many others may be a basis to terminate a patient from the practice. A physician, however, cannot refuse to give a patient an appointment because the patient has not paid the bill without first terminating the patient-physician relationship. Terminating the patient-physician relationship can be accomplished by sending the patient a certified, return receipt letter.

Once the patient is released, be sure to follow some specific guidelines to minimize the chance of being sued for abandonment. Observe the following principles as a matter of your risk management strategy:

- First, put the notice in writing. The reason may or may not be stated, but can be one of the following:
  - If for noncompliance, say so clearly in the letter.
  - If for personality conflict, an unpaid bill, or for a reason not to be made public, avoid stating the reason in writing.
- Send the letter by certified mail, return receipt requested. Keep the receipt in the patient's file, along with a copy of the letter. (See Figure 13-1 for a sample of a Patient Discharge Letter.)

The requirement for alternative care, amount of time a physician is required to give a patient to seek alternative health care and other matters related to patient termination varies in each state. Contact your local medical society, state medical board, or seek counsel from an attorney for the answer.

The patient-physician relationship is the foundation of medical law. The legal rights and obligations of both patients and physicians rest upon it.

[Name]

[Address]

[City, State, Zip]

Dismissal Letter

Date: _____

Dear _____

Individuals receiving outpatient services at one of our practice locations may be involuntarily terminated for inability or unwillingness to comply with their plan of treatment or other policies of (NAME OF YOUR PRACTICE).

A physician-patient relationship is established when the physician provides service to a person to address medical needs, whether the service was provided by mutual consent or implied consent, or was provided without consent pursuant to a court order. Once a physician-patient relationship is established, a person remains a patient until the relationship is terminated.

Patients may be involuntarily terminated if they meet one or more of the following criteria:

   a. The patient (or parent/guardian) harasses or threatens the therapist or other department staff.

   b. The patient misuses or abuses medication.

   c. The patient refuses to comply with treatment recommendations and plans.

   d. The patient (or parent/guardian) violates policies of (NAME OF YOUR PRACTICE)

   e. The patient fails to comply with (NAME OF YOUR PRACTICE) policy on patient attendance.

We are dismissing _____ from our practice for the following reason:

_____

_____

_____

Please note we will continue care for 30 days from the receipt of this letter. However, you must find alternative health care. Once you have found another provider, please complete an authorization to release medical records providing us with your new providers' information, and we will send all medical records to them.

Sincerely,

_____

(PHYSICIAN NAME)
(NAME OF PRACTICE)

FIGURE 13-1   Sample Discharge Letter (Certified Mail with Return Receipt Requested)

Rights of the Patient

The physician and staff members must be aware of certain legal rights that belong to the patient as provided by CMS. They include:

- The right to choose the physician from whom to receive treatment

- The right to say whether medical treatment will begin and to set limits on the care provided

- The right to know before the treatment begins:
  - What it will consist of
  - What effect it will have on the body
  - What are the inherent dangers
  - What it will cost

Consent to Treatment

Legal consequences for treating a patient without properly informed consent include civil actions, which may result in monetary damages. Informed consent also has specific ethical requirements for physicians articulated in the AMA Ethical Guidelines. For emphasis, take note of the following:

- Treating a patient with the patient's consent, but failing to explain the inherent risks of a procedure, could result in a charge of negligence.

- State statutes vary, but generally contain provisions related to the necessary elements of informed consent, civil and criminal penalties for failure to adequately inform the patient, the role of the patient, and situations in which informed consent may not be necessary. There are special provisions related to medical research (regulated by the Food and Drug Administration). Mentally incompetent adults and children require special treatment under consent provisions.

Implied consent is reflected in the patient's actions, such as having a prescription filled or accepting an injection.

Expressed consent is an oral or written acceptance of the treatment. Obtain the written form of expressed consent when the proposed treatment involves surgery, experimental drugs or procedures, or high-risk diagnostic or treatment procedures.

Fraud and Abuse

Any medical practice treating Medicare patients must be aware of the strict fraud and abuse rules governing Medicare billing. The Office of Inspector General (OIG) is responsible for identifying and eliminating fraud and abuse. The OIG carries out this mission through a nationwide network of audits, investigations, and inspections of physician offices.

The most common inspection by the OIG is the Medicare audit to identify inconsistencies in billing, coverage, and payment of bills for particular services.

The Centers for Medicare and Medicaid Services (CMS) defines Medicare fraud as "knowingly and willfully making or causing a false statement or representation of a material fact made in application for a Medicare benefit of payment." Fraud occurs when a physician knowingly bills Medicare for a service that was not rendered or when the physician overstates or exaggerates a particular service.

Some examples of Medicare fraud are as follows:

■ An indication that there may be deliberate application of duplicate reimbursement

■ Any false representation with respect to the nature of charges for services rendered

■ A claim for uncovered services billed as services that are covered

■ A claim involving collusion between the physician and recipient resulting in higher costs or charges

Medicare abuse refers to activities that may directly or indirectly cause financial losses to the Medicare program or the beneficiary. Abuse generally occurs when the physician operates in a manner that is inconsistent with accepted business and medical practices.

The most common types of abuse are:

■ The overuse of medical services (eg, repeated lab testing when results are normal)

■ Up-coding and overuse of office visits

■ Waiving copayments for patient's deductible portion. Physicians are required to collect the 20 percent Medicare copayment from the Medicare patient. Routinely waiving the copayment, unless in very unusual cases, such as extreme financial hardship, is considered a fraudulent activity.

For more information, go to www.cms.gov/FraudAbusefor Consumers/04_Rip_Offs_Schemes.asp.

The Medical Record

A well-documented, legible, structured medical record is the physician's first line of defense if there is a malpractice suit. The medical record is a form of communication among health care professionals about the patient's condition. This documentation identifies the patient, supports the diagnosis, justifies the treatment, and documents the results of treatment.

The medical record is confidential. The information is private; it should remain secure and not be made public. While the record belongs to the physician, the information belongs to the patient.

Authorization to Release Records

Records are the heart of systematic patient care. Excellent record keeping is one of the most effective tools in patient care and in preventing claims. Paper medical charts may still preferred by many physicians. However the electronic health record (EHR) is becoming the preferred means for maintaining medical records even from a liability standpoint. EHRs are the next step in the continued progress of health care that can strengthen the relationship between patients and clinicians. The benefit of availability and the timeliness of retrieving data enables providers to make better decisions and provide better care. The EHR automates access to information and has the potential to streamline the clinician's workflow. The EHR also has the ability to support other care-related activities directly or indirectly through various interfaces, including evidence-based decision support, quality management, and outcomes reporting. For example, the EHR can improve patient care by:

- Reducing the incidence of medical errors by improving the accuracy and clarity of medical records
- Making the health information available, reducing duplication of tests, reducing delays in treatment, and keeping patients well informed to take better decisions
- Reducing medical error by improving the accuracy and clarity of medical records

The following are key elements of a good medical record:

- **Uniform Records.** Medical records should be uniform within the practice. All records should include specific sections for lab, X-ray, progress notes, etc. Records should include a problem list. In this format, the record is organized for easy scanning by all health care professionals who subsequently use the chart.
- **Secure Pages.** When utilizing a paper medical chart, all pages of the record should be in chronological order with fasteners to prevent pages from being lost.

- **Organization.** Organize records for easy and accurate retrieval. Whatever system is used, it should be logical and clear to all staff members and physicians (eg, active versus inactive patients, color coding for chronic problems or frequent diagnoses, etc).

- **Timeliness.** Make all entries in the record, whether written, entered electronically, or dictated, at the time of the patient contact. Include the date and the time of the exam or contact. The greater the time lapse between the exam and the entry, the less credible the medical record becomes.

- **Legible Records.** Records must be legible. Health care professionals with illegible handwriting should dictate their notes or use electronic health records (EHR). This helps to avoid misinterpretations that result in improper treatment.

- **Dictated Records.** Dictated notes must be proofread and signed. The statement *dictated but not read* does not relieve the physician from responsibility for what was transcribed. At best, the statement alerts another health care professional that the note has not been proofed and may not be correct.

- **Accurate Records.** Recording all information in objective and concise terms is important. Never include extraneous information, subjective assessments, or derogatory comments about the patient. Include direct quotations from the patient. Reduce the essential information to the least possible number of words.

- **Corrections.** Never improperly or unlawfully alter a medical record. Do not obliterate an entry with a marker or correction fluid. If an error has been made, draw a single line through the inaccurate entry and enter the necessary correction. Date, time, and initial the correction in the margin. Making an addendum to a medical record is also acceptable. It should be made after the last entry noting the current date and time, and both entries should be cross-referenced. A record that appears to have been altered implies that a cover-up has occurred.

- **Derogatory Comments.** Never criticize or make derogatory comments about another health care professional or organization to the patient or in the medical record. A negative comment can undermine a patient's confidence in the previous health care worker and contribute to or cause a decision to pursue a legal claim regardless of causation and/or who was responsible.

- **Patient Telephone Calls.** Document all patient telephone calls in the medical record. When speaking to a patient while you are away from the office, and the medical record is not available, record notes on a call pad regarding any prescriptions or medical advice given over the telephone. The sheet can be presented for entry into the chart when you return to the office.

- **Conversations.** Address and document all patient/family worries or concerns in the patient record. Record the source of the information, if other than the patient.

- **Important Instructions.** Always document important warnings and instructions given to the patient at the time of discharge. Documenting discharge instructions may help prove a patient's noncompliance. Juries are less sympathetic toward noncompliant patients.

- **Informed Consent.** To reinforce the signed informed consent form, always document information disclosed during the informed consent process.

- **Potential Complications.** Document all possible complications that might occur. Failure to recognize a complication in time to prevent injury is a common basis for a lawsuit. Proving negligence is difficult if the record shows prior awareness that a complication might occur.

Medical Records Documentation

A great deal of emphasis has been placed recently on the thorough documentation of patient encounters. Not only is documentation critical to reduce the possibility of malpractice, it is also a necessity in claiming proper reimbursement.

Many physicians have been unsuccessful in defending malpractice suits due to incomplete or illegible medical records. Following are some general recommendations for loss prevention initiatives:

- Fasten or scan all materials into the chart.
- If not utilizing an EHR, dictate progress notes and have them transcribed, if possible.
- Clearly identify allergies on the chart.
- Enter the patient's name on every page in the chart.
- The physician should initial every entry in the medical record.
- Financial data should not be kept in the chart.

Table 13-1 is a sample of a medical records checklist form that can be used when checking a patient's chart. To minimize risk, audit 10 to 20 charts periodically to assure that these guidelines are being met.

Documentation to Support Level of Service

Most managed care organizations (MCOs) have definite guidelines for documenting patient encounters. Sometimes they conduct post-payment audits in the physician's office to assure that the documentation on the

TABLE 13-1   Medical Records Checklist Form

MEDICAL RECORDS CHECKLIST			
	Yes	No	N/A
Patient name on all pages			
All pages secured with fasteners or scanned into electronic record			
Forms organized with tabs for easy access			
Organized chronologically			
Legible entries			
Missed appointments documented			
Telephone message documented			
Allergies uniformly documented			
Entries dated, timed, and initialed			
Dictation proofread and initialed			
Only standard abbreviations used			
Diagnostic reports initialed prior to filing			
Reason for visit documented			
Clinical findings (positive/negative) documented			
Treatment plan documented			
Entries are objective			
Patient instructions documented			
Patient education materials given/documented			
Medication list			
1. Current			
2. Prescriptions			
3. Refills			
4. Allergies			
Informed consent on chart			
Consultation reports on chart			
Problem list kept current			

patient's medical chart supports the service that was charged, and to assure that the physician took the proper steps to reach a satisfactory diagnosis. Medicare also conducts post-payment audits and will usually request that the physician mail in photocopies of specific patient records. Both MCOs and Medicare will require the physician to repay any amount paid for a service that is not supported by proper documentation. These repayments can sometimes amount to thousands of dollars.

To avoid this type of risk, begin during the start-up phase to set up the patient records according to the guidelines in this chapter, and make thorough documentation as convenient and efficient as possible. Existing charts (inherited from other practitioners) can be converted over time and information organized for efficiency. Preprinted forms are recommended for progress notes, medication records, telephone calls, and other reports.

Charting the Patient's Progress

Using a standard format to record the patient's visit will assure that every encounter includes all the components that are necessary for complete documentation. The Medicare Learning Network (MLN) has published evaluation and management documentation guidelines available at http://www.cms.gov/MLNEdWebGuide/25_EMDOC.asp. The MLN publication is designed to provide education on medical record documentation and evaluation and management (E/M) billing and coding considerations. The "1995 Documentation Guidelines for Evaluation and Management Services" and the "1997 Documentation Guidelines for Evaluation and Management Services" are included in this publication. Carriers and A/B Medicare Administration Contractors review using both the 1995 and 1997 documentation guidelines (whichever is more advantageous to the physician).

The publication provides definitions and documentation guidelines for the three key components of E/M services and for visits, which consist predominately of counseling or coordination of care. The three key components—history, examination, and medical decision making—appear in the descriptors for office and other outpatient services, hospital observation services, hospital inpatient services, consultations, emergency department services, nursing facility services, domiciliary care services, and home services.

The descriptors for the levels of E/M services recognize seven components, which are used in defining the levels of E/M services. These components are:

- History
- Examination
- Medical decision making
- Counseling
- Coordination of care
- Nature of presenting problem
- Time

The 1995 and 1997 documentation guidelines require the following:

I. Documentation of History

   A. Chief Complaint (CC)

     The CC is a concise statement describing the symptom, problem, condition, diagnosis, physician recommended return, or other factor that is the reason for the encounter.

   B. History of Present Illness (HPI)

     The HPI is a chronological description of the development of the patient's present illness from the first sign and/or symptom or from the previous encounter to the present. It includes the following elements:

       i. Location

      ii. Quality

     iii. Severity

      iv. Duration

      v. Timing

      vi. Context

     vii. Modifying factors

    viii. Sssociated signs and symptoms

      ix. Review of systems (ROS)

      x. Past, family, and/or social history (PFSH)

   C. Review of Systems (ROS)

     An ROS is an inventory of body systems obtained through a series of questions seeking to identify signs and/or symptoms, which the patient may be experiencing or has experienced.

     For purposes of ROS, the following systems are recognized:

- Constitutional symptoms (eg, fever, weight loss)
- Eyes
- Ears, Nose, Mouth, Throat
- Cardiovascular
- Respiratory
- Gastrointestinal
- Genitourinary
- Musculoskeletal
- Integumentary (skin and/or breast)
- Neurological
- Psychiatric
- Endocrine

- Hematologic/Lymphatic
- Allergic/Immunologic

D. Past, Family, and/or Social History (PFSH)

The PFSH consists of a review of three areas:

   i. Past history (the patient's past experiences with illnesses, operations, injuries, and treatments)

   ii. Family history (a review of medical events in the patient's family, including diseases which may be hereditary or place the patient at risk)

   iii. Social history (an age-appropriate review of past and current activities)

II. Physical Examination under 1995 Guidelines

A. ***Problem Focused***—a limited examination of the affected body area or organ system

B. ***Expanded Problem Focused***—a limited examination of the affected body area or organ system and other symptomatic or related organ system(s)

C. ***Detailed***—an extended examination of the affected body area(s) and other symptomatic or related organ system(s)

D. ***Comprehensive***—a general multisystem examination or complete examination of a single organ system

For purposes of examination, the following ***body areas*** are recognized:

   i. Head, including the face

   ii. Neck

   iii. Chest, including breasts and axillae

   iv. Abdomen

   v. Genitalia, groin, buttocks

   vi. Back, including spine

   vii. Each extremity

For purposes of examination, the following ***organ systems*** are recognized:

   i. Constitutional (eg, vital signs, general appearance)

   ii. Eyes

   iii. Ears, nose, mouth, and throat

   iv. Cardiovascular

   v. Respiratory

   vi. Gastrointestinal

   vii. Genitourinary

   viii. Musculoskeletal

      ix. Skin

      x. Neurologic

     xi. Psychiatric

    xii. Hematologic/Lymphatic/Immunologic

III. Physical Examination under 1997 Guidelines (Table 13-2)

   A. General Multi-System Examinations

      i. To qualify for a given level of multisystem examination, the following content and documentation requirements should be met:

        a. *Problem-Focused Examination*—should include performance and documentation of one to five elements identified by a bullet (·) in one or more organ system(s) or body area(s).

        b. *Expanded Problem-Focused Examination*—should include performance and documentation of at least six elements identified by a bullet (·) in one or more organ system(s) or body area(s).

        c. *Detailed Examination*—should include at least six organ systems or body areas. For each system/area selected, performance and documentation of at least two elements identified by a bullet (·) is expected. Alternatively, a detailed examination may include performance and documentation of at least twelve elements identified by a bullet (·) in two or more organ systems or body areas.

        d. *Comprehensive Examination*—should include at least nine organ systems or body areas. For each system/area selected, all elements of the examination identified by a bullet (·) should be performed, unless specific directions limit the content of the examination. For each area/system, documentation of at least two elements identified by a bullet is expected.

   B. Single Organ System Examinations

      i. The single organ system examinations recognized by CPT are described in detail in Table 13-3. Variations among these examinations in the organ systems and body areas identified in the left columns and in the elements of the examinations described in the right columns reflect differing emphases among specialties. To qualify for a given level of single organ system examination, the following content and documentation requirements should be met:

        a. *Problem-Focused Examination*—should include performance and documentation of one to five elements

TABLE 13-2   General Multi-System Examination

CONTENT AND DOCUMENTATION REQUIREMENTS

General Multi-System Examination

System/Body Area	Elements of Examination
Constitutional	• Measurement of **any three of the following seven** vital signs: 1) sitting or standing blood pressure, 2) supine blood pressure, 3) pulse rate and regularity, 4) respiration, 5) temperature, 6) height, 7) weight (may be measured and recorded by ancillary staff) • General appearance of patient (eg, development, nutrition, body habitus, deformities, attention to grooming)
Eyes	• Inspection of conjunctivae and lids • Examination of pupils and irises (eg, reaction to light and accommodation, size and symmetry) • Ophthalmoscopic examination of optic discs (eg, size, C/D ratio, appearance) and posterior segments (eg, vessel changes, exudates, hemorrhages)
Ears, Nose, Mouth and Throat	• External inspection of ears and nose (eg, overall appearance, scars, lesions, masses) • Otoscopic examination of external auditory canals and tympanic membranes • Assessment of hearing (eg, whispered voice, finger rub, tuning fork) • Inspection of nasal mucosa, septum and turbinates • Inspection of lips, teeth and gums • Examination of oropharynx: oral mucosa, salivary glands, hard and soft palates, tongue, tonsils and posterior pharynx
Neck	• Examination of neck (eg, masses, overall appearance, symmetry, tracheal position, crepitus) • Examination of thyroid (eg, enlargement, tenderness, mass)
Respiratory	• Assessment of respiratory effort (eg, intercostal retractions, use of accessory muscles, diaphragmatic movement) • Percussion of chest (eg, dullness, flatness, hyperresonance) • Palpation of chest (eg, tactile fremitus) • Auscultation of lungs (eg, breath sounds, adventitious sounds, rubs)
Cardiovascular	• Palpation of heart (eg, location, size, thrills) • Auscultation of heart with notation of abnormal sounds and murmurs Examination of: • carotid arteries (eg, pulse amplitude, bruits)

(*continued*)

TABLE 13-2   General Multi-System Examination (*continued*)

	• abdominal aorta (eg, size, bruits) • femoral arteries (eg, pulse amplitude, bruits) • pedal pulses (eg, pulse amplitude) • extremities for edema and/or varicosities
Chest (Breasts)	• Inspection of breasts (eg, symmetry, nipple discharge) • Palpation of breasts and axillae (eg, masses or lumps, tenderness)
Gastrointestinal (Abdomen)	• Examination of abdomen with notation of presence of masses or tenderness • Examination of liver and spleen • Examination for presence or absence of hernia • Examination (when indicated) of anus, perineum and rectum, including sphincter tone, presence of hemorrhoids, rectal masses • Obtain stool sample for occult blood test when indicated
Genitourinary	**MALE:** • Examination of the scrotal contents (eg, hydrocele, spermatocele, tenderness of cord, testicular mass) • Examination of the penis • Digital rectal examination of prostate gland (eg, size, symmetry, nodularity, tenderness) **FEMALE:** Pelvic examination (with or without specimen collection for smears and cultures), including • Examination of external genitalia (eg, general appearance, hair distribution, lesions) and vagina (eg, general appearance, estrogen effect, discharge, lesions, pelvic support, cystocele, rectocele) • Examination of urethra (eg, masses, tenderness, scarring) • Examination of bladder (eg, fullness, masses, tenderness) • Cervix (eg, general appearance, lesions, discharge) • Uterus (eg, size, contour, position, mobility, tenderness, consistency, descent or support) • Adnexa/parametria (eg, masses, tenderness, organomegaly, nodularity)
Lymphatic	Palpation of lymph nodes in **two or more** areas: • Neck • Axillae • Groin • Other

(*continued*)

TABLE 13-2 General Multi-System Examination (*continued*)	
Musculoskeletal	• Examination of gait and station • Inspection and/or palpation of digits and nails (eg, clubbing, cyanosis, inflammatory conditions, petechiae, ischemia, infections, nodes) Examination of joints, bones and muscles of **one or more of the following six** areas: 1) head and neck; 2) spine, ribs and pelvis; 3) right upper extremity; 4) left upper extremity; 5) right lower extremity; and 6) left lower extremity. The examination of a given area includes: • Inspection and/or palpation with notation of presence of any misalignment, asymmetry, crepitation, defects, tenderness, masses, effusions • Assessment of range of motion with notation of any pain, crepitation or contracture • Assessment of stability with notation of any dislocation (luxation), subluxation or laxity • Assessment of muscle strength and tone (eg, flaccid, cog wheel, spastic) with notation of any atrophy or abnormal movements
Skin	• Inspection of skin and subcutaneous tissue (eg, rashes, lesions, ulcers) • Palpation of skin and subcutaneous tissue (eg, induration, subcutaneous nodules, tightening)
Neurologic	• Test cranial nerves with notation of any deficits • Examination of deep tendon reflexes with notation of pathological reflexes (eg, Babinski) • Examination of sensation (eg, by touch, pin, vibration, proprioception)
Psychiatric	• Description of patient's judgment and insight Brief assessment of mental status including: • Orientation to time, place and person • Recent and remote memory • Mood and affect (eg, depression, anxiety, agitation)

Content and Documentation Requirements

Level of Exam	Perform and Document:
Problem Focused	**One to five** elements identified by a bullet.
Expanded Problem Focused	**At least six** elements identified by a bullet.
Detailed	**At least two** elements identified by a bullet **from each of six areas/systems** OR **at least twelve** elements identified by a bullet **in two or more areas/systems**.
Comprehensive Perform	**All elements** identified by a bullet in **at least nine** organ systems or body areas and document **at least two** elements identified by a bullet **from each of nine areas/systems**.

Source: Available at www.cms.gov/MLNProducts/Downloads/MASTER1.pdf. Accessed June 30, 2011.

identified by a bullet (·), whether in a box with a shaded or unshaded border.

  b. *Expanded Problem-Focused Examination*—should include performance and documentation of at least six elements identified by a bullet (·), whether in a box with a shaded or unshaded border.

  c. *Detailed Examination*—examinations other than the eye and psychiatric examinations should include performance and documentation of at least twelve elements identified by a bullet (·), whether in box with a shaded or unshaded border.

  • Eye and psychiatric examinations should include the performance and documentation of at least nine elements identified by a bullet (·), whether in a box with a shaded or unshaded border.

  d. *Comprehensive Examination*—should include performance of all elements identified by a bullet (·), whether in a shaded or unshaded box. Documentation of every element in each box with a shaded border and at 13 least one element in each box with an unshaded border is expected.

IV. Medical Decision Making under Both 1995 and 1997 Guidelines (Table of Risk, Table 13-4)

  A. The levels of E/M services recognize four types of medical decision making (straightforward, low complexity, moderate complexity, and high complexity). Medical decision making refers to the complexity of establishing a diagnosis and/or selecting a management option as measured by:

    i. The number of possible diagnoses and/or the number of management options that must be considered.

    ii. The amount and/or complexity of medical records, diagnostic tests, and/or other information that must be obtained, reviewed, and analyzed.

    iii. The risk of significant complications, morbidity and/or mortality, as well as comorbidities, associated with the patient's presenting problem(s), the diagnostic procedure(s), and/or the possible management options.

TABLE 13-3   Single Organ System Examination

Eye Examination

System/Body Elements of Examination Area	Elements of Examination
Constitutional	
Head and Face	
Eyes	• Test visual acuity (Does not include determination of refractive error) • Gross visual field testing by confrontation • Test ocular motility including primary gaze alignment • Inspection of bulbar and palpebral conjunctivae • Examination of ocular adnexae including lids (eg, ptosis or lagophthalmos), lacrimal glands, lacrimal drainage, orbits and preauricular lymph nodes • Examination of pupils and irises including shape, direct and consensual reaction (afferent pupil), size (eg, anisocoria) and morphology • Slit lamp examination of the corneas including epithelium, stroma, endothelium, and tear film • Slit lamp examination of the anterior chambers including depth, cells, and flare • Slit lamp examination of the lenses including clarity, anterior and posterior capsule, cortex, and nucleus • Measurement of intraocular pressures (except in children and patients with trauma or infectious disease) Ophthalmoscopic examination through dilated pupils (unless contraindicated) of: • Optic discs including size, C/D ratio, appearance (eg, atrophy, cupping, tumor elevation) and nerve fiber layer • Posterior segments including retina and vessels (eg, exudates and hemorrhages)
Ears, Nose, Mouth and Throat	
Neck	
Respiratory	
Cardiovascular	
Chest (Breasts)	
Gastrointestinal (Abdomen)	
Genitourinary	

(continued)

TABLE 13-3   Single Organ System Examination (*continued*)

Lymphatic	
Musculoskeletal	
Extremities	
Skin	
Neurological/Psychiatric	Brief assessment of mental status including • Orientation to time, place and person • Mood and affect (eg, depression, anxiety, agitation)

Content and Documentation Requirements

Level of Exam	Perform and Document:
Problem Focused	**One to five** elements identified by a bullet.
Expanded Problem Focused	**At least six** elements identified by a bullet.
Detailed	**At least nine** elements identified by a bullet.
Comprehensive Perform	**All** elements identified by a bullet; document every element in each box with a shaded border and at least one element in each box with an unshaded border.

Genitourinary Examination

System/Body Area	Elements of Examination
Constitutional	• Measurement of **any three of the following seven** vital signs: 1) sitting or standing blood pressure, 2) supine blood pressure, 3) pulse rate and regularity, 4) respiration, 5) temperature, 6) height, 7) weight (may be measured and recorded by ancillary staff) • General appearance of patient (eg, development, nutrition, body habitus, deformities, attention to grooming)
Head and Face	
Eyes	
Ears, Nose, Mouth and Throat	
Neck	• Examination of neck (eg, masses, overall appearance, symmetry, tracheal position, crepitus) • Examination of thyroid (eg, enlargement, tenderness, mass)
Respiratory	• Assessment of respiratory effort (eg, intercostal retractions, use of accessory muscles, diaphragmatic movement) • Auscultation of lungs (eg, breath sounds, adventitious sounds, rubs)
Cardiovascular	• Auscultation of heart with notation of abnormal sounds and murmurs • Examination of peripheral vascular system by observation (eg, swelling, varicosities) and palpation (eg, pulses, temperature, edema, tenderness)

(*continued*)

TABLE 13-3 Single Organ System Examination (*continued*)

Chest (Breasts)	[See genitourinary (female)]
Gastrointestinal (Abdomen)	• Examination of abdomen with notation of presence of masses or tenderness • Examination for presence or absence of hernia • Examination of liver and spleen • Obtain stool sample for occult blood test when indicated
Genitourinary	**MALE:** • Inspection of anus and perineum Examination (with or without specimen collection for smears and cultures) of genitalia including: • Scrotum (eg, lesions, cysts, rashes) • Epididymides (eg, size, symmetry, masses) • Testes (eg, size, symmetry, masses) • Urethral meatus (eg, size, location, lesions, discharge) • Penis (eg, lesions, presence or absence of foreskin, foreskin retractability, plaque, masses, scarring, deformities) Digital rectal examination including: • Prostate gland (eg, size, symmetry, nodularity, tenderness) • Seminal vesicles (eg, symmetry, tenderness, masses, enlargement) • Sphincter tone, presence of hemorrhoids, rectal masses
Genitourinary (*continued*)	**FEMALE:** Includes **at least seven of the following eleven** elements identified by bullets: • Inspection and palpation of breasts (eg, masses or lumps, tenderness, symmetry, nipple discharge) • Digital rectal examination including sphincter tone, presence of hemorrhoids, rectal masses Pelvic examination (with or without specimen collection for smears and cultures) including: • External genitalia (eg, general appearance, hair distribution, lesions) • Urethral meatus (eg, size, location, lesions, prolapse) • Urethra (eg, masses, tenderness, scarring) • Bladder (eg, fullness, masses, tenderness) • Vagina (eg, general appearance, estrogen effect, discharge, lesions, pelvic support, cystocele, rectocele) • Cervix (eg, general appearance, lesions, discharge) • Uterus (eg, size, contour, position, mobility, tenderness, consistency, descent or support)

(*continued*)

TABLE 13-3   Single Organ System Examination (*continued*)

	• Adnexa/parametria (eg, masses, tenderness, organomegaly, nodularity) • Anus and perineum
Lymphatic	• Palpation of lymph nodes in neck, axillae, groin and/or other location
Musculoskeletal	
Extremities	
Skin	• Inspection and/or palpation of skin and subcutaneous tissue (eg, rashes, lesions, ulcers)
Neurological/ Psychiatric	Brief assessment of mental status including • Orientation (eg, time, place and person) and • Mood and affect (eg, depression, anxiety, agitation)

Content and Documentation Requirements

Level of Exam	Perform and Document:
Problem Focused	**One to five** elements identified by a bullet.
Expanded Problem Focused	**At least six** elements identified by a bullet.
Detailed	**At least twelve** elements identified by a bullet.
Comprehensive Perform	**All** elements identified by a bullet; document every element in each box with a shaded border and at least one element in each box with an unshaded border.

Hematologic/Lymphatic/Immunologic Examination

System/Body Elements of Examination Area	Elements of Examination
Constitutional	• Measurement of **any three of the following seven** vital signs: 1) sitting or standing blood pressure, 2) supine blood pressure, 3) pulse rate and regularity, 4) respiration, 5) temperature, 6) height, 7) weight (may be measured and recorded by ancillary staff) • General appearance of patient (eg, development, nutrition, body habitus, deformities, attention to grooming)
Head and Face	• Palpation and/or percussion of face with notation of presence or absence of sinus tenderness
Eyes	• Inspection of conjunctivae and lids
Ears, Nose, Mouth and Throat	• Otoscopic examination of external auditory canals and tympanic membranes • Inspection of nasal mucosa, septum and turbinates • Inspection of teeth and gums • Examination of oropharynx (eg, oral mucosa, hard and soft palates, tongue, tonsils, posterior pharynx)

(*continued*)

TABLE 13-3 Single Organ System Examination (*continued*)

Neck	• Examination of neck (eg, masses, overall appearance, symmetry, tracheal position, crepitus) • Examination of thyroid (eg, enlargement, tenderness, mass)
Respiratory	• Assessment of respiratory effort (eg, intercostal retractions, use of accessory muscles, diaphragmatic movement) • Auscultation of lungs (eg, breath sounds, adventitious sounds, rubs)
Cardiovascular	• Auscultation of heart with notation of abnormal sounds and murmurs • Examination of peripheral vascular system by observation (eg, swelling, varicosities) and palpation (eg, pulses, temperature, edema, tenderness)
Chest (Breasts)	
Gastrointestinal (Abdomen)	• Examination of abdomen with notation of presence of masses or tenderness • Examination of liver and spleen
Genitourinary	
Lymphatic	• Palpation of lymph nodes in neck, axillae, groin, and/or other location
Musculoskeletal	
Extremities	• Inspection and palpation of digits and nails (eg, clubbing, cyanosis, inflammation, petechiae, ischemia, infections, nodes)
Skin	• Inspection and/or palpation of skin and subcutaneous tissue (eg, rashes, lesions, ulcers, ecchymoses, bruises)
Neurological/ Psychiatric	Brief assessment of mental status including • Orientation to time, place and person • Mood and affect (eg, depression, anxiety, agitation)

Content and Documentation Requirements

Level of Exam	Perform and Document:
Problem Focused	**One to five** elements identified by a bullet.
Expanded Problem Focused	**At least six** elements identified by a bullet.
Detailed	**At least twelve** elements identified by a bullet.
Comprehensive Perform	**All** elements identified by a bullet; document every element in each box with a shaded border and at least one element in each box with an unshaded border.

Musculoskeletal Examination

System/Body Area	Elements of Examination
Constitutional	• Measurement of **any three of the following seven** vital signs: 1) sitting or standing blood pressure, 2) supine blood pressure, 3) pulse rate and regularity, 4) respiration, 5) temperature, 6) height, 7) weight (may be measured and recorded by ancillary staff)

(*continued*)

TABLE 13-3   Single Organ System Examination (*continued*)

	• General appearance of patient (eg, development, nutrition, body habitus, deformities, attention to grooming)
Head and Face	
Eyes	
Ears, Nose, Mouth and Throat	
Neck	
Respiratory	
Cardiovascular	• Examination of peripheral vascular system by observation (eg, swelling, varicosities) and palpation (eg, pulses, temperature, edema, tenderness)
Chest (Breasts)	
Gastrointestinal (Abdomen)	
Genitourinary	
Lymphatic	• Palpation of lymph nodes in neck, axillae, groin and/or other location
Musculoskeletal	• Examination of gait and station Examination of joint(s), bone(s) and muscle(s)/ tendon(s) of **four of the following six** areas: 1) head and neck; 2) spine, ribs and pelvis; 3) right upper extremity; 4) left upper extremity; 5) right lower extremity; and 6) left lower extremity. The examination of a given area includes: • Inspection, percussion and/or palpation with notation of any misalignment, asymmetry, crepitation, defects, tenderness, masses or effusions • Assessment of range of motion with notation of any pain (eg, straight leg raising), crepitation or contracture • Assessment of stability with notation of any dislocation (luxation), subluxation or laxity • Assessment of muscle strength and tone (eg, flaccid, cog wheel, spastic) with notation of any atrophy or abnormal movements NOTE: For the comprehensive level of examination, all four of the elements identified by a bullet must be performed and documented for each of four anatomic areas. For the three lower levels of examination, each element is counted separately for each body area. For example, assessing range of motion in two extremities constitutes two elements.
Extremities	[See musculoskeletal and skin]

(*continued*)

TABLE 13-3   Single Organ System Examination (*continued*)

Skin	• Inspection and/or palpation of skin and subcutaneous tissue (eg, scars, rashes, lesions, cafe-au-lait spots, ulcers) in **four of the following six** areas: 1) head and neck; 2) trunk; 3) right upper extremity; 4) left upper extremity; 5) right lower extremity; and 6) left lower extremity. NOTE: For the comprehensive level, the examination of all four anatomic areas must be performed and documented. For the three lower levels of examination, each body area is counted separately. For example, inspection and/or palpation of the skin and subcutaneous tissue of two extremities constitutes two elements.
Neurological/ Psychiatric	• Test coordination (eg, finger/nose, heel/knee/shin, rapid alternating movements in the upper and lower extremities, evaluation of fine motor coordination in young children) • Examination of deep tendon reflexes and/or nerve stretch test with notation of pathological reflexes (eg, Babinski) • Examination of sensation (eg, by touch, pin, vibration, proprioception) Brief assessment of mental status including • Orientation to time, place and person • Mood and affect (eg, depression, anxiety, agitation)

Content and Documentation Requirements

Level of Exam	Perform and Document:
Problem Focused	**One to five** elements identified by a bullet.
Expanded Problem Focused	**At least six** elements identified by a bullet.
Detailed	**At least twelve** elements identified by a bullet.
Comprehensive Perform	**All** elements identified by a bullet; document every element in each box with a shaded border and at least one element in each box with an unshaded border.

Neurological Examination

System/Body Area	Elements of Examination
Constitutional	• Measurement of **any three of the following seven** vital signs: 1) sitting or standing blood pressure, 2) supine blood pressure, 3) pulse rate and regularity, 4) respiration, 5) temperature, 6) height, 7) weight (may be measured and recorded by ancillary staff) • General appearance of patient (eg, development, nutrition, body habitus, deformities, attention to grooming)
Head and Face	

(*continued*)

TABLE 13-3   Single Organ System Examination (*continued*)

Eyes	• Ophthalmoscopic examination of optic discs (eg, size, C/D ratio, appearance) and posterior segments (eg, vessel changes, exudates, hemorrhages)
Ears, Nose, Mouth and Throat	
Neck	
Respiratory	
Cardiovascular	• Examination of carotid arteries (eg, pulse amplitude, bruits) • Auscultation of heart with notation of abnormal sounds and murmurs • Examination of peripheral vascular system by observation (eg, swelling, varicosities) and palpation (eg, pulses, temperature, edema, tenderness)
Chest (Breasts)	
Gastrointestinal (Abdomen)	
Genitourinary	
Lymphatic	
Musculoskeletal	• Examination of gait and station Assessment of motor function including: • Muscle strength in upper and lower extremities • Muscle tone in upper and lower extremities (eg, flaccid, cog wheel, spastic) with notation of any atrophy or abnormal movements (eg, fasciculation, tardive dyskinesia)
Extremities	[See musculoskeletal]
Skin	
Neurological	Evaluation of higher integrative functions including: • Orientation to time, place and person • Recent and remote memory • Attention span and concentration • Language (eg, naming objects, repeating phrases, spontaneous speech) • Fund of knowledge (eg, awareness of current events, past history, vocabulary) Test the following cranial nerves: • 2nd cranial nerve (eg, visual acuity, visual fields, fundi) • 3rd, 4th and 6th cranial nerves (eg, pupils, eye movements)

(*continued*)

TABLE 13-3   Single Organ System Examination (*continued*)

Neurological (*continued*)	• 5th cranial nerve (eg, facial sensation, corneal reflexes) • 7th cranial nerve (eg, facial symmetry, strength) • 8th cranial nerve (eg, hearing with tuning fork, whispered voice and/or finger rub) • 9th cranial nerve (eg, spontaneous or reflex palate movement) • 11th cranial nerve (eg, shoulder shrug strength) • 12th cranial nerve (eg, tongue protrusion) • Examination of sensation (eg, by touch, pin, vibration, proprioception) • Examination of deep tendon reflexes in upper and lower extremities with notation of pathological reflexes (eg, Babinski) • Test coordination (eg, finger/nose, heel/knee/shin, rapid alternating movements in the upper and lower extremities, evaluation of fine motor coordination in young children)
Psychiatric	

Content and Documentation Requirements

Level of Exam	Perform and Document:
Problem Focused	**One to five** elements identified by a bullet.
Expanded Problem Focused	**At least six** elements identified by a bullet.
Detailed	**At least twelve** elements identified by a bullet.
Comprehensive Perform	**All** elements identified by a bullet; document every element in each box with a shaded border and at least one element in each box with an unshaded border.

Psychiatric Examination

System/Body Area	Elements of Examination
Constitutional	• Measurement of **any three of the following seven** vital signs: 1) sitting or standing blood pressure, 2) supine blood pressure, 3) pulse rate and regularity, 4) respiration, 5) temperature, 6) height, 7) weight (may be measured and recorded by ancillary staff) • General appearance of patient (eg, development, nutrition, body habitus, deformities, attention to grooming)
Head and Face	
Eyes	
Ears, Nose, Mouth and Throat	
Neck	
Respiratory	

(*continued*)

TABLE 13-3   Single Organ System Examination (*continued*)

Cardiovascular	
Chest (Breasts)	
Gastrointestinal (Abdomen)	
Genitourinary	
Lymphatic	
Musculoskeletal	• Assessment of muscle strength and tone (eg, flaccid, cog wheel, spastic) with notation of any atrophy and abnormal movements • Examination of gait and station
Extremities	
Skin	
Neurological	
Psychiatric	• Description of speech including: rate; volume; articulation; coherence; and spontaneity with notation of abnormalities (eg, perseveration, paucity of language) • Description of thought processes including: rate of thoughts; content of thoughts (eg, logical vs. illogical, tangential); abstract reasoning; and computation • Description of associations (eg, loose, tangential, circumstantial, intact) • Description of abnormal or psychotic thoughts including: hallucinations; delusions; preoccupation with violence; homicidal or suicidal ideation; and obsessions • Description of the patient's judgment (eg, concerning everyday activities and social situations) and insight (eg, concerning psychiatric condition) Complete mental status examination including • Orientation to time, place and person • Recent and remote memory • Attention span and concentration • Language (eg, naming objects, repeating phrases) • Fund of knowledge (eg, awareness of current events, past history, vocabulary) • Mood and affect (eg, depression, anxiety, agitation, hypomania, lability)

(*continued*)

TABLE 13-3   Single Organ System Examination (*continued*)

Content and Documentation Requirements

Level of Exam	Perform and Document:
Problem Focused	**One to five** elements identified by a bullet.
Expanded Problem Focused	**At least six** elements identified by a bullet.
Detailed	**At least nine** elements identified by a bullet.
Comprehensive Perform	**All** elements identified by a bullet; document every element in each box with a shaded border and at least one element in each box with an unshaded border.

Respiratory Examination

System/Body Area	Elements of Examination
Constitutional	• Measurement of **any three of the following seven** vital signs: 1) sitting or standing blood pressure, 2) supine blood pressure, 3) pulse rate and regularity, 4) respiration, 5) temperature, 6) height, 7) weight (may be measured and recorded by ancillary staff) • General appearance of patient (eg, development, nutrition, body habitus, deformities, attention to grooming)
Head and Face	
Eyes	
Ears, Nose, Mouth and Throat	• Inspection of nasal mucosa, septum and turbinates • Inspection of teeth and gums • Examination of oropharynx (eg, oral mucosa, hard and soft palates, tongue, tonsils and posterior pharynx)
Neck	• Examination of neck (eg, masses, overall appearance, symmetry, tracheal position, crepitus) • Examination of thyroid (eg, enlargement, tenderness, mass) • Examination of jugular veins (eg, distension; a, v or cannon a waves)
Respiratory	• Inspection of chest with notation of symmetry and expansion • Assessment of respiratory effort (eg, intercostal retractions, use of accessory muscles, diaphragmatic movement) • Percussion of chest (eg, dullness, flatness, hyperresonance) • Palpation of chest (eg, tactile fremitus) • Auscultation of lungs (eg, breath sounds, adventitious sounds, rubs)
Cardiovascular	• Auscultation of heart including sounds, abnormal sounds and murmurs • Examination of peripheral vascular system by observation (eg, swelling, varicosities) and palpation (eg, pulses, temperature, edema, tenderness)

(*continued*)

TABLE 13-3   Single Organ System Examination (*continued*)

Chest (Breasts)	
Gastrointestinal (Abdomen)	• Examination of abdomen with notation of presence of masses or tenderness • Examination of liver and spleen
Genitourinary	
Lymphatic	• Palpation of lymph nodes in neck, axillae, groin and/or other location
Musculoskeletal	• Assessment of muscle strength and tone (eg, flaccid, cog wheel, spastic) with notation of any atrophy and abnormal movements • Examination of gait and station
Extremities	• Inspection and palpation of digits and nails (eg, clubbing, cyanosis, inflammation, petechiae, ischemia, infections, nodes)
Skin	• Inspection and/or palpation of skin and subcutaneous tissue (eg, rashes, lesions, ulcers)
Neurological/ Psychiatric	Brief assessment of mental status including • Orientation to time, place and person • Mood and affect (eg, depression, anxiety, agitation)

Content and Documentation Requirements

Level of Exam	Perform and Document:
Problem Focused	**One to five** elements identified by a bullet.
Expanded Problem Focused	**At least six** elements identified by a bullet.
Detailed	**At least twelve** elements identified by a bullet.
Comprehensive Perform	**All** elements identified by a bullet; document every element in each box with a shaded border and at least one element in each box with an unshaded border.

Skin Examination

System/Body Area	Elements of Examination
Constitutional	• Measurement of any **three of the following seven** vital signs: 1) sitting or standing blood pressure, 2) supine blood pressure, 3) pulse rate and regularity, 4) respiration, 5) temperature, 6) height, 7) weight (may be measured and recorded by ancillary staff) • General appearance of patient (eg, development, nutrition, body habitus, deformities, attention to grooming)
Head and Face	
Eyes	• Inspection of conjunctivae and lids

(*continued*)

TABLE 13-3   Single Organ System Examination (*continued*)

Ears, Nose, Mouth and Throat	• Inspection of lips, teeth and gums • Examination of oropharynx (eg, oral mucosa, hard and soft palates, tongue, tonsils, posterior pharynx)
Neck	• Examination of thyroid (eg, enlargement, tenderness, mass)
Respiratory	
Cardiovascular	• Examination of peripheral vascular system by observation (eg, swelling, varicosities) and palpation (eg, pulses, temperature, edema, tenderness)
Chest (Breasts)	
Gastrointestinal (Abdomen)	• Examination of liver and spleen • Examination of anus for condyloma and other lesions
Genitourinary	
Lymphatic	• Palpation of lymph nodes in neck, axillae, groin and/or other location
Musculoskeletal	
Extremities	• Inspection and palpation of digits and nails (eg, clubbing, cyanosis, inflammation, petechiae, ischemia, infections, nodes)
Skin	• Palpation of scalp and inspection of hair of scalp, eyebrows, face, chest, pubic area (when indicated) and extremities • Inspection and/or palpation of skin and subcutaneous tissue (eg, rashes, lesions, ulcers, susceptibility to and presence of photo damage) in **eight of the following ten** areas: • Head, including the face and • Neck • Chest, including breasts and axillae • Abdomen • Genitalia, groin, buttocks • Back • Right upper extremity • Left upper extremity • Right lower extremity • Left lower extremity NOTE: For the comprehensive level, the examination of at least eight anatomic areas must be performed and documented. For the three lower levels of examination, each body area is counted separately. For example, inspection and/or palpation of the skin and subcutaneous tissue of the right upper extremity and the left upper extremity constitutes two elements.

(*continued*)

TABLE 13-3   Single Organ System Examination (*continued*)

Skin (*continued*)	• Inspection of eccrine and apocrine glands of skin and subcutaneous tissue with identification and location of any hyperhidrosis, chromhidroses or bromhidrosis
Neurological/ Psychiatric	Brief assessment of mental status including • Orientation to time, place and person • Mood and affect (eg, depression, anxiety, agitation)

Content and Documentation Requirements

Level of Exam	Perform and Document:
Problem Focused	**One to five** elements identified by a bullet.
Expanded Problem Focused	**At least six** elements identified by a bullet.
Detailed	**At least twelve** elements identified by a bullet.
Comprehensive Perform	**All** elements identified by a bullet; document every element in each box with a shaded border and at least one element in each box with an unshaded border.

Source: www.cms.gov/MLNProducts/downloads/eval_mgmt_serv_guide-ICN006764.pdf. Accessed July 1, 2011.

TABLE 13-4   Table of Risk

Level of Risk	Presenting Problem(s)	Diagnostic Procedure(s) Ordered	Management Options Selected
Minimal	• One self-limited or minor problem, eg, cold, insect bite, tinea corporis	• Laboratory tests requiring venipuncture • Chest X-rays • EKG/EEG • Urinalysis • Ultrasound, eg, echocardiography • KOH prep	• Rest • Gargles • Elastic bandages • Superficial dressings
Low	• Two or more self-limited or minor problems • One stable chronic illness, eg, well controlled hypertension, non-insulin dependent diabetes, cataract, BPH • Acute uncomplicated illness or injury, eg, cystitis, allergic rhinitis, simple sprain	• Physiologic tests not under stress, eg, pulmonary function test • Non-cardiovascular imaging studies with contrast, eg, barium enema • Superficial needle biopsies • Clinical laboratory tests requiring arterial puncture • Skin biopsies	• Over-the-counter drugs • Minor surgery with no identified risk factors • Physical therapy • Occupational therapy • IV fluids without additives
Moderate	• One or more chronic illnesses with mild exacerbation, progression, or side effects of treatment • Two or more stable chronic illnesses • Undiagnosed new problem with uncertain prognosis, eg, lump in breast • Acute illness with systemic symptoms, eg, pyelonephritis, pneumonitis, colitis	• Physiologic tests under stress, eg, cardiac stress test, fetal contraction stress test • Diagnostic endoscopies with no identified risk factor • Deep needle or incisional biopsy • Cardiovascular imaging studies with contrast and no identified risk factors, eg, arteriogram, cardiac catheterization	• Minor surgery with identified risk factors • Elective major surgery (open, percutaneous or endoscopic) with no identified risk factors • Prescription drug management • Therapeutic nuclear medicine • IV fluids with additives • Closed treatment of fracture or dislocation without manipulation

(continued)

TABLE 13-4   Table of Risk

Moderate *(continued)*	• Acute complicated injury, eg, head injury with brief loss of consciousness	• Obtain fluid from body cavity, eg, lumbar puncture, thoracentesis, culdocentesis	
High	• One or more chronic illnesses with severe exacerbation, progression, or side effects of treatment • Acute or chronic illnesses or injuries that pose a threat to life or bodily function, eg, multiple trauma, acute MI, pulmonary embolus, severe respiratory distress, progressive severe rheumatoid arthritis, psychiatric illness with potential threat to self or others, peritonitis, acute renal failure • An abrupt change in neurologic status, eg, seizure, TIA, weakness, sensory loss	• Cardiovascular imaging studies with contrast with identified risk factors • Cardiac electrophysiological tests • Diagnostic endoscopies with identified risk factors • Discography	• Elective major surgery (open, percutaneous or endoscopic) with identified risk factors • Emergency major surgery (open, percutaneous or endoscopic) • Parental controlled substances • Drug therapy requiring intensive monitoring for toxicity • Decision not to resuscitate or to de-escalate care because of poor prognosis

Source: www.cms.gov/MLNProducts/downloads/eval_mgmt_serv_guide-ICN006764.pdf. Accessed June 30, 2011.

Organizing the Patient File

Having every patient's chart organized in the same order saves time. It takes less time to locate a specific report or item the physician needs to properly treat the patient. Figure 13-2 is an example of how a patient's chart might be organized for greater efficiency.

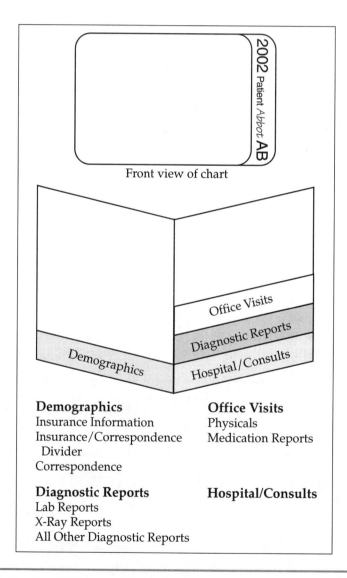

Front view of chart

Demographics
Insurance Information
Insurance/Correspondence
  Divider
Correspondence

Office Visits
Physicals
Medication Reports

Diagnostic Reports
Lab Reports
X-Ray Reports
All Other Diagnostic Reports

Hospital/Consults

FIGURE 13-2   Sample Patient's Chart Map

Conclusion

Risk management is vital to the success of your practice. Be mindful of your liabilities in every aspect of your practice. In addition to having the proper insurance coverage for your liabilities, be sure to have the proper procedures and protocols in place to lessen your exposure to risk.

References

1. Dunevitz B. Risk management program can mean the difference between success and legal failure. *MGM Update.* 2000; 39.

2. Department of Health and Human Services, Centers for Medicare & Medicaid Services, Medicare Learning Network, Documentation Guidelines for Evaluation and Management (E/M) Services. www.cms.gov/MLNEdWeb Guide/25_EMDOC.asp. Accessed June 30, 2011.

3. Department of Health and Human Services, Centers for Medicare & Medicaid Services. 2010. Medicare Learning Network, Evaluation and Management Services Guide. December. www.cms.gov/MLNProducts/downloads/eval_mgmt_serv_guide-ICN006764.pdf. Accessed June 30, 2011.

4. Department of Health and Human Services, Centers for Medicare & Medicaid Services. Medicare Learning Network, 1995 Documentation Guidelines for Evaluation & Management Services. www.cms.gov/MLNProducts/Downloads/1995dg.pdf. Accessed June 30, 2011.

5. Department of Health and Human Services, Centers for Medicare & Medicaid Services. Medicare Learning Network, 1997 Documentation Guidelines for Evaluation and Management Services. www.cms.gov/MLNProducts/Downloads/MASTER1.pdf. Accessed June 30, 2011.

14

Establishing Financial Controls and Developing Policies and Procedures

Introduction

For the success of any practice, it is important to develop, implement, and follow policies and procedures that touch various aspects of daily tasks. A formal policy manual should be developed to address administrative and accounting procedures and protocols. Every medical practice should have checks and balances in place for managing cash to ensure that all monies are properly credited. Management should also be aware of the risks within a practice for embezzlement and fraud and the steps to take towards the prevention of dishonest activity.

Preparing written policies is a good exercise in thinking through the processes and examining their validity and accuracy. It is also a good opportunity to recognize inefficient processes that need to be addressed to ensure quality patient care and staff efficiency. A well-written policies and procedures manual will provide a training and orientation guide for new employees and serve as an ongoing reference for the office staff. The master manual should always be updated and readily available to any staff member. Many payers also request to review the current policy and procedure manual during their onsite practice reviews.

This chapter discusses various administrative and financial controls, policies, and procedures that should be addressed by practices. It also encompasses the content, preparation, and maintenance of a manual that defines the policies and procedures for accounting and cash controls, prevention of fraud and embezzlement, appointment scheduling, and the various administrative protocols that are necessary.

Policies and Procedures

Every medical practice should develop appropriate policies and procedures for the various tasks and functions performed throughout the non-clinical departments of the practice. An experienced practice administrator or manager can be an asset in the development of these guidelines. The manager must initially receive approval from the physician or managing partner on all policies and procedures. Going forward, the physician should clearly outline the manager's level of authority for any future policies so that the physician will not have to approve all minor administrative changes or new processes.

A policies and procedures manual should address the following situations and should include step-by-step processes for each task in the office:

- Sample forms with explanations of when to use them, how to complete them, to whom the form should be sent, etc.
- Patient scheduling procedures, including protocols for each physician and type of visit. (Most current practice management systems can be programmed to handle customized schedules by physician and specific type of visit.) This should also include guidelines for new patients and applicable paperwork, current medications list, authorizations if required, etc.
- Overview of HIPAA requirements and privacy policies. The importance of this should be emphasized and include the ramifications that will occur if an employee fails to follow these federal guidelines.
- Chart set up and filing standards.
- How to register a patient, demographics verification, patient flow, etc.
- Front desk and checkout collection policies.
- How to handle patient walk-ins and sales representatives.
- Protocols for releasing patient records.
- Guidelines for referring patients and a list of preferred providers by specialty, including labs, X-ray centers/hospitals, etc.
- Procedures for handling patient calls for numerous situations, including medical issues (how to triage), prescription refills, test results, and so on.
- Billing and collection policies.
- Guidelines for handling daily patient collections at the time of service, posting payments, depositing checks and cash, etc.
- Protocols for closing and daily/monthly reconciliation.
- Office safety and hygiene rules and guidelines including OSHA requirements.

The office should also maintain updated phone lists of frequently called numbers (insurance carriers, equipment vendors, and so on), physician contact numbers, and other emergency information, for distribution to all applicable staff positions.

Accounting and Cash Controls

It is essential for each practice to have strong accounting and cash controls in place to help ensure a profitable business. A physician's first priority is to provide quality care to patients in a timely and ethical manner. However, a medical practice must also be properly managed like a business with efficient procedures in place to provide a good working environment for employees, a safe and comfortable atmosphere for patients, and a sound financial foundation for profitability.

Each practice needs to establish guidelines for accounting controls, and the staff involved will vary depending on the size of a practice. For example, in smaller practices, the physician (or senior partner) should probably sign all checks over a certain dollar amount rather than the practice manager or administrator. This allows him or her to control payments and help ensure that payments are being made to valid vendors. Below are situations that should be addressed by practices of any size.

- Monitor check numbers and require a physician or trusted manager to sign all checks. (If the manager is responsible for reconciling the bank account and making deposits, he or she should not have authorization to sign checks, as there should be a separation of duties.)
- Require supporting documentation for all checks.
- Monitor check numbers and make sure each check is properly issued with no missing check numbers.
- Establish guidelines for petty cash and create a log for all withdrawals, including reason, date, amount, and to whom.
- Balance the ledger of payments daily.
- A physician should sign off on all bank reconciliations not performed by an outside accounting firm.
- Utilize an accounting firm, when possible, for quarterly reviews.

Patients typically have the option to pay for services via check, credit card, or cash. Checks and cash need to be managed to ensure proper credit is applied to the patient's account and checks and cash are posted and deposited on a timely basis, preferably daily. The administrative staff should write the patient's chart or account number on each cash receipt and each check to correlate them to the account to which they apply. There needs to be a separation of duties to maintain a full check and balance routine for these types of transactions. The employee who accepts payments from patients should complete a receipt for all cash payments and give the original to the patient with a copy placed in the collection box/drawer. A different employee, typically the office or accounting manager, should create deposit slips based upon the cash receipts and the checks in the daily collection. A random audit should be conducted routinely by checking the patient's record in the practice management system to ensure cash and checks are properly posted to the applicable account. This provides a double check to make sure all cash and checks are handled properly by the staff. Also, management needs to listen to all patient complaints regarding any payments not applied to their account; this could be an indication of embezzlement.

Fraud and Embezzlement

Unfortunately, fraud and embezzlement within a practice are common occurrences across the country. Practices fall victim to these types of crimes for several reasons. First, physicians are focused on patient care and clinical protocols. Many providers are removed from financial management and have not established controls for monitoring and preventing embezzlement. Office managers frequently have numerous responsibilities and so many tasks to handle that it can be difficult to complete all work on a daily or even a weekly basis.

Employees can more easily commit fraud in a practice due to:

- Easy access to funds, cash, and/or checks
- Unquestioning practice owners
- Autonomy of positions
- Physicians focused on medical rather than financial responsibilities
- Many practices are too small to justify sufficient staff to assure good internal controls, and they cannot segregate duties

One way to help protect the practice financially against employee fraud or embezzlement is to bond employees. Only those employees who handle cash, credit cards, or checks need to be bonded. Physicians could find this form of insurance well worth the premiums to avoid falling prey to these types of criminal acts. There are cases of employees who have embezzled amounts in excess of $300,000 over a period of years.

The controls listed under the accounting and cash controls section can help prevent fraud. Additionally, employee audits and having a clear policy of checks and balances can help prevent dishonesty. Many corporations require all employees to take vacations; this can help identify potential issues that may come to light during an employee's absence. Develop a clear message in the policies and procedures manual that embezzlement or dishonesty will not be tolerated and the practice will prosecute to the full extent of the law.

Physicians and management need to aware of certain warning signs of cash misappropriation that could lead to financial improprieties. Some warning signs include:

- A decrease in cash to total assets
- A decrease in the ratio of cash to credit card transactions
- Unexplained cash discrepancies
- Altered or forged deposit slips
- An increase in soft expenses
- Vendor name consisting of initials or a vendor address that is a post office box
- Excessive voiding, missing, or destroyed checks

Some practices experience patient fraud through misrepresentation of insurance information. The front desk staff needs to verify the identification of all patients to confirm a match to the name on the insurance card. They should require a photo ID and thoroughly review the picture to compare to the patient. If the practice has a practice management/EMR system that allows the capture of a digital photo, the front desk should utilize this feature for all patients, which then allows them to visually confirm the patient on each subsequent visit. The photo ID presented by the patient during the initial visit must be first authenticated by asking for date of birth, zip code, and comparison of signatures on drivers licenses and another resources (eg, credit card, etc) to ensure the patient presented in the ID is the actual patient and is indeed covered by the insurance carrier.

In summary, following protocols for procedures and accounting controls will assist the practice with efficiency and accuracy and help reduce liability. The cash and accounting controls will also contribute to the financial success of a practice. Written guidelines will assist current and future employees in the performance of their jobs. They also assist with cross-training to cover duties when someone is on vacation or ill. Additionally, the written policies provide guidance for the training of new hires. It is essential to keep all policies and procedures current so they are valid at any given time. Although time constraints in a busy practice make it difficult to amend written procedures, it is important to update the manual on a monthly basis as needed.

Understanding possible fraud and embezzlement challenges will help a practice monitor and prevent such occurrences. Checks and balances are essential for practices of all sizes. Unfortunately, some practices have been the victim of employee embezzlement for years without discovering the missing funds. Establish financial controls, follow the procedures, and do not be afraid to confront an employee if there is suspicion. And, if there is proof of fraud or embezzlement, pursue and prosecute under the guidance of a legal expert.

Types of Appointment Schedules

Inefficient patient scheduling can significantly impede the progress of your day. There are many effective methods from which to choose. Experiment with different appointment schedules to learn what works best for the practice.

- **Typical format.** One patient scheduled every 15 minutes, with an extra 15 minutes allowed for complete physicals or new patients.
- **Wave method.** Three patients scheduled to arrive on the hour and half hour based on the concept that one patient will always be early, another on time, and the third 5 to 10 minutes late.
- **Need method.** Patients for follow-up visits or minor illnesses are scheduled back to back. New patients, procedures, or physicals are scheduled as the first and last patient each morning and each afternoon.
- **Open access.** Patients are seen on the day they call with designated time slots for types of visits.

Whatever method is used, let the office staff know that it is imperative patients wait no longer than 15 minutes without the office manager being made aware of the situation. The staff should also be responsible for keeping the patients informed of any delays. Patients usually do not mind waiting an extra few minutes if they are regularly updated and given the opportunity to reschedule. Telephone confirmation of all appointments will significantly reduce the number of appointments not kept (no-shows). This should be done one to two days prior to the scheduled appointment.

Your own responsibility for maintaining a prompt appointment schedule cannot be overstated. Being kept waiting is still the number one complaint of most patients. Patient satisfaction is crucial in today's health care market, and being on time goes a long way toward achieving patient satisfaction.

TABLE 14-1   Ten Tips for Efficient Scheduling

1. Arrange office hours to fit community needs. Consider seeing patients during evening hours two or three times a week or Saturday mornings.
2. Use an appointment scheduler customized according to physician preferences. In a partnership or group, scheduling preferences may vary by physician. Provide for evening and weekend coverage and vacations.
3. Establish an office policy for screening telephone calls. Be sure to set aside specific times for callbacks.
4. When an emergency results in a delay, explain the situation to waiting patients; give them a choice of waiting or rescheduling. Contact patients that are not yet in the office.
5. When a patient requests an appointment time that is already filled, offer at least two other times that are available. Chances are the patient will choose one of the other times offered.
6. Identify more lengthy appointment types and high risk, no-show patients (ie, new patients) and send them written or oral reminders.
7. If canceling an appointment is necessary, notify the patient as soon as possible.
8. If the physician makes house calls or visits to other institutions, schedule these trips realistically so they do not conflict with office hours.
9. Do not overcrowd the schedule. Allow two or three times during the day for catching up, work-ins, or emergencies.
10. On slow days, consider keeping a standby list available of patients who can be called in on short notice in case of cancellation.

Consider the pointers in Table 14-1 when addressing scheduling issues. These tips will improve access and increase efficiencies, benefiting you and your patients. Ensure that your staff has this information available to them through the policies and procedures manual.

Developing a Policies and Procedures Manual

The policies and procedures manual should be prepared with greater detail and bound separately from the employee handbook (discussed in Chapter 11). Each employee should sign a form that will be maintained in the employee's personnel file acknowledging that the policies and procedures have been read. All updates and changes to the policies should be included in the manual as well.

The Policies and Procedures Manual should accomplish the following:

- Provide step-by-step guidelines for completion of each task in the office
- Identify key personnel to use as resources for each task
- Include samples of forms and office documents to be used
- Advise about miscellaneous office matters (eg, location of keys, daily start-up and end-of-day processes, supply ordering, etc)

Specific policies and instructions should address the following functions:

- Handling incoming phone calls
- Scheduling patient appointments
- Patient registration and check-in
- Office collections routine
- Medical records protocols and prerequisites
- Charge capture procedures
- Completing a superbill appropriately
- Coding and billing processes
- Accounts receivable protocols
- Closing and reconciling day's activities
- Purchasing supplies and equipment
- Cleaning laboratory equipment
- Performing tests and ancillary procedures in the office (ie, EKG, labs, X-rays)
- Referring a patient for tests in other facilities and physician offices.
- Handling test results and referral follow-up (eg, notifying the patient, physician's responsibilities)

The office administrator or manager must assume responsibility for the preparation of the policies and procedures manual in the early stages with input from the physician(s). How each policy or procedure will be carried out or conducted should be clearly defined. After the initial office set-up phase, this task can be turned over to the administrative staff for updates and maintenance. Figure 14-1 is an example of an appointment scheduling policy. Use it as a format for writing a specific manual.

ABC Medical Practice Policies and Procedures Manual

Appointment Scheduling

When the doctor is in the office and running more than _____ minutes late:
• Notify patients already in reception area and those arriving:

Suggest opportunity to reschedule? ❑ Yes ❑ No
• Call patients not yet at office? ❑ Yes ❑ No

When calling suggest opportunity to reschedule? ❑ Yes ❑ No

When the doctor is in the office and running more than _____ minutes late:
• Notify patients already in reception area and those arriving:

Suggest opportunity to reschedule? ❑ Yes ❑ No

If doctor is delayed at hospital, ER, nursing home, or other location:
• Notify patients already in reception area and those arriving:

Suggest opportunity to reschedule? ❑ Yes ❑ No
• Call patients not yet at office? ❑ Yes ❑ No

When calling suggest opportunity to reschedule? ❑ Yes ❑ No

Patients calling to cancel appointments should be asked the following questions:

_____
_____
_____

Be sure to document in chart and appointment book.

Call patients on *early call-in*—those scheduled later in the week who might like to come in earlier.

Instruction/statements to callers who have previously been a *no-show:*

_____
_____

Instructions/statements to patients being *worked-in:*

_____
_____

FIGURE 14-1   Sample Policy: Appointment Scheduling

Office policy on non-emergency *drop-ins:*

_____

_____

Policy for when more than one family member hopes to be seen in an appointment time
reserved for just one:

_____

_____

Office policy for patients arriving more than _____ minutes late:

_____

_____

Office policy for patients arriving early:

_____

_____

Office policy to follow when pharmaceutical sales representatives arrive without an
appointment:

_____

_____

Source: ©1993 AMA Financing & Practice Services, Inc

FIGURE 14-1   Sample Policy: Appointment Scheduling (*continued*)

Conclusion

For a myriad of reasons, every practice must have policies and procedures in place for "how we do that here." Some of the issues to be
addressed are efficiency, structure, and liability. Many of the ways your
practice does things will change as the staff grows and the practice
builds its patient base. Written policies and procedures are essential
for training and holding the staff accountable for the delivery of quality
patient care.

15

Marketing and Business Development Considerations

A rapidly changing health care environment is challenging physicians to adopt strategies to attract new patients, maintain the loyalties of existing patients, and do it in a cost effective manner. One vital strategy is effective marketing. If the term *marketing* is a concern or it contains negative connotations, think of these strategies as building or expanding the practice.

Practice Building Guidelines for the Future

With any marketing effort, developing guidelines is important. Clarify your thoughts and plans on paper and follow these suggestions:

- **Define your objectives.** Define these for the short term (less than one year); then define them for the long term (more than one year). Express them in a way that they can be quantified and tracked so that progress can be noted and successes and failures can be measured.

- **Be realistic.** Practically all professionals automatically say, "I'd like to double my practice." It is not that simple! Determine how much time and energy can be spent to achieve that goal. To play conservatively, figure that the budget must amount to 20 percent to 33 percent of the targeted increase in income to generate an equally conservative 33 percent to 50 percent in revenue.

- **Remember cash flow.** Many strategies call for 50 percent to 75 percent of the marketing budget to be spent in the beginning stages of marketing development. This usually means that the first large sum of cash needs to be in the bank at the start of the program, so it cannot come out of unexpected cash flow.

- **Identify the target groups.** Define the groups that the practice is trying to reach. Describe the target populations by the chief characteristics of age, sex, location, educational level, income, ethnicity/religion, blue-collar workers versus white-collar workers, and lifestyle. Choose only those factors that are most important, usually income, education, sex, age, and location. If business is targeted, describe it by industry, industry position, yearly sales, number of employees, and location.

- **Create a different, one-page marketing plan for each target.** For example, set up separate plans for other practitioners from whom to generate referrals, senior citizens, blue-collar workers, 18- to 34-year-old females, and so on. Then rank those groups, targeting the easiest first.

- **Define what the target groups want.** What are the characteristics most important to the target group in selecting a physician? Is it experience, hours, location, price? What will make each group need/want to visit you? What do you offer that they cannot do without?

- **Define the physician.** Strengths? Weaknesses? What is different or special about what you offer? Identify your unique, defining characteristics: education, expertise, years of experience, credentials. What does the practice offer in terms of location, hours, pricing, and special equipment?

- **Analyze the main competitors.** Analyze your competitors with whom the practice will compete in the service area. Do not ignore the indirect competitors outside the profession to whom prospects could turn as a substitute, such as chiropractors, podiatrists, or psychologists. Chart each competitor's strengths and weaknesses.

- **How to compete.** How does the practice rate against those main competitors? Where can the practice best compete? List primary points, then secondary points. Can the targets be serviced well, or is the practice going too far outside its area of expertise? Assume you have good, solid experience, but that a competitor has more. If that competitor does not promote experience and the practice does, the practice will have the reputation for experience with the public. The same is true for any other advantage.

- **Determine the budget.** How much can the practice afford now? Reconcile the budget with the goals, realizing that you may have to scale back on your original plan.

- **Choose a strategy.** Should it be internal promotion? Website? Direct mail? Newspapers? Public relations? Seminars? Is this strategy the most effective one? Weigh the pros and cons of various vehicles against each other.

- **Choose the timing.** List events, both external and internal, that will affect the campaign over the period that has been specified. Choose the time of year, which months, and what week to take action. If the practice has seasonal peaks, promote heavily upon entering those busier periods, not during the practice lows. Dollars and efforts must work a lot harder in low periods when prospects are not already looking for services.

- **Plan the execution.** Assign responsibilities. Set a schedule with deadlines for all steps on a master time line.

Developing Marketing Strategies

The strategies that are employed to attract new patients are generally very tangible, such as direct mail, online advertisements, or those placed in a newspaper. These are called external marketing strategies. Internal strategies are directed toward retaining the patient base, building trust, and increasing loyalty through subliminal, yet deliberate, activities. The physician and staff accomplish these through friendliness and efficiency, expressed by communication and concern. This chapter provides some suggestions on both internal and external marketing strategies.

The Marketing Budget

As the first year's operational budget is established, include a specific amount for marketing expenses. Establishing a marketing budget is an extremely important step in the development of the practice's promotional efforts. There are many ways to advance your practice, and every method has its costs. Do not think of your budget as an expense, rather as an investment in the success of your practice. If you do not expend the necessary time and money, you may suffer the consequences in loss of patients to the competition.

Obtain quotes on the development and printing of a practice brochure, appointment and business cards, letterhead, other stationery, and educational materials. Also obtain pricing on website development, unless you intend to create this yourself (refer to the Website Development section of this chapter for more information). Factor these costs into the first year's budget and include the costs of any other marketing expense you might have such as newspaper announcements, direct mail marketing campaign, or an online advertisement on a variety of websites (eg, metro area newspaper websites, etc).

The Marketing Plan

Just as you have planned for the furniture and equipment needs in starting your practice, you will want to establish a marketing plan. The plan need not be complicated or formal, but it is imperative that it is thought out, easy to follow, and committed to paper. Share this plan with your staff. They will become an integral part of your marketing efforts.

Four months before opening

- Check sources such as The Welcome Wagon (www.welcomewagon .com) and groups that present information to new residents. Supply handout items for their distribution; items might include refrigerator magnets with the contact information of your practice or other promotional items that provide your address, contact information, and website.

- Set up a system to track how patients are referred to the practice. One method is to use a referral log, a simple grid that lists the various sources of referral. Referrals come from various sources (eg, your website, online web searches, local Chamber of Commerce offices, a presentation made at a civic group, another physician or patient, etc). Always ask patients the name of the patient, physician, or other individual who referred him or her to you. As a nice touch, send a thank-you note to that person.

- Attend meetings and join civic or business networking groups that will enhance your presence in the community. Consider joining and advertising with your local Chamber of Commerce office, as they receive numerous calls from newly relocated individuals looking for places to do business. If you have children in the local school system, join the Parent Teacher Association. Offer to speak to these organizations on medical topics. Tell the Medical Staff Secretary at your hospital(s) that you are available for public speaking engagements.

- Check with local hospitals to see if these institutions have planned health fairs or health screenings in the future. Offer to participate.

Three months before opening

- Develop a practice brochure. An attractive, well-prepared brochure provides your patients with all the information they need about the practice. Include a short paragraph about yourself, your specialty, and your education. Add a professional photograph. If the budget does not permit a professionally prepared brochure, use computer software and a laser printer to print information about your practice. (See the Brochure Contents section in this chapter for an outline of a practice brochure.)

Two months before opening

■ Design and place an order for announcement cards to send to local physicians and other health care professionals. You can opt to purchase a distribution list of local addresses from a direct mail marketing company to send to prospective patients as well. In either case, these announcements should clearly show your name, specialty, address, website, and telephone number; mail a minimum of two weeks before opening.

■ Order stationery, business cards, and appointment cards with the letterhead and logo if one has been developed. Order only small amounts to begin. Changes may need to be made later.

One month before opening

■ Order patient education materials for the practice. Use a rubber stamp to imprint your name, address, phone number, and website on the front of every piece of educational information that is handed out or placed in the waiting room. Placing laser-printed labels with the same information on your materials is an alternative to consider. This information may find its way to another potential patient.

■ Consider enrolling with an email distribution company to send announcements, monthly newsletters, health tips, etc. Staying in constant contact with your patients will put you in the forefront of their minds when a need arises. Email is tremendously important to consumers—over 45% of all consumers (patients) rate it of higher importance than postal mail or the phone – even among seniors and older adults. Over 70% of all age groups are using email more and more each year.[1]

■ Visit the hospital(s) where you will be on staff. Introduce yourself to the department heads and nursing staff.

■ If you are providing treatment for work injuries, rehabilitation, or other occupationally related services, visit employers in the area; introduce yourself and the services you provide. Take copies of your practice brochure and your business cards. Meet with the person responsible for overseeing treatment of workers' compensation injuries and the benefits coordinator.

■ Join state and local medical societies as appropriate, attend meetings and introduce yourself to possible referral sources.

Two weeks before opening day

■ Draft an advertisement that includes your name, address, telephone number, and website address. It should define and briefly describe your specialty and services that will be offered. Also, indicate the hours of operation. Prior to publishing, check your state's medical board to ensure consistency with its advertising policy. Submit your advertisement for placement in the local newspaper and run the ad online on the newspaper's website.

- Meet with your staff to share the marketing plan and ask for ideas. Patients who call for an appointment will want to know a little about you. Tell your staff about yourself so they can discuss your credentials with potential patients. Explaining to your staff the types of services provided by your specialty is also helpful. Keep in mind that your staff is marketing the practice's services to patients as well. If necessary, hand out copies of your curriculum vitae to your staff for further reference.

- Conduct office staff training on telephone communications to patients and referring physicians. If you receive a referral from a physician you have not previously met, it is a good idea to speak to that physician yourself. Put these protocols in writing and make them a part of the policies and procedures manual. Tell your staff how much time is needed for specific types of appointments. Relationship building is a powerful marketing tool that is often overlooked, so allow extra time for patients' first visits to discuss their needs.

Website Development

In today's market, practices that offer their patients quick and easy access to information will have an advantage over their competition; developing and maintaining a website provides this access. There are several advantages to creating a website for your practice including increased visibility to prospective patients, enhanced patient services (ie, contact information or patient forms available for download), and better overall practice image. An effective, well-planned website does not have to be expensive, but it does need to contain crucial pieces of information.

- Patients want the ability to visit your website and easily find contact information, such as your address and directions to your office, phone number, and hours of operation. Make sure this is in plain view on the homepage, not hidden at the bottom of the page or elsewhere. Consider including a picture of your building to help visitors recognize your location.

- Internet searches could likely land a potential patient on your doorstep. Make sure to include an About Us section. Imagine you were talking to a potential patient: how would you describe your practice and offerings? Most likely, you would use simple, direct language. Use the same approach on your website. Introduce the providers in your practice and include a picture and a short description of their backgrounds. If desired, include expanded information about specific procedures or services performed.

- Make the patient visit smoother and shorter by making necessary patient forms available for download. For example, you may want to include new patient registration forms, pre-examination questionnaires, pre- or post-operative instructions, or other helpful information.

- If your practice participates in social media outlets, such as Facebook, Twitter, LinkedIn, or other sites, make the appropriate icons visible and link them to the correct landing page.

Once you have collected this information, you are ready to build the website. Several options are available. You can hire an advertising or web development firm; make sure you receive several quotes and do not hesitate to negotiate. A less expensive option is to find a do-it-yourself web-development website. Performing a Google search with the parameters "create a website" will display numerous options that are as low as $9.95 per month[2] to maintain. Regardless of the tactic you choose to build your practice website, keep in mind that it is an extension of your business and should be well planned and maintained.

Advertising

Like all aspects of business, advertising trends change over time. In years past, advertising in the printed telephone business directory was a cost effective means to attract new patients. While this method may still be effective in smaller, rural communities or even for tight budgets, the fact is that advertising trends have changed. Today, most information is obtained via the Internet. Statistics reveal that the number of people in the United States that search for information they need online will reach nearly 80% of the population by 2014.[3] There are many places to investigate when looking into placing an online ad. *Yellow Pages* now offers online advertising,[4] as do local newspaper websites. In some cases, one price will provide both a print and an online advertisement. When choosing the appropriate venue to advertise, keep in mind your marketing budget. For instance, if online advertising does not fit into your budget, do not rule out advertising as a whole; rather, be wise in selecting highly visible areas that fit your budget. Proper research will ensure you get the most out of every dollar spent.

Before designing an ad (whether for online or for print), evaluate what other colleagues and competitors are doing. Then browse other ads to compare styles, design, size, and text. What makes the ad stand out from the rest? Which ads are more attractive? The goal is to make the practice's ad unique and to grab the individual's attention. Achieving this without discrediting the practice with a cluttered distasteful ad is very important.

The following checklist will help the practice create an effective, powerful, and attractive advertisement.

- Are the practice's name, specialty, location, and telephone number the most prominent elements in the ad?
- Has the name of the practice been included with the name(s) of the physician(s) in the practice?
- Have any special qualifications such as board certification been included?
- Are area locators, such as cross streets or building names, mentioned with the listing of the office address? For online ads, Google maps may be useful.
- Have all extended hours been listed?
- Have all special services been included?
- If the practice has a logo or slogan, was it included in the ad?
- Have the ad sizes for competitors been reviewed to determine an appropriate-sized ad for the practice?
- Should boldface type be used to call attention to the ad?
- Does the chosen typeface correspond to the character of the practice?
- Does the ad reflect the image that the practice hopes to project?
- Is the ad clear, concise, and professional in appearance?

Creating a Medical Practice Brochure

A practice brochure creates many marketing opportunities. It provides an image of the practice to current and prospective patients and referral sources. The brochure provides a quick overview about available services, office policies, practice philosophy, and easy-to-locate contact information. It also saves staff time by addressing repetitive questions, such as where the physician has hospital privileges or how insurance is billed. The brochure will serve as a compact reference about the practice that can be left in numerous locations for potential patients to pick up.

How to Create a Brochure

The best resources for creating a brochure are colleagues and other professional businesses. To obtain ideas, collect samples of attractive brochures from a variety of businesses. Using an Internet search engine will provide a vast array of brochure ideas. Free or inexpensive templates can be found online. A typical brochure has six to eight panels of information and its folded dimensions are 3½" × 8½". If you prefer a larger option, consider a brochure with folded dimensions of 8.5" x 6". Write the copy or hire a professional to help with the writing. The goal of the brochure is to clarify practice policies, written in language that is clear, concise, and easy to understand. Make sure to use a design that is professional and uncluttered.

Brochure Contents

The practice brochure should contain the following information:

- **Introduction to the practice.** Begin by including the name, address, telephone number, and website of the practice. Provide a brief history of the practice and state the patient care and philosophy.

- **Professional profile of the physician(s).** Introduce each physician in the practice and include details on training, board certification, areas of special interest, and personal information. For example, "Dr. Doe is married and has two school-aged children," or "Dr. Smith enjoys working in underserved countries one month each year." Include a professional picture of each physician to help patients with name and face recognition.

- **Explanation of specialty.** Quite frequently, physicians and their staffs are not aware that patients do not know or understand a physician's specialty and the part of the anatomy to which it pertains. They assume that once a patient gets as far as the reception room, the patient has a thorough understanding of why he or she is there. To educate the patient about the practice, include a description, in simple terms, of the practice specialty and the special services and procedures that can be provided. The more informed a patient is before the visit, the more confidence he or she has in the care that is received.

- **Office policies.** One primary objective of a practice brochure is to educate and inform patients about practice policies. It serves as a reference and reminder to established patients and provides guidelines and standards for new patients before incurring services.

Key areas to highlight include:

- **Office hours.** This is especially critical if appointment times are beyond the typical practice hours (ie, evening, Saturday hours). Stating office hours will also reduce after-hours calls to the answering service and consequently reduce overhead expenses.

- **How to schedule and cancel appointments.** If patients are asked to use a different telephone number for scheduling appointments, publicize it. If there are a lot of no-show patients, it is very important to establish and state the policy that will discourage this and encourage compliance. Charging $25 for a no-show or a late cancellation (within 24 hours of scheduled appointment) is customary for practices. If a patient abuses either policy three times, he or she should receive a letter discharging him or her from care within a reasonable period (ie, 30 days). To protect the practice, send the letter via certified mail, return receipt requested. You can also send this message via e-mail and use a read receipt to indicate the message has been received and read. Print these emails and place in the patient's file for record keeping.

■ **Hospital affiliations.** The insurance industry may influence a patient's selection of both a hospital and a physician. Therefore, including hospital affiliations in the practice brochure is important.

■ **Financial policies.** Generally, the most frequently asked questions pertain to the practice's financial policies. Document these policies in the brochure to inform patients about their financial responsibility. Include the forms of accepted payment (ie, cash, check, and credit card; note which cards you accept). Most practices follow the policy that they expect payment when they render services unless the patient makes other arrangements. This policy should be stated.

Identify the insurance plans in which the practice participates. Also state whether the practice accepts Medicare assignment and/or Medicaid and TRICARE. Include billing information, such as when the patient should expect to receive a statement, and so forth. Be sure to include the telephone number to call regarding billing questions.

■ **Special services.** Health care consumers will look for practices that offer one-stop shopping. List all services that the practice offers, such as laboratory and radiology services. Also list special procedures or testing that is offered (eg, infertility tests, nutrition counseling, pain management, etc).

■ **Telephone calls.** If the practice has an established office policy regarding prescription refills, print it in the brochure. Patients need to know how to handle routine prescription refills. Informing them of the policy makes the office more efficient and responsive to the patient's requests.

Notifying patients that an answering service will respond to calls after normal office hours is important. Patients appreciate knowing a voice is always on the other end of the line, and that the physician will get their message. Consider printing the answering service telephone number for the rare occasion the office forgets to sign off to the service after hours. Printing the physician's cell phone or pager number is not advisable.

- **Map of office location.** Including a map of the office location is as important as printing the name and telephone number of the practice. The map should include landmarks, such as a hospital, a lake, a park, or something with which the patient may be familiar. If the office is close to the hospital, it adds a competitive marketing edge. It is to the physician's benefit to include this information.

Building Patient Satisfaction

The most important component to building patient satisfaction is a customer service-oriented attitude that extends to each aspect of patient and practice interaction. Physicians and their practice staff need to know how patients want to be treated. Although high quality care should be the ultimate goal, providers have little chance of realizing that without retaining a steady patient base.

Satisfied patients are more likely to:

- Remain with a physician
- Refer others to a physician
- Follow physician orders
- Pay bills on time
- Refrain from filing malpractice suits

Alternatively, dissatisfied patients:

- Will leave a practice because of an attitude of indifference by staff
- Will tell multiple people about their negative experience
- Will complain most frequently about poor communication
- Frequently just leave a practice without even bothering to voice their displeasure
- Will continue with a physician as a patient if a complaint is resolved in their favor

So, what does it take to provide the kind of customer service that results in attracting, retaining, and satisfying patients? This section will examine five key components that patients consider as important as having a physician who is technically competent:

- Attentiveness and good communication
- Appointment scheduling
- Attractive offices
- Appropriate follow-up
- Amiable and skilled staff

Attentiveness and Good Communication

Attracting and retaining patients can be as simple as making every patient feel comfortable and appreciated and providing a personal touch to patient relationships. Yet, patients often complain that their physician does not give them enough time and the medical office staff does not listen to their questions and concerns. A starting point in positive patient attentiveness and communication is to improve listening skills, because poor listening is a strong precursor to poor performance. Keys to good listening in any patient interaction are:

- Focus on what the patient is saying while listening for key facts and feelings.

- Acknowledge what has been heard and ask questions for clarification.

- Respond to the patient clearly, specifically, and empathetically.

Be as positive as possible in all communication with patients. The emphasis should be on what can be accomplished rather that what cannot be done. For example, instead of, "We can't refill your prescription without a doctor's appointment," try, "We will be happy to refill that medication. The doctor will want to see you first, so when is a good time to come in?" This type of language demonstrates a caring desire to serve and a team mentality.

Bring some personality and warmth to all patient encounters. Enter the exam room prepared by taking a moment to review the chart. Use the patient's name and have an understanding of the reason for their visit. Make sure to jot down personal notes in the chart to have an icebreaker for the next visit. Instead of rushing through the visit, start the encounter by taking a moment to chat about the weather or their family, or something that will make a personal connection. Communicate that you are going to work together as a team to resolve their concerns.

Saying the correct things efficiently but with an attitude of indifference will not leave a patient satisfied and wanting to return; however, showing a sincere caring attitude will result in contented, loyal patients. Skills can be taught; attitude has to come from within.[5]

Appointment Scheduling

Since appointment timeliness is so important to patient satisfaction and retention, physicians are encouraged to be punctual and attentive to the appointment schedule. A patient's time is valuable, too. Patients waiting ten or fewer minutes rate their satisfaction as "good" to "very good."[6] Since occasional delays are unavoidable no matter how efficiently a practice is run, make a habit of explaining all delays, giving patients the opportunity to reschedule if they desire. Acknowledge and apologize for the wait when the patient is called from the waiting room. The frustration of delays may be mitigated if patients have something to do in a waiting room. Some practices have jigsaw puzzle tables, crossword puzzle books, electric massage chairs, computers, and current magazines that appeal to the patient base. Be creative!

In order to ensure timeliness, a physician practice may need to see fewer patients, lengthen appointment times, factor in gaps to allow for following up with emergencies, add a mid-level provider to assist with overload, or assess practice operations to identify the root cause of delays. Surveys show that patient satisfaction directly correlates to the amount of time the physician spends with a patient; therefore, make sure that the schedule allows adequate time with each patient. Show patients respect by valuing their time.

Attractive Offices

Ensure that external and internal signage makes it easy for patients to locate the practice office and the exterior landscaping and painting showcase a well-maintained facility. Initial curb appeal should make an excellent first impression.

Create a pleasant reception area by providing a tastefully decorated living room effect. Use table lamps rather than fluorescent lighting. Plants should be alive and healthy. Play easy-listening music or tune in to a non-confrontational television show. Make sure the front desk is inviting and free of clutter. As the patient walks from the waiting room to the exam room, they should see an orderly clean office. Exam rooms and restrooms should be clean and odor free. Dispensers of antibacterial gel should be available, especially during flu season.

Patients will feel much more positive about returning to the practice if they have encountered a warm welcoming environment.

Appropriate Follow-Up

Start the follow-up process by sending a welcome letter to patients after they have made their initial appointment. Thank them and enclose a practice brochure.

Between office visits, patients expect to receive prompt callbacks for lab results or questions and concerns that they may have. Policies should be established designating the number of days for lab results to be forwarded, the number of hours for message callbacks to be completed, and the expectation that prescription refills will be completed the same day as requested. Make patients aware of the practice policies in order to manage their expectations. Keeping track of patient needs once they leave the office can seem to be a daunting task, but developing a system to track prescription requests, out-of-office concerns, and referrals will enable the physician's practice to ensure that each patient receives a complete cycle of care. Providing educational material can help patients become better informed so that they are empowered to assume some ownership in assisting with their healing process.

When an office visit is completed, request that every patient take a simple satisfaction survey. This can easily be done at checkout. Many practices have a computer at the checkout station for capturing responses quickly; paper copies should be available for patients who are not as electronically adept. A four point rating scale, such as "Needs Improvement," "Satisfactory," "Above Average," and "Excellent" can be used to gauge patient satisfaction and areas where improvement is needed. Figure 15-1 is a sample patient satisfaction survey. Key issues to assess include:

- Ease of securing an appointment
- Wait time after arrival
- Telephone accessibility of office
- Promptness of requested return calls and receipt of test results
- Courtesy of front desk personnel
- Courtesy of medical staff
- Helpfulness of the appointment

In lieu of satisfaction surveys, some practices hold informal focus groups several times a year with a sampling of their patients. When asked what can be done to improve their experience with the practice, these patients are able to offer helpful feedback and even solutions. Monitoring patient satisfaction is an ongoing process that is never complete.

Amiable and Skilled Staff

The Ritz Carlton Hotel Company, known for quality customer service, trains employees using a simple three-step process.[7]

1. Greet each customer using his or her name.
2. Meet the customer's needs.
3. Wish the customer a warm farewell and use their name again.

Personal Information (Optional)

Name _____   Male/Female   Age _____

Please circle the physician you saw today:

Belle C, M.D.	Mallory C, M.D.	Jackson G, M.D.
Jake T, M.D.	Ella G, M.D.	Beau H, M.D.

Please check the response that indicates how well you think we are doing in the following areas:	GREAT 4	GOOD 3	OK 2	POOR 1
Scheduling your appointment				
Was the staff member who scheduled your appointment courteous and helpful?				
Was the time between your call and your scheduled appointment satisfactory?				
When you checked in/out for your appointment				
Were the patient services specialists at the front desk and check out courteous?				
Did you find the waiting and exam rooms comfortable and clean?				
Did the physician see you at your appointment time?				
Medical care staff				
Was the nursing staff courteous, friendly, and caring?				
Were you treated with dignity and respect?				
Physician				
How would you rate the clarity of the physician's explanation of your condition and treatment options?				
Was the physician courteous, sensitive, and personable?				
Follow-up				
Was your follow-up appointment or procedure scheduled at a time that was convenient for you?				
Did you receive your results in a timely manner?				
Overall				
How would you rate your overall experience?				
Would you return to this facility in the future?				
Would you recommend this physician?				

Additional Feedback:

FIGURE 15-1   ABC Medical Practice: Patient Satisfaction Survey

Medical practice staff trained to follow these three steps will be positive advocates for the practice and will be the front-runners for satisfying patients and building loyalty.

Greet Each Customer (Patient) Using His or Her Name

Expect staff to acknowledge patients immediately upon arrival with courtesy, making eye contact, and using a pleasant expression and tone of voice. When talking with patients and other employees, they should use words that express respect, patience, and understanding. Each staff member and physician should have visible identification and introduce themselves by name and title when first meeting a patient.

If patients have been adequately prepared before they enter the practice, the practice has a head start on making a positive first impression. Forms that need to be filled out should be available on the practice website or offered by mail to ensure that patients have the information needed before they arrive. This will lessen the stress of having to hurry and complete daunting amounts of paperwork. A well-designed website can also be a source of reassurance to patients because they have the opportunity to familiarize themselves with the practice and physician prior to their visit.

Remember that patients arriving at the practice may be ill, worried about their health, or concerned about time they are missing from work. The calm, caring demeanor of staff members with whom they have initial contact makes an excellent first impression.

Meet the Customer's (Patient's) Needs

Like any other business, physicians and staff should treat patients like the valued paying customers they are and reflect that mindset throughout the entire patient experience. Take the time to find and hire staff determined to meet patient needs regardless of the extra work involved, and the practice will have no problem attracting and retaining patients. Find out what patients want and train staff to deliver it.

Physicians set the tone for practice operations. Staff will observe the physicians' attitudes toward patient service and follow that lead. High patient satisfaction cannot be achieved when staff is unhappy; patients easily detect a dysfunctional atmosphere fostered by quarreling, dissatisfied employees. The actions and attitudes of the lowest paid employee could have considerable financial repercussions on the entire practice, and even on physician income. When a patient calls, the person who answers the telephone is their first contact with the practice, so it is essential that person is courteous, helpful, and well informed. The telephone needs to be answered quickly and cheerfully. Staff members should identify themselves by name. They should be knowledgeable and equipped with staff member extensions, practice policies, and a triage matrix that delineates who handles what, when to transfer, etc.

Office conversation should be carefully monitored. Personal conversations, discussions about employees, office politics, and other patients should never be overheard in public areas. Empower staff by giving them the autonomy they need to do their jobs. Let them suggest policies, procedures, and solutions to problems. Hold educational sessions to give them the tools needed to make each patient visit memorable. If there is a sincere desire to take care of patients, physicians and staff will do whatever is needed to make that happen.

Wish the Customer (Patient) a Fond Farewell and Use Their Name Again

Customers/patients will remember the first and last minutes of their visit more vividly than anything else; thus, the staff member who checks out the patient must make a lasting warm impression and leave them with the feeling they are leaving friends who care about them.

Building true customer loyalty by determining to offer the best possible customer service is one of the ultimate drivers of enduring business/practice growth. Happy patients are likely to come back and recommend others to the practice.

Conclusion

Building a medical practice takes a concerted effort and careful planning. Typically, in the early stages of practice start up, marketing funds are limited. Be sure to spend all marketing dollars wisely and appropriately in the area and specialty. If help is needed, get assistance from a reliable and experienced health care consultant who can keep the practice focused on initiatives that are most likely to be beneficial. Further, practice building encompasses every aspect of customer service to achieve patient satisfaction. Staff training and investment in delivering caring attention to the patient will ensure patient retention and continual build up of the patient base.

References

1. Marketing Sherpa. *Email Marketing Benchmark Guide 2008*. www.market ingsherpa.com. Accessed June 9, 2011.

2. BuildYourSite.com. www.buildyoursite.com/website-builder.php?gclid=CJins qfm5agCFaNl7AodLHhbFg. Accessed May 13, 2011.

3. New Media Trend Watch. www.newmediatrendwatch.com/markets-by-country/17-usa/123-demographics. Accessed August 4, 2011.

4. Yellow Pages. www.yellowpages.com.

5. Deming, Vasudha. What Customer Service Skills Are Most Valuable? www.impactlearning.com/what-customer-service-skills-are-most-valuable. Accessed June 1, 2011.

6. Johnson, Lee J, JD. *Foster Good Patient Relations by Minimizing Wait Times.* www.modernmedicine.com/modernmedicine/Modern+Medicine+Now/ Foster-good-patient-relations-by-minimizing-wait-t/ArticleStandard/Article/ detail/678693. Accessed June 1, 2011

7. Smith, Gregory P. *Customer Service Is Not a Four-Letter Word. Manager Wise.* www.managerwise.com/article.phtml?id=483. Accessed June 1, 2011.

PART THREE

Trends and Strategies for the Future

Chapters 16 through 20 address ongoing trends and upcoming changes that every practicing physician needs to know to survive and thrive in the dramatic evolution of health care delivery. Topics in this section include physician alignment strategies, practice acquisition, structuring equity, physician diversification, practice mergers, and review of the planning process.

CHAPTER

Physician Alignment Strategies

Although physicians and hospitals have worked together for years, their roles have been somewhat competitive. Competition has increased in recent years as many physician practices have expanded their services into competitive diagnostic testing, surgical and other procedural services. Physician-hospital integration occurred at a record pace in the 1990s, only to be halted (abruptly, in many instances), even entailing separation of that integrated relationship through hospital divestiture. Entering the second decade of the 21st century, physician-hospital integration (now termed "alignment") is prominent again. Although many of the structures look very similar to earlier models, alignment is a broader term and encompasses more than employment (though employment is a major part).

One major driver of alignment is the likelihood of a changing payment structure. CMS (and specifically, Medicare) have already started this process through its accountable care structure, which is set to become a reality in 2012 and years following. While the debate runs rampant as to whether accountable care organizations (ACOs) will in fact become the standard for health care delivery, it is undeniably true that the providers, primarily physicians, and hospitals, will have to adapt to a changing system for measuring and quantifying payment. That system, largely based upon shared savings, reduced costs and demonstrated quality, will continue to drive more and more physician/hospital integration. This chapter explores various alternatives to alignment, considering the models that are being applied, and reviewing the pros and cons of each.

Drivers of Alignment

Hospitals and physicians are continuing to integrate, working within various alignment scenarios, for many reasons. Currently, the most prominent reasons include:

- Private practice profits and physician incomes are declining
- Physicians prefer a greater quality of life (prefer to work fewer hours with more predictable income)
- Physician supply shortages, especially in primary care
- A new attitude among physicians and hospitals, allowing physicians to maintain greater control
- Limited forms of alignment, realizing moderate success
- Legitimate ability to increase physician compensation
- Ability to improve physician recruitment and retention success
- Cost savings through some economies of scale in expense and asset purchase controls
- Increasing malpractice insurance cost and ability to leverage that through partnering with a larger organization
- Responding to an apparent changing payment paradigm through ACOs, patient-centered medical homes, and related entities

These are all viable possibilities/realities that are promoting the overall alignment models between hospitals and physicians. Although economic reasons may be a major factor, it is not just about economics; it transcends to the physician's desire for a better quality of life within their professional careers and personal lives and the reality that payment is being structured more and more toward a single bundled payment, meaning that physicians and hospitals will receive one payment from the government and/or commercial payers.

Alignment Challenges

Alignment initiatives still have many challenges as physicians and hospitals do not always see eye to eye in the way they manage, operate, and administer the physician practice. It remains very true that hospitals and physician practices operate very differently. In fact one of the major reasons the integration efforts of the 1990s failed was that hospitals forced physician practices to be managed and administered similar to a hospital department—not a physician practice. Indeed, the two are very different, particularly in the following areas:

- Culture
- Operations
- Autonomy and control
- Trust
- Competition
- Revenue sharing

There are cultural differences, for example, that must be handled somewhat differently as hospitals are much more bureaucratic and regimented in their day-to-day structures. Physicians typically still run their practice as a small business, whereas many hospitals/health systems are multimillion/multibillion dollar entities. Yet the two have to work together to become a congruent entity relative to those very different cultures.

From an operational standpoint, this also has to be considered. Hospitals typically work as designated departmental/service line entities, and this simply does not apply (unless it is perhaps a multispecialty group) for medical practices. Thus, operations have to be clearly defined and structured for hospitals to realize the opportunities possible through their management and ownership of physician practices.

Another challenge with alignment is issues of autonomy and control. Loss of physician ownership, especially when the physicians are accustomed to making all their decisions, is a major obstacle to overcome within any alignment strategy, especially full alignment. Physicians who desire less responsibility from day-to-day practice management and other areas of running their businesses may be more willing to give up control. But even these individuals at times find the situation challenging. Although in alignment physicians usually maintain some control over their clinical decision making, much can change relative to daily business and administrative decisions. Governance and leadership issues, therefore, are a major challenge within alignment structures, especially those that involve full alignment (ie, employment or something close to employment).

In addition, for years hospitals and physicians have experienced a huge obstacle relative to trust. Lack of trust is a major challenge no matter what the alignment effort. A lot of baggage may exist due to past experiences. Moreover, many physician groups have in fact become competitors of hospitals for ancillary services such as ambulatory surgery centers and diagnostic testing. This is a tough issue to overcome, especially as hospitals continue to experience tighter margins. Efforts must be made to establish trust between hospitals and physicians; without at least some level of confidence that the partners will come through and do what they say they will do, the alignment structure will likely fail.

Competition is also a challenge. Physicians resist giving up their ancillary services, although in many instances, payment is much better under a hospital-owned entity in terms of managed care contracting with commercial payers, and even more often is the case with Medicare payment through hospital outpatient department rates. Physicians and hospitals must overcome the attitude of the two entities being competitors as opposed to partners.

Yet another challenge to alignment is the concept of sharing revenue. As accountable care becomes more the norm, Medicare (and perhaps many commercial insurers) will likely limit the level of payment on every procedure, encounter, and overall charge. In fact, much discussion centers on the fact that the ultimate payment methodology will be bundled wherein both the physician (ie, professional) and the hospital (ie, technical/facility/hospital charges) will be blended together. Getting used to some form of shared revenue will be a challenge, as is now evident within many alignment structures.

In summary, the challenges relative to alignment are numerous, yet are possible to overcome—especially if the parties are willing to look at the win–win opportunities that alignment offers. This may be more common as alignment transactions become more standard.

Alignment Models

What are some of the actual alignment models between hospitals and physicians and what are their characteristics? First, the terms alignment and integration are fairly interchangeable. The forms (or models) of alignment can be classified as three major groups: *limited, moderate,* and *full alignment.* The choices are varied and hospitals and physicians have many options. While most groups use the full alignment model, the limited and moderate alternatives also are worthy of consideration. Further, there can be blends or hybrid models wherein certain limited or moderate forms of alignment are "wrapped around" the full forms of alignment, as explored here.

Limited Alignment Models

While these do not entail a great deal of integration/affiliation, they can be a good start toward hospitals and physicians working together. And in fact, from the physicians' standpoint, they can result in an economic as well as a non-economic value proposition.

Managed Care Networks

Managed care networks are, in the purest forms of alignment, a health care model in which a health plan contracts with more than one physician group or independent practice association (IPAs) and may contract with single and multispecialty groups that work out of their own office facilities. As the accountable care initiative unfolds, these networks are resurging in prominence as physicians seek ways to coordinate delivery of care to a group of patients. IPAs and/or physician/hospital organizations (PHOs) are the primary method wherein physicians collectively work with managed care organizations. Many PHOs and IPAs have been in existence for years, going back to the 1990s in a form of affiliation in which they provided a common base for physicians and hospitals to negotiate payment with commercial payers. While the Federal Trade Commission has challenged many of these entities for antitrust violations, and in fact has limited their ability to negotiate fee-for-service contracts unless the physician practices are clinically integrated, they still have some level of viability throughout the industry.

IPAs and PHOs are formed to promote the ability for the members (ie, hospitals and physicians) to jointly contract for payment. While clinical integration in and of itself is a major undertaking, some PHOs and IPAs have qualified to become clinically integrated. As such, they are free to negotiate fee-for-service contracts. Conversely, the majority of these entities have not become clinically integrated, yet they can have some value, especially when utilizing a messenger model for representing their constituencies in managed care contracting. A messenger model does not entail direct negotiation representation for payment. However, it does allow for the transmission of fee schedules to and from the managed care payer to the provider within the PHO/IPA entity. Thus, the IPA or PHO may facilitate individual negotiation, but not collectively bargain on behalf of the physician members. Many PHOs and IPAs perform other functions for their members, such as delegated credentialing, group purchasing, and facilitation of electronic medical records systems.

Although PHOs and IPAs have traditionally been limited in their ability to serve their basic purpose of fee negotiations, they are now starting to receive renewed interest through formation of a platform or foundation for accountable care organizations. Many entities believe that their IPAs or PHOs can be the conduit between various provider physician groups and the hospital to form an ACO. They are limited forms of alignment, nonetheless, and represent a limited or restricted ability to affiliate.

Call Coverage Stipends

Physicians are becoming more and more dissatisfied with the responsibilities they have for unassigned emergency department (ED) call. Traditionally, ED call was regarded as an avenue for practice building; it has quickly moved away from this as physicians largely encounter patients without insurance or with limited coverage. These patients often become no-pay patients.

Therefore, for the distinct privilege of covering the ED, physicians are no longer able to realize any significant payment or fees for their services. As a result, many physicians have informed hospitals that they can no longer provide call coverage without some form of compensation. The ways to compensate physicians for call vary and can apply to those that are employed (as in a fully aligned model). The key issue is whether the pay-for-call arrangement for physicians qualifies as a significant enough burden on that physician to justify some form of compensation.

Often, compensation is in the form of a daily stipend, but it also can be structured as a fee-for-service payment, meaning the physician is compensated (perhaps up to Medicare rates) but only for self-pay patients. Compensation of physicians in this context is regulated by Stark guidelines for hospitals and usually requires some justification based on fair market value calculations.

Pay for call can be a form of alignment between hospitals and physicians, albeit quite limited. Nevertheless, although pay for call can be rendered within the employment model, most hospitals believe the responsibilities and duties of call are implicit within the employment compensation arrangement.

Medical Directorships

Responsibilities for medical directorships have existed for many years. Roles and levels of responsibility varied in the past, but this is changing. As a limited form of alignment, physicians can be bonded to a hospital through directorship of a specific department or service of the hospital. For example, often a general surgeon is in charge of the hospital's wound care center which is a serious responsibility that requires ongoing clinical oversight. It justifies some form of compensation, usually in a fair market value (FMV) determined amount per hour worked. It may be a monthly or even annual stipend total largely contingent upon the amount of time actually worked.

Although medical directorships can be a major part of the overall alignment strategy, they are limited forms of alignment in that the physicians are not employed nor do they have long-term commitments to the hospitals.

Recruitment Guarantees

Hospitals have long helped physician practices (ie, private practices) recruit based upon demonstrated community need and community benefit requirements. The Stark laws have allowed for such recruitment support arrangements where the hospitals can supplement/subsidize the privately recruited physician's income and some other areas of support such as malpractice payments, school tuition payments, etc, as long as they are deemed within FMV. In the normal setting, this is structured as a loan that is forgiven over a specific subsequent period. The recruitment guarantee period is usually no more than two years and usually limited to one year—the initial 12 months that the physician is a part of the practice and ramping up productivity. While the physician is not obligated to work for the hospital—only obligated to remain within the defined service area—the normal relationship between the hospital and physician is such that that the provider remains active and loyal to the hospital. This is not a requirement; hence, this is a very limited form of alignment.

Moderate Alignment Models

More moderate alignment arrangements that entail greater integration are management services organizations, shared savings, quality incentives, joint ventures, and clinical co-management/service line management initiatives.

Management Services Organizations

Management services organizations, often referred to as MSOs, provide an opportunity for physicians and hospitals to work together. Typically, MSOs are entities that provide administrative oversight, which can encompass a range of services from revenue cycle management to personnel, accounting, human resources, and other functions. It can also take the form of an information services organization (ISO). An ISO is an entity that may be jointly formed as an alignment strategy to provide information technology support and assistance to private medical practices within the hospital's medical staff.

MSOs have a role in certain sectors to promote alignment/affiliation among hospitals and physicians. However, those formed as a partnership between physicians and hospitals are somewhat rare. Some private groups will form their own management companies and contract with hospital-employed physicians for management services. This is another form of moderate alignment in that it is an arms-length agreement between the hospital and the physician for management services, as the services must be charged at a FMV rate. This does allow for a moderate profit to the managing entity, yet not at a level that can be deemed, under Stark laws, as inurement or as purchasing referrals.

Shared Savings

Shared savings, also called gainsharing, are prominent parts of alignment strategies, and they will increase in importance as a component of accountable care and accountable care organization strategies. Shared savings programs are targeting specific areas wherein physicians within a particular service line or specialty work with the hospital to identify areas where expenses can be controlled. The shared savings concept also relates to the opportunity to develop a more streamlined delivery of care, which is at the core of health care reform.

Shared savings programs are difficult to quantify and are usually limited in life, meaning that once a specific initiative is identified for a shared savings program, it cannot be repeated year after year. Moreover, shared savings programs are often part of a larger co-management or service line management agreement (discussed below).

Quality Incentives

Quality initiatives as a joint effort are a way to attain a moderate level of hospital and physician alignment. The ability to recognize quality outcomes is a major part of health care reform. Compensating physicians, whether they are employed or contracted through a co-management or service line management agreement is a viable way to achieve moderate alignment. The anticipation that the government will continue to recognize greater amounts of compensation through demonstrated quality outcomes is a major motivator for these structures. Although the physician quality and reporting system (PQRS) (formerly PQRI or physician quality reporting initiative) has been in place for several years, it has not attained the amount of interest and enhanced payment that was hoped for in the future. Likewise, commercial payers, which have not largely participated in a pay-for-performance/quality performance pay program to this point, are anticipated to engage in payment for meeting quality thresholds in the future.

Joint Ventures

Joint ventures are a valid consideration within an overall alignment strategy, but they must be structured very carefully to assure a long-term positive working relationship (eg, fair and equitable terms and conditions between the hospital and physicians) and to meet regulatory requirements pertaining to joint ventures. Joint ventures can take on various structures and formations, such as MSOs and ISOs. Joint real estate ventures are very popular among physicians and hospitals.

Block leases are a part of the joint venture alternative. In these agreements, the lessee (usually physician surgeons) agree to rent a facility, such as an operating room, within an ambulatory surgery center (ASC), often with staffing and other support systems included for a defined period each week or month. During that defined period, the lessee will have virtually complete authority over the running of the facility, analogous to any other lease.

Joint ventures are subject to regulations and must be carefully structured to be in accord with current law. For example, the under arrangement joint venture ceased to be legal in 2009.

Clinical Co-Management/Service Line Management

As previously mentioned, clinical co-management and service line management arrangements are popular forms of moderate alignment wherein hospitals and physicians work together to establish the parameters for co-managing a complete service line. Figures 16-1 through 16-6 identify common forms of co-management agreements.

Clinical co-management entails specific clinical protocols and structures within a particular service line: for example, orthopedics. The

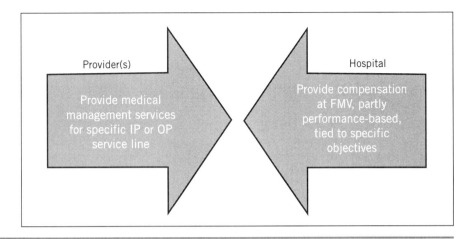

FIGURE 16-1   Service Line Co-Management Arrangement Description

FMV = Fair market value; IP = Inpatient; OP = Outpatient

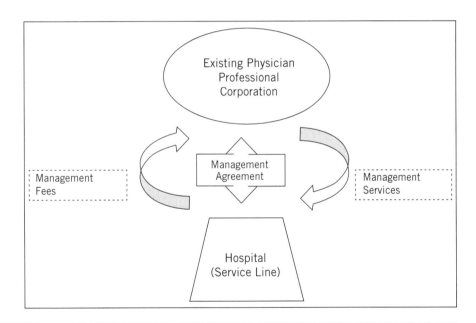

FIGURE 16-2   Co-Management: Model A

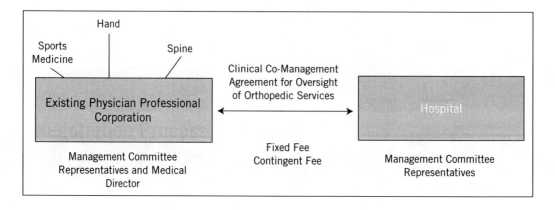

FIGURE 16-3   Example: Orthopedic Surgery

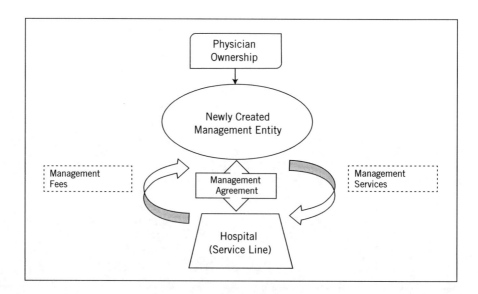

FIGURE 16-4   Co-Management: Model B

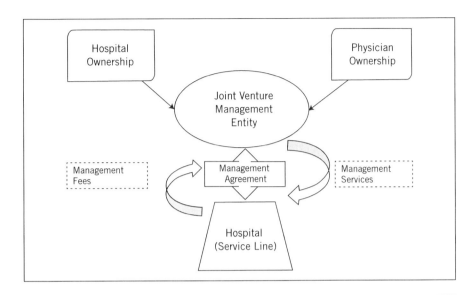

FIGURE 16-5   Co-Management: Model C

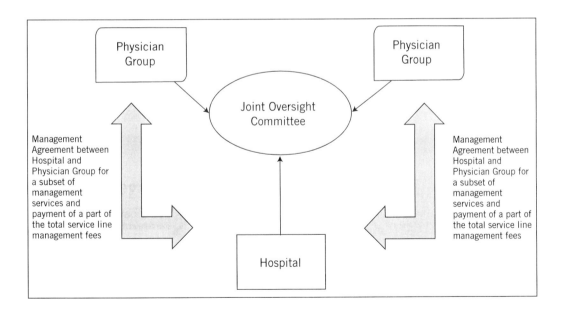

FIGURE 16-6   Co-Management: Model D

physicians can come from a varied number of practices, and whether the binding agreement between the hospital and physicians is a separately formed limited liability company (or some other legal entity) or simply a management agreement (or even potentially a joint venture), the relationship is formed within these alternatives.

Service line management is a slightly broader form of co-management in that it encompasses all services that the physicians within a particular specialty might provide within the hospital. The key is that these services are provided within the hospital—they are not practice or clinic oriented. Service line management is a part of the alignment strategy because hospitals are looking to specialists such as orthopedic surgeons, neurosurgery, general surgery, and cardiology to assist them in operating and managing these respective departments. The key is that this is within the hospital service line, not the practice or clinic.

Both clinical co-management and service line management can be added to fuller forms of alignment. Often called "wraparound" agreements, these arrangements are essentially in addition to a basic form of alignment, perhaps as an employment or a professional services agreement (discussed below). In addition, co-management and service line agreements can encompass other features of alignment that we have discussed, ie, pay-for-call, medical directorships, and quality and shared savings programs. Although a much more all-encompassing form of alignment, they fall short of full integration.

Full Alignment/Integration

Highly integrated models are those that include but are typically termed as full alignment, which is usually either in the form of employment (ie, W-2) or professional services agreement (PSA) (ie, 1099).

Employment

Employment is the highest form of alignment in that it fully integrates the hospital with the applicable physicians. Physicians are employed and receive their compensation in the form of salaries and bonuses with typical benefits for health insurance, retirement, Social Security withholdings, etc. Benefits are paid based upon several criteria, some of which could include the wraparounds of lesser forms of alignment (ie, clinical co-management, quality, shared savings, pay-for-call, etc). Generally, medical directorships are subject to a separate contract and not a part of the employment contract, although this is not an absolute requirement.

Under a standard employment structure, physicians are typically paid a base salary with incentives tied to various criteria, mostly focused on individual and/or group productivity. Often, the productivity is tied to a metric of performance such as dollars charged net of adjustments (or perhaps even gross before such adjustment), collections, and work relative value units (wRVUs). wRVUs are very popular and allow for a measurement of productivity that does not consider the effect of payer contracts and specific payment. For this reason, the physicians and hospital are usually more in sync because the issues of actual dollars generated are not a factor in determining actual compensation. wRVUs are derived from CPT codes with specific values assigned per code. The number of RVUs (and specifically wRVUs) generated by the physician has nothing to do with payer mix; thus, it is perceived to be a much fairer way of measuring productivity.

In addition, most compensation structures of employed physicians include considerations of such items as quality and some cost savings as the payment paradigm continues to shift toward these things. Non-productivity based incentives, therefore, are a major part of the overall consideration and are appropriate under the employed structure.

While the purpose of this chapter is not to delve deeply into compensation structures (for either employment or any other mode of integration), we refer the reader to previous American Medical Association books specifically written on this topic, such as *Physician Compensation Strategies, Second Edition* (American Medical Association; 2004). Another credible resource on RVUs is *RVUs at Work: Relative Value Units in the Medical Practice* (Greenbranch Publishing, LLC; 2009).

Professional Services Agreements—"Employment Lite"

Professional services agreements (PSAs), which have existed for some time, are the legal contracts that document any such agreement between a hospital and physician. However, in specifically considering this in the context of full alignment, we refer to the PSA as a very similar approach to employment, but it functions through an independent contractor format. PSAs are, therefore, often referred to in this context as "employment lite." Although there are various scenarios within the PSA models, Figure 16-7 illustrates four basic models.

---

1. *Global Payment PSA*: Hospital contracts with Practice for Global Payment; practice retains all management responsibilities

2. Hospital employs physicians; practice entity retained and contracts with hospital; for administrative management—staff not employed by hospital

3. *Traditional PSA*: Hospital contracts with physicians for professional services; hospital employs staff and owns administrative structure

4. Hospital employs/contracts with physicians; practice entity spun-off into a jointly owned MSO/ISO

FIGURE 16-7   Four Possible PSA Models

Of the four basic models, Models 1 and 3 are the most popular and applied most often.

Global Payment PSA

Under the global payment PSA, the hospital contracts with the practice for a global payment. Essentially, this means the hospital becomes the payer source to the physician practice. However, the practice remains independent—in effect, an independent contractor. The physicians are still employed by the practice. They can be partners as well, but their official employment relationship is with the practice not the hospital; the practice contracts for professional services with the hospital. Thus, the physicians, as it relates to the hospital, are self-employed with no benefits coming from the hospital. The practice invoices the hospital for actual services rendered. Usually, this is based upon a particular metric of productivity, which is most often wRVUs, then converted to dollars. The hospital pays the practice directly without any withholdings, as it would if they were employees. Instead, the hospital issues a 1099 to the practice (not individual physicians), and the practice is responsible for providing benefits, withholding taxes, etc, from the individual physicians.

Thus, the global payment model has characteristics of employment yet stops significantly short of it. It is a comprehensive alignment strategy requiring less integration than employment. The hospital engages the practice which continues to employ the physicians to provide comprehensive services through a PSA. The practice is compensated globally. Often this is called the "top line" of its income statement.

The global payment PSA, as well as the traditional PSA (to be discussed below), can be structured to entail additional wraparound services. These could include such things as:

- Multispecialty diagnostic and procedural services
- Clinical management and coordination
- Administrative, supervisory, teaching, and research functions
- Medical directorships
- Complete service line and clinical co-management
- Call responsibilities
- Shared savings (sometimes previously referred to as gainsharing, though gainsharing is somewhat different than shared savings)
- Quality incentives

All of these forms of compensation, including the global payment, must be at fair market value or commercially reasonable rates.

Under the global payment PSA model, the practice may retain the ancillaries; however, usually they will sell or lease them to the hospital. The hospital will then be able to bill at its negotiated rates, including if it chooses to bill provider-based and/or at hospital outpatient department rates. Generally, hospitals are reimbursed at higher rates than physicians in private practice, even for providing the same services. Although hospitals cannot pay directly for these increased payments in the physicians' compensation, physicians benefit indirectly through the establishment of these relationships with hospitals. A word of caution regarding provider-based billing under the global payment PSA: legal experts differ on whether this is permissible under the global payment PSA in that provider-based billing regulations established by CMS call for the entity that is in charge of the service and doing the provider-based billing, must be in control of the management of that entity. Some believe that this is still structurally possible under the global payment PSA; however, others dispute that the PSA equates to management control. It is essential to seek competent legal counsel for deciding how best to structure these arrangements.

Another feature regarding the global payment PSA model is that the accounts receivable going forward are owned by the hospital, as are the payer contracts, because they are negotiated by the hospital. Thus, the hospital establishes the fee structure. The practice is clearly an agent providing professional services to support the hospital, just as it would if it were under the employment setting in this regard. The practice continues to be responsible for covering its overhead and must make ends meet just as it does within a private practice setting. As for the billing, this could be done by the practice, but through a third-party management contract because the receivables under the global payment PSA are owned by the hospital.

Figure 16-8 illustrates some of the key features of the PSA global payment model relative to practice versus hospital responsibilities and/or ownership.

As for the benefits of the global payment model, this provides many of the goals of employment without actually going as far as employment (hence, the term "employment lite"). It also allows the physicians to maintain a level of independence and autonomy from the hospital, providing more flexibility and structure. It gives both the hospital and the physician's practice opportunities to increase and enhance their bottom lines, and entails a form of full alignment.

Other benefits of this alignment strategy include bonus opportunities for exceptional performance, a stable relationship with the hospital, particularly if there had been some lack of trust going forward prior to this arrangement, and many opportunities to expand services together. Ultimately, employment lite provides an easy transition to full employment.

While there are many benefits to this model, there are some disadvantages. First, it is still a form of full alignment, which means the practice will have to forgo some level of independence and autonomy. While the global payment PSA entails giving up less autonomy (which indeed is a reason why many hospitals do not prefer it), the practice is still not fully independent and autonomous after the transaction is completed. In

Global Payment Model		
	Practice	**Hospital**
Real Estate Ownership	X	
Medical Equipment Ownership (Non-Ancillary)	X	
Medical Equipment Ownership (Ancillary)	*	*
Employees' Employer	X	
Billing Tax ID		X
Recipient of Insurance Payments		X
Owner of Ancillary Profits/Income	*	*
Party Responsible for Billing/Collections	X	
Provider of Malpractice Insurance	X	
Managed Care Contracting Negotiations		X
MD Employment Status	X	
*Depends upon negotiated agreement		

FIGURE 16-8   PSA: Global Payment Model

addition, this model entails the practice giving up its contractual negotiations with payers. While many would consider this to actually be a plus, enabling the hospital to realize higher reimbursement through both "strength in numbers" and outright better reimbursement in many cases from Medicare (through provider-based billing and hospital outpatient rates on ancillaries), the practice still gives up this major area of work/responsibility. It would be somewhat difficult to retrieve this, and even to retrieve the expertise going back into a private practice setting. Thus, once the global payment PSA is in place, it often is a segue to employment later. This means that the practice has less recourse (at least in practicality) to go back into a fully private setting.

Another disadvantage to the global payment PSA is that inherently hospitals prefer a traditional PSA wherein they employ the staff and control all of the operations. This is often a point of contention and in some circles is of concern from a regulatory standpoint—vis-à-vis, being able to do provider-based billing.

Yet another possible disadvantage of the global payment PSA would be that the practice still has to decide on its physician/provider income distribution plan. Again, some might consider this an advantage in that the practice still has the ability to decide how it divides up the monies available for distribution to the physicians. Yet in some groups, this is such a volatile issue that if its responsibility can be transitioned over to a hospital, like employment, it takes away a major area of concern and potential conflict within the practice.

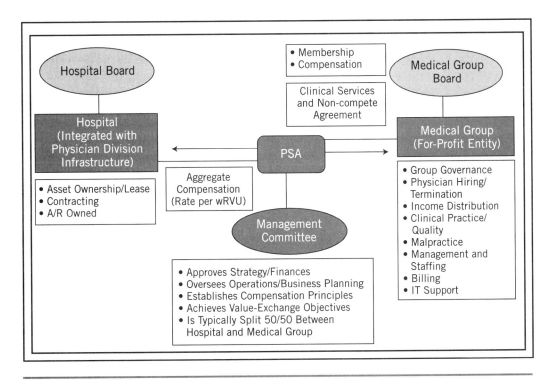

FIGURE 16-9   PSA: Global Payment Example

Thus, there are both advantages and disadvantages to the PSA model. In most cases, physicians prefer it over employment, and especially if they are not yet a hundred percent certain that "full" alignment with a health system is their preference.

The PSA global payment model is further illustrated in Figure 16-9.

Figure 16-9 provides a visual illustration of the structure of the global payment PSA. The medical practice as a for-profit entity remains intact; the hospital may be for profit or not for profit, but the two are tied together through the PSA. Typically, there is also a joint management committee that is structured for purposes of governance and day-to-day oversight. However, both entities retain their individual ability to govern and lead themselves.

Finally, there is also usually a non-compete or some sort of restrictive covenant wherein the physicians make a long-term commitment (generally the PSA global payment model is of a duration of three to five years with the ability to renew) under such a structure.

As for the traditional PSA model, this is similar to the global payment with one major difference. The hospital still contracts with the physicians for professional services who retain their practice identity and separate legal entity. However, in such a structure, the hospital employs the staff and owns the administrative structure. This means that the hospital can actually own the facilities or lease them directly from the owner as well as the equipment, or it can lease these from the practice. But the most critical point of understanding in the traditional PSA model is that the hospital takes on the responsibility of management of the practice. The payment is not the top line as with the global payment PSA; rather, it is just the payment attributable to the physician's compensation and benefits. (Obviously, benefits are not provided separately, as the practice is contracted and the physicians are still employed by the practice.)

Thus, under the traditional PSA model, the physicians are still not employed by the hospital, but the staff and other administrative/management responsibilities are under the auspices, control, and oversight of the hospital. Theoretically, under the global payment PSA, the payment structure is often established as two major components: one is the physician's compensation component (often paid on a wRVU basis), and the other is the appropriate amount to offset the practice's overhead. That payment could be on a wRVU basis, but is often better received and ultimately negotiated as a mostly fixed (with some variable expenses allowed) payment to the practice. Thus, the traditional PSA model is similar except the hospital assumes the responsibility of the practice overhead and does not pay this to the practice as a form of payment.

As for provider-based billing opportunities, there is no question that this would allow qualification for this form of billing when the hospital has complete control over all management of the practice entity.

The traditional PSA model is further illustrated in Figure 16-10.

In Figure 16-10, it is evident that the hospital or health system has many points of responsibility under the traditional PSA model with one being contracting with the physician practice for professional services. Essentially all other things remain under its oversight/ownership.

As for the ancillaries, under the PSA model—whether traditional or global models—the practice can sell or lease to a hospital in accordance with fair market value limitations and commercial reasonableness. When properly structured, there should be no legal impediments to such a transaction; however, it does require very knowledgeable health care legal counsel to navigate through such structures.

The benefits of the hospital assuming ancillary responsibilities include relieving the practice of the expense of such services (along with the profits, which have dwindled due to payment reductions from both Medicare and private payers). Payment for these services (particularly at the private practice level) continues to decrease, especially those paid by the government. Ideally, a practice may be made whole through its compensation. But this cannot be tied directly to any additional payment that the hospital receives from the payers, particularly from the government. Again, in some PSA settings, the ancillaries are retained by the practice.

The impact of ancillary payment going to hospitals and the Medicare portion billed as a hospital outpatient department is very significant.

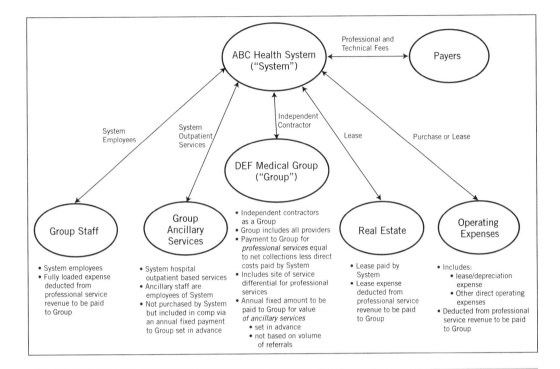

Professional and Technical Fees (between ABC Health System and Payers)

ABC Health System ("System")

Payers

System Employees

System Outpatient Services

Independent Contractor

Lease

Purchase or Lease

DEF Medical Group ("Group")

Group Staff

- System employees
- Fully loaded expense deducted from professional service revenue to be paid to Group

Group Ancillary Services

- System hospital outpatient based services
- Ancillary staff are employees of System
- Not purchased by System but included in comp via an annual fixed payment to Group set in advance

- Independent contractors as a Group
- Group includes all providers
- Payment to Group for *professional services* equal to net collections less direct costs paid by System
- Includes site of service differential for professional services
- Annual fixed amount to be paid to Group for value *of ancillary services*
  - set in advance
  - not based on volume of referrals

Real Estate

- Lease paid by System
- Lease expense deducted from professional service revenue to be paid to Group

Operating Expenses

- Includes:
  - lease/depreciation expense
  - Other direct operating expenses
- Deducted from professional service revenue to be paid to Group

FIGURE 16-10   PSA: Traditional Example

Figure 16-11 illustrates the variability of payment for hospitals versus private practices for two ancillary code procedures.

As for the other PSA models, they are variations of the two major ones explained. In one example, the hospital could actually employ the physicians, and the physicians could retain the practice entity for all management and administrative services and would contract with the hospital for such. Although rare, this scenario can happen, particularly if the physicians are more entrepreneurial and want to retain that infrastructure. Another reason they might want to do this (which also applies to the global payment PSA) is that it would enable the physicians to return to fully private practice with their infrastructure intact; thus simplifying the transition. Hospitals do not favor such a scenario and thus, do not tend to favor the global payment PSA model or the model wherein the physicians may be employed, but the practice management entity is retained separately.

A final model could be a variation of all three models where the hospital could either contract or employ the physicians and the practice management entity is spun off into a jointly owned MSO/ISO.

Thus, "employment lite" is a model of significant interest and as a form of full alignment. It provides much opportunity for the hospitals and the physicians to accomplish the goals and objectives of integration.

Reimbursement for physician's professional fees and the reimbursement to a hospital under HOPPS for 78452 and 93306						
HCPCS Code	Modifier	Short Description	Carrier Locality[1]	Non-facility Price	HOPPS Non-facility Price	Variance
78452	Global	Ht muscle image spect, mult	1020201	$439.73	$833.64	$393.91
78452	TC	Ht muscle image spect, mult	1020201	$358.86	$752.77	$393.91
78452	26	Ht muscle image spect, mult	1020201	$80.88	NA	NA
93306	Global	Tte w/doppler, complete	1020201	$237.90	$509.56	$271.66
93306	TC	Tte w/doppler, complete	1020201	$166.59	$438.26	$271.67
93306	26	Tte w/doppler, complete	1020201	$71.30	NA	NA

[1]Based on zip code

- The potential for increased reimbursement is evident for these codes. The conversion to HOPPS rates (ie $439.73 to $833.64 for 78452, and $237.90 to $509.56 for 93306) represents an 89.6% increase for 78452 and an increase of 114.2% for 93306.
- It is possible to quantify the potential increase in reimbursement under HOPPS using a practice's actual operating data (ie volume and payer mix).

HOPPS = hospital outpatient prospective payment system

FIGURE 16-11   HOPPS versus Global Practice Rate

Strategic Considerations and Alternatives

Physicians and hospitals have various alternatives to consider in light of their perspectives. Few practices should be without an alignment strategy. Whatever the strategy, hospitals and physicians should carefully consider the current health care environment and realize that it is much better to function in partnership rather than as competitors.

In the context of starting, buying, and owning a medical practice, physicians should be aware of their opportunities for alignment with hospitals and also with other practices. This gives them a clearer insight as to all their options and again, as we have emphasized throughout this chapter, does not require them completely to sell out and be employed (although this is a viable alternative).

Figure 16-12 illustrates the opportunities and alternatives for the various alignment models, summarizing the basic concepts and compensation framework for each one. The strategies for physicians to align with hospitals enable opportunities for additional compensation. This must be structured in a manner that is within legal and regulatory parameters and all compensation must be at fair market value, at commercially reasonable rates, and genuine effort must be expended to realize these possibilities.

Opportunities and Alternatives		
Strategy	**Basic Concept**	**Compensation Framework**
Managed Care Networks (IPAs, PHOs)	• Loosely formed alliances • Primarily for contracting purposes • Limited in ability unless clinically integrated • Being used as a platform for ACO development	• No true impact on pay unless through improved payer contracts • If used as platform for ACO, could result in distribution of incentives received
Call Coverage Stipends	• Compensation for the personal, financial, and risk burden associated with ED coverage	• Payment can come in the form of a daily stipend, fee for service payment, or hybrid payment
Medical Directorships	• Payment for defined administrative services • Must be a true need for the services	• Typically paid via a market-based hourly rate
Recruitment/Incubation	• Traditional style of a hospital financially supporting a new recruit	• Allows existing physicians in practice to not see a decrease in their pay as a new physician comes on board
Management Services (MSO)	• Services such as revenue cycle, human resources, IT, etc • Can be hospital-owned, joint venture, private practice owned	• Can provide an additional revenue stream

FIGURE 16-12 Opportunities and Alternatives

Opportunities and Alternatives (*continued*)

Strategy	Basic Concept	Compensation Framework
Equity Model Assimilation	• Tiles all entities via legal agreements • Can jointly contract with payers	• Can result in increased profitability through better payer contracts and other efficiencies

Target Cost Objectives	• Focus to ensure delivery of cost effective care while still maintaining quality	• Savings shared with providers
		  • Percentage
		  • Hourly fee
		  • Fixed fee

Provider Equity (joint ventures, investments)	• Joint ventures such as specialty hospital, surgery centers, etc	• Can provide an additional revenue stream to private practice physicians
Clinical Co-management/ Service Line Management	• Provision of administrative services and work toward certain strategic initiatives within a service line	• Involves hourly payment for administrative time and incentive payment for achieving established metrics
Employment	• Traditional employment arrangement with a hospital	• Typically includes productivity payment and potentially some other incentives for quality, cost control
Employment Lite (PSA model)	• Allows practice to remain private, but hedge payer risk • Hospital owns receivables	• Hospital provides payment, oftentimes on wRVU basis, which is intended to provide FMV compensation, benefits, and other overhead costs incurred by practice

FIGURE 16-12   Opportunities and Alternatives (*continued*)

Conclusion

This chapter has reviewed the possibilities for physician/hospital alignment strategies, including a reasonably detailed summary of the various models that currently exist. While many physicians are not ready for full alignment and are also quite disinterested in employment or even a PSA "employment lite" model, there are many other opportunities that can lead to improvements in their overall practice bottom line through genuine partnering efforts with hospitals. As accountable care continues to be a major part of the health care delivery system, it is important for every physician and practice to develop an alignment strategy. It is appropriate to dedicate the time and resources to attain some form of integration, even if it is somewhat limited. While there are a few specialties that have very little opportunity, due to their having virtually no involvement with hospitals (eg, allergists, dermatologists, etc), this is a small minority of physician specialists. Thus, having an alignment strategy is imperative. Time will tell how far accountable care and newer forms of payment progress within the health care industry. However, at this time, based upon what we know and what we believe will occur in the near future, it is imperative that physicians and hospitals work even more closely together than ever before.

CHAPTER 17

Practice Acquisition

Among the many entities that consider the acquisition of medical practices are hospitals, major health care systems, medical groups, private practices, and other health care organizations, as well as individual physicians. The process of buying a medical practice requires a thorough review so that both buyer and seller are assured that a fair and objective transaction has resulted. The process includes due diligence, an independent valuation, negotiations, agreements, tax considerations, completion of a financial statement, and perhaps, most importantly, a thoroughly defined transitioning process.

Due Diligence

The due diligence process is a very complex and detailed undertaking. It includes a thorough evaluation and assessment of the key issues relative to a potential target. These include areas such as general management, human resources, legal and tax issues, financial standing, and information technology. The goal of the due diligence process is to equip the prospective buyer with the information to make a sound business decision relative to the acquisition and to assess the potential risks and challenges that may be faced post-acquisition.

The first step for the practice buyer is to determine exactly what is being acquired, and the scope of the due diligence should be consistent with this determination.

Identifying the right practice to purchase is a significant part of the process and a major reason why due diligence should be completed. Buying a medical practice is based on sound business analysis and the assessment of practice characteristics. The prospective buyer must identify a practice that fits the predetermined and defined goals of a strategic plan or an overall strategy for the acquisition. Without such a match, the acquisition may be unsound.

Medical Practice Business Fundamentals

The target practice's value to its potential buyer lies in its value-added characteristics and how it fits the overall strategy of the new owner. The following are some business fundamentals that affect not only the value of the practice but also its future economic viability:

- **Market position.** The ability to attract and retain patients; the relative market status of the practice and its current and prospective market share; and the practice's estimated utilization by type of patient.

- **Regulatory position.** The type and volume of regulation of the medical practice. This includes its regulatory history, malpractice liability history, and relationships with third-party payers, governmental entities, and other regulators.

- **Operations.** The effectiveness and the efficiency of operations and the quality and adequacy of staffing; the overall quality of management, including financial management.

- **Physical facilities.** The quality and general condition of the physical facilities and equipment and the capacity for growth. This includes the estimated requirements for capital expenditure (Cap Ex) in the future.

- **Financial position.** The ability to sustain and grow revenue. The practice's debt coverage, liquidity, and capital structure.

The following list outlines the key areas of review within each of the five business fundamentals illustrated above.

- Market position produces projected patient utilization by patient type and payer classification.
- Regulatory position produces information concerning the following:
  - Expected reimbursement rates
  - Malpractice insurance premiums
  - Insurance reserves
  - Conformity to billing and safety codes
  - Conformity to other state, local, and federal codes and regulations
- Operations produce information regarding the following:
  - Operating expenses and staffing
  - Efficiency and effectiveness of office management
  - Information regarding contractual arrangements
  - Information regarding partnership arrangements or other special arrangements

- Physical facilities produces the following:
    - Projected capital expenditures for new or remodeled physician facilities
    - Projected capital expenditures for equipment in the next 1 to 3 years
    - Accountability for maintenance costs in the next 1 to 3 years and current condition from functional regulatory competitive standpoints
- Financial position results in the following:
    - Operating income and expenses projected for the next 1 to 3 years
    - Projections for capital expenditures and other reserves, extraordinary expenses, and any other items that will affect cash flow (including interest and principal on debt obligations and required payments to investors and/or partners)

A comprehensive due diligence based on these business fundamentals is used to form the foundation for valuation calculations (discussed later in this chapter).

Since the emphasis of this review is on the business and operations side of an acquisition, the clinical aspect is not addressed herein. However, the clinical operations demand equal and thorough consideration. Clinical review is more subjective, being based on the proficiency and professional credentials of providers, including physicians, mid-level providers, technicians, and others. These credentials are difficult to assess and should be completed by a clinician, possibly the prospective buyer of the practice. Accessing references, patient surveys, and the general reputation within the medical community provides helpful information to complete this process.

Operational Due Diligence

The due diligence process, depending on its area of focus, can be broken down into two types: operational due diligence and financial due diligence. The former focuses on the various operational and managerial aspects of the practice, whereas the latter primarily reviews and analyzes the practice's historical and prospective financial performance. Operational due diligence and financial due diligence are often closely correlated.

Key areas of review in the process of an operational due diligence are discussed in detail in the following pages.

Ownership

One of the first areas of due diligence review is the practice's current ownership structure. This information is important for the acquirer for its determination of ownership structure to be in place post-acquisition and to identify any issues that might potentially affect the acquisition and transition of ownership.

- If the practice is a professional corporation, complete a thorough due diligence of the assets and liabilities.

- The assets of a sole proprietorship are often not delineated from those of the practice and those that are personal. A comprehensive review of tax returns should clearly separate them.

- Similarly, in a partnership, partners share the assets. The partnership can then lease or use the assets in another way, but ownership remains that of the individual partners.

- Two contemporary hybrids of ownership formed and approved in many states include a limited liability company and a limited liability partnership. (See Chapter 2 for a discussion of these hybrids.) In the acquisition of a limited liability company, identify the assets you are purchasing and state that any practice assets not identified remain the property of the current owners.

Health Provider Matters

The most valuable assets of any medical practice are its physicians and other providers. The utilization of their time is likewise valuable. A complete due diligence process must review and analyze the following key areas relative to the providers:

- **General information:** This includes each provider's specialty, subspecialty, full-time equivalent (FTE) status, ownership status, compensation, and leadership role.

- **Physician schedules and hours:** This assesses each provider's work schedule, current and prospective capacity, and growth potential.

- **Physician productivity:** This measures each provider's charges, payments, and relative value units (RVUs). Given the fact that gross charges are primarily determined based on the practice's fee schedule, collections and work only RVUs (wRVUs) are considered the most objective productivity metrics for productivity analysis purposes. In analyzing physician productivity, a variety of industry benchmark resources can be used. These include the *Physician Compensation and Productivity Survey* published by the Medical Group Management Association (MGMA), *Physician Compensation and Productivity Survey* by Sullivan, Cotter and Associates, Inc, and *Medical Group Compensation and Financial Survey* by the American Medical Group Association (AMGA).

Practice Demographics

A demographic analysis of the practice will reveal the types of patients in the area and the area's economic stability. It is also a valid resource for determining the practice's potential future growth. A demographic analysis provides data to detect both current and future earnings potential and the most viable type of delivery, eg, managed care or fee-for-service.

Patient demographics are dictated in many respects by the payers regardless of the population. Therefore, it is important to track the pulse of the payers' situation within the demographic area under consideration. There may be significant discounting of fees, whether from Medicare, Medicaid, private and commercial payers, etc, or there may be some stabilization of the payers as to reimbursement. Further, the age of the patient base will often indicate the degree of governmental involvement (ie, Medicare). A payer mix analysis will indicate the degree of indigent Medicaid service patients.

Managed Care Penetration

Managed care consists of many payer and reimbursement systems. In its simplest application, managed care takes the form of a preferred provider network paid on a discounted fee-for-service basis. Managed care penetration and market maturity significantly affect reimbursement to the physician. Sometimes reimbursement equates to participation in a capitated payment system, which requires the physician to a set dollar amount per covered member per month, without regard to the amount of medical care he or she provides for an individual patient.

The practice buyer must learn the status of managed care contracts and the projected after-acquisition managed care penetration. This information should be analyzed in detail using a 1- to 3-year projection and on a broader scale for subsequent years. Managed care is a moving target and difficult to evaluate. However, good information based on existing trends of the practice and the managed care market greatly facilitates the process. If possible, assess and review any outstanding or proposed contracts before the acquisition.

In summary, the prospective buyer should have a managed care strategy planned for the acquired practice. This strategy should consider the following:

- Ability to remain on existing managed care contract panels
- Desirability of remaining on existing managed care contract panels
- Ability to renegotiate any unfavorable reimbursement arrangements

- Opportunities for expansion of additional managed care contracts
- Desirability and capacity to expand to additional managed care contracts

Personnel

The depersonalization of health care has not diminished the patient's preference for a hands-on, personal health care experience. Patients are distinguishing practices based on those that offer personalized care. A well-trained staff is an indispensable part of the practice's personality, and the retention of knowledgeable, well-informed, loyal employees is essential to the continuum of practice efficiency, productivity, and patient satisfaction.[1]

To ensure a smooth transition, it is important to understand the practice's current staffing arrangement. Key areas of review include the name, position, pay rate, date of hire, and employment status of each individual employee of the practice. In reviewing these, it is important to identify whether any of the family members of the physician is on the payroll. In addition, the practice's existing benefit program (eg, group insurance, paid time off, and retirement plan) should also be reviewed.

Practice Facility

The physical location of the practice and the lease agreement are major factors to consider in the offer to buy the practice. Is the location inappropriate for future expansion? Is the facility too small or too large? Is the facility personally owned by the physician or leased from a third party? Location refers not only to the street address but also to accessibility (eg, the ground floor, an elevator), parking, appearance, etc.

A favorable lease that allows an assignment or a sublease to another party is a positive feature in an acquisition. The remaining term on the lease also influences the assessment of the practice's stability. Determine if the remaining duration is sufficient to assure a fixed or known rental rate. A lease term that will soon expire, requiring renegotiation or perhaps even a move, negatively influences the acquisition.

The furnishings and aesthetic presentation of the practice influence the decision to purchase. Ideally, the facility is tastefully and colorfully decorated with durable, comfortable furnishings. The color scheme and decor should harmonize with the type and size of the practice. For example, a pediatric practice would be bright and cheerful, appealing to children; the décor of an obstetrics/gynecology practice would appeal to women, etc.

The general state of upkeep and maintenance of the facilities is also important; list the condition of these assets in the contract. Similarly, evaluate and test the clinical equipment to be sure it is functional.

Patient Scheduling and Billing

A thorough review of the practice's daily patient scheduling and billing process can help the prospective acquirer identify potential issues and/or risks within the practice's operations and thereby ensure these issues are resolved during the transition.

To review this, the easiest way is to simply follow the patient from the time he/she calls the practice to the time his/her bill is paid (both patient responsibility and insurance responsibility). During this process, you will be able to review the practice's patient scheduling practice, coding and compliance process, check-in/check-out practice, billing and collection functions, and the patient flow. One of the best ways to gather this information is an onsite review where the reviewer interviews various personnel to find out how the practice operates and interacts. In smaller organizations, this may be a day-long meeting with the office administrator; for larger organizations, this will entail multiple days meetings with the department heads and employees who can provide hands-on information as to how the practice operates on a day-to-day basis.

Accounts Receivable

An acquisition does not always include accounts receivable (A/R). Either the purchaser buys the accounts at a discount, due to aging and noncollectibles, or the outstanding account balances remain the responsibility of the seller. The seller also realizes the proceeds from those collections.

If the acquirer desires to assume the ownership of the practice's existing A/R, a thorough due diligence based on the aging and historical collection rates would be an important component of the due diligence process. The reviewer should also give particular attention to the credit policies and collection protocols.

It is equally important to fully understand, through the due diligence process, the method of collecting. For example, this process may be outsourced through an application service provider (ASP) and/or a business service provider (BSP). With the ASP approach, the practice is not limited to its existing purchased software (and, to a certain extent, hardware) because the ASP is hosting the information system for the practice. With the BSP approach, the entire practice accounts receivable management function is outsourced with the hosting or ASP services. These factors should be analyzed closely not only to determine the success or lack thereof of this initiative, but to also understand the cost relative to the revenue generated. As the valuation process is considered later in this chapter, this will become even more important.

Plan for the transfer and collection of accounts if the purchase includes them. A change in ownership may cause delays in payments. Accounts receivable can be grouped according to the third-party payer system and the reimbursement schedule used in the practice (including Medicaid and Medicare).

Computer Software and Hardware System

The backbone of any medical practice is its information system. The prospective acquirer should review in depth the existing information system at the practice and access its compatibility to the buyer's desired system. If there is a need to switch the practice to a different system, this will be an added cost. This switch will also cause significant downtime for training on the new system components, decreasing productivity and causing a strain for the practice personnel.

Any ASP/BSP system that is in place must be thoroughly analyzed. The overall effect of owning complete software and hardware systems versus the cost of leasing through the ASP must be considered.

An additional consideration is a paperless office (ie, electronic health records [EHR]). If such a system exists, the due diligence process should not only consider the effectiveness and efficiency that is rendered by the EHR system but, in some cases, the opposite effect. In some practices, both employees and providers have not accepted the concept of EHR and have, in effect, inhibited its growth, development, and usefulness. This must be thoroughly reviewed in the due diligence process because problems are likely to continue after purchase of the practice. On the other hand, an effective and efficient EHR system will undoubtedly influence the future viability of the practice as well as enhance and improve operational efficiencies.

Medical Records

Medical records hold certain value for the medical practice, and they reveal a great deal about the ongoing value of the entity. The buyer should consider the following aspects concerning medical records:

- **Establish your own criteria for an active patient.** If 2,000 active charts are represented, what services were actually rendered to these patients? Have they all been seen in the practice within the last two years? Was the visit for physician services or merely to receive an injection?

- **Prior arrangements with another physician.** Did the selling physician have a close call-sharing or space-sharing arrangement with another physician? What are the chances that patients will opt to see the known physician instead of the new buyer?

- **Responsibility for medical records.** Are you assuming responsibility for all medical records or just the active ones? If you assume responsibility for all, where and how will you store them? How many of them must be stored and how long will you be required to maintain them? What will be the cost of storing the old records? Have records of deceased patients been marked? Do they have year tabs for easy purging?

- **Records purging.** Purged records must be burned or shredded. Do you have resources for this?
- **Condition of records.** What is the condition of these records? Will the buyer have to upgrade the records to a more modern file system? At what cost?
- **Legibility.** Are the records legible? If you cannot read them, how useful will they be?
- **Storage.** If old X-ray film exists in the practice that may require special storage, do you have this storage capability?

Financial Due Diligence

Financial due diligence relies on information provided by the practice's financial documents. Typical financial documents to review include tax returns, financial statements, productivity statements, and other internal managerial reports. In the process of a financial due diligence, the following are key areas of consideration:

- Revenue performance
- Provider productivity and growth potential
- Expense structure
- Required capital expenditure
- Liabilities and debt services
- Leases

Financial due diligence lays out the foundation for the practice valuation, and it is a key component of the transaction review process.

Valuation

Completion of the practice acquisition is based on a thorough due diligence process of its operations as well as a valuation of the practice's fair market value.

Valuation Goals

The objective of an appraisal is to express an unambiguous and professional opinion relative to the value of the practice. Following

appropriate procedures, the appraiser collects and analyzes all information, including concise summaries provided by the owner and requested
by the appraiser. An appraisal is expressed as a single dollar amount or
as a range of dollar amounts.

To ensure that the negotiation and transaction is facilitated by a
high quality appraisal, it is important to select only a highly qualified,
professional appraiser. Also, you should carefully scrutinize the profes-
sionalism and credentials of the firm and/or consultant and make sure
the selected firm and consultant have expertise in health care valuations and familiarity with the health care industry.

Many firms conduct independent appraisals of medical practices.
Most perform thorough and comprehensive valuations and conduct
themselves professionally. On rare occasion you may find others that are
less professional and who compromise their work to oblige their clients,
inaccurately slanting the report to achieve the most or least amount of
value in the practice.

Both the buyer and the seller benefit from the appraisal. In a
transaction, either party can engage with a valuation firm to complete
an independent appraisal of the practice. If the appraiser conducts
work impartially, the valuation conclusion will be no different whether
the seller or the buyer engages the independent appraiser. However,
since there is a certain level of subjectivity in an appraisal, it is very
typical to have slight differences in valuation conclusions from two
appraisers.

In the interest of cost savings, the buyer and seller may mutually
agree to hire an independent appraiser and share the expense. Sharing
the cost of an independent appraiser is appropriate for a prospective
seller and buyer, especially when discussions have already begun. This
ensures that the outcome will be a valuation performed at arms' length.
The appraisal fee should in no way be contingent on the total appraised
value of the practice. An independent appraiser is one who has no vested
financial interest in either the valuation or the transaction.

Achieving Valuation Goals

Achieving the following goals is very important in the completion of the
medical practice's independent valuation:

- **Determination of true business enterprise value.** Business
  enterprise value is the sum of the following:
  - Net working capital
  - Tangible assets
  - Intangible assets

  Alternatively, business enterprise value is the total invested capital value of the entity, which is the combination of stockholders'
  equity and long-term debt.

- **Fair market value.** Determination of the fair market value total is an extension of the business enterprise value. IRS Revenue Ruling 59-60 IRC Sec. 2031 defines fair market value as "the price at which property would exchange hands between a willing buyer and a willing seller, neither being under the compulsion to buy nor sell, and both having knowledge of all the relevant facts as of the date of the valuation."[2]

- **Knowledge of the medical practice's operations.** Obtaining knowledge of the operations of the practice is a goal for any independent valuation of a medical practice. This includes an understanding of the day-to-day business activity and the financial operating results, including profit and loss and balance sheet reporting. For example, a business may have historically experienced good operating results, yet due to lack of attention, it has accumulated excessively high accounts receivable which it may or may not have the ability to collect. Therefore, the practice is not in as good of financial condition as in previous years. Knowing this is important to the appraiser as the valuation is completed.

- **Compensation characteristics.** The independent appraiser must understand how physician compensation is allocated and distributed in this practice. Compensation consists of salary or distribution of earnings and the total of fringe benefits, retirement plan contributions, and other nonstandard practice operating expense items.

The appraiser's goals must be consistent no matter who has requested the valuation—the buyer or the seller. The valuation lays the groundwork for the negotiation process that eventually results in the agreed sales price.

Enterprise Value and Equity Value

In general, acquisition of a medical practice can be structured as either an asset purchase or an equity purchase. The key difference between the two methodologies is that in a stock purchase the buyer acquires the seller's share of interest in all assets, liabilities, and off-balance sheet items, whereas in an asset purchase the buyer can pick and choose which assets it wants to acquire and which liabilities it wants to assume.

With respect to the two types of transactions, there are two distinct types of values that an appraiser can calculate in the valuation of the practice: enterprise value and equity value.

Enterprise value (EV), also referred to as invested capital value, is an economic measure reflecting the value pertaining to the entire business entity. For a typical medical practice, the term enterprise value is representative of the sum of the value for equity shareholders (ie, equity value) and the value for debt holders. For a practice that relies on equity financing, its enterprise value is equivalent to equity value.

The majority of the hospital-physician transactions are structured as an asset purchase in a debt-free setting. The advantage of this is that the hospital will not be responsible for any unknown or uncertain liabilities that may exist prior to the acquisition. When this is the case, the proper value to base the transaction price on is enterprise value. Under this arrangement, the buyer of the practice does not assume the practice's existing interest-bearing debt, and the practice will use the proceeds from the transaction to pay off its existing liabilities. In contrast, a stock purchase is based on the equity value. The buyer of the practice assumes the equity interest of the practice and will continue to be responsible for its existing liabilities.

Valuation Approaches

There are three broad approaches to value a business:

- Cost (asset-based) approach
- Market approach
- Income approach

Cost Approach

Cost approach is based on the theory of substitution. Under this approach, there are the net asset value (NAV) method and the excess earnings method.

The net asset value method values the practice by adjusting its assets and liabilities to reflect their fair market value. In this method, the appraiser takes into consideration various intangible items that are not reported on the balance sheet for accounting purposes. Examples of these intangible items include accounts receivable (for practices that use the cash basis of accounting) and pending lawsuits.

It is important to note that in most cases the book value of an asset is unrelated to its fair market value. For example, for tax purposes, practices tend to depreciate the majority of its tangible assets (ie, furniture and equipment) using accelerated depreciation method; the result of this is that very little tangible asset value (ie, book value) is reported in the balance sheet. For valuation purposes, however, since these assets play a critical role in the practice's ability to generate revenue, they still present significant value from a fair market value standpoint. Therefore, to determine the fair market value of these assets, the appraiser should consider factors such as the working condition, expected remaining useful life, and the market price of similar items in the market place.

The excess earnings method is essentially a combination of cost approach and income approach, but it relies heavily on the value of the practice's fair market value in tangible assets. This method values the practice based on the sum of its value in tangible assets and intangible assets; the latter is derived by capitalizing the earnings in excess of the estimated amount of earnings solely attributable to the tangible assets. Although still widely used in valuations of professional service firms, the excess earnings method has a number of problems that prevents it as a viable method for valuing medical practices. This method derives the value largely based on the practice's past performance, which is unrealistic given the changes that have occurred and are expected to occur in the health care industry. Other issues with this method include the high level of subjectivity related to the assumptions based on which the value is determined.

The cost approach of valuation is mostly applied in valuations of capital-intensive business, such as real estate holding or financial holding companies, where the majority of the entity's value is driven by the assets held by the business. This approach is often used for valuing financially distressed companies and for businesses on a basis other than a going concern. The cost approach is not a preferred approach for valuing service-oriented entities such as medical practices.

Due to the many pitfalls associated with this approach, Business Valuation Standards (BVS)-III specifies that "the asset approach should not be the sole appraisal approach used in assignment relating operating companies appraised as going concerns unless this approach is customarily used by sellers and buyers. In such cases, the appraiser must support the selection of this approach."

Market Approach

As with the cost approach, market approach is also based on the principle of substitution, meaning a prudent investor will pay no more for a property than it would cost to acquire a substitute property with the same utility.[3]

There are two primary methods within this approach:

- Guideline public company method
- Merger and acquisition (transaction) method

The guideline public company method derives the business value based on market multiples dictated by market prices of actively traded stocks in the same or similar line of business. The merger and acquisition method, on the other hand, calculates the value based on the multiples suggested by comparable transactions that occurred within a reasonable time frame.

The market approach is easy to understand and apply. However, the guideline public company method is virtually impossible to apply in valuation of many small health care entities, particularly private medical practices, due to the fact that there are no publicly traded physician clinics in the marketplace. The merger and acquisition method is a more viable method for medical practice valuations.

In constructing the merger and acquisition method analyses, one must pay attention to the market transactions' timeliness and comparability. Typically, at least five comparable transactions are needed for a meaningful analysis. However, due to various limitations within the transaction database, often it is difficult to obtain a sufficient amount of data to support valid market-approach calculations.

In FMV-based valuations, the most prominent pitfall within the merger and acquisition method is that it is very difficult to isolate the synergy effect in the reported transaction prices. Unlike public companies, transactions of closely held companies are not required to be disclosed to the public. Thus, while a large number of transactions have occurred, specific terms surrounding these transactions are difficult to obtain. Moreover, transaction data from various resources typically lack consistency.

In the valuation of medical practices, valuation conclusions are rarely based on the merger and acquisition method due to the various disadvantages outlined above. However, this method is frequently used to provide a sanity check to measure the overall reasonableness of the valuation conclusions.

Income Approach

The income approach is the most widely used approach in the determination of the FMV medical practices. The discounted cash flow (DCF) method within the approach calculates the practice value based on the present value of its expected future economic benefit streams (ie, cash flows).

The DCF method relies on appropriate and realistic projections of the practice's future cash flows. This method involves a detailed financial pro forma analysis, typically for 5 to 7 years, based on the appraiser's professional judgment. The basis of the forecasts and assumptions applied in the DCF method should be reasonable and defensible based on the historical and market data available.

In the Instruction Program Textbook, the IRS expressed strong preference for the DCF method. The most prominent advantage of the DCF model is that it allows the appraiser to take into consideration a variety of key factors that determines the value of a practice:

1. **Growth expectations:** These consider the practice's future earning capacity, the providers' ability to grow, and expected changes

in the provider base. For two practices with the same current earning levels and risks, the one that is expected to grow more has a higher value.

In general, the practice's historical track record provides the best indication of its future performance. In order to support his/her pro forma assumptions, it is essential that the appraiser completes an extensive analysis of the practice's historical productivity data and thoroughly documents how this affects the value; the most widely used financial analysis techniques include trending, benchmarking, and ratio analysis.

2. **Post-transaction physician compensation:** For most medical practices, physician compensation is the single largest expense item, representing between 20 and 50% of the medical revenue. Since the post-transaction compensation is a key component of the ramifications received by physician shareholders, it plays a crucial role in determination of the practice value.

   The FMV valuation of the practice sets forth the amount of the upfront purchase price of the practice. It measures the future economic benefits (after physician compensation is paid) to be received by any willing buyer of the practice. Subsequent to the transaction, the physician shareholders take away a portion of the future cash flows to be received by the buyers. As a result, the amount of post-transaction physician compensation has an inverse relationship to the practice value (ie, up-front purchase price). That is, the greater the post-transaction physician compensation, the lower the practice value.

   In order to accurately measure the practice's FMV, it is critical that the pro forma and DCF calculation reflect the actual physician compensation plan to be provided to the physician-owners post transaction. Various fringe benefits, which are considered as a component of the physician compensation, must also be applied. In instances that a specific compensation plan is not available at the time the valuation is performed, the appraiser will apply an estimated FMV compensation amount for the initial valuation and adjust the valuation when the actual compensation becomes available.

3. **Expected changes in payer reimbursement:** In most cases, medical practices rely heavily on third-party reimbursement. Changes in payer reimbursement have a large impact on medical practice value. Therefore, it is imperative that the practice valuation takes into consideration the expected reimbursement changes. This places great importance on retaining an experienced health care business appraiser who is able to skillfully and accurately determine the extent of future reimbursement change on the practice value.

Standard of Value

The standard of value is the type of value being used to determine valuation. It determines the assumptions and considerations that an appraiser applies in the process of deriving the value of the practice. Different standards of value may yield significantly different valuation conclusions. Therefore, it is critical that, when working with business appraisal professionals, the users of the appraisal, such as hospital and practice executives, understand the distinction between standards of value.

There are three distinct standards of value typically used by valuation professionals:

- Fair market value (FMV)
- Fair value (FV)
- Investment value (IV)

Fair Market Value

Fair market value is the most widely used and common standard of value in business valuations in the United States. Within transactions between physicians and tax-exempt entities, it is mandatory that the purchase prices do not exceed fair market value.

The Internal Revenue Service (IRS) Revenue Ruling 59–60 defines fair market value as "the price at which the property would change hands between a willing buyer and a willing seller, when the former is not under any compulsion to buy and the latter is not under any compulsion to sell; both parties having reasonable knowledge of relevant facts."

The definition of FMV in the Stark law is "the value in arm's length transactions, consistent with the general market value." General market value means the prices that an asset would bring as the result of bona fide bargaining between well-informed buyers and sellers who are not otherwise in a position to generate business for the other party, or the compensation that would be included in a service agreement as the result of a bona fide bargaining between well-informed parties who are not otherwise in a position to generate business for the other party, on the date of acquisition of the asset of at the time of the service agreement. Usually, the fair market price is the price at which bona fide sales have been consummated for assets of like type, quality, and quantity in a particular market at the time of acquisition or the compensation that has been included in bona fide service agreements with comparable terms at the time of the agreement, where the price of compensation has not been determined in any manner that takes into account the volume or value of anticipated or actual referrals."[4]

In addition, FMV is defined by the American Society of Appraisers Business Valuation Standards as "the price, expressed in terms of cash equivalents, at which property would change hands between a hypothetical willing and able buyer and a hypothetical willing and able seller acting at arm's length in an open and unrestricted market, when neither is under compulsion to buy or sell and when both have reasonable knowledge of the relevant facts."[5]

Fair Value

Fair value in the context of legal proceedings is typically used in stockholder dissenting and shareholder oppression cases. There is not a standard definition for fair value for legal purposes; rather, it varies from jurisdiction to jurisdiction.

Fair value in the context of financial reporting purposes is defined by the new exposure draft[6] on fair value measure as "the price at which an asset or liability could be exchanged in a current transaction between knowledgeable, unrelated willing parties."

In medical practice valuations, fair value is typically used in marital dissolution cases for shareholders.

Investment Value

Investment value, sometimes also called strategic value or synergy value, is defined as the value to a particular buyer (or a small handful of buyers). It is different from fair market value in that investment value considers the unique synergy(ies) a particular buyer would realize as a result of acquiring the asset.

Uniqueness of Value in Health Care

The health care industry possesses unique characteristics that require a highly specialized valuation process. This is because health care is a highly regulated industry. Health care overall and medical practices specifically are subjected to and becoming increasingly affected by governmental regulations.

Transactions of health care entities are regulated by IRS statute, federal anti-kickback statute, and Stark self-referral law. These laws will affect not only the transaction price and the structure of the alignment transaction but also the ongoing physician/hospital relationship. Thus, proper valuation analyses must be performed in regards to both the up-front transaction price (practice business valuation) and the post-transaction compensation plan provided to the physician owners of the practice (physician compensation valuation).

From a valuation perspective, in transactions of a wide variety of health care entity transactions, it is mandatory that these valuations be constructed based on fair market value. These include physician-hospital transactions and any transactions that involve Medicare reimbursable designated health services as defined by the Stark law.

Subsequent sections of this chapter closely review these concepts. Practice characteristics should be a part of the evaluation process to learn whether the acquisition is viable.

Negotiation Process

The acquisition of a medical practice inevitably entails the process of negotiation. Both parties, buyer and seller, must recognize that the negotiation will establish the foundation of cooperation, which ultimately affects the successful transition of the practice. The buyer and seller must create an environment in which they can structure a fair and equitable agreement in a spirit of compromise. They must be aware of the need to maintain this environment and monitor the conduct of their respective legal representation and consultants. In most cases, the physician-to-physician relationship is the critical component in consummating the sale of the practice. Due to the various legal and compliance issues that physician-hospital transactions must comply with, it is also important to make sure that both parties are aware and comply with these regulations.

The key negotiation points to consider follow:

- Determine exactly what assets are to be purchased.
  - Specify the purchase price of the acquired assets.
  - If purchase price is not separated by asset, at least assign totals in groups or blocks of assets.
- Determine exactly the liabilities to be assumed, if any.
  - Compile a list of the assumed liabilities. Specify a dollar amount for each.
  - Secure an indemnity contract for any liabilities uncovered after the closing.
- Determine how to pay the unassumed liabilities.
  - Specify who will pay the unassumed liabilities: buyer or seller.
  - Specify a time for payment of the liabilities.
- Allocate the purchase price in total and, where appropriate, by line item for the tangible and intangible assets.

Other matters for negotiation pertain to personnel issues. What employee benefits, if any, will be transitioned with the practice? For example, accrued vacation or sick leave may not necessarily be carried forward to the new practice. What about pension plans? These points of negotiation will probably require compromise by the seller for a willing buyer to assume such potential liability.

Other items of negotiation are specific to each situation. They could relate to any points that either the buyer or seller perceives important and inherent to the transaction. Discussing and resolving issues that may create potential discrepancies is best done before consummation of the purchase.

Typically, four types of issues may arise between the buyer and the seller during the negotiation process.

- *Type 1* issues can be considered simple because both parties have a high level of agreement and compatibility and virtually no possibility exists for these issues to remain unresolved.

- *Type 2* issues are those with mixed compatibility or agreement and are resolved through a spirit of compromise.

- *Type 3* issues are the deal breakers. These types of issues lend themselves to very little compatibility, compromise, or agreement and, as a result, have the potential to cause the acquisition to fail. Address any such issue early in the process so neither party will waste time in negotiating a deal doomed for failure.

- *Type 4* issues are either financially or nonfinancially related. The nonfinancial issues are normally more subjective in nature, related to personality, ego, or emotion. Financial issues are usually clear-cut and easy to discover early in the negotiation process.

Fortunately, most negotiation issues are easily resolved. Although deal-breaker issues are seldom encountered, they are more significant in that they are apt to remain unresolved and lead to a failed transaction.

Written Legal Agreement

A purchase and sale agreement can be drafted by either party, but a legal representative for each party should then review the agreement regardless of who originates it. This agreement is the final document that legally testaments the purchase of the practice. It should thoroughly record all appropriate prices and exchanges and all representations and warranties.

The major components of the purchase and sale agreement include:

- List of definitions
- Assets to be included or excluded
- General purchase and sale language
- Current liabilities to be assumed by the purchaser

- Purchase price
  - Methodology for establishing price
  - Specific price adjustments (eg, for liabilities)
  - Manner and timing of payment
  - Stock swap (where appropriate)
- Representations and warranties of seller
  - Financial statements
  - Duly organized entity (such as a corporation, partnership, LLC)
  - Status of existing contracts, liens, leases, etc
- Representations and warranties of purchaser
  - Authority to enter agreement
  - Fully binding representations
  - Stock transfer authority (where applicable)
- Obligations and agreements of both parties before closing (such as conducting business normally before closing)
  - Continued access to information
  - Public announcements
  - Continued confidentiality

Tax Considerations

Both the buyer and the seller should fully understand, anticipate, and plan for tax implications associated with the transaction. Most implications relate to the structure of the assets purchased and the ownership status (ie, the acquired legal entity). Seek advice on tax issues from your accountant, attorney, or a consultant familiar with practice acquisition.

Probably the single most important determinant of tax implication of the purchase price and the payout terms is the structure of transaction (ie, stock purchase or asset purchase). This issue is essentially identical to that of any other business acquisition. However, state laws must be reviewed to clarify who may own stock in a business that provides professional services.

To avoid an unfavorable tax position, the seller generally prefers to sell stock rather than assets. In an asset sale, the seller pays taxes on the difference between the paid purchase price and the basis (or cost) of the asset sold. This asset basis may be higher for tax purposes because the Internal Revenue Service (IRS) recognizes accounts receivable on the books as of the sale date, creating a tax liability for the practice. Later, when the seller assigns dividends from the post-tax proceeds from the sale, individual shareholders likely will be taxed on an individual level for those amounts, resulting in double taxation. By selling stock, the individual shareholders avoid this situation and pay tax only on the difference between the purchase price and their basis in the stock. In 1986, a tax reform act occurred wherein corporate liquidations result in corporate level tax under the General Utilities Rule. Now, the general rule under Internal Revenue Code (IRC) Section 336(a) states "the corporation must recognize gain under the distribution of its assets and a complete liquidation as though the property is sold to the distributee at fair market value." A stock purchase usually has no immediate tax consequence for the buyer.

Tax recognition can only be delayed; it cannot be avoided. Consider the liability and tax issues when acquiring assets or stock. In an asset purchase, the buyer assumes no corporate liabilities that may arise from acts or occurrences before the sale date. The seller is responsible for identifying known or potential liabilities and taking appropriate steps to pay them from the proceeds of the sale. In a stock transaction, the corporation acquired is still live and any liabilities are the responsibility of the new owners. If the new owner buys assets (as opposed to stock), he or she must select the new legal entity. Chapter 2 reviews this topic as a part of the various options for establishing the medical practice. Simultaneously, certain tax aspects are addressed.

Financing Process

Rare is the physician who does not have to gain access to financing to complete the practice acquisition. The financing process consists of raising capital from lenders who will usually want to see a business plan for the practice. Based upon this information the lender will decide whether, how, and when to provide financing to support the practice.

Raising Capital

The buyer will need initial capital to complete the practice acquisition. The purchase price depends on existing factors such as the size of the practice, number of locations, amount of equipment, total goodwill, etc. The capital needed varies depending on the purchaser's ability to access available investment capital versus the need to raise the capital, either by a loan or other means.

In addition to accessing capital for acquisition, a buyer needs start-up capital to infuse into the business. Working capital is needed for operating expenses, particularly if there is a lag in collections of accounts receivable beyond the normal 60- to 90-day shortfall of cash. The buyer should complete a pro forma analysis of all possible cash needs, as if the buyer were starting a new practice. Appendix F is an example of a pro forma analysis.

In addition to working capital, the buyer should also consider equipment and other capital needs in this analysis. Sufficient capital will enable the practice to function from the outset with adequate property, plant, and equipment to reach optimum productivity. Medical groups have an even greater need for capital, and the process for securing a loan is more complicated. Comprehensive and thorough analysis or a formalized business plan can help in these situations.

Preparing a Business Plan

Most lenders require a business plan for large loan applications, up to $100,000 for a solo practice, or $250,000 or more for a group practice. Provide the plan to your lender when applying for the following classifications of financing:

- Start-up capital
- Working capital
- Property and equipment acquisition
- Major practice expansion

More comprehensive than a pro forma statement, the business plan includes a market analysis and projections of practice operating results (ie, billings, collections, expenses, capital needs, and timing of incurred expenses and collections). It should be conservative and realistic and make projections for at least a 3- to 5-year period. The calculations of cash flow needs will indicate how much capital is required to finance the practice. In an existing practice, the historical operating results are the primary source of information. In a practice anticipating changes that may potentially vary from previous operating results (plus or minus), the projections should be considered in more detail with greater analysis.

Typically, a business plan should include the following:

- *Analysis of strategic objectives* includes services provided (including ancillary services) and specialty services (including laboratory and X-ray).
- *Management analysis.* Every good organization should have a clear description of its management. This includes the physicians and reflects other administrative functions such as preparation of payroll, purchasing, accounting duties, etc.
- *Service area analysis* includes data as it relates to the potential within the practice's primary and secondary service areas. This sets the stage for the ability to penetrate the market area and achieve needed volume increases.

- *Managed care analysis.* The dominance of managed care has a significant bearing on the overall business plan. This includes a thorough analysis of the opportunities and the potential limitations on revenue production.

- *Planned services and programs.* Consider opportunities for expansion among the service providers. This may include the ability to complete more intricate and expanded medical procedures within the specialty and within the hospital.

- *Pro forma income statements* may be similar to or perhaps more expanded than the one presented in Appendix F.

Lender Evaluation

The lender will thoroughly analyze the business plan and loan application. The buyer must respond to basic questions, such as: How will the monies be used? What is the amount of the proposed loan? How will it be repaid? From the answers, the lender gains assurance that the buyer understands the transaction and determines whether to arrange the loan. Preparing the pro forma analysis and/or business plan is essential to achieving positive results.

Key Credit Ratios

A lender considers the key ratios listed in Figure 17-1 when analyzing the credit worthiness of a loan. Figure 17-1 provides a summary of these key ratios.

The Transitioning Process

When the acquisition is accomplished, attention is turned to the transitioning process.

Operational Changes

Efficient and productive operational procedures should remain unchanged. If an in-depth review of operations finds deficiencies (and these should have been found during due diligence), new procedures should be established and implemented immediately after the acquisition. A practice's value depends on its potential to continue a favorable earnings trend. The success of a service-oriented business, with income dependent on patients, is contingent on efficient operations and happy personnel.

Item	Computation	Target
Debt service coverage	$$\frac{\text{Net income (after physician compensation)} + \text{Interest and depreciation}}{\text{Principal and interest payments}}$$	1.5 times or greater
Debt to capitalization	$$\frac{\text{Total debt (including leases)}}{\text{Current liabilities}}$$	75% or less
Return on equity	$$\frac{\text{Net income}}{[(\text{Equity at beginning of year}) + (\text{Equity at end of year})] \div 2}$$	10% or more
Current ratio	$$\frac{\text{Current assets}}{\text{Current liabilities}}$$	2.0, 1.0, or better
Day cash balance	$$\frac{\text{Cash}}{\text{Annual operating expenses} \div 260 \text{ days}}$$	At least 20 days

FIGURE 17-1   Key Credit Ratios

Patient Relations

Most patients do not react negatively to an acquisition and figure it will not affect them. Typically, patients are not aware of which physicians are owners and which are not. It will be beneficial to express to the patients, at the outset, the expected improvements under new ownership, including increased services, greater access to physicians, and more efficient care. With each visit, the practice has an opportunity to make a positive impression on the patient with the care that it delivers.

Employee Relations

Perhaps the most crucial aspect of transitioning a practice concerns the employees. They will naturally be anxious and uncertain about potential changes in policies and procedures and be fearful of their job security, and a decrease in their own empowerment, and autonomy. The most consequential uncertainty will be the effect on salaries and benefits. Although income is not always the most important element of job satisfaction, it ranks high on the list. Acquisitions usually do not result in employee pay reductions. Change may, however, affect subsequent pay raises and reduce benefits, particularly health insurance. If changes are

TABLE 17-1   Benefits Comparison

	Benefits Before	Benefits After	Comments
Medical	Yes	Yes	Better
Dental	No	Yes	N/A
Disability	Yes	Yes	Equal
Pension	Yes	Yes	Better
Paid time off	Yes	Yes	Equal

expected after the acquisition takes place, the new owner should conduct a benefits comparison before and after the purchase (see Table17-1) to demonstrate the actual effect of proposed changes that will occur.

Unless there are glaring operational and control deficiencies that must be corrected right away, other changes in policies and procedures should be clearly defined and slowly implemented. Communication is fundamental to maintaining stable employee relations. Thus, it is important to educate the employees about the benefits of the changes before they become effective.

The buyer may also consider establishing a forum for employees to express their feelings and ideas at regularly scheduled staff meetings and encourage employees to openly participate. Empirical studies show that these communications are valuable and generally very productive to the overall well-being of the new practice. In addition, supervisors and managers should practice an open door policy so employees can discuss their concerns in private. Management should also acknowledge that employees should be provided with time to adjust and adapt to the new routines. Another useful tool is an employee recognition program during the transition process to help soften the impact of change. Be considerate and sensitive to employees as they adapt to reorganization.

Accounts Receivable

The practice should have a complete credit history that includes all information relating to accounts receivable. This requires the physician purchasing the practice to work closely with the seller in transferring the data. Depending on the type of transaction, this may be an easy process if the new owner is able to simply take on the information system of the previous owner. A more difficult transition occurs when the new owner institutes a completely new billing system. Policies and procedures would need to be redefined, and a program for total and complete compliance within the billing processes reviewed and established or reestablished. Existing protocols relative to payment plans would be difficult to change because the patients are used to the old system.

Regulatory Matters

The practice's responsibilities for complying with regulatory issues is immense and growing. These regulatory issues must be examined within the transitioning or due diligence process. In addition to the requirements of Stark and anti-kickback statutes, there are currently numerous stipulations relative to proper coding and documentation, billing processes, and the like. There are requirements for meeting all Health Insurance Portability and Accountability Act of 1996 (HIPAA) stipulations, which could entail enforcement of policies and procedures relative to both privacy and security.

Conclusion

The process of buying a medical practice includes many key components so that the buyer and seller are assured that a fair and objective transaction has occurred. These components include due diligence, independent valuation, negotiations, agreements, tax considerations, and completion of a financial statement. Another important consideration in the buying process is a thoroughly defined transition plan for the practice.

References

1. Grandinetti D. 2000. Make the most of your staff. *Medical Economics* 77:56, 63-6.
2. Pratt S, Reilly R, Schweihs R. 2000. *Valuing a Business: The Analysis and Appraisal of Closely Held Companies*. 4th edition. New York: McGraw-Hill.
3. American Society of Appraisers. *The Market Approach to Value*. 2008.
4. Stark Law—442 CFR 411.351-Definitions. http://law.justia.com/cfr/title42/42-2.0.1.2.11.html#42:2.0.1.2.11.10.35.2. Accessed August 29, 2011.
5. American Society of Appraisers. *Business Valuation Standards*. v 6.0. 2008; page 25; Washington, DC: American Society of Appraisers.
6. Exposure Draft Proposed Statement of Financial Accounting Standards, Fair Value Measurements; Financial Accounting Standards Board; No. 12-1-100, June 23, 2004.

18

Structuring of Equity

While there has been a dramatic increase in hospital employment of physicians over the last several years, the fact remains that many physicians are still in private practice. Accordingly, practice buy-in and buy-out scenarios continue to be a reality that must be addressed as physicians enter and exit ownership of the private medical practice. Potential practice purchasers and sellers must evaluate the various alternatives pertaining to the acquisition and divestiture of partnership interests. Often referred to as buying in and buying out of practice ownership, the process is of critical importance and has long-lasting effects on the practice's welfare and success. It requires thorough planning and design, fitting the specific profile of the practice to its partners.

Equity Track Considerations

Most corporations have agreements with their shareholders that encompass the terms for buy in and buy out. Physician practices should do the same. In most cases, equity agreements are created during the formative stages of the practice and are outlined in the company's operating agreements. When a new practice is being formed, one of the decisions the existing partners must make is how the buy–sell process will work. This is not as much an issue when a solo practitioner starts a practice, unless the physician proactively addresses these areas to create an avenue for adding new shareholders in the future. Additionally, at certain points in time, a practice may choose to review and revise their equity agreements to stay current with changes occurring in the market or to respond to specific issues they are facing as a practice. These could include recruitment issues, lack of ability to fund the current buy-out plan, as well as a host of other potential concerns.

If a physician has the opportunity to become an owner, there should be a process outlined for achieving ownership. This process should be outlined early on in the physician's tenure, if not at the time he or she joins the practice. A prescribed process, referred to as the equity track process, is implemented over time for the physician to reach the point of purchase. Although this does not guarantee the physician an ownership interest, the equity track process should define what the expectations and requirements are in order to qualify for ownership. From the beginning of employment, the physician should understand these requirements and work toward meeting the goals and objectives of partnership.

The equity track process can be developed in a number of ways ranging from a physician simply being at the practice for a specified period of time, a certain productivity level that must be achieved, and/or a specific monetary value that must be paid to existing partners. In later sections of this chapter, various scenarios and processes for becoming a partner are reviewed.

The Buy-In Process

The acquisition of an ownership interest in the practice is what the equity track process is all about; ie, the current owners must decide how the new physician will buy into the ownership of the practice and, to that end, become a partner. The incoming or aspiring partner physician must understand all buy-in requirements which should be outlined in writing (including any revisions). Of course, this also applies to the existing partners who need to understand how the buy in will be calculated and how it will be paid. Due to the infrequency of buy/sell transactions, many of the existing partners are not familiar with the terms. The entire process should be defined at the beginning of the employment relationship to avoid potential problems in the future.

This is a common oversight in many instances, in that physician employment contracts do not include the provisions and specific requirements for becoming a partner. While rarely the norm, some employment contracts deliberately do not include such provisions in order to allow the practice flexibility as circumstances change. If such is the case, it is still beneficial to directly note in the initial draft of the employment contract that the buy-in process and associated requirements will be defined later. Alternatively, coinciding with the extension of an employment contract, the practice could issue the physician a letter that outlines the fact that the buy-in process and requirements will be addressed later (if it is desired not to include this information in the employment contract). While there is always a fear that specific documentation of the buy-in process will be too binding on the practice, the buy-in agreement can always be amended and likely should be reviewed and amended on a regular basis. This type of evolving agreement makes it possible for all parties to understand how the buy in will be calculated and paid and keep it continually refreshed and consistent with market trends. We note that the legal process to modify the buy in is rather straightforward, but the decision making that must occur, in terms of agreement with the existing partners, may not be so easy.

Physician Eligibility for Buy In

There is substantial flexibility in how practices determine how or when a physician should become eligible to buy into a practice and, as a result, many methodologies exist. All of the methodologies can largely be consolidated into two specific approaches: (1) years of service and (2) level of productivity.

A common occurrence is for a practice to simply state that after a certain number of years as an employed physician, the physician is eligible to become a shareholder. In most instances, this is within two to five years after becoming employed by the practice with most practices being at the lower end of the range. A methodology sometimes used involves a practice developing a stair-step approach, where the physician gradually gains equity in the practice over a period of years. Another important consideration, especially in today's market due to the number of physicians considering employment by hospitals as opposed to joining a private practice, is the time requirement is often waived altogether or limited to a short period of one year. A physician who can make the same or more money under a hospital employment arrangement may see an extended or expensive buy-in process as unattractive.

As an example, consider the following example of buy-in language from a Texas medical practice.

2.4 Admission of New Equity Members.

(a) The Company may, from to time, admit as additional Equity Members individuals who are duly licensed to practice medicine in the State of Texas. The admission of an additional Equity Member and the terms and conditions of such admission shall require the approval of a [specified number] of the Equity Members. Unless otherwise determined by a [specified number] of the Equity Members, an individual will be admitted as an Equity Member only after being a Clinical Member for at least two years.

(b) Unless otherwise determined by a [specified number] of the Equity Members, a new Equity Member will be required to pay to the Company a buy-in amount equal to such new Equity Member's Interest multiplied by the excess of the fair market value of the fixed tangible assets of the Company as of the date such new Equity Member is being admitted to the Company over any liabilities of the Company associated with such assets, all as determined in the reasonable discretion of a Required Interest of the Equity Members.

(c) No Person shall be admitted as an additional Equity Member unless such Person executes, acknowledges, and delivers to the Company such documents as the Company may deem necessary or advisable to effect the admission of such Person as an additional Equity Member, including (without limitation) the written acceptance and adoption by such Person of the provisions of this Agreement and the entering into an Employment Agreement on terms mutually acceptable to such Person and the Company.

In this example, after two years the physician may have the ability to become a clinical member of the practice, and after a total of four years (two years after becoming a clinical member), the physician is granted full shareholder rights.

Table 18-1 outlines the key differences between a clinical member and a full shareholder. As a clinical member (after two years of employment), the physician gains some benefits of being a shareholder but only achieves full shareholder status after four years of employment. This stair-step approach is beneficial for practices that want to lengthen the partnership track, as it provides some benefit before becoming a full shareholder while still keeping the incentive to achieve full shareholder status.

Another very common method for determining partnership eligibility is tying it to productivity. A variety of productivity metrics could be used with the most common ones being cash collections or work relative value units (wRVUs). Most practices will establish a threshold or quota that the buying-in physician must achieve before being considered for shareholder status. Instead of considering raw professional productivity, a bottom line approach can be used, focusing on profitability. For example, the buying-in physician may be required to fully cover any financial loss that existed when he started and then generate a certain level of profit for the partners of the practice. Once this occurs, the physician would be eligible to buy in. Some other examples of productivity qualifications are outlined below:

TABLE 18-1   Comparison of Clinical Member and Full Shareholder

	Clinical Member	Shareholder
Equity interest	No	Yes
Voting rights	No	Yes
Participate in shareholder income distribution plan	Yes	Yes
Share in ancillary profits	No	Yes

- An orthopedic surgeon must achieve collections of $60,000 per month for four consecutive months.

- A family practice physician must achieve annual wRVUs equivalent to the 50th percentile as outlined in the latest Physician Compensation and Production Survey from the Medical Group Management Association.

- Clinical member status will be granted after achieving the 60th percentile for collections with full shareholder status granted once 85th percentile collections are achieved.

- The physician must achieve wRVUs that are consistent with the average wRVUs for the other practice physicians.

The productivity thresholds can obviously take many forms. The key is that the thresholds be achievable by a reasonable physician over an appropriate period of time and reflect the culture of the practice. If the culture of the practice is very high producers, the thresholds should likely be established at a corresponding (high) level. Unachievable metrics will likely create a disincentive for the physician, potentially causing him or her to leave the practice. Similarly, metrics that are inconsistent with the practice could create disharmony across the entire physician base. Due to the fact that private practices are competing against hospitals for new physicians, there is a heightened sense of awareness relative to the reasonableness of the buy in.

Establishing Practice Buy-In Value

The key question relative to the buy-in process is how much money is involved and how the buy-in amount is calculated. There are many possible ways to structure the purchase price and factors to which it can be tied. The following four alternatives are some of the key formula approaches used.

Alternative 1: Set Purchase Price

A common form of buy in is a preestablished purchase price. In these instances, practices simply establish an amount that is associated with becoming a shareholder, and this figure applies to each new shareholder that is added. As an example, the purchase price could be $50,000. Thus, every new partner added is required to pay $50,000, which is then reallocated to the existing shareholders.

This is by far the simplest buy-in method as it requires very little work when a buy-in event occurs. Further, it is very easy to inform new physicians of what will be required and maintains consistency over time. It also limits the cost of the buy-in process because there is no need for a formal valuation and may require less work from legal counsel to accomplish.

Alternative 2: Tangible Assets

Another very common approach that is not quite as simple and consistent as having a set purchase price is determining the value based on the practice's tangible assets. While the practice may desire to inventory and assign a value to their assets themselves, or simply use the net book value of their assets, the best practice is to use an independent third party to perform a tangible asset valuation. This is because only looking at the net book value can undervalue certain assets if depreciation has been accelerated. Also, it can place no value on assets that may be fully depreciated but are still in full use. Thus, the best practice is to value using an in-place valuation methodology wherein the assets actually being used are considered and are valued based on their current status and functionality. In such cases, an independent valuation firm is hired to value the practice's tangible assets, which is then used to assign a value to the interest the new physician is purchasing. The value is calculated on the basis of only owned tangible assets, less any debt associated with those assets. Thus, any assets that are leased are excluded from the calculation. As an example, consider the following:

- Value assigned to tangible assets, less debt: $500,000
- Current shareholders: 8

The purchase price is calculated by determining the equity interest the new physician will purchase. As there will be 9 shareholders after the new physician purchases an equity interest, in order to obtain an equal interest, the physician will need to purchase 1.39% interest from each physician. Thus, the interest he or she is purchasing is 11.11% interest. When multiplied by the full practice tangible asset value, the buy-in interest totals $55,550.

Alternative 3: Full Practice Valuation

Another, less common but still often used method of determining the purchase price of the practice is by performing a business valuation of the practice, which takes into consideration both the tangible and intangible assets associated with the practice. As intangible assets are also being considered, in many cases this will result in a significantly higher value than the other methods outlined earlier. This can largely be impacted by the valuation methodologies applied, necessitating a highly qualified valuator.

The higher value can prove to be beneficial to the existing partners as they are able to generate higher incomes when new physicians buy into the practice. However, this can be a significant inhibitor to recruitment as physicians, who are also struggling to begin paying down their student loans do not also want to be encumbered by a large buy-in amount. This is especially the case now in that the physician could become employed by a hospital, have little risk associated with managing a practice, and still generate a fair market value wage.

Alternative 4: Gifted Equity

The least common of these four approaches is to have no purchase price. The equity is essentially transferred without cost to the buying-in physician. In some cases, when the practice has been able to generate substantial profit from the employed physician's financial performance over the period of employment, such a process can make financial sense. In this case, the shareholder physicians consider the profits reaped when the physician was an employed physician to be sufficient to cover any buy in that would otherwise occur.

In other instances, for a variety of reasons, the shareholder physicians may choose to give equity to a buying-in physician even when it does not make as much financial sense. This could be a result of a child joining a parent's practice or a means of enticing a physician from a recruiting perspective. Another reason may be the physician has already been participating in the shareholder income distribution plan and therefore very little would change if the physician were admitted as a partner.

While there may be limited benefits in such a method from a financial perspective, operationally speaking this is clearly a very easy approach to effect.

In many situations, the purchase price is a blending of several of the alternatives outlined earlier. Consider the following examples:

- A physician is gifted a partial (less than equal) interest in the practice after a period of three years and then, once certain productivity thresholds are met, is able to purchase the remaining interest based on the value of the tangible assets.

- The purchase price is based on the lesser of the value of the tangible assets or $50,000.

- The value assigned to the entire practice, for purposes of calculating the purchase price for a single physician, will be based on the business valuation (both tangible and intangible) but will be no lower than $750,000 and no higher than $950,000.

Examples of Buy-In Alternatives

The method of purchase largely involves the (1) timing of the payment process and (2) treatment from a tax perspective. There are several alternatives that typically exist relative to the timing of the payment, which we explore below.

Immediate Physician Buy In

The first is an up-front payment when the option to become a share-holder is available. In this scenario, regardless of the purchase price, the physician is required to submit the required funds in a lump sum at the onset of becoming a shareholder. Depending on the amount of the buy in and the physician's financial situation, this could require him or her to borrow money to fund the buy in. The borrowing could be in the form of a small-business loan from a local bank or a loan from the practice at a market rate of interest. Depending on the economic climate and/or the financial situation of the physician (eg, level of student loans), it could be difficult for the physician to borrow the adequate level of funds, thus making becoming a shareholder challenging. Further, the practice may not have the funds to lend to the physician to fund his or her buy in. If financing can be secured or if the buy-in amount is minimal so that funding is not necessary, an upfront payment is a legitimate alternative. In most situations a buy in that was based on a specific purchase price or only on the tangible assets would likely best effectuate this buy-in methodology.

Buy In over Several Years via an Equity Track Formula

The second alternative, which is commonly used, is payment over time. Thus, the physician may be allowed a period of 12 to 48 months to complete the buy-in process. This option tends to be more functional for new physicians than having to secure funds for an upfront payment. The key question with this approach is when the physician is granted full share-holder status in terms of voting rights, profit distributions, etc. The full shareholder status can be granted either at the onset of the buy-in process, incrementally, or at the conclusion of the buy-in process. Typically, an incremental approach is not taken because of the difficulty it creates in calculating physician compensation, etc. Thus, the key options are either at the inception or conclusion. The preferred method tends to be granting full shareholder status at the inception of the buy-in process.

Buy In at the End of the Eligibility Period

A buy in at the end of the eligibility period can be achieved by establish-ing the valuation total and a correlated buy-in amount at the beginning of the buy-in period or some time thereafter, including at the time of buy in, which is at the end of the eligibility period. The new physician part-ner does not have to pay any of this amount until the end of the equity track period, say 3 to 5 years. This arrangement allows the physician to accumulate excess earnings and then contribute at the end of that period. Of course, the disadvantage is that the equity interest is purchased with after-income tax dollars. A slight advantage is the ability to accumulate excess monies and privately earn a return on that investment before having to contribute to the buy in. But, the earnings on this corpus is likely not sufficient to cover the tax liability that could otherwise have been avoided (by using pre-tax dollars). Also, the practice buy-in amount could be established at the beginning of the buy-in period but not paid until some years later. The physician could, in theory, have a fixed buy-in price that is lower than the value of the practice would have dictated (ie, buy-in percentage interest times the valuation). In theory, he or she would be paying for an equity interest after an appreciation of value is actually realized over the value initially established. Obviously, this would be the case if the arrangement were established at the time of the buy in some years after initial employment. However, it is still possible to accumulate wealth and contribute a portion of that wealth to the practice buy in some years later.

Fund Receivables Through a Compensation Formula

In certain instances, the buying-in physician must also purchase part of accounts receivable. In essence, the buying-in physician is faced with the responsibility of paying for receivables that were initially built during the first few weeks or months of working at the practice. During that time, the physician received full compensation. Although productivity may have been good, it was probably not enough to fund the direct and indirect overhead (including the compensation) of the employed physician (now a prospective partner). Consequently, when the partnership is achieved, the receivables that the new physician is required to pay to offset those initially fronted dollars becomes part of the buy in. In some cases, this initial loss could be covered through an income guarantee arrangement with a local hospital. If such is the case, the physician should not be required to repay this loss (ie, the value of his or her receivables).

Most buy-in plans quantify the amount of the receivables along with the value of the practice. As a consequence, the following components could equal the total buy-in amount:

- Accounts receivable
- Fixed assets
- Intangible value or goodwill

Most methodologies for funding these receivables via the buy-in payment allow the new physician to pay his or her share in pre-tax dollars. Some require payment in after-tax dollars, which is unattractive.

If the practice is a subchapter S or corporation, partnership, or LLC in which the earnings are passed through, and if the new partner held a portion of that equity during the buy-in period, that portion of the earnings, unless reallocated to the senior physician in the form of compensation, would be passed through and taxes would be paid by the new physician. If allocated strictly to the senior physician and paid in the form of compensation, the new physician would have not paid any taxes on those reallocated amounts; ie, the senior physician would be responsible for the income taxes on those earnings.

The other key discussion point relative to the method of purchase is how the buy in is treated from a tax perspective. The buy in can take the form of either a post-tax or a pre-tax transaction. In a post-tax transaction, the physician is paid a salary, less any applicable withholdings for taxes and benefits, and then pays the purchase price by using this take-home pay. In a pre-tax transaction, the buy-in amount is withheld within the practice before the physician's compensation is calculated. Thus, the physician's gross compensation is less because the buy in for that period has been withheld.

As an example, consider a physician with an annual salary of $400,000, which includes a buy-in amount of $60,000. For the year when the buy in occurs, the physician's annual salary could be reduced to $340,000 to allow for the buy in to occur. The $60,000 would then be redistributed to the shareholder physicians and included in their compensation.

The pre-tax method is favorable in that it reduces the buying-in physician's tax liability during the buy-in period because of the lower gross income. The pre-tax method makes little to no difference from the perspective of the partner physicians. The pre-tax method tends to be how most practices structure buy-in transactions.

Practice Buy Out

While the buy-in process occurs at the beginning of the physician's life cycle with the practice, the buy-out process occurs at the end of this life cycle. A physician buy out occurs for several reasons, including retirement, death, disability, pursuing other opportunities, and termination. In most cases, the buy-out process is not impacted by the reason for the buy out, with the exception of termination. In some cases, if a shareholder violates the terms of his or her employment agreement with the practice or the operating agreement, the shareholder may forfeit his or her equity interest or receive a limited buy out. An example of this is provided in the sample buy-out language near the beginning of this chapter. Other than these limited instances, the same buy-out process will apply regardless of the reason.

As in the buy-in process, there are several factors that must be considered when appropriately structuring how the buy out will occur.

Some of these can be correlated with the buy-in process, while others are considerations that do not apply to the buy-in process. This section outlines the key areas of focus relative to structuring the most effective buy out for the practice, focusing on various alternatives, where applicable.

Determining the Buy-Out Amount

In many instances, practices will correlate the buy-in process and the buy-out process. This is not to say that they specifically mirror each other, but they have similar characteristics. The prime example is in the amount of funds involved. A common term used within the health care industry in terms of structuring buy-sell agreements is *easy in/easy out*. This means that the buy-in process requires limited funds from the purchasing physician, while the buy-out process also entails limited funds in terms of the physician's payout from the practice. Thus, from an economic standpoint, there is consistency between the two equity events.

Logically speaking, this makes sense because otherwise the transactions would be out of balance. For example, it would be unreasonable to have someone pay a substantial sum of money to purchase an equity interest in a practice only to have the operating agreement assign limited funds to the equity interest when the buy out occurs. This would be akin to purchasing a share of stock at $1000 knowing that in several years it could only be sold for $100. No one would be willing to make such an investment. However, ownership in a medical practice is different from purchasing stock in a publicly traded company, as most of the value associated with the medical practice is realized in the years of ownership through the compensation that is earned. Most practices pay out all funds as compensation; thus, very little value remains in the company, at least from a tangible perspective. Hence, the need for a minimal buy out.

Thus, while it does not have to be the case, typically the buy-in and buy-out process are correlated in terms of the funds involved. If limited funds are required to purchase an equity interest in the practice, the physician should expect a similar result when selling the equity interest. Similarly, if a physician pays a substantial amount for the equity interest, it would only be reasonable to expect a similar payout when leaving the practice.

The buy-out amount can be calculated in a manner similar to the buy-in purchase. In fact, the purchase price can also establish the value for the buy out. This makes sense in that the two equity events are dealing with the same equity. However, as noted, the buy in and buy out do not necessarily have to be correlated.

To reiterate some of the buy-in concepts and how they would apply to the buy out, this section outlines various alternatives.

Alternative 1: Established Value

Similar to the buy-in process, the value associated with the practice can be an established amount. While it would make sense for the buy-in amount and the buy-out amount to mirror each other, this does not have to be the case. For example, the buy in could be established at $40,000 while the buy out was established at $70,000. The opposite could be true as well.

Having an established amount has many benefits. It still recognizes some value associated with the equity interest, while maintaining it at a level that is functional for the practice from a cash flow perspective. Further, limited costs are incurred with each equity transaction, as there is less need for third-party appraisals of the business and legal costs.

The accounts receivable are typically paid out to the physician in addition to any established purchase price.

Alternative 2: Tangible Assets

At the time of each equity event, the practice can have an independent appraiser place a value on the practice's tangible assets and let the assigned value establish the buy-out amount. Then, the physician's share of the tangible assets and any collections generated from his or her existing accounts receivable balance would compose the buy out.

Alternative 3: Full Practice Valuation

Finally, the value can be derived on the basis of the value associated with the entire practice, including both intangibles and tangibles.

As this method typically entails a higher valuation and resultant buy-out amount, the practice must proactively plan for such an occurrence. This includes regularly setting aside funds well before the equity event occurs so that it can be funded through existing practice assets. Alternatively, an installment payment process should be instituted wherein the departing physician is paid over a period of years.

As in the buy-in process, limitations can be established relative to the buy-out amount. For example, the buy-out amount could be based on the lesser of the physician's share of the value placed on the tangible assets or $75,000. Thus, there is benefit in having an independent valuator assess the value of the assets involved, but then there is a limitation on the maximum exposure of the practice from a payout standpoint.

Alternative 4: No Value Assigned

A final method of handling the buy-out process is not to assign any value to the practice. Thus, the physician essentially leaves with nothing. This would make sense only if the physician did not pay anything for the equity interest when he or she went through the buy-in process.

Considering how medical practices function, with literally all available cash being paid out as compensation to the physicians, this process makes sense in that all the value could be assumed to have been extracted while the physician was a shareholder of the practice.

Even if no value is assigned to the practice, the physician typically does retain ownership of his or her accounts receivable, which are paid out as they are collected. Thus, the physician still receives some payout on leaving. However, as the payout is funded from accounts receivable, it has no negative cash flow impact on the practice.

Paying for the Buy Out

A key issue with the buy-out process is having the funds available to accomplish the transaction, especially when a substantial buy out is involved. The majority of medical practices distribute all excess earnings, leaving very little compensation within the practice to fund replacement of equipment, expansion of services, and buy out of departing physicians. Thus, when a physician is leaving the practice and is eligible to receive a sizeable buy out, the practice must come up with the funds to fund it. This typically involves either a reduction in compensation for the existing physicians or borrowing money. Alternatively, the practice must plan for these buy-out events well ahead of time through retaining funds in the corporation for this purpose.

Funding the buy out through debt is not in the best interest of the remaining physicians, as the debt is not tied to any tangible asset and the existing physicians are still left with paying off the debt over a period of years. An immediate reduction in compensation in the year of the physician's departure is likely not tolerable either. Accordingly, an alternative approach must be considered, which typically involves the practice paying the buy out over a period of years.

For large buy outs, the payments can extend over a period of five years, whereas smaller buy outs are limited to a period of 12 to 24 months. Funding the buy out over a period of years keeps the practice from having to borrow money and limits the reduction in the remaining physicians' compensation to a specific period. It is up to the practice whether interest is charged on any unpaid balance. For example, if the buy out was $60,000, the practice could pay interest on any unpaid balance at market rates.

Depending on how the buy out is structured, another means of funding it is through the profits of a newly added employed physician. This approach typically applies only when a retiring physician is replaced with an employed physician. Once the employed physician's productivity reaches the expected level (which should happen rather quickly, as he or she is taking over the existing patient base of the retiring physician), the retiring physician is paid any profits generated by the newly employed physician. This is in lieu of the profits being paid to the existing shareholders. Thus, from a cash flow perspective, the buy out has no impact on the existing shareholders, as it is contingent on the profits generated by the employed physician. When this type of approach is applied, it tends to be for a limited period of time, typically 24 months. After that time, the profits generated by the employed physician either increase his or her compensation or are paid to the existing shareholders.

Another key factor that exists relative to the funding of a physician buy out pertains to the death of the physician. In this case, the buy out is funded through any life insurance proceeds the practice receives on policies held against the deceased physician. While not all practices hold life insurance policies on their physicians that are payable to the practice, this is key for situations where a significant buy out exists, as it can cause potentially irreparable harm to the practice if it is suddenly faced with a significant equity buy out.

One aspect of the buy-out process that should be considered is a potential waiting period. In many instances, it makes sense to require physicians to be shareholders of the practice for at least five years before buying out, particularly if the buy out is somewhat more lucrative than the buy in. Further, practices often need to limit the number of physicians who can buy out during a given period. For example, the practice may limit equity events to one physician buying out per 12- to 24-month period. This will allow the practice to better handle buy outs from a cash flow perspective.

Key Points to the Buy-In/Buy-Out Process

When buy-in and buy-out agreements are created, the following key considerations should be a part of the process:

- Define the buy-in/buy-out terms at the same time to ensure that they make sense when considered together.
- Define the terms for obtaining an equity interest at the onset of a potential shareholder's employment.
- Establish the eligibility requirements for becoming a shareholder.
- Establish the buy-in purchase price at an appropriate balance that is significant enough to be meaningful but not unattractive.
- Structure the payment process associated with the buy in so that it is functional for younger physicians who may also be managing substantial student loans.
- Where possible, structure the buy in to occur on a pre-tax basis.
- Require that certain criteria are met before guaranteeing partnership to ensure that some discretion can be applied by the existing shareholders.

- Consider these key factors when determining the appropriate buy-in formula: recruitment, practice size, culture, philosophies, and economics.

- Real estate buy ins should be handled separately from the practice buy in. If possible, the real estate should be housed in a separate legal entity.

- From the onset of employment, ensure that prospective shareholders understand the governance and leadership terms and conditions that will apply as a shareholder.

- Allow existing owners to have some level of greater control from a governance and leadership perspective. Some powers may also be reserved for the original owners.

- Ensure that the prospective partner fits within the culture of the practice before an equity interest is offered. This should include a focus on attitude, collegiality, productivity, and expense/savings control.

- Limit the number of buy outs that can occur at the same time.

- To the extent possible, ensure that the buy in and buy out are somewhat aligned.

- Ensure that the buy-out method is such that the practice can fund it without a substantial impact on operations or the existing physicians' compensation.

- Structure the payout to occur over a period of years as opposed to a lump sum.

- Regularly review the practice's operating agreements to ensure that the buy-sell structure is consistent with the practice's intent and industry standards.

Conclusion

Physicians in private medical practice must address equity issues as new physicians are added to the practice, as well as when they exit ownership. The plans in place must be designed to fit the profile of the practice and its partners. Likewise, physicians considering entry into a practice must be able to evaluate the various alternatives pertaining to the acquisition and divestiture of partnership interests. The process of buy in and buy out of practice ownership is of critical importance and has long-lasting effects on the practice's welfare and success.

CHAPTER 19

Physician Diversification

As reduction in payment continues to place more and more pressure on medical practice, the basic business model of the traditional medical practice is changing. Many physicians now realize that to enhance their personal wealth through their business, they must consider alternatives to the traditional outpatient medical practice. Depending on the specialty, there are opportunities to build value and increase overall profitability by diversifying.

Many physicians believe that diversification requires some sort of professional affiliation. Others may find the intrusion of business issues and risk into the practice as offensive. Yet, many physicians today are aggressively seeking opportunities to build lucrative business ventures in the context of their given medical specialty and training. To assure a good fit within the organization's business model and with its physicians, professional values and personal temperament are key to diversifying successfully. As part of the review of the medical practice in transition, it is important to evaluate the alternatives and the possibilities pertaining to such diversification.

Alternatives to the Traditional Business Model

By definition, a business model is defined by size, structure, and services offered. This business model can be changed in many ways. For example, some practices increase their size by adding physicians or merging with other practices. Others achieve business diversification by forming separate entities so that they can invest in ancillary services and facilities. For example, a group of surgeons who own individually managed outpatient practices may come together to form a new company that invests in and owns ancillary ventures such as an ambulatory service center (ASC). Others from specialties such as orthopedics, otolaryngology, urology, ophthalmology, general surgery, pain management, gynecology, and gastroenterology may build and operate an ASC (see Table 19-1). This

TABLE 19-1   Ancillary Services

Specialty	Ancillary Venture
Anesthesiology/Pain management	ASC
Cardiology	Catheterization lab
Dermatology	Surgery center
Endocrinology	Nutrition center/Health education
Family practice	Laboratory and diagnostic wellness centers
Gastroenterology	ASC/Endoscopy center
Hematology/Oncology	Cancer center including radiation oncology
Infectious disease	Laboratory diagnostic wellness centers
Internal medicine	Laboratory diagnostic subspecialty ventures
Nephrology	Renal center
Obstetrician/Gynecologist	Surgery center
Ophthalmology	Surgery center, optical shop
Pediatrics	Diagnostic and laboratory
Podiatry	Surgery center
Pulmonary medicine	Sleep centers
General surgery	Surgery center
Plastic and reconstructive surgery	Surgery center
Urgent care	Walk-in clinic, urgent care center
Urology	Continence center, surgery center
Orthopedic surgery	Surgery center

arrangement opens up a new area of financial opportunity because the ASC does not generate revenue from professional charges. Rather, it generates income from the technical/facility fees.

Although incorporating ancillary services or an ancillary venture into the overall business model may require a separate legal entity, it can be a viable business venture that complements or even augments the basic practice. Such diversification comes with a great deal of risk, including managed care and reimbursement issues, demographics, financial strength of the local economy, and imbalances between supply and demand for comparable services. These risks must be evaluated and measured by the diversified physician-owned organization and addressed within its overall business strategy. The physicians must be willing to accept the worst outcomes from these risks, even loss of income.

Of course, diversification does come with rewards, including increased personal income and net worth. Another reward comes in the form of improved quality of life. Often, surgeons express frustration with the lack of control they have over scheduling the operating room facilities at the local hospital. After constructing their own ASC, they have much more flexibility. This leads to more efficiency not only within the ASC but within their outpatient practice.

Another reward comes from the physician's ability to expand his/her presence throughout the community for the delivery of health care services. The physician who traditionally looked to the local hospital for support in these ventures can be even more independent and reap the benefits of such diversification but still stay within his or her level of clinical expertise.

As an alternative, many physicians look for diversification partners. This arrangement mitigates the risk and allows for a more communal attitude toward the delivery of care. In many instances, the physician partners with a local hospital(s). For the community's long-term welfare, it is best that both physicians and hospitals be successful. In some markets, challenges can result when physicians go out on their own and try to provide services that traditionally have been provided by the hospital. However, it can be a challenge to join hospitals and independent physicians in such a venture. With the advent of accountable care organizations (ACOs) or other similar patient management vehicles, this is likely to occur more frequently. In addition, there are real estate opportunities, such as medical office buildings and other facilities, that are technically outside of the realm of the day-to-day physician practice. These truly qualify as diversification, although they are somewhat outside of the immediate realm of their clinical expertise.

The many alternatives available to the physician must be evaluated and weighed as they relate to the following:

- Overall impact on the community
- Relational impact between the physician and other physicians
- Physician and hospitals
- Physician and the community at large
- Financial return on investment
- Legal requirements relative to physicians investing in such health care entities

Business Opportunities

One of the biggest challenges for any physician is to expand the business. What strategies are available for the physician to do this? If the physician is devoted only to his outpatient practice, growth will be limited. This physician can work longer hours, expand to new locations, or add providers. These options come with added cost and increased risk, and there is the question of viability because the market for such traditional services is mature and spending is in fact decreasing. In addition, the physician must decide whether there should be a reinvestment in the practice infrastructure, including information technology.

This is a challenge because most approaches to revenue growth lack creativity and fail to take advantage of emerging technology and consumer trends and demands. Instead, most physicians focus on capturing shrinking premium dollars and market shares for their individual practice, perpetuating a sickness model, even while the population around them is becoming more concerned about wellness and maintaining health. To avoid such stagnation, many physicians are thinking retail.

Thinking Retail

Webster's defines *retail* as "the sale of commodities or goods in small quantities to ultimate consumers."[1] Thinking retail involves taking the perspective of the consumer, in this case the patient, and developing service features and attributes that will prompt the consumer to purchase directly from the business owner, the physician. Of course, many traditional health services will continue (perhaps always) to be sold through wholesaling intermediaries (ie, insurance and managed care companies). However, the physician should not assume that it is no longer important to seek good managed care contracts with insurance companies. Rather, it should be understood that this is just one of many components in the customer acquisition and retention process.

The historical orientation of facility-based providers and the traditional system of payment is focused on large-scale purchasers. This includes the federal government (Medicare, Federal Employee Health Program, TRICARE, etc), state and local governments (Medicaid), private third parties mostly through insurance companies, and managed care organizations. The insurers have consolidated and the government entities continue to provide payment in ever-diminishing returns. Thus, more and more pressure exists for the providers of health care. Unfortunately, it is not unusual to hear physicians express the view that they have little control over the services they provide; it is the health plans, including government payers, that dictate what will be paid. In many market places, this approach has led to the view of traditional health care services as a commodity. As a result, many ancillary ventures that focus on certain specific areas have been developed by physicians to try to rebalance their ability to control how they practice. Private for-profit companies have also approached physicians in an aggressive manner. The concept of thinking retail about the business has evolved. While we do not want to minimize the importance and the overall priority of physicians providing quality health care, this business approach must be considered.

A number of socioeconomic trends are promoting this move to a more retail-oriented marketplace, including the changing population, technology, and the cost of health care. Opportunities exist to sell preventive screening services (diabetes, cancer), improve home accessibility and functionality, run support groups, sell information on social and medical services, provide cosmetic pharmaceuticals and vitamins, and even provide housing and living alternatives, all within the framework of delivering health care. The largest demographic group, the baby boomers, is now at an age where they frequently seek health care services. Baby boomers have traditionally valued convenience, control, and customer service. They do not hesitate to obtain alternative services or to find different ways to obtain health care, particularly if it means better service for the cost.

Physicians interested in entering the retail market could likely sell the following to the growing baby-boomer population: self-help books and tapes; computer-oriented educational programs; quick tests for blood pressure level, and other health status indicators at shopping malls; and alternative therapies such as massage, biofeedback, and acupuncture. In addition, boutique medicine, ie, arrangements wherein a select number of patients pay the physician an annual fee for full and complete access to services, is appearing in certain markets. Other physicians are taking their practice to the patient. For example, the physician may go to a business person's office or home to treat basic cold or flu.

The baby boomer has stimulated demand for many physician services. Cosmetic surgeries, such as tummy tucks, vein treatment, hair replacement, facelifts, and other cosmetic surgeries, are being performed in nonclinical settings and essentially are paid out of pocket on a fee-for-service basis.

The tremendous technological advances that have been introduced to our society in the last few decades offer new revenue opportunities. They provide this through information access, self-diagnosis, and even home testing capability. The ability to test and measure cholesterol, blood sugar, protein levels, HIV, pregnancy, and even help parents diagnose ear infections has grown into a major industry.

Researchers are working on ways to detect other diseases, such as strep throat, ulcers, and even venereal disease. Interactive systems take blood pressure and pulse and monitor medication usage, making self-care or home health care feasible for the chronically ill and attractive for their caregivers.

The Internet offers significant help via chat rooms for both chronic and acute illnesses, providing a variety of information online. Accuracy is still a major concern with this information.

While not all of these have applicability to the physician, many do. Moreover, the physician must be savvy, understanding that they are a part of the overall health care delivery system. Physicians must have a heightened awareness of the innovations and be willing to include them in their practice as a viable alternative to more traditional methods. Ultimately, these may provide better and more efficient services to patients at an effectively lower cost.

Retailing methodologies also apply to the way health care is presented in the marketplace. For example, traditionally some health care providers have minimized the importance of facility aesthetics, environment, and surroundings when treating patients. Believing that the health care environment does not matter severely limits opportunity and growth. Today, many physicians are thinking more about facility convenience, accessibility, and aesthetics so that the overall practice experience is much more pleasant (realizing that there are limitations to this given the degree of illness extant). Such improvements do not have to cost a lot; high-quality customer service is often most important to patients.

Another retail strategy is to offer related products and services to stimulate additional spending. Although this may be perceived as taboo, it is very much a part of today's medical experience. For example, expectant mothers will soon need to select a pediatrician or a family practitioner for newborn care. What process does the obstetrician have in place to help her make that selection? More obstetricians are also offering other women's services, such as spa-related services. What better way to follow through on this than to provide nutritional counseling services in the office? One must consider what impact the Stark regulations have on the desired services to offer.

Diversification is a fact of life in health care today. Just look at successful retailers such as Walmart and Home Depot, which are extremely diversified. The way to succeed in this area is to look at business opportunities from the patient's point of view. For example, what type of health care services are available for adolescents who believe they are too old to go to a pediatrician and too cool to go to their parent's general practitioners? There is obviously a niche to be addressed in this and many other areas of the medical practice.

The Possibilities of Partnering

Many reasons exist for aligning with other providers including the following:

- Strength in numbers
- Creating a name-brand identity
- Assuring cost effective services
- Diversification of payers (spread out the payer mix)
- Expansion of patient base

The preceding list represents basic yet very real reasons for forming such strategically aligned organizations.

There are several possibilities for partnering among physicians and ancillary or diversified ventures. The most logical is for fellow providers or physicians to come together in such a venture. Occasionally, physicians find non-physician entities or individuals to partner with; these partnerships often take the form of joint ventures between physicians and hospitals.

Partnership Evaluation Facets: Relational

Each partnership should be evaluated to make sure it is a good fit for all involved. Fit is not always based on the financial or fiscal ramifications of the partnership. Considerations to be evaluated include the following:

- Attributes of potential partners
- Community orientation
- Ability to develop links with other health care providers
- Ability to develop an integrated information system
- Effectiveness in negotiating managed care contracts
- Capital investment potential
- Profitability potential
- Expense reduction potential
- Cultural compatibility
- Ability to achieve the goals of the partnership

Partnership Evaluation Facets: Financial

Areas that should be assessed to make sure the partnership makes good business sense include the following:

- Fundamentally solid fiscal base
- Realistic strategic plan with a sound feasibility study
- Ability to expand
- Adequate community involvement
- Strong market penetration
- Similar practice goals/objectives
- Strategically viable location (both physically and services offered) in the community

Any proposed joint venture or partnership should include the following in its business plan and/or contracts:

- Purpose of the partnership
- Legal structure
- Assets/liabilities

- Governance
- Management
- Valuation
- Profit and loss sharing
- Capitalization/working capital
- Human resources
- Partnership exit
- Covenants not to compete
- Tax-exemption issues if applicable

Failed Partnerships

Despite efforts to create the ideal partnership, some mergers or partnerships do fail. Usually, they fail when there is a lack of planning and coordination, eg, making key strategic decisions after the partnership has been formed. Other times partnerships fail because they are thought to be the "silver bullet" but end up not solving existing problems. There may be clashes at the highest levels of the organization, or physicians who are not able to get along and work together. Control is also a major factor. Some physicians give up control when they take on an equity partner and are simply not ready to do this.

When is the best time to create a partnership or joint venture? Usually, when partners who are both financially stable are able to take the time to look for the right opportunity and to put together a well-planned and coordinated initiative. The ability to assess organizational strengths and weaknesses and acquire partners who will be strong contributors to the organization are also important for success. Physicians who are willing to work together and truly function as partners will assure success.

Hospital Alignment

Although many physicians would prefer to be independent, many are aligning more closely with hospitals. Hospitals and physicians participating in integrated delivery systems should realize that success cannot be achieved independent of each other. While the dynamics of physician employment by hospitals is changing, physicians and hospitals are still able to work collaboratively to benefit both parties in the marketplace. Refer to Chapter 1 for a more detailed review.

In addition, there are strategic reasons for maintaining collaborative initiatives. Increased understanding of the market through broad-based services gives increased visibility in the community to both the physician and the hospital. More comprehensive services may also be the result. Another viable reason for joining forces is to pursue contract opportunities through consolidated systems to negotiate contracts. Lastly, another reason to come together is to attract quality managers and physicians in a desired practice setting for new physicians.

The overriding physician integration principles should include a shared mission and values, a structure that will thrive in a managed care environment (especially in capitation arrangements), a genuine spirit of partnership, and a culture that promotes physician creativity, leadership, and long-term relationships between the hospital and the physician.

The ability to form a strong physician–physician, physician–investor, or physician–hospital partnership requires the partners to do the following:

- **Set a quality standard.** Although every physician must be clinically competent, the partners should be at the forefront of their respective fields, intolerant of less than high quality care.

- **Make entrepreneurial contributions to the partnership.** Every partner should participate in the entity's management, organization, and administrative structuring. Being a partner also means accepting the risks as well as the rewards. An individual who wants to practice good medicine for a guaranteed income should be an employee, not an owner/investor.

- **Make personal contributions to the partnership.** A partner must clearly add value to the entity by the work product and the output of that product. The result is increased revenues or other improvements within the practice. Ownership demands more time, energy, and commitment than one could expect from an employee.

The Political Fallout

Political fallout is possible after the formation of a partnership or diversified health care venture. For example, the surgeon who invests in the building and operation of an ASC may be alienated from the hospital and other physicians. Certainly, this type of surgical specialist depends on referrals for continued viability. Such considerations should become part of the feasibility study, which is used to evaluate the proposed venture, in this case whether to build the ASC.

Political fallout may occur within the very group that is considering investing in the ancillary venture. For example, a multispecialty group may not have the backing of all of its partners for the investment in certain ancillary ventures. Or the ASC that is to be constructed by a multispecialty group may not generate a great deal of interest among its primary care physicians. Thus, the overall initiative needs to be thoroughly discussed and agreed on before moving ahead, and all decisions should be made with the best interests of the entire group in mind.

Legal Constraints and Considerations

There are, of course, legal considerations relative to ancillary ventures and physician diversification. Both state and federal regulations require physicians and other health care entities to be in compliance relative to the delivery of services, regardless of the format under which they are practicing. Most regulations, whether they are federal anti-kickback statutes, Stark regulations, or other laws, focus on ensuring that the cost or delivery of care is not being impugned or in any way being taken advantage of by the actions of the physicians. The Stark regulations prohibit a physician from making referrals for certain designated health services payable by Medicare to an entity with which he or she (or an immediate family member) has a financial relationship (ownership, investment, or compensation), unless an exception applies. Designated health services (DHS) include the following services and supplies:

- Clinical laboratory services
- Physician therapy, occupation therapy, and speech-language therapy
- Radiology and radiation therapy (now includes nuclear medicine)
- Durable medical equipment and supplies
- Parenteral/enteral nutrients
- Prosthetics
- Home health services
- Outpatient prescription drugs
- Inpatient and outpatient hospital services

Physician Self-Referral (Stark Laws) Regulations

The Omnibus Budget Reconciliation Act of 1989 (OBRA 1989), which bars self-referrals for clinical laboratory services under the Medicare program, became effective January 1, 1992. This provision is known as Stark I. In 1993, Congress expanded the law to apply to 10 additional health services known as Stark II, which became effective in 1995. The Stark law, which actually incorporates three separate regulations, governs physician self-referral for Medicare and Medicaid patients. (The law is named for US Congressman Pete Stark, who sponsored the initial bill.)

The 11 designated health services from which physicians are barred from self-referring include:

- Clinical laboratory services
- Physical therapy services
- Occupational therapy services
- Radiology services
- Radiation therapy services
- Durable medical equipment and supplies
- Parenteral and enteral nutrients, equipment, and supplies
- Prosthetics, orthotics, prosthetic devices, and supplies
- Home health services
- Outpatient prescription drugs
- Inpatient and outpatient hospital services

Penalties for violation of Stark I and II include denial of payment for the designated health services, refund of amounts collected in violation of the provision, and civil monetary penalties up to $15,000 for each service. Physicians and entities entering into an arrangement to circumvent the referral restriction law are subject to civil monetary penalties of up to $100,000 per occurrence.[2]

Phase III of Stark II, the final rule, was published in 2007. It did not change the designated health services, but it does clarify some provisions for office space and equipment lease arrangements, eliminated the safe harbor for fair market value, modified the definition of physician in a group practice, and made other changes.

Other proposed statutes and regulations may impact Stark in the near future. These include the 2008 Medicare proposed physician fee schedule limits per-click (or per unit of service) compensation that applies when a physician leases space or equipment to an entity that performs designated health services (DHS) and then refers patients to that DHS entity. CMS believes these arrangements give physicians the incentive to make unnecessary DHS referrals. The agency has requested comments on other arrangements in which an entity performing DHS pays the owners of space and/or equipment per unit of time or per unit of service and in which the units reflect referrals from the space and/or equipment owners. The proposed limit on per-click compensation was not included in the final rule. However, this provision was included in the Medicare hospital inpatient prospective payment system (IPPS) rulemaking for FY 2009 and went into effect October 1, 2009.

Exceptions

As with the anti-kickback statute, there are exceptions to the general Stark rule prohibiting a physician from making a referral for certain designated health services payable by Medicare to an entity with which the physician or an immediate family member has a financial relationship. Some exceptions are similar to the safe harbors listed in the anti-kickback statute. The exceptions fall into three categories:

- *Those based on compensation, investments, and ownership.* These exceptions apply to physician services personally provided by the physician, ancillary services provided by the ordering physician or another member of the group or supervised by the ordering physician, services furnished to enrollees of risk-based Medicare health maintenance organizations, and services furnished in ambulatory surgery centers or end-stage renal disease facilities.

- *Those based on both ownership and investment.* These exceptions include ownership or investment in publicly traded securities and mutual funds and certain hospital exceptions.

- *Those based on compensation only.* These exceptions deal with office rental, equipment rental, employee relationships, group practice arrangements within hospitals, and group purchasing arrangements.

The Stark law, however, is based on fact rather than intent. Whether or not people intended to violate these laws, if they are in violation—well, they are in violation! Unlike the anti-kickback statute, which can apply to any health care provider, this law currently pertains only to physicians, defined as doctors of medicine, osteopathic physicians, dentists, or doctors of dental surgery, podiatrists, optometrists, and chiropractors. Recently, questions have been raised pertaining to Stark laws and mid-level providers. This applicability is still being tested.

Conclusion

Physician diversification will continue to be a key topic of discussion over the next few years. It is important for individual providers to define their personal and practice goals as they consider the many options in the market today.

References

1. Merriam-Webster Dictionary Online. www.merriam-webster.com/dictionary/retail. Accessed March 18, 2011.

2. US Department of Health and Human Services, Centers for Medicare and Medicaid Services. *42 CFR Parts 411 and 424, Medicare Program; Physicians' Referrals to Health Care Entities With Which They Have Financial Relationships (Phase III); Final Rule.* http://edocket.access.gpo .gov/2007/pdf/07-4252.pdf. September 5, 2007.

20

Practice Mergers

When owners of a medical practice consider strategic growth alternatives, one of the multiple options they will likely weigh is the possibility of merging with another practice. Practices have been coming together to form larger entities for many years. Just like any other company, the opportunity to merge with another group can be a significant step toward future growth and success. Conversely, when you consider any type of merger, the far majority of them end up failing compared to those that turn out to be successful. As such, merging two practices will involve a monumental task that requires significant planning, preparation, and execution by the key stakeholders involved. Regardless of whether a merger makes business sense, if those driving the merger do not conduct adequate planning and execute their strategy effectively, the likelihood of failure will more often than not outweigh the probability of success. Nevertheless, a merger can be one of the most advantageous strategies that a health care entity can pursue. The key distinction, however, is that this strategy must be executed properly in order for it to ultimately generate the expected returns.

Merger Strategy and Types

When considering the prospect of a merger, one must first ask, "Why merge?" Some mergers may be driven by the simple lack of alternatives; some are for growth. A medical group's partners should constantly be thinking about their long-term strategies and objectives for the business; if a goal is to grow, then the prospect of merging with another entity should always be open for consideration and exploration. Mergers among medical practices are very common, because in many cases this is the only way these entities can achieve any sort of real economies of scale or scope. Physicians operating an existing medical practice with a reasonable patient base are typically unable to broadly expand their own individual services. For instance, otolaryngologists may be able to expand into allergy services; however, they are not likely to extend beyond that within their specialty. Likewise, a group of cardiologists might expand into vascular services or add a vascular imaging unit; however, going beyond that with procedures that are more specialized will require additional training and certification. The more likely prospect would be to add one or more new physicians. Alternatively, that existing group can reach out to other established groups to discuss the prospect of joining in a partnership that would allow both parties to reap significant gains from the advantage of the combined entity. They would be able to extend the scope of their services, while gaining economies of scale, which can be beneficial in increasing volume, gaining purchasing leverage, and attaining a more advantageous position in managed care contracting.

Historically, this concept has also been the largest factor driving the growth of the modern multi-specialty group, which often encompasses multiple different and unique specialty groups that merge to form a larger and more powerful organization. A key characteristic of the multi-specialty group model is that even though a physician or group of physicians within an established specialty does not have a significant flexibility to extend their own range of services, they can partner with physicians in other specialties to form a more dynamic health care delivery organization.

The multi-specialty group model represents one type of practice merger that is common in today's environment. Other types of mergers include solo physicians combining their individual practices to form a group; a group of internal medicine or primary care physicians combining with another comparable group; a group of specialists merging with another group within their same specialty for the purpose of growing volume and increasing market share; and, situations involving groups merging into a larger group model, such as an independent practice association, management services organization, or even a health system's employed physician network. In all of these cases, though, the reason for the merger is usually to achieve some degree of scale (ie, volume growth, market share, new patients, etc), scope (ie, new services, additional locations, extended geography, etc) or both.

Due Diligence

Within any merger process, due diligence is perhaps the most critical element, even more so than the negotiations of economic terms and a deal's financial consideration. The reason for this is that rarely will a merger fail due to the economics of the deal; more mergers fail than succeed primarily due to non-economic considerations. A transaction's non-economic consideration refers to the qualitative aspects of a deal, which includes culture, operational dynamics, human resources and personnel, adherence to certain clinical processes, and/or tools, etc. Frequently, this boils down to simply whether a group of physicians can get along well while working together. Before a merger closes, the parties on both sides must conduct due diligence on the financial, operational, and other quantitative aspects of the entities as well as the qualitative dynamics involved.

The due diligence process can be a very complex and detailed undertaking, and it should be approached as a process. Further, parties in a transaction should never attempt to conduct their own due diligence internally without any external and/or independent counsel. In any merger, there will be a number of challenges to overcome, in order to achieve success; therefore, entities that are merging should take every precaution and step that they can to minimize their risk of failure. One of those steps will be to engage outside advisors that can assist throughout the transaction process, a key aspect of which is due diligence.

Within the scenario of a practice merger, due diligence will typically include a full assessment of the entities involved with an analysis of productivity, revenue, and expenses, as well as the assets of the practices (both tangible and intangible). Due diligence also reviews processes relative to information systems and electronic health records (EHR). (See Chapter 18.)

In addition, the due diligence evaluation should include a forward-looking analysis that considers not only the state of the merging entities today, but how they will operate in the newly merged entity going forward. This element is the most critical and is often the missing link that if done properly bridges a particular merger with success. While two separate entities may be extremely efficient, profitable, and valuable as separate entities, simply putting them together does not necessarily double those efficiencies, profits, or value. In fact, putting two well balanced organizations together can actually result in diminishing benefits as a result of redundancies or overlap in weaknesses. Just as one might assume that the positives of two practices should equal one positive that is twice as large as it used to be, one must also consider the same affect the merger will have on the entities' weaknesses which can often have more impact than the positives.

In any merger, there will be certain synergies, which are the complementary aspects of the two businesses, and how those synergies will result in value going forward. Alternatively, combining two entities will also mean combining those entities' weaknesses which typically are referred to as redundancies, gaps, or diseconomies. These are the negative elements that will outweigh the synergies much faster than the synergies will be able to generate value; therefore, the focus within the merger strategy should always first be on reducing weaknesses or threats and then accentuating the synergies. However, simply accentuating synergies will rarely make up for the losses associated with the combined entity's weaknesses. Those weaknesses will often be detrimental to the growth of the organization, eroding the practice's foundation. This ultimately will mean the combined entity will not be able to benefit from synergies until it addresses the negative aspects of each organization.

Within the due diligence process, one or likely both of the parties will conduct valuation analysis, which is addressed in further detail in Chapter 18. However, the valuation is a key component of a transaction's financial due diligence, and while every transaction will ultimately have a set valuation, when it is all said and done throughout the due diligence process, the valuation is typically an evolving and constantly moving target. Due diligence and valuation analysis of mergers will often include some specific methodologies, which include DuPont analysis, Accretion/Dilution analysis, SWOT analysis, Porter's Five Forces, and Scenario analysis.

DuPont analysis is an approach to evaluating a company's potential return on equity and is often used in evaluating the value of a future, combined entity once a merger is completed. This approach ultimately allows for a better understanding of the superior value based on return on equity in comparison against comparable entities. Likewise, the Accretion/Dilution analysis method involves evaluating the impact of a specific transaction on the value of a company's equity. It essentially attempts to answer the question as to whether a specific deal increases (ie, is accretive) or decreases (ie, is dilutive) a company's value.[1] Both the DuPont model and Accretion/Dilution analysis are typically reserved for transactions involving larger companies. Most of the time, their application is specifically relevant to publicly traded companies, where specific quantitative elements, such as return on equity and earnings per share, can be obtained more easily. For smaller, private entities like medical practices, the DuPoint model and Accretion/Dilution analysis will not be directly applicable in the conventional sense of those methods, partially due to the fact that these models are intrinsically focused on measuring the share value of the ongoing entity after a transaction is complete.

There are many ways that companies can apply some of the same principles and approaches of these analyses to the due diligence assessment of a medical practice. For instance, while a practice may not have earnings per share (EPS) information, there are ways to conduct the practice assessment which will tell whether the impact of certain parameters will have the effect of increasing value or decreasing it. For instance, how should you deal with real estate when one or both of the merging entities own property? Should you extend the transaction to purchasing real estate which is likely in a separate entity? Or perhaps the real estate is owned within the same entity that is being merged; however, the shareholders of the other entity do not want to include real estate in the deal. Then you will have to deal with carving the real estate out of the deal, putting it into a separate entity, and adjusting the transaction's value based on those changes. But, if there is openness to consider the deal either with or without the property, this type of analysis can provide a helpful reading on which approach would be most optimal for shareholders going forward. The same mind-set can be carried over to analyzing the returns that investors (ie, shareholders) will get from a specific investment which will inevitably be involved in any merger. The analyst will just need to be innovative in how he or she reviews the relevant data in a practice merger and applies the appropriate analysis to the specific situation in a manner that makes sense.

Other types of analytical methods used in due diligence are more focused on the qualitative aspects of a deal or those elements of a transaction that cannot be fully quantified. These include SWOT analysis and Porter's Five Forces analysis, among others. SWOT—Strengths, Weaknesses, Opportunities, and Threats—analysis is one of the most commonly applied analysis methodologies used in businesses of all shapes and sizes. SWOT analysis is also very helpful when analyzing the likely go-forward impact of a merger or acquisition, because it digs into the most critical elements of a transaction that will make it either successful or unsuccessful. However, when using SWOT analysis, one should not just identify the four parameters and then assume the task is complete. Identifying the key items in each category is just the first step. One of the helpful aspects of SWOT analysis is that an analyst can assess both quantitative and qualitative parameters in their analysis. Once you have identified the key items, you should then attempt to quantify their impact. Even if the parameter does not seem to be directly quantifiable, you can still attempt to place a quantifiable value on the impact of that variable. For instance, if you identify loss of market share as a potential threat, you should not just end the analysis assuming you could lose market share. You should attempt to determine (1) how much market share would likely be lost; (2) what value does that likely loss of market share equate to (ie, decline in revenues, increase in expenses, diminishing profitability and volume, etc), and (3) what is a reasonable assumption of probability that this threat could become a reality? This analysis will require some subjective assumptions; however, this is much more actionable and rigorous than simply identifying a threat, because calling out a threat without any sort of solution or actionable approach to dealing with it is meaningless. Further, the same can be said of opportunities. You may identify that a proposed merger could potentially present the opportunity to garner leverage in purchasing and supply chain management. However, without knowing how much value can be attributed to that potential opportunity, you really cannot determine whether this opportunity justifies the merger. It could be that although gaining purchasing power would be a benefit, the potential value from that opportunity does not outweigh other identified threats and weaknesses; therefore, you would have a clear assessment as to the likely impact of those considerations.

Porter's Five Forces (PFF) was an analytical approach to industry analysis and business strategy developed by Harvard Business School Professor Michael Porter in 1979 as an alternative to SWOT analysis, which Porter did not believe was rigorous enough. While PFF is more commonly used with larger organizations, the simple model has been used frequently in evaluating specific situations or events, such as mergers, new business unit launches, new product/service offerings, investment under consideration, etc. PFF models take into consideration five key elements: (1) the threat of entry of new competitors; (2) the intensity of competitive rivalry; (3) the threat of substitute products/ services; (4) the bargaining power of customers/buyers; and (5) the bargaining power of suppliers. The idea is to be able to look at the key qualitative and quantitative elements of each category and conduct a broad, systemic analysis of each category as a separate silo as well as the aggregation of the different elements combined. You can then apply that analysis and the key elements to a valuation or some other quantitative metric that will generate an output variable illustrating the likely outcome of each of the elements and their parameters. Similar to SWOT analysis, a PFF model is most beneficial in applying it as a guide in an overall assessment; as with SWOT analysis, this model should be used in conjunction with a valuation or some sort of analysis that allows the analyst to quantify key elements of the analysis.

One other type of global analysis tool that should be applied in merger due diligence is scenario analysis, often referred to as *if, then analysis,* because it simply attempts to evaluate the qualitative and quantitative effects of a certain chain of events resulting from a specific action such as a merger. Rather than simply conducting scenario analysis on its own, this approach usually is applied within the other methods used. For instance, when you conduct valuation analysis, the analyst should typically include a model that is adjustable based on some specific inputs (ie, scenarios). A typical analysis would be "if we were to change 'variable X' by a specified percentage, then the 'Y variable'—typically the entity's valuation—will change by a certain percentage or dollar amount."

With all of these models, it is essential to understand that analysts will never be able to consider every possible outcome, contingency, or variable. These approaches represent a very small sample of the many different approaches you can take to due diligence to evaluate a merger. However, the most critical thing to keep in mind is that all of the analysis in the world will never be able to mitigate every ounce of risk in a merger. The idea is to reduce gaps and limit risks to an amount that makes sense and can be justified from an investment standpoint. If the organization can justify the investment—the financial investment as well as non-economic investment that a merger will require—based on the amount of expected risk, then they can typically justify to their partners, shareholders, and others, to move forward.

Most mergers fail due to two pitfalls: (1) the parties involved never conducted any real due diligence analysis and essentially just assumed the combined entity would be successful because it made sense in theory, or (2) the parties conducted such extensive due diligence analysis that they essentially eliminated any of the potential value of the deal when they eliminated the risk, because value in a free market economy never comes without risk. Many investors or strategic companies going through a merger will go to the extreme with quantified models of risk and return; however, they fail to consider the non-economic variables, and the net outcome in the long run is often failure.

Finally, we should note that due diligence is not exclusively about financial and business operations analysis. This is also the phase where the companies' legal counsel will conduct their review of contracts, litigation, regulatory compliance, etc. Legal due diligence is a critical and essential element of every merger or acquisition. However, the parties should be fully aware that due diligence does not solely apply to the legal review done by their attorneys. Due diligence should be composed of financial, operational, and legal due diligence, all conducted separately in a vacuum at first and then aggregated to assess any overlapping or contributing factors that span multiple categories. For instance, if your legal counsel identifies a potential legal or regulatory issue in due diligence, and when the list of issues is aggregated, you realize that your financial due diligence team identified the same legal or regulatory issue, then you know this is something that needs further consideration. Potentially, this could even prevent the deal from closing. Rarely does one single issue arise in due diligence that kills a deal; it is typically the recurrence of complementary issues that ultimately equal a major risk to the parties involved that will justify walking away from a deal. In all cases, due diligence should be confirmatory in nature, meaning the justification for a deal should already have been made before diligence even begins. However, to make a merger or acquisition truly successful, the parties should be able to approach due diligence with a healthy level of skepticism to ensure they are not going in a deal with blinders on. In this regard, it is always beneficial for parties in a merger to engage a financial advisory or consulting firm to assist throughout the due diligence process.

Once the due diligence process is complete, the merging entities will both be equipped with the information, data, and analysis that will allow them to make a rationale business decision relative to the transaction.

Post-Merger Integration

In many merger cases, whether it is a multibillion dollar merger of publicly traded companies, or mergers of small medical practice entities, the single most detrimental factor that ultimately results in failure of the merger is the lack of a post-merger integration plan. Often, the typical response is that once they figure out the details of the transaction and deal with the challenges of that process, they can then think about how they are going to make the merger work after the transaction. However, this is the first loose rock in the impending descent down a slippery slope that more often than not results in a merger failing. The key issue here is that when you are considering a strategic transaction of some

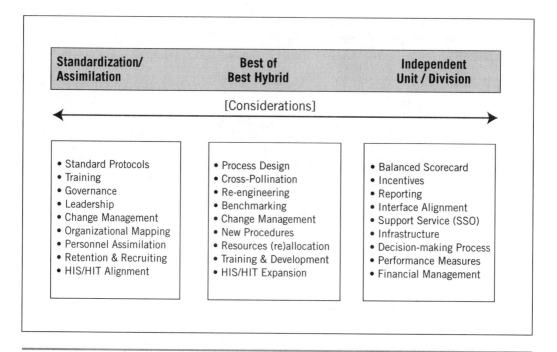

FIGURE 20-1   Continuum of Integration Strategies

Source: Coker Group, 2010.

sort (ie, a merger of two or more operating businesses) and you cannot develop a plan for post-merger integration, then you ultimately have not adequately justified the merger at all. The merger must have both strategic and financial value for the stakeholders involved, which in a going concern will mean some sort of future growth and/or value. As such, post-merger integration is a misnomer because it alludes to an event that occurs after a merger is completed. Post-merger integration should begin long before companies even start the merger transaction process.

Post-merger integration can ultimately incorporate a range of different strategies and approaches; however, the goal of integration typically is considered on some form of continuum as illustrated in Figure 20-1.

Typically, the integration process should incorporate some key defined steps or phases. First, conduct integration planning. This should begin prior to a deal closing and likely will occur in conjunction with due diligence, because the analysis conducted in the due diligence process can usually be applied to the post-merger integration planning process. Once the integration planning is completed, the companies should develop an integration road map or plan. This will be the defined plan for the short-term post-merger transition and long-term post-merger integration. Integration transition focuses more on maintaining current levels of productivity and ensuring that the recently closed deal does not have any direct negative effects on the newly merged entity. After a merger, there will typically be some sort of initial decline in productivity or increase in costs associated with getting the deal done; however, the first priority of post-merger integration is achieving a stable and sustainable transition process while mitigating and/or reducing as many risks as possible.

Alternatively, post-merger integration focuses on the comprehensive, long-term strategy that will guide the newly merged entity in achieving the full value and potential of the merger. Worded differently, the focus of integration is on making those synergies identified in due diligence a reality.

The roadmap should be a detailed, comprehensive, and dynamic plan that outlines the key parameters of the integration, including tasks, timeline, budget, personnel, and governance. The roadmap will outline in detail what steps need to occur to achieve integration, and each step or task will have a designated time frame associated with it. In some cases, each task will have a cost that can be factored into a budget. However, this is not always the case, so you will typically need to develop milestones or subprojects built into the overall integration process. Each subproject or milestone period should have a cost factor attributed to a line item in an overall integration budget. The integration should also have a defined, and if possible dedicated, team to manage and drive the integration process. You can have the greatest plan in the world on paper; however, if there is no one person or team driving the execution of that plan, it will be a waste of time. Finally, the integration process needs a defined governance structure associated with it, so there is a defined working group, committee, or steering group that is responsible for making decisions associated with the integration as well as being responsible for managing the budget and timeline of the overall integration.

Once the roadmap is in place, you will start staging for execution. This simply refers to the time prior to the deal closing where you can attempt to get everything in place that you possibly can before closing, so that when the transaction is completed, you can immediately effect the integration execution plan.

This brings us to integration execution. We already discussed the two phases of integration execution above (ie, transition and integration), but this is where the plan is put into action. If your roadmap is as comprehensive and specific as it should be, the execution aspect of integration should not be overwhelming. However, regardless of how extensive your planning is, the integration process will always involve continuous changes and unexpected events or situations that arise to throw the plan offtrack. Therefore, when you are conducting your planning, it is critical to give yourself enough flexibility once you are in the execution phases to make the necessary adjustments and on-the-ground changes to the plan as needed without having to toss the entire plan and completely start from scratch.

As previously discussed, the first few weeks after a deal closes, the primary focus should be on transitioning the companies into the newly merged single entity as seamlessly as possible. In this phase, your roadmap should tell you where certain employees, groups, assets, systems, and infrastructure elements should be located within the new entity. If the merger model is truly a best of best hybrid where you are taking the best elements of each business and combining them to get the most optimal result, then the evaluation conducted during due diligence should have defined what those elements are and how they need to be structured post-transaction. You should know where the potential pitfalls and gaps are, as well as have a real understanding of the high areas of value which you should focus on first. Throughout this process, the most critical element is understanding that the transition should center on minimizing losses in productivity, revenue, and growth as the transition is in progress.

Once the organization gets through the initial transition element of post-merger integration, which will typically last anywhere from four weeks to two years, depending on the size of the organizations involved, the long-term integration plan will then become the priority. We mentioned before about the impact of not having any focus on post-merger integration; however, even those businesses that do consider post-merger integration often fail to separate transition and true long-term integration, and this can have detrimental effects on the long-term success and effectiveness of a merger. Ultimately, it is not possible to define the latter segment of integration because it will always be dynamic and different for each particular entity and every transaction. The critical point to keep in mind, however, is that long-term integration focuses on achieving the true value from a merger, while the transition period focuses on minimizing negative effects from the transaction. One is about minimizing negatives, and the other is about maximizing positives. Both are critical and both segments depend on each other to make each achieve maximum effectiveness.

Conclusion

In this chapter, we considered some of the key elements of mergers between health care entities. We considered the different types of mergers as well as common strategies pursued when two or more organizations consider merging. We also looked at some of the critical aspects of executing a merger, including the role of due diligence and the most optimal approaches to that process. Finally, we considered the importance of post-merger integration and how this is often the most critical, yet most commonly neglected, aspect of a merger regardless of the size of the organizations involved.

Reference

1. Accretion Dilution Analysis, *Investopedia.com*. Accessed April 2011.

Professional Associations

American Academy of Family Physicians
11400 Tomahawk Creek Parkway
Leawood, KS 66211-2672
Telephone: (913) 906-6000
E-mail: fp@aafp.org
http://www.aafp.org

American College of Obstetricians and Gynecologists
409 12th Street, SW, P.O. Box 96920
Washington, DC 20090-6920
http://www.acog.com/

The American Academy of Pediatrics
141 Northwest Point Boulevard
Elk Grove Village, IL 60007-1098
Telephone: (847) 434-4000
Fax: (847) 434-8000
http://www.aap.org/

American Academy of Otolaryngology–Head and Neck Surgery
1650 Diagonal Road
Alexandria, VA 22314-2857
Telephone: (703) 836-4444
http://www.entnet.org/

The American College of Cardiology
Heart House
2400 N Street NW
Washington DC 20037
Telephone: (800) 253-4636, ext. 5603 or (202) 375-6000
Fax: (202) 375-7000
http://www.acc.org/

American Academy of Neurology
1080 Montreal Avenue
St. Paul, MN 55116
Telephone: (651) 695-2717
http://www.aan.com/

American Academy of Ophthalmology
655 Beach Street
San Francisco, CA 94109
Telephone: (415) 561-8500
http://www.aao.org/

American College of Surgeons
633 N. Saint Clair Street
Chicago, IL 60611-3211
Telephone: (312) 202-5000
Fax: (312) 202-5001
E-mail: postmaster@facs.org
http://www.facs.org/

American Urological Association
1000 Corporate Boulevard
Linthicum, MD 21090
Telephone: (410) 689-3700
Fax: (410) 689-3800
http://www.auanet.org/

**American Academy of Orthopaedic
Surgeons**
6300 North River Road
Rosemont, IL 60018-4262
Telephone: (847) 823-7186 or
    (800) 356-AAOS
Fax: (847) 823-8125
AAOS Fax on Demand: (800) 999-2939
http://www.aaos.org/

**American Association of
Neurological Surgeons**
5550 Meadowbrook Drive
Rolling Meadows, IL 60088
Telephone: (847) 378-0500 or
    (888) 566-AANS (2267)
Fax: (847) 378-0600
E-mail: info@aans.org
http://www.aans.org

American Psychiatric Association
1000 Wilson Boulevard, Suite 1825
Arlington, VA 22209-3901
Telephone: (703) 907-7300
E-mail: apa@psych.org
http://www.psych.org/

Renal Physicians Association
1700 Rockville Pike, Suite 220
Rockville, MD 20852
Telephone: (301) 468-3515
Fax: (301) 468-3511
http://www.renalmd.org/

**American Academy of Physical
Medicine and Rehabilitation**
9700 W. Bryn Mawr Ave., Suite 200
Rosemont, IL 60018
Telephone: (847) 737-6000
Fax: (847) 737-6001
E-mail: info@aapmr.org
http://www.aapmr.org/

**American Academy of Physician
Assistants**
2318 Mill Road, Suite 1300
Alexandria, VA 22314-1552
Telephone: (703) 836-2272
Fax: (703) 684-1924
http://www.aapa.org/

**American Academy of Nurse
Practitioners**
P.O. Box 12846
Austin, TX 78711
Telephone: (512) 442-4262
Fax: (512) 442-6469
E-mail: admin@aanp.org
http://www.aanp.org/

**American Academy of Allergy,
Asthma & Immunology**
555 East Wells Street, Suite 1100
Milwaukee, WI 53202
Telephone: (414) 272-6071
Patient Information and Physician
    Referral Line: 1 (800) 822-2762
http://www.aaaai.org/

**The American Academy of Child
and Adolescent Psychiatry**
3615 Wisconsin Avenue, NW
Washington, DC 20016-3007
Telephone: (202) 966-7300
Fax: (202) 966-2891
http://www.aacap.org/

**The American Academy of
Dermatology**
930 E. Woodfield Road
Schaumburg, IL 60173-4927
Telephone: (866) 503-SKIN
Fax: (847) 240-1859
http://www.aad.org/

**American Academy of Facial Plastic
and Reconstructive Surgery**
310 S. Henry Street
Alexandria, VA 22314
Telephone: (703) 299-9291
Fax: (703) 299-8898
http://aafprs.org

American Academy of Insurance Medicine
100 – 32 Colonnade Road
Ottawa ON K2E 7J6
Telephone: (613) 226-9601
Fax: (613) 721-3581
http://www.aaimedicine.org/

American Academy of Pain Medicine
4700 W. Lake Avenue
Glenview, IL 60025
Telephone: (847) 375-4731
Fax: (847) 375-6477
E-mail: info@painmed.org
http://www.painmed.org/

American Academy of Sleep Medicine
2510 North Frontage Road
Darien, IL 60561
Telephone: (630) 737-9700
Fax: (630) 737-9790
http://www.aasmnet.org/

The American Association for Thoracic Surgery
500 Cumming Center, Suite 4550
Beverly, MA 01915
Telephone: (978) 927-8330
Fax: (978) 524-8890
http://www.aats.org/

American Association of Clinical Endocrinologists
245 Riverside Avenue, Suite 200
Jacksonville, FL 32202
Telephone: (904) 353-7878
Fax: (904) 353-8185
http://www.aace.com/

American Association of Public Health Physicians
1605 Pebble Beach Blvd.
Green Cove Springs, FL 32043
Telephone: (904) 860-9208
Fax: (904) 529-7761
http://www.aaphp.org/

American College of Chest Physicians
3300 Dundee Road
Northbrook, IL 60062-2348
Telephone: (847) 498-1400
Fax: (847) 498-5460
E-mail: accp@chestnet.org
http://www.chestnet.org/

American College of Emergency Physicians
1125 Executive Circle
Irving, TX 75038-2522
Telephone: (800) 798-1822
http://www.acep.org/

American College of Gastroenterology
P.O Box 342260
Bethesda, MD 20827-2260
Telephone: (301) 263-9000
http://www.acg.gi.org/

American Gastroenterological Association
4960 Del Ray Avenue
Bethesda, MD 20814
Telephone: (301) 654-2055
Fax: (301) 654-5920
http://www.gastro.org/

American College of Medical Quality
5272 River Road, Suite 630
Bethesda, MD 20816
Telephone: (301) 718-6516
Fax: (301) 656-0989
http://www.acmq.org/

American College of Occupational and Environmental Medicine
25 Northwest Point Blvd.,
   Suite 700
Elk Grove Village, IL 60007-1030
Telephone: (847) 818-1800
Fax: (847) 818-9266
http://www.acoem.org/

**American College of Physicians—
American Society of Internal
Medicine**
190 N. Independence Mall West
Philadelphia, PA 19106-1572
Telephone: (800) 523-1546, x2600 or
   (215) 351-2600
http://www.acponline.org/

**American College of Physician
Executives**
400 North Ashley Drive, Suite 400
Tampa, FL 33602
Telephone: (800) 562-8088
Fax: (813) 287-8993
http://www.acpe.org/

**American College of Preventive
Medicine**
455 Massachusetts Avenue, N.W.,
   Suite 200
Washington, DC 20001
Telephone: (202) 466-2044
Fax: (202) 466-2662
http://www.acpm.org/

**American College of Radiation
Oncology**
5272 River Road, Suite 630
Bethesda, MD 20816
Telephone: (301) 718-6515
Fax: (301) 656-0989
http://www.acro.org/

American College of Radiology
1891 Preston White Drive
Reston, VA 20191-4397
Telephone: (800) 227-5463
http://www.acr.org/

American College of Rheumatology
2200 Lake Boulevard NE
Atlanta, GA 30319
Telephone: (404) 633-3777
Fax: (404) 633-1870
E-mail: acr@rheumatology.org
http://www.rheumatology.org/

American Geriatrics Society
40 Fulton Street, 18th Floor
New York, NY 10038
Telephone: (212) 308-1414
Fax: (212) 832-8646
http://www.americangeriatrics.org/

**American Orthopaedic Foot and
Ankle Society**
6300 N. River Road, Suite 510
Rosemont, IL 60018
Telephone: (800) 235-4855
Fax: (847) 692-3315
http://www.aofas.org/

American Roentgen Ray Society
44211 Slatestone Court
Leesburg, VA 20176-5109
Telephone: (703) 729-3353
Fax: (703) 729-4839
http://www.arrs.org/

**American Society for Dermatologic
Surgery**
5550 Meadowbrook Drive,
   Suite 120
Rolling Meadows, IL 60008
Telephone: (847) 956-0900
http://www.asds.net

**American Society for
Gastrointestinal Endoscopy**
1520 Kensington Road, Suite 202
Oak Brook, IL 60523
Telephone: (630) 573-0600
Fax: (630) 573-0691
http://www.asge.org/

**American Society for Reproductive
Medicine**
1209 Montgomery Highway
Birmingham, AL 35216-2809
Telephone: (205) 978-5000
Fax: (205) 978-5005
http://www.asrm.org/

American Society for Surgery of the Hand
6300 North River Road, Suite 600
Rosemont, IL 60018-4256
Telephone: (847) 384-8300
Fax: (847) 384-1435
E-mail: info@assh.org
http://www.assh.org

American Society for Therapeutic Radiology and Oncology
8280 Willow Oaks Corporate Drive, Suite 500
Fairfax, VA 22031
Telephone: (703) 502-1550
Fax: (703) 502-7852
http://www.astro.org/

American Society of Abdominal Surgeons
824 Main Street, 2nd Floor, Suite 1
Melrose, MA 02176-3195
Telephone: (781) 665-6102
Fax: (781) 665-4127
http://www.abdominalsurg.org/

American Society of Addiction Medicine
4601 North Park Avenue, Upper Arcade Suite 101
Chevy Chase, MD 20815
Telephone: (301) 656-3920
Fax: (301) 656-3815
E-mail: Email@asam.org
http://www.asam.org/

American Society of Anesthesiologists
520 N. Northwest Highway
Park Ridge, IL 60068-2573
Telephone: (847) 825-5586
Fax: (847) 825-1692
E-mail: communications@asahq.org
http://www.asahq.org/

The American Society of Bariatric Physicians
2821 South Parker Road, Suite 625
Aurora, CO 80014
Telephone: (303) 770-2526
Fax: (303) 779-4834
E-mail: bariatric@asbp.org
http://www.asbp.org/

American Society of Cataract and Refractive Surgery
4000 Legato Road, Suite 700
Fairfax, VA 22033
Telephone: (703) 591-2220
Fax: (703) 591-0614
http://www.ascrs.org/

American Society of Clinical Oncology
2318 Mill Road, Suite 800
Alexandria, VA 22314
Telephone: (571) 483-1300
membermail@asco.org
http://www.asco.org/

American Society for Clinical Pathology
33 West Monroe Street, Suite 1600
Chicago, IL 60603
Telephone: (312) 541-4999
E-mail: info@ascp.org
http://www.ascp.org/

American Society of Colon and Rectal Surgeons
85 W. Algonquin Road, Suite 550
Arlington Heights, IL 60005
Telephone: (847) 290-9184
Fax: (847) 290-9203
http://www.fascrs.org/

American Society of Hematology
2021 L Street NW, Suite 900
Washington, DC 20036
Telephone: (202) 776-0544
Fax: (202) 776-0545
E-mail: ash@hematology.org
http://www.hematology.org/

American Society of Plastic Surgeons
Plastic Surgery Foundation
444 E. Algonquin Road
Arlington Heights, IL 60005
Telephone: 1 (888) 4-PLASTIC—
1 (888) 475-2784
http://www.plasticsurgery.org/

American Thoracic Society
25 Broadway
New York, NY 10004
Telephone: (212) 315-8600
Fax: (212) 315-6498
http://www.thoracic.org/

College of American Pathologists
325 Waukegan Road
Northfield, IL 60093
Telephone: (800) 323-4040
Fax: (847) 832-7000 in Illinois
http://www.cap.org/

The Endocrine Society
8401 Connecticut Avenue, Suite 900
Chevy Chase, MD 20815
Telephone: (301) 941-0200
Fax: (301) 941-0259
E-mail: endostaff@endo-society.org
http://www.endo-society.org/

North American Spine Society
7075 Veterans Blvd
Burr Ridge, IL 60527
Telephone: (630) 230-3600
E-mail: info@spine.org
http://www.spine.org/

Radiological Society of North America, Inc.
820 Jorie Boulevard
Oak Brook, IL 60523-2251
Telephone: (630) 571-2670
Fax: (630) 571-7837
http://www.rsna.org/

Society of American Gastrointestinal Endoscopic Surgeons
11300 West Olympic Boulevard, Suite 600
Los Angeles, CA 90064
Telephone: (310) 437-0544
Fax: (310) 437-0585
http://www.sages.org/

Society of Cardiovascular & Interventional Radiology
3975 Fair Ridge Drive, Suite 400 North
Fairfax, VA 22033
Telephone: (800) 488-7284 or (703) 691-1805
Fax: (703) 691-1855
http://www.sirweb.org/

Society of Critical Care Medicine
500 Midway Drive
Mount Prospect, IL 60056
Telephone: (847) 827-6869
Fax: (847) 827-6886
E-mail: info@sccm.org
http://www.sccm.org/

Society of Nuclear Medicine
1850 Samuel Morse Drive
Reston, VA 20190-5316
Telephone: (703) 708-9000
Fax: (703) 708-9015
http://www.snm.org/

The Society of Thoracic Surgeons
633 N. Saint Clair Street, Floor 23
Chicago, IL 60611-4267
Telephone: (312) 202-5800
Fax: (312) 202-5801
http://www.sts.org/

B

IRS Instructions and Form 2553

The following instructions for Form 2553 are available at www.irs.gov/pub/irs-pdf/i2553.pdf.

The form itself can be accessed at www.irs.gov/pub/irs-pdf/f2553.pdf.

Instructions for Form 2553

Department of the Treasury
Internal Revenue Service

(Rev. December 2007)
Election by a Small Business Corporation

Section references are to the Internal Revenue Code unless otherwise noted.

What's New

For tax years ending on or after December 31, 2007, certain corporations (entities) with reasonable cause for not timely filing Form 2553 can request to have the form treated as timely filed by filing Form 2553 as an attachment to Form 1120S, U.S. Income Tax Return for an S Corporation. An entry space for an explanation of reasonable cause was added to page 1 of the form. See *Relief for Late Elections*.

General Instructions

Purpose of Form

A corporation or other entity eligible to elect to be treated as a corporation must use Form 2553 to make an election under section 1362(a) to be an S corporation. An entity eligible to elect to be treated as a corporation that meets certain tests discussed below will be treated as a corporation as of the effective date of the S corporation election and does not need to file Form 8832, Entity Classification Election.

The income of an S corporation generally is taxed to the shareholders of the corporation rather than to the corporation itself. However, an S corporation may still owe tax on certain income. For details, see *Tax and Payments* in the Instructions for Form 1120S.

Who May Elect

A corporation or other entity eligible to elect to be treated as a corporation may elect to be an S corporation only if it meets all the following tests.

1. It is (a) a domestic corporation, or (b) a domestic entity eligible to elect to be treated as a corporation, that timely files Form 2553 and meets all the other tests listed below. If Form 2553 is not timely filed, see *Relief for Late Elections* on page 2.

2. It has no more than 100 shareholders. You can treat a husband and wife (and their estates) as one shareholder for this test. You can also treat all members of a family (as defined in section 1361(c)(1)(B)) and their estates as one shareholder for this test. For additional situations in which certain entities will be treated as members of a family, see Notice 2005-91, 2005-51 I.R.B. 1164. All others are treated as separate shareholders. For details, see section 1361(c)(1).

3. Its only shareholders are individuals, estates, exempt organizations described in section 401(a) or 501(c)(3), or certain trusts described in section 1361(c)(2)(A).

For information about the section 1361(d)(2) election to be a qualified subchapter S trust (QSST), see the instructions for Part III. For information about the section 1361(e)(3) election to be an electing small business trust (ESBT), see Regulations section 1.1361-1(m). For guidance on how to convert a QSST to an ESBT, see Regulations section 1.1361-1(j)(12). If these elections were not timely made, see Rev. Proc. 2003-43, 2003-23 I.R.B. 998.

4. It has no nonresident alien shareholders.

5. It has only one class of stock (disregarding differences in voting rights). Generally, a corporation is treated as having only one class of stock if all outstanding shares of the corporation's stock confer identical rights to distribution and liquidation proceeds. See Regulations section 1.1361-1(l) for details.

6. It is not one of the following ineligible corporations.

a. A bank or thrift institution that uses the reserve method of accounting for bad debts under section 585.

b. An insurance company subject to tax under subchapter L of the Code.

c. A corporation that has elected to be treated as a possessions corporation under section 936.

d. A domestic international sales corporation (DISC) or former DISC.

7. It has or will adopt or change to one of the following tax years.

a. A tax year ending December 31.
b. A natural business year.
c. An ownership tax year.
d. A tax year elected under section 444.
e. A 52-53-week tax year ending with reference to a year listed above.
f. Any other tax year (including a 52-53-week tax year) for which the corporation establishes a business purpose.

For details on making a section 444 election or requesting a natural business, ownership, or other business purpose tax year, see the instructions for Part II.

8. Each shareholder consents as explained in the instructions for column K.

See sections 1361, 1362, and 1378, and their related regulations for additional information on the above tests.

A parent S corporation can elect to treat an eligible wholly-owned subsidiary as a qualified subchapter S subsidiary. If the election is made, the subsidiary's assets, liabilities, and items of income, deduction, and credit generally are treated as those of the parent. For details, see Form 8869, Qualified Subchapter S Subsidiary Election.

When To Make the Election

Complete and file Form 2553:
• No more than two months and 15 days after the beginning of the tax year the election is to take effect, or
• At any time during the tax year preceding the tax year it is to take effect.

For this purpose, the 2 month period begins on the day of the month the tax year begins and ends with the close of the day before the numerically corresponding day of the second calendar month following that month. If there is no corresponding day, use the close of the last day of the calendar month.

Example 1. No prior tax year. A calendar year small business corporation begins its first tax year on January 7. The two month period ends March 6 and 15 days after that is March 21. To be an S corporation beginning with its first tax year, the corporation must file Form 2553 during the period that begins January 7 and ends March 21. Because

Cat. No. 49978N

the corporation had no prior tax year, an election made before January 7 will not be valid.

Example 2. Prior tax year. A calendar year small business corporation has been filing Form 1120 as a C corporation but wishes to make an S election for its next tax year beginning January 1. The two month period ends February 28 (29 in leap years) and 15 days after that is March 15. To be an S corporation beginning with its next tax year, the corporation must file Form 2553 during the period that begins the first day (January 1) of its last year as a C corporation and ends March 15th of the year it wishes to be an S corporation. Because the corporation had a prior tax year, it can make the election at any time during that prior tax year.

Example 3. Tax year less than 2 1/2 months. A calendar year small business corporation begins its first tax year on November 8. The two month period ends January 7 and 15 days after that is January 22. To be an S corporation beginning with its short tax year, the corporation must file Form 2553 during the period that begins November 8 and ends January 22. Because the corporation had no prior tax year, an election made before November 8 will not be valid.

Relief for Late Elections

A late election to be an S corporation generally is effective for the tax year following the tax year beginning on the date entered on line E of Form 2553. However, relief for a late election may be available if the corporation can show that the failure to file on time was due to reasonable cause.

To request relief for a late election when the tax year beginning on the date entered on line E ends on or after December 31, 2007, a corporation that meets the following requirements can explain the reasonable cause in the designated space on page 1 of Form 2553.
• The corporation fails to qualify to elect to be an S corporation (see *Who May Elect* on page 1) solely because of the failure to timely file Form 2553.
• The corporation has reasonable cause for its failure to timely file Form 2553.
• The corporation has not filed a tax return for the tax year beginning on the date entered on line E of Form 2553.
• The corporation files Form 2553 as an attachment to Form 1120S no later than 6 months after the due date of Form 1120S (excluding extensions) for the tax year beginning on the date entered on line E of Form 2553.
• No taxpayer whose tax liability or tax return would be affected by the S corporation election (including all shareholders of the S corporation) has reported inconsistently with the S corporation election on any affected return for the tax year beginning on the date entered on line E of Form 2553.
Similar relief is available for an entity eligible to elect to be treated as a corporation (see the instructions for Form 8832) electing to be treated as a corporation as of the date entered on line E of Form 2553. For more details, see Rev. Proc. 2007-62, 2007-41 I.R.B. 786.

To request relief for a late election when the above requirements are not met, the corporation generally must request a private letter ruling and pay a user fee in accordance with Rev. Proc. 2008-1, 2008-1 I.R.B. 1 (or its successor). However, the ruling and user fee requirements may not apply if relief is available under the following revenue procedures.
• If an entity eligible to elect to be treated as a corporation (a) failed to timely file Form 2553, and (b) has not elected to be treated as a corporation, see Rev. Proc. 2004-48, 2004-32 I.R.B. 172.
• If a corporation failed to timely file Form 2553, see Rev. Proc. 2003-43, 2003-23 I.R.B. 998.

• If Form 1120S was filed without an S corporation election and neither the corporation nor any shareholder was notified by the IRS of any problem with the S corporation status within 6 months after the return was timely filed, see Rev. Proc. 97-48, 1997-43 I.R.B. 19.

Where To File

Generally, send the original election (no photocopies) or fax it to the Internal Revenue Service Center listed below. If the corporation files this election by fax, keep the original Form 2553 with the corporation's permanent records. However, certain late elections can be filed attached to Form 1120S. See *Relief for Late Elections* above.

If the corporation's principal business, office, or agency is located in:	Use the following address or fax number:
Connecticut, Delaware, District of Columbia, Illinois, Indiana, Kentucky, Maine, Maryland, Massachusetts, Michigan, New Hampshire, New Jersey, New York, North Carolina, Ohio, Pennsylvania, Rhode Island, South Carolina, Vermont, Virginia, West Virginia, Wisconsin	Department of the Treasury Internal Revenue Service Center Cincinnati, OH 45999 Fax: (859) 669-5748
Alabama, Alaska, Arizona, Arkansas, California, Colorado, Florida, Georgia, Hawaii, Idaho, Iowa, Kansas, Louisiana, Minnesota, Mississippi, Missouri, Montana, Nebraska, Nevada, New Mexico, North Dakota, Oklahoma, Oregon, South Dakota, Tennessee, Texas, Utah, Washington, Wyoming	Department of the Treasury Internal Revenue Service Center Ogden, UT 84201 Fax: (801) 620-7116

Acceptance or Nonacceptance of Election

The service center will notify the corporation if its election is accepted and when it will take effect. The corporation will also be notified if its election is not accepted. The corporation should generally receive a determination on its election within 60 days after it has filed Form 2553. If box Q1 in Part II is checked, the corporation will receive a ruling letter from the IRS that either approves or denies the selected tax year. When box Q1 is checked, it will generally take an additional 90 days for the Form 2553 to be accepted.

Care should be exercised to ensure that the IRS receives the election. If the corporation is not notified of acceptance or nonacceptance of its election within 2 months of the date of filing (date faxed or mailed), or within 5 months if box Q1 is checked, take follow-up action by calling 1-800-829-4933.

If the IRS questions whether Form 2553 was filed, an acceptable proof of filing is (a) a certified or registered mail receipt (timely postmarked) from the U.S. Postal Service, or its equivalent from a designated private delivery service (see Notice 2004-83, 2004-52 I.R.B. 1030 (or its successor)); (b) Form 2553 with an accepted stamp; (c) Form 2553 with a stamped IRS received date; or (d) an IRS letter stating that Form 2553 has been accepted.

Do not file Form 1120S for any tax year before the year the election takes effect. If the corporation is now required to file Form 1120, U.S. Corporation Income Tax Return, or any other applicable tax return, continue filing it until the election takes effect.

End of Election

Once the election is made, it stays in effect until it is terminated or revoked. IRS consent generally is required for another election by the corporation (or a successor corporation) on Form 2553 for any tax year before the 5th tax year after the first tax year in which the termination or revocation took effect. See Regulations section 1.1362-5 for details.

Specific Instructions

Part I

Name and Address

Enter the corporation's true name as stated in the corporate charter or other legal document creating it. If the corporation's mailing address is the same as someone else's, such as a shareholder's, enter "C/O" and this person's name following the name of the corporation. Include the suite, room, or other unit number after the street address. If the Post Office does not deliver to the street address and the corporation has a P.O. box, show the box number instead of the street address. If the corporation changed its name or address after applying for its employer identification number, be sure to check the box in item D of Part I.

Item A. Employer Identification Number (EIN)

Enter the corporation's EIN. If the corporation does not have an EIN, it must apply for one. An EIN can be applied for:
• Online–Click on the EIN link at *www.irs.gov/businesses/small.* The EIN is issued immediately once the application information is validated.
• By telephone at 1-800-829-4933.
• By mailing or faxing Form SS-4, Application for Employer Identification Number.

If the corporation has not received its EIN by the time the return is due, enter "Applied For" and the date you applied in the space for the EIN. For more details, see the Instructions for Form SS-4.

Item E. Effective Date of Election

 Form 2553 generally must be filed no later than 2 months and 15 days after the date entered for item E. For details and exceptions, see When To Make the Election *on page 1.*

A corporation (or entity eligible to elect to be treated as a corporation) making the election effective for its first tax year in existence should enter the earliest of the following dates: (a) the date the corporation (entity) first had shareholders (owners), (b) the date the corporation (entity) first had assets, or (c) the date the corporation (entity) began doing business.

 When the corporation (entity) is making the election for its first tax year in existence, it will usually enter the beginning date of a tax year that begins on a date other than January 1.

A corporation (entity) not making the election for its first tax year in existence that is keeping its current tax year

should enter the beginning date of the first tax year for which it wants the election to be effective.

A corporation (entity) not making the election for its first tax year in existence that is changing its tax year and wants to be an S corporation for the short tax year needed to switch tax years should enter the beginning date of the short tax year. If the corporation (entity) does not want to be an S corporation for this short tax year, it should enter the beginning date of the tax year following this short tax year and file Form 1128, Application To Adopt, Change, or Retain a Tax Year. If this change qualifies as an automatic approval request (Form 1128, Part II), file Form 1128 as an attachment to Form 2553. If this change qualifies as a ruling request (Form 1128, Part III), file Form 1128 separately. If filing Form 1128, enter "Form 1128" on the dotted line to the left of the entry space for item E.

Item F

Check the box that corresponds with the S corporation's selected tax year. If box (2) or (4) is checked, provide the additional information about the tax year, and complete Part II of the form.

Signature

Form 2553 must be signed and dated by the president, vice president, treasurer, assistant treasurer, chief accounting officer, or any other corporate officer (such as tax officer) authorized to sign.

If Form 2553 is not signed, it will not be considered timely filed.

Column K. Shareholders' Consent Statement

For an election filed before the effective date entered for item E, only shareholders who own stock on the day the election is made need to consent to the election.

For an election filed on or after the effective date entered for item E, all shareholders or former shareholders who owned stock at any time during the period beginning on the effective date entered for item E and ending on the day the election is made must consent to the election.

If the corporation timely filed an election, but one or more shareholders did not timely file a consent, see Regulations section 1.1362-6(b)(3)(iii). If the shareholder was a community property spouse who was a shareholder solely because of a state community property law, see Rev. Proc. 2004-35, 2004-23 I.R.B. 1029.

Each shareholder consents by signing and dating either in column K or on a separate consent statement. The following special rules apply in determining who must sign.
• If a husband and wife have a community interest in the stock or in the income from it, both must consent.
• Each tenant in common, joint tenant, and tenant by the entirety must consent.
• A minor's consent is made by the minor, legal representative of the minor, or a natural or adoptive parent of the minor if no legal representative has been appointed.
• The consent of an estate is made by the executor or administrator.
• The consent of an electing small business trust (ESBT) is made by the trustee and, if a grantor trust, the deemed owner. See Regulations section 1.1362-6(b)(2)(iv) for details.
• If the stock is owned by a qualified subchapter S trust (QSST), the deemed owner of the trust must consent.
• If the stock is owned by a trust (other than an ESBT or QSST), the person treated as the shareholder by section 1361(c)(2)(B) must consent.

Continuation sheet or separate consent statement. If you need a continuation sheet or use a separate consent statement, attach it to Form 2553. It must contain the name, address, and EIN of the corporation and the information requested in columns J through N of Part I.

Column L

Enter the number of shares of stock each shareholder owns on the date the election is filed and the date(s) the stock was acquired. Enter -0- for any former shareholders listed in column J. An entity without stock, such as a limited liability company (LLC), should enter the percentage of ownership and date(s) acquired.

Column M

Enter the social security number of each individual listed in column J. Enter the EIN of each estate, qualified trust, or exempt organization.

Column N

Enter the month and day that each shareholder's tax year ends. If a shareholder is changing his or her tax year, enter the tax year the shareholder is changing to, and attach an explanation indicating the present tax year and the basis for the change (for example, an automatic revenue procedure or a letter ruling request).

Part II

Complete Part II if you checked box (2) or (4) in Part I, Item F.

Note. Corporations cannot obtain automatic approval of a fiscal year under the natural business year (box P1) or ownership tax year (box P2) provisions if they are under examination, before an appeals (area) office, or before a federal court without meeting certain conditions and attaching a statement to the application. For details, see section 7.03 of Rev. Proc. 2006-46, 2006-45 I.R.B. 859.

Box P1

A corporation that does not have a 47-month period of gross receipts cannot automatically establish a natural business year.

Box Q1

For examples of an acceptable business purpose for requesting a fiscal tax year, see section 5.02 of Rev. Proc. 2002-39, 2002-22 I.R.B. 1046, and Rev. Rul. 87-57, 1987-2 C.B. 117.

Attach a statement showing the relevant facts and circumstances to establish a business purpose for the requested fiscal year. For details on what is sufficient to establish a business purpose, see section 5.02 of Rev. Proc. 2002-39.

If your business purpose is based on one of the natural business year tests provided in section 5.03 of Rev. Proc. 2002-39, identify which test you are using (the 25% gross receipts, annual business cycle, or seasonal business test). For the 25% gross receipts test, provide a schedule showing the amount of gross receipts for each month for the most recent 47 months. For either the annual business cycle or seasonal business test, provide the gross receipts from sales and services (and inventory costs, if applicable) for each month of the short period, if any, and the three immediately preceding tax years. If the corporation has been in existence for less than three tax years, submit figures for the period of existence.

If you check box Q1, you will be charged a user fee of $3,200 ($1,500 if your request is received before February 2, 2008) (subject to change by Rev. Proc. 2009-1 or its successor). Do not pay the fee when filing Form 2553. The service center will send Form 2553 to the IRS in Washington, DC, who, in turn, will notify the corporation that the fee is due.

Box Q2

If the corporation makes a back-up section 444 election for which it is qualified, then the section 444 election will take effect in the event the business purpose request is not approved. In some cases, the tax year requested under the back-up section 444 election may be different than the tax year requested under business purpose. See Form 8716, Election To Have a Tax Year Other Than a Required Tax Year, for details on making a back-up section 444 election.

Boxes Q3 and R2

If the corporation is not qualified to make the section 444 election after making the item Q2 back-up section 444 election or indicating its intention to make the election in item R1, and therefore it later files a calendar year return, it should write "Section 444 Election Not Made" in the top left corner of the first calendar year Form 1120S it files.

Part III

In Part III, the income beneficiary (or legal representative) of certain qualified subchapter S trusts (QSSTs) may make the QSST election required by section 1361(d)(2). Part III may be used to make the QSST election only if corporate stock has been transferred to the trust on or before the date on which the corporation makes its election to be an S corporation. However, a statement can be used instead of Part III to make the election. If there was an inadvertent failure to timely file a QSST election, see the relief provisions under Rev. Proc. 2003-43.

Note. Use Part III only if you make the election in Part I. Form 2553 cannot be filed with only Part III completed.

The deemed owner of the QSST must also consent to the S corporation election in column K of Form 2553.

Paperwork Reduction Act Notice. We ask for the information on this form to carry out the Internal Revenue laws of the United States. You are required to give us the information. We need it to ensure that you are complying with these laws and to allow us to figure and collect the right amount of tax.

You are not required to provide the information requested on a form that is subject to the Paperwork Reduction Act unless the form displays a valid OMB control number. Books or records relating to a form or its instructions must be retained as long as their contents may become material in the administration of any Internal Revenue law. Generally, tax returns and return information are confidential, as required by section 6103.

The time needed to complete and file this form will depend on individual circumstances. The estimated average time is:

Recordkeeping . . . . 9 hr., 48 min.

Learning about the law or the form . . . . 2 hr., 33 min.

Preparing, copying, assembling, and sending the form to the IRS . . . . 4 hr., 1 min.

If you have comments concerning the accuracy of these time estimates or suggestions for making this form simpler, we would be happy to hear from you. You can write to Internal Revenue Service, Tax Products Coordinating Committee, SE:W:CAR:MP:T:T:SP, 1111 Constitution Ave. NW, IR-6526, Washington, DC 20224. Do not send the form to this address. Instead, see *Where To File* on page 2.

Form **2553**
(Rev. December 2007)

Department of the Treasury
Internal Revenue Service

Election by a Small Business Corporation

(Under section 1362 of the Internal Revenue Code)

▶ See Parts II and III on page 3 and the separate instructions.
▶ The corporation can fax this form to the IRS (see separate instructions).

OMB No. 1545-0146

Note. This election to be an S corporation can be accepted only if all the tests are met under **Who May Elect** on page 1 of the instructions; all shareholders have signed the consent statement; an officer has signed below; and the exact name and address of the corporation and other required form information are provided.

Part I   Election Information

Type or Print	Name (see instructions)	**A** Employer identification number
	Number, street, and room or suite no. (If a P.O. box, see instructions.)	**B** Date incorporated
	City or town, state, and ZIP code	**C** State of incorporation

D Check the applicable box(es) if the corporation, after applying for the EIN shown in **A** above, changed its ☐ name or ☐ address

E Election is to be effective for tax year beginning (month, day, year) (see instructions) . . . . . ▶ ___/___/___

Caution. A corporation (entity) making the election for its first tax year in existence will usually enter the beginning date of a short tax year that begins on a date other than January 1.

F Selected tax year:

(1) ☐ Calendar year

(2) ☐ Fiscal year ending (month and day) ▶ _____

(3) ☐ 52-53-week year ending with reference to the month of December

(4) ☐ 52-53-week year ending with reference to the month of ▶ _____

If box (2) or (4) is checked, complete Part II

G If more than 100 shareholders are listed for item J (see page 2), check this box if treating members of a family as one shareholder results in no more than 100 shareholders (see test 2 under **Who May Elect** in the instructions) ▶ ☐

H Name and title of officer or legal representative who the IRS may call for more information	**I** Telephone number of officer or legal representative ( )

If this S corporation election is being filed with Form 1120S, I declare that I had reasonable cause for not filing Form 2553 timely, and if this election is made by an entity eligible to elect to be treated as a corporation, I declare that I also had reasonable cause for not filing an entity classification election timely. See below for my explanation of the reasons the election or elections were not made on time (see instructions).

Sign Here ▶

Under penalties of perjury, I declare that I have examined this election, including accompanying schedules and statements, and to the best of my knowledge and belief, it is true, correct, and complete.

Signature of officer	Title	Date

For Paperwork Reduction Act Notice, see separate instructions.   Cat. No. 18629R   Form **2553** (Rev. 12-2007)

Form 2553 (Rev. 12-2007) | | | | | Page **2**

Part I   Election Information (continued)

J Name and address of each shareholder or former shareholder required to consent to the election. (See the instructions for column K.)	K Shareholders' Consent Statement. Under penalties of perjury, we declare that we consent to the election of the above-named corporation to be an S corporation under section 1362(a) and that we have examined this consent statement, including accompanying schedules and statements, and to the best of our knowledge and belief, it is true, correct, and complete. We understand our consent is binding and may not be withdrawn after the corporation has made a valid election. (Sign and date below.)		L Stock owned or percentage of ownership (see instructions)		M Social security number or employer identification number (see instructions)	N Shareholder's tax year ends (month and day)
	Signature	Date	Number of shares or percentage of ownership	Date(s) acquired		

Form **2553** (Rev. 12-2007)

Form 2553 (Rev. 12-2007)   Page **3**

Part II   Selection of Fiscal Tax Year (see instructions)

Note. All corporations using this part must complete item O and item P, Q, or R.

O   Check the applicable box to indicate whether the corporation is:

1. ☐ A new corporation **adopting** the tax year entered in item F, Part I.
2. ☐ An existing corporation **retaining** the tax year entered in item F, Part I.
3. ☐ An existing corporation **changing** to the tax year entered in item F, Part I.

P   Complete item P if the corporation is using the automatic approval provisions of Rev. Proc. 2006-46, 2006-45 I.R.B. 859, to request **(1)** a natural business year (as defined in section 5.07 of Rev. Proc. 2006-46) or **(2)** a year that satisfies the ownership tax year test (as defined in section 5.08 of Rev. Proc. 2006-46). Check the applicable box below to indicate the representation statement the corporation is making.

1. Natural Business Year ▶ ☐ I represent that the corporation is adopting, retaining, or changing to a tax year that qualifies as its natural business year (as defined in section 5.07 of Rev. Proc. 2006-46) and has attached a statement showing separately for each month the gross receipts for the most recent 47 months (see instructions). I also represent that the corporation is not precluded by section 4.02 of Rev. Proc. 2006-46 from obtaining automatic approval of such adoption, retention, or change in tax year.

2. Ownership Tax Year ▶ ☐ I represent that shareholders (as described in section 5.08 of Rev. Proc. 2006-46) holding more than half of the shares of the stock (as of the first day of the tax year to which the request relates) of the corporation have the same tax year or are concurrently changing to the tax year that the corporation adopts, retains, or changes to per item F, Part I, and that such tax year satisfies the requirement of section 4.01(3) of Rev. Proc. 2006-46. I also represent that the corporation is not precluded by section 4.02 of Rev. Proc. 2006-46 from obtaining automatic approval of such adoption, retention, or change in tax year.

Note. If you do not use item P and the corporation wants a fiscal tax year, complete either item Q or R below. Item Q is used to request a fiscal tax year based on a business purpose and to make a back-up section 444 election. Item R is used to make a regular section 444 election.

Q   Business Purpose—To request a fiscal tax year based on a business purpose, check box Q1. See instructions for details including payment of a user fee. You may also check box Q2 and/or box Q3.

1. Check here ▶ ☐ if the fiscal year entered in item F, Part I, is requested under the prior approval provisions of Rev. Proc. 2002-39, 2002-22 I.R.B. 1046. Attach to Form 2553 a statement describing the relevant facts and circumstances and, if applicable, the gross receipts from sales and services necessary to establish a business purpose. See the instructions for details regarding the gross receipts from sales and services. If the IRS proposes to disapprove the requested fiscal year, do you want a conference with the IRS National Office?

☐ Yes   ☐ No

2. Check here ▶ ☐ to show that the corporation intends to make a back-up section 444 election in the event the corporation's business purpose request is not approved by the IRS. (See instructions for more information.)

3. Check here ▶ ☐ to show that the corporation agrees to adopt or change to a tax year ending December 31 if necessary for the IRS to accept this election for S corporation status in the event (1) the corporation's business purpose request is not approved and the corporation makes a back-up section 444 election, but is ultimately not qualified to make a section 444 election, or (2) the corporation's business purpose request is not approved and the corporation did not make a back-up section 444 election.

R   Section 444 Election—To make a section 444 election, check box R1. You may also check box R2.

1. Check here ▶ ☐ to show that the corporation will make, if qualified, a section 444 election to have the fiscal tax year shown in item F, Part I. To make the election, you must complete **Form 8716,** Election To Have a Tax Year Other Than a Required Tax Year, and either attach it to Form 2553 or file it separately.

2. Check here ▶ ☐ to show that the corporation agrees to adopt or change to a tax year ending December 31 if necessary for the IRS to accept this election for S corporation status in the event the corporation is ultimately not qualified to make a section 444 election.

Part III   Qualified Subchapter S Trust (QSST) Election Under Section 1361(d)(2)*

Income beneficiary's name and address	Social security number
Trust's name and address	Employer identification number

Date on which stock of the corporation was transferred to the trust (month, day, year) . . . . ▶ / /

In order for the trust named above to be a QSST and thus a qualifying shareholder of the S corporation for which this Form 2553 is filed, I hereby make the election under section 1361(d)(2). Under penalties of perjury, I certify that the trust meets the definitional requirements of section 1361(d)(3) and that all other information provided in Part III is true, correct, and complete.

_____   _____
Signature of income beneficiary or signature and title of legal representative or other qualified person making the election   Date

*Use Part III to make the QSST election only if stock of the corporation has been transferred to the trust on or before the date on which the corporation makes its election to be an S corporation. The QSST election must be made and filed separately if stock of the corporation is transferred to the trust **after** the date on which the corporation makes the S election.

Printed on recycled paper   Form **2553** (Rev. 12-2007)

Sample Medical Office Building Lease

THIS LEASE, made this 1st day of August, 2011, between ANY MANAGEMENT SERVICES, INC., a Kansas corporation, ("Lessor"), and JOHN DOE, MD, ("Lessee").

WITNESSETH:

Lessor hereby leases to Lessee and Lessee leases from Lessor the premises containing 1,041 square feet of the 2,082 square feet and made a part hereof (the "leased premises"), in the ANYPLACE PROFESSIONAL ARTS BUILDING subject to the following terms and conditions:

1. TERM. The term of this lease shall be one year, commencing on the 1st day of August 2010 and ending on the 1st day of August 2011. If Lessor, for any reason whatsoever, cannot deliver possession of the leased premises to Lessee at the commencement of the term of this lease as above specified, this lease shall not be void or voidable, nor shall Lessor be liable to Lessee for any loss or damage resulting there from, but in such event, there shall be a proportionate reduction of rent covering the period between the commencement of said term and the time when Lessor can deliver possession of the leased premises to Lessee.

2. RENT. Lessee covenants to pay Lessor, without demand and without set-off or deduction, at Lessor's office or at such other place as Lessor may from time to time designate in writing, the following rental:

Annual rent will be payable in advance in successive, equal installments on the first day of each and every calendar month during the term of the lease. Rental for a fractional calendar month shall not be prorated.

3. LEASE YEAR. The term "lease year" shall mean a period of twelve consecutive full calendar months. The first lease year shall begin on the date of commencement of the term if such date of commencement shall occur on the first day of a calendar month; if not, then on the first day of the calendar month next following such date of commencement. Each succeeding lease year shall commence on the anniversary date of the first lease year.

4. USE. Lessee covenants and agrees so long as this lease remains in force, to continuously use and occupy the premises solely as offices for the practice of medicine, for no other purpose or purposes whatsoever without the prior written consent of Lessor. Lessee shall not do or permit anything to be done or kept on the leased premises that would increase insurance rates or cause a cancellation of any insurance on the building in which the leased premises are located. Lessee shall not do or permit to be done any act or thing on the leased premises that disturbs the quiet enjoyment of any other occupant of the building in which the leased premises are located.

5. MAINTENANCE AND REPAIRS. Lessee shall keep and maintain the leased premises, including all glass, glass windows, and glass doors and their appurtenant sills and frames, and all appliances, equipment, plumbing and utility line thereon in good condition and repair, ordinary wear and tear excepted, and keep the same free from filth, nuisance or danger of fire, and in all respects and at all times use and maintain said premises in a manner which will fully meet and comply with all health, police and fire regulations and ordinances and all other laws which are now in force or which may hereafter be enacted by the City of Anytown, Anywhere, Any County, Any State, the United States of America, or any other governmental body or agency now or hereafter having jurisdiction of the leased premises.

6. ALTERATIONS. Lessee shall not erect or install any exterior or interior signs or advertising or window or door lettering and shall not make any alteration, additions or improvements in the leased premises without the prior written consent of Lessor. All alterations, additions or improvements made upon consent of Lessor by the Lessee shall be made at the Lessee's expense. All alterations, additions or improvements, including all fixtures, partitions, counters, venetian blinds and linoleum, irrespective of which party may have paid the cost thereof excepting only movable office furniture put in at the expense of the Lessee, shall be the property of Lessor, and shall remain upon and be surrendered with the leased premises as a part thereof, at the termination of this lease, without disturbance, molestation, or injury. Once Lessee receives written consent from Lessor for alterations or additions, the Lessor reserves the right of prior inspection and approval of the written contracts of the contractor, material personnel, and subcontractors before they are entered into. Each such contract should provide that it cannot be modified in any way without utilizing a written change order approved in writing both by Lessee and by Lessor.

Additionally, there should be no changes in the subcontractors and material personnel and contractor to whom Lessor has consented to without Lessor's further written consent. Lessee will be required to give to Lessor a check to be held in escrow equal to the total amount of the contracted changes to insure that funds are available in full for such construction. In the event the aforementioned escrow procedure is not followed, then Lessee agrees to pay when due all bills for labor, services, materials, supplies or equipment furnished to or for Lessee in or about the leased premises and keep the leased premises and the building of which the leased premises are a part of free from all liens or claims to the liens of mechanics and material personnel for work done or materials furnished to Lessor. In the event a lien is placed on the building in which the leased premises are a part and therefore in violation hereof, Lessee agrees to either pay the lien or have it bonded within ten (10) days after the filing thereof.

7. UTILITIES. Lessor shall furnish the leased premises with heat and air conditioning, as required to meet normal seasonal demands, plus water and elevator service when necessary or applicable, electrical service for normal lighting and small business machines (exclusive of computers) during the hours of 8:00 am to 6:00 pm, Monday through Friday and 8:00 am to 1:00 pm on Saturdays, with Sundays and holidays excepted.

Lessee shall pay for the installation, use and maintenance of all telephone service required by Lessee during its occupancy of the leased premises.

8. ASSIGNMENT AND SUBLETTING. Lessee shall not assign this lease or any part thereof, without the written consent of Lessor, and shall not sublet or allow any other person, firm, or corporation to come in with or under Lessee, without like consent. No assignment or subletting (with or without the consent of Lessor) shall release Lessee under this lease nor shall Lessee permit this Lease or any interest herein or in the same tenancy hereby created to become vested in or owned by any other person by operation of law or otherwise. The power of Lessor to give or withhold its consent to any assignment or subletting shall not be exhausted by the exercise thereof on one or more occasions, but the same shall be a continuing right and power with respect to any type of transfer, assignment, or subletting.

If Lessee shall make any assignment of this lease or shall make any subletting hereunder in any way not authorized by the terms hereof, the acceptance by Lessor or any rental from any person claiming as assignee, sublessee, or otherwise shall not be construed as a recognition of or consent to such assignment or subletting or as a waiver of the right of Lessor hereafter to collect any rent from Lessee, it being agreed that the Lessor may at any time accept rent and other moneys due under this lease from any person offering to pay same without thereby acknowledging the person so paying as a tenant in place of Lessee herein above named, and without releasing said Lessee.

9. LESSOR'S USE OF BUILDING. Lessor reserves the exclusive right to use the building in which the leased premises are located and every part thereof, except the interior of the leased premises, for advertising purposes. The Lessor reserves the right to enter and be upon the leased premises at any time and from time to time to repair, maintain, alter, improve and remodel the building, including the right to change, alter, close or add entrance ways, and to add additional stories to the building, and each part thereof. Lessee shall not be entitled to any compensation, damages or abatement or reduction in rent on account of any such repairs, maintenance, alterations, improvements or remodeling or adding of additional stories thereto. Lessor reserves the right at any time and from time to time to enter and be upon the leased premises for the purposes of examining same, to show the same to prospective purchasers and mortgagees, and for cleaning and for such repairs, alteration, additions, installations, and removals, as Lessor may deem proper or useful for serving the leased premises, or the building. During the 120 days prior to the expiration of this lease, Lessor shall have the right to place upon the windows and doors of the leased premises any usual or ordinary "to let" or "to lease" signs, and at reasonable hours, to enter upon the leased premises and exhibit same to prospective lessees.

10. RISK OF LOSS INSURANCE. The Lessor shall not in any event be responsible for loss of property from or for damage to person or property occurring in or about the leased premises, however caused, not the intentional and willful fault of the Lessor, and particularly not for any damage from steam, gas, electricity, water, plumbing, rain, snow, leakage, breakage, or overflow, whether originating in the leased premises, premises of other tenants, or any part of the building whatsoever.

Lessee agrees to indemnify and hold harmless the Lessor from and against all claims of whatever nature arising from any accident, injury, or damage to person or property during the term hereof in or about the leased premises or arising from any accident, injury or damage to personal property occurring outside the leased premises but within the property of which the leased premises is a part, where such accident, injury or damage results or is claimed to have resulted from an act, omission, or negligence on the part of Lessee, or on the part of any of its licensees, agents, invitees, servants, or employees. This indemnity agreement shall include indemnity against all costs, claims, expenses, penalties, liens, and liabilities incurred in or in connection with any such claim or proceeding brought thereon and the defense thereof.

Lessee agrees to maintain a policy of general public liability and property damage insurance under which the insurer agrees to indemnify Lessor and to hold it harmless from and against all costs, expenses and/or liability arising out of or based upon any and all claims, accidents, injuries and damages heretofore mentioned in Section 11. Each such policy shall be approved as to form and insurance company by Lessor, and shall be noncancellable with respect to Lessor except upon ten (10) days' written notice to Lessor, and a duplicate original thereof shall be delivered on injury (or death) to any one person, and $25,000 with respect to property damage.

Lessor and Lessee agree:
(a) that in the event the leased premises or its contents are damaged or destroyed by fire or other insured casualty, the rights, if any, of either party against the other with respect to any such damage or destruction are hereby waived; and (b) that all policies of fire and/or extended coverage or other insurance covering the leased premises or its contents shall contain a clause or endorsement provided in substance that the insurance shall not be prejudiced if the assured have waived right of recovery from any person or persons prior to the date and time of loss or damage, if any.

11. DAMAGE/CONDEMNATION. In case during the term hereof the leased premises become untenantable by fire, Providence, or casualty, then rent shall abate, with proportionate refund of any prepayment, from the time of such occurrence until Lessor restores the premises; provided that if the building of which the leased premises are a part or any part thereof be so injured as in the opinion and at the option of the Lessor the possession of the leased premises is needed by the Lessor for demolition, reconstruction, sale, or any purpose whatsoever, the Lessor may by written notice to Lessee wholly terminate the term of this lease.

In the event the building of which the leased premises is a part shall be taken, in whole or in part, by condemnation or the exercise of the right of eminent domain, the Lessor may terminate this lease by written notice to lessee and prepaid rent shall be proportionately refunded. All damages awarded for such taking, whether for the fee or the leasehold interest, shall belong to and be the property of Lessor, except that Lessee shall be entitled to compensation for removal of trade fixtures owned by Lessee. The lessee retains the right and option to cancel said rental agreement if damages prevent the conduct of business beyond a ninety (90) day period.

12. DEFAULTS. If Lessee shall fail to pay any rent or any other sum of money due hereunder when due and shall fail to pay the same within ten (10) days after notice from Lessor that the same is overdue, or if Lessee shall violate or fail to perform any other provision and shall fail to correct or perform the same within thirty (30) days after notice thereof from lessor, then this lease shall be in default and at any time thereafter Lessor may at its option
(a) terminate this lease,
(b) re-enter, take possession of the leased premises, and remove all persons and property there from (such property as may be removed may

be stored in a public warehouse or elsewhere at the cost of, and for the account of Lessee), all without notice or legal process and without being deemed guilty of trespass, or liable for any loss or damage occasioned thereby. If Lessee shall after default voluntarily give up possession to Lessor, deliver to Lessor the keys to the premises, or both, such actions shall be deemed to be in compliance with Lessor's rights and the acceptance thereof by Lessor shall not be deemed to constitute a surrender of the leased premises. Should Lessor elect to re-enter, as herein provided, or should it take possession pursuant to legal proceedings or pursuant to any notice provided for by law, it may either terminate this lease or it may from time to time without terminating this lease, make such alterations and repairs as may be necessary in order to relet the premises, and relet said premises or any part thereof for such term or terms (which may be for a term extending beyond the term of this lease) and at such rental or rentals and upon such other terms and conditions as Lessor in its sole discretion may deem advisable; upon each such reletting all rentals received by the Lessor from such reletting shall be applied; first, to the payment of any indebtedness other than rent due hereunder from Lessee to Lessor; second, to the payment of any costs and expenses of such reletting, including brokerage fees and attorney's fees and of costs of such alterations and repairs; third, to the payment of rent due and unpaid hereunder, and the residue, if any, shall be held by Lessor and applied in payment of future rent or damage as the same may become due and payable hereunder. If such rentals received from such reletting during any month be less than that to be paid during that month by Lessee hereunder, Lessee shall pay any such deficiency to Lessor, the same to be calculated and paid monthly. No such reentry or taking possession of said leased premises by Lessor shall be construed as an election on its part to terminate this lease unless a written notice of such intention be given to Lessee or unless the termination thereof be decreed by a court of competent jurisdiction. Notwithstanding any such reletting without termination, Lessor may at any time thereafter elect to terminate this lease for such previous breach. Should Lessor at any time terminate this lease for any breach, in addition to any other remedies it may have, it may recover from Lessee all damages it may incur by reason of such breach, including the cost of recovering the leased premises, reasonable attorney's fee, and including the worth at the time of such termination of the excess, if any, of the amount of rent and charges equivalent to rent reserved in this lease for the remainder of the stated term over the then reasonable rental value of the leased premises for the remainder of the stated term, all of which amounts shall be immediately due and payable from Lessee to Lessor.

In case suit shall be brought for recovery of possession of the leased premises, for the recovery of rent or other amount due under the provision of this lease, or because of the breach of any other covenant herein contained on the part of Lessee to be kept or performed, and a breach shall be established, Lessee shall pay to Lessor all expenses incurred therefore, including a reasonable attorney's fee.

Lessor shall not be obligated to notify Lessee of the due date of rent nor demand payment thereof on its due date, the same being expressly waived by Lessee. The acceptance of any sum of money from Lessee after the expiration of any 10-day or 30-day notice as above provided shall be taken to be a payment on account by Lessee and shall not constitute a waiver by Lessor of any rights, nor shall it reinstate the lease or cure a default on the part of Lessee.

13. ABANDONMENT. If Lessee shall vacate or abandon the leased premises, the same shall constitute a default under this lease and Lessor shall have all of the same rights and remedies against Lessee as herein granted and reserved to Lessor by paragraph 13 of this lease upon a default of Lessee in this lease.

For the purposes of this lease, the leased premises shall be deemed to be vacant if Lessee shall cease to operate its business in the leased property.

Upon the expiration of the lease and if the leased premises should be vacated at any time, or abandoned by the Lessee, or this lease should terminate for any cause, and at the time of such expiration, vacation, abandonment, or termination, the Lessee or Lessee's agents, subtenants or any other person should leave any property of any kind or character on or in the premises, the fact of such leaving of property on or in the leased premises shall be conclusive evidence of intent by the Lessee, Lessee's agents or subtenants, to abandon such property so left in or upon the lease premises, and such leaving shall constitute abandonment of the property. It is understood and agreed by and between the parties hereto that none of Lessor's servants, agents or employees, have or shall have the actual or apparent authority to waive any portion of this paragraph, and the Lessee shall have no right to leave any such property upon the leased premises without the written consent in writing, signed by the Lessor.

Lessor, its agents, or attorneys, shall have the right and authority without notice to lessee, Lessee's agents or subtenants, or anyone else, to remove and destroy, or to sell or authorize disposal of such property, or any part thereof, without being in any way liable to the Lessee therefore, the said property received therefore shall belong to the Lessor as compensation for the removal and disposition of said property.

14. SUBORDINATION. This lease shall be subject and subordinate to any existing or future mortgage or deed of trust placed by Lessor on the leased premises or the building in which the leased premises are located, provided however, that Lessor may, at its option at any time by written document duly recorded in the Office of the Register of Deeds in and for Any Town, Any State, cause this lease to become superior to any mortgage or deed of trust on the building, or any portion thereof. Further, at Lessor's option, this lease may be assigned by Lessor to any mortgagee as additional security for any loan to Lessor, and Lessee upon request shall acknowledge receipt of notice of each such assignment. Such assignment may be recorded and Lessee shall, upon notice of each such assignment, comply with the terms thereof. Lessee shall, without charge at any time, and from time to time, within ten (10) days after request by Lessor, deliver a written instrument to Lessor or any other person, firm, or corporation specified by Lessor, duly executed and acknowledged, certifying:

(a) that Lessee has accepted the premises, is in occupancy and is paying rent on a current basis with no offsets or claims, or if he is not paying rent on a current basis or if Lessee does have off-sets or claims, Lessor shall specify the status of its rental payments and the basis and amount claimed due as off-sets or claims;

(b) that this lease is unmodified and in full force and effect, or if there has been any modification, that the same is in full force and effect as so modified, and identifying any such modification;

(c) whether or not there are then existing any off-sets or defenses in favor of Lessee against the enforcement of any of the terms covenants and conditions of this lease by Lessor, and if so, specifying the same, and also whether or not Lessor has observed and performed all of the terms, covenants and conditions on the part of Lessor to be observed and performed, and if not, specifying the same;

(d) the dates to which minimum rent, additional rent and all other charges equivalent to rent hereunder have been paid.

15. BANKRUPTCY. The filing of any petition in bankruptcy or insolvency or for reorganization under the Bankruptcy Act by or against Lessee, or the making of a voluntary assignment by Lessee for the benefit of its general creditors, or the filing by Lessee of any petition for an arrangement or composition under the Bankruptcy Act, or the appointment of a receiver or trustee after notice and hearing to take charge of Lessee's business, or of any other petition or application seeking relief of debtors, shall automatically constitute a default in this lease by Lessee for which Lessor may, at any time or times thereafter, at its option, exercise any of the remedies and options provided to Lessor in subparagraphs (a) and (b) of paragraph 13 of this lease for a default in this lease by Lessee, provided, however, that if such petition be filed by a third party against Lessee, who desires in good faith to defend against the same and Lessee is not in any way in default of any obligation hereunder at the time of the filing of such petition, and Lessee within ninety (90) days thereafter procures a final adjudication that it is solvent and a judgment dismissing such petition, this lease shall be fully reinstated as though such petition had never been filed. In the event of termination as provided for in this paragraph, Lessee shall pay forthwith to Lessor as liquidated damages, the difference between the value of the rent reserved in this lease at the time of such termination and the then reasonable rental value of the leased premises for the residue of said term.

16. LIEN ON PROPERTY. All property of Lessee in the leased premises during the term hereof shall be held and found by a lien for payment of rent and full performance of all agreements to be performed by Lessee, and in the event of default, Lessor may foreclose such lien and take possession, in person or by agent, of all property in the leased premises, and sell same therein or elsewhere at any time. Such sale shall bar Lessee's rights of redemption.

17. NOTICES. Every notice required or permitted hereunder shall be in writing and shall be deemed duly served for all purposes only if

(a) upon the Lessor, by depositing a copy thereof in the United States mail, registered, postage prepaid, addressed to Lessor, C/O, 222 Any Street, Any Town, Any State 99999 or at such other place or places as Lessor from time to time may designate in writing as the place for the payment of rent hereunder; or if

(b) upon the Lessee, by depositing a copy thereof in the United States mail, registered, postage prepaid, addressed to Lessee at the address of the leased premises. Each such notice shall be deemed given as of the date it is so deposited in the United States mail.

18. RULES AND REGULATIONS. Lessee will abide by and perform the Rules and Regulations attached hereto and made a part hereof, and will abide by and perform all such reasonable Rules and Regulations as Lessor may hereafter make according to Lessor's judgment for the general good of the leased premises.

19. HEIRS, SUCCESSORS, ETC. Subject to the provisions of paragraph 11 of this lease, all covenants, conditions, and agreements herein contained shall be binding upon and inure to the benefit of the parties hereto and their respective heirs, legal representative, successors, and assigns.

20. LIQUIDATED DAMAGES. Lessee shall, as liquidated damages, pay double rent for all the time Lessee retains possession of the leased premises, or any part thereof, after the termination of this lease, whether by lapse of time or by election of Lessor.

21. NO WAIVER. No waiver of any covenant or condition of this lease by Lessor shall be deemed to imply or constitute a further waiver of the same covenant or condition or of any other covenant or condition of this lease. Whenever in this lease Lessor reserves or is given the right and power to give or withhold its consent to any action on the part of Lessee, such right and power shall not be exhausted by the exercise on one or more occasions, but shall be a continuing right and power during the entire term of this lease.

22. DIRECTORY. A directory will be maintained in the lobby of the building by Lessor, with the names and suite number of the Lessee of the building properly numbered and lettered but will be renewed and changed at the expense of the Lessee.

23. KEYS AND INSPECTION. Lessee will be supplied, free of charge, with two keys for each corridor door entering the leased premises. All such keys shall remain the property of the Lessor. No additional locks shall be allowed on any door of the leased premises. Lessor and Lessor's designees shall have the reasonable right at all times to enter the leased premises, by pass key or otherwise.

24. OPTION TO RENEW. Lessee shall have the right to extend this lease for an additional period of four (4) years provided Lessee shall exercise this option in writing at least 180 days prior to the termination date of the lease. The renewal period shall be governed by the same terms and conditions as the original lease with the exception that rental during the four (4) year extension period shall be subject to negotiation and the mutual agreement of the parties at that time taking into account the then prevailing rental rate in the building. In this regard, said agreement on the rent must be reached 90 days prior to the expiration of the original term hereof or Lessee's renewal option shall be of no force and effect and become null and void.

25. PARKING. Lessor shall provide and maintain for the use of Lessee's patients, invitees, and guests of Lessee in common with other Lessees, an off-street parking facility that shall be adjacent to said building and on the above-described real property. Lessor reserves the right to allocate parking space for Lessor and other tenants and/or their employees in such building and shall designate such space reserved for Lessee and other tenants in building. Lessor shall provide maintenance of the parking lot, the lighting and cleaning thereof, and removal of ice, snow, and trash, subject to the provisions herein. Upon written request Lessee will furnish Lessor or its authorized agent the state automobile license number or numbers assigned to its automobile or automobiles and those of all persons employed on the leased premises.

26. TERMINATION OF LEASE. In the event of Lessee's death, or in the event of his continuing disability, that is, in the event Lessee is unable, for a period of nine (9) months, to perform his full-time duties by reason of disability resulting from injury, sickness, disease, insanity, or other cause, and in the event Lessee is disabled for a period of less than nine (9) months, and then returns to the performance of his full-time duties, but is unable for a period of nine (9) months following such return to continue the full performance of his duties, Lessor, at its option, may terminate this lease by giving Lessee such 30 days notice as aforesaid, then Lessee (or, if he be deceased, his personal representative) may, provided the circumstances outlined herein shall obtain, at his option, terminate this lease by giving Lessor 30 days notice.

Should Lessee desire to terminate this lease for any other reason, he may do so by providing Lessor with one hundred eighty (180) days advanced written notice of his intention to vacate the premises. Rental charges will stop at the end of the 180-day period.

IN WITNESS WHEREOF, the undersigned parties have executed duplicate copies of this lease agreement.

LESSOR: ANY MANAGEMENT SERVICES, INC.
LESSEE; John Doe, MD Name, President
Date

RULES AND REGULATIONS
Lessee agrees to the following rules and regulations of the Lessor.
Lessee:
—Will take good care of the premises at all times, keeping them clean and free from danger or damage by fire, open windows, open faucets, or improper handling of apparatus or equipment of all kinds;
—Will conform to parking regulations as may be promulgated by Lessor and will require that its agents, clerks, employees and invitees do the same. Also agrees to provide Lessor with the state license numbers of the cars of all its employees as requested by Lessor;
—Will not attach or detach any window shade, blind, screen, or drapery without Lessor's consent and will abide by Lessor's rules and desires with respect to maintaining uniform curtains, draperies, and window shades at all windows and hallways so that the building will present a uniform appearance;
—Will conduct Lessee's business on the leased premises so as not to interfere with any other tenant in the building and will not play or permit to be played in the leased premises any musical instrument, phonograph, or radio, or any sound equipment, other than that which might be supplied by the Lessor, or introduce or operate anything which may increase insurance rates of the building;
—Will not permit animals, birds, or bicycles to be brought or kept in or about the building;
—Will not move into or through any part of the building any furniture, fixtures, apparatus, or supplies or any article of weight or bulk except in such manner and at such times as Lessor may approve;
—Will not permit cooking or installation of refrigerators without written consent of Lessor;
—Will not overload the building floors or place thereon any weight exceeding one hundred (100) pounds per square foot;
—Will have all decorating, carpentry work, or any labor required for the installation of Lessee's equipment, furnishing, or other property, performed at its expense and only by the employees of Lessor or with the consent of Lessor by persons duly authorized by Lessor;
—Will not install any electrical lighting or power equipment in the premises without first obtaining the written approval of Lessor;
—Will not allow anything to be placed outside windows or on ledges nor permit anything to be thrown by Lessee or others there from;
—Will not use the water closets, urinals, and other water fixtures for any other purpose than that for which they were constructed;

—Will not mark, paint, drill into, or in any way deface the windows, doors, walls, ceiling, partitions, floors, or the wood, stone, or aluminum work in the building and shall not put therein any spikes, hooks, screws, or nails without Lessor's written consent;

—Will abide by and perform all such reasonable rules and regulations as Lessor may now or hereafter make which are according to Lessor's judgment for the general good of the building and its tenants.

APPENDIX

D

Federal Tax Forms

Appendix D contains samples of the following IRS forms: Form 941-SS, Employer's Quarterly Federal Tax Return (available at www.irs .gov/pub/irs-pdf/f941ss.pdf) and Form 940, Employer's Annual Federal Unemployment (FUTA) Tax Return (available at www.irs.gov/pub/ irs-pdf/f940.pdf). Updates of the forms can be sought through the Internal Revenue Service by visiting www.irs.gov.

Form **941-SS for 2011:** **Employer's QUARTERLY Federal Tax Return**
(Rev. January 2011)
Department of the Treasury — Internal Revenue Service

American Samoa, Guam, the Commonwealth of the Northern
Mariana Islands, and the U.S. Virgin Islands

OMB No. 1545-0029

(EIN)
Employer identification number ☐☐ – ☐☐☐☐☐☐☐

Name *(not your trade name)*

Trade name *(if any)*

Address

Number   Street   Suite or room number

City   State   ZIP code

Report for this Quarter of 2011
(Check one.)

☐ **1:** January, February, March
☐ **2:** April, May, June
☐ **3:** July, August, September
☐ **4:** October, November, December

Prior-year forms are available at
www.irs.gov/form941ss.

Read the separate instructions before you complete Form 941-SS. Type or print within the boxes.

Part 1:   Answer these questions for this quarter.

1   Number of employees who received wages, tips, or other compensation for the pay period
including: *Mar. 12* (Quarter 1), *June 12* (Quarter 2), *Sept. 12* (Quarter 3), *or Dec. 12* (Quarter 4)   1 ☐

2

3

4   If no wages, tips, and other compensation are subject to social security or Medicare tax   ☐ Check and go to line 6e.

	Column 1		Column 2
5a Taxable social security wages	☐	× .104 =	☐
5b Taxable social security tips	☐	× .104 =	☐
5c Taxable Medicare wages & tips	☐	× .029 =	☐

For 2011, the employee social
security tax rate is 4.2% and the
Medicare tax rate is 1.45%. The
employer social security tax rate
is 6.2% and the Medicare tax
rate is 1.45%.

5d   Add *Column 2* line 5a, *Column 2* line 5b, and *Column 2* line 5c . . . .   5d ☐

5e   Section 3121(q) Notice and Demand—Tax due on unreported tips (see instructions) . . . . .   5e ☐

6a   Reserved for future use.
6b   Reserved for future use.   **Do Not Complete Lines 6a-6d**
6c   Reserved for future use.
                                                                            6d

6e   Total taxes before adjustments (add lines 5d and 5e) . . . .   6e ☐

7   Current quarter's adjustment for fractions of cents . . . .   7 ☐

8   Current quarter's adjustment for sick pay . . . .   8 ☐

9   Current quarter's adjustments for tips and group-term life insurance . . . .   9 ☐

10   Total taxes after adjustments. Combine lines 6e through 9 . . . . . .   10 ☐

11   Total deposits, including prior quarter overpayments . . . .   11 ☐

12a   COBRA premium assistance payments (see instructions) . . . .   12a ☐

12b   Number of individuals provided COBRA premium assistance . . . ☐

13   Add lines 11 and 12a . . . .   13 ☐

14   Balance due. If line 10 is more than line 13, enter difference and see instructions . . . . .   14 ☐

15   Overpayment. If line 13 is more than line 10, enter difference ☐   Check one: ☐ Apply to next return. ☐ Send a refund.

▶ You **MUST** complete both pages of Form 941-SS and **SIGN** it.

Next ▶

For Privacy Act and Paperwork Reduction Act Notice, see the back of the Payment Voucher.   Cat. No. 17016Y   Form **941-SS** (Rev. 1-2011)

Name *(not your trade name)*

Employer identification number (EIN)

Part 2: Tell us about your deposit schedule and tax liability for this quarter.

If you are unsure about whether you are a monthly schedule depositor or a semiweekly schedule depositor, see *Pub. 80 (Circular SS)*, section 8.

16

17   Check one: ☐   Total taxes (line 10) on this return are less than $2,500 or total taxes on the return for the preceding quarter were less than $2,500, and you did not incur a $100,000 next-day deposit obligation during the current quarter. If you meet the *de minimis* exception based on the prior quarter and line 10 for the current quarter is $100,000 or more, you must provide a record of your federal tax liability. If you are a monthly schedule depositor, complete the deposit schedule below; if you are a semiweekly schedule depositor, attach Schedule B (Form 941). Go to Part 3.

☐   You were a monthly schedule depositor for the entire quarter. Enter your tax liability for each month and total liability for the quarter, then go to Part 3.

Tax liability: Month 1   [.   ]

Month 2   [.   ]

Month 3   [.   ]

Total liability for quarter   [.   ]   Total must equal line 10.

☐   You were a semiweekly schedule depositor for any part of this quarter. Complete *Schedule B (Form 941): Report of Tax Liability for Semiweekly Schedule Depositors*, and attach it to Form 941-SS.

Part 3: Tell us about your business. If a question does NOT apply to your business, leave it blank.

18   If your business has closed or you stopped paying wages . . . . ☐ Check here, and

enter the final date you paid wages   [   ] .

19   If you are a seasonal employer and you do not have to file a return for every quarter of the year   . . . ☐ Check here.

Part 4: May we speak with your third-party designee?

Do you want to allow an employee, a paid tax preparer, or another person to discuss this return with the IRS? See the instructions for details.

☐ Yes.   Designee's name and phone number   [   ]   [   ]

Select a 5-digit Personal Identification Number (PIN) to use when talking to IRS.   [ ][ ][ ][ ][ ]

☐ No.

Part 5: Sign here. You MUST complete both pages of Form 941-SS and SIGN it.

Under penalties of perjury, I declare that I have examined this return, including accompanying schedules and statements, and to the best of my knowledge and belief, it is true, correct, and complete. Declaration of preparer (other than taxpayer) is based on all information of which preparer has any knowledge.

✗ Sign your name here   [   ]   Print your name here   [   ]

Print your title here   [   ]

Date   [   ]   Best daytime phone   [   ]

Paid Preparer Use Only   Check if you are self-employed . . . ☐

Preparer's name   [   ]   PTIN   [   ]

Preparer's signature   [   ]   Date   [   ]

Firm's name (or yours if self-employed)   [   ]   EIN   [   ]

Address   [   ]   Phone   [   ]

City   [   ]   State   [   ]   ZIP code   [   ]

Form **941-SS** (Rev. 1-2011)

Form 941-V(SS), Payment Voucher

Purpose of Form

Complete Form 941-V(SS), Payment Voucher, if you are making a payment with Form 941-SS, Employer's QUARTERLY Federal Tax Return. We will use the completed voucher to credit your payment more promptly and accurately, and to improve our service to you.

If you have your return prepared by a third party and make a payment with that return, please provide this payment voucher to the return preparer.

Making Payments With Form 941-SS

To avoid a penalty, make your payment with Form 941-SS **only if:**

• Your net taxes for either the current quarter or the preceding quarter (line 10 (previously line 8) on Form 941-SS) are less than $2,500, you did not incur a $100,000 next-day deposit obligation during the current quarter, and you are paying in full with a timely filed return, or

• You are a monthly schedule depositor making a payment in accordance with the Accuracy of Deposits Rule. See section 8 of Pub. 80 (Circular SS), Federal Tax Guide for Employers in the U.S. Virgin Islands, Guam, American Samoa, and the Commonwealth of the Northern Mariana Islands, for details. In this case, the amount of your payment may be $2,500 or more.

Otherwise, you must make deposits by electronic funds transfer. See section 8 of Pub. 80 (Circular SS) for deposit instructions. Do not use Form 941-V(SS) to make federal tax deposits.

Caution. *Use Form 941-V(SS) when making any payment with Form 941-SS. However, if you pay an amount with Form 941-SS that should have been deposited, you may be subject to a penalty. See* Deposit Penalties *in section 8 of Pub. 80 (Circular SS).*

Specific Instructions

Box 1—Employer identification number (EIN). If you do not have an EIN, apply for one on Form SS-4, Application for Employer Identification Number, and write "Applied For" and the date you applied in this entry space.

Box 2—Amount paid. Enter the amount paid with Form 941-SS.

Box 3—Tax period. Darken the circle identifying the quarter for which the payment is made. Darken only one circle.

Box 4—Name and address. Enter your name and address as shown on Form 941-SS.

• Enclose your check or money order payable to the "United States Treasury." Be sure to enter your EIN, "Form 941-SS," and the tax period on your check or money order. Do not send cash. Do not staple Form 941-V(SS) or your payment to Form 941-SS (or to each other).

• Detach Form 941-V(SS) and send it with your payment and Form 941-SS to the address in the Instructions for Form 941-SS.

Note. You must also complete the entity information above Part 1 on Form 941-SS.

✂ - - - - - - - - - - - ▼ **Detach Here and Mail With Your Payment and Form 941-SS.** ▼ - - - - - - - - - - - ✂

Form **941-V(SS)** Department of the Treasury Internal Revenue Service	**Payment Voucher** ▶ Do not staple this voucher or your payment to Form 941-SS.	OMB No. 1545-0029 20**11**

1 Enter your employer identification number (EIN).	2 **Enter the amount of your payment.** ▶	Dollars	Cents

3 Tax period	4 Enter your business name (individual name if sole proprietor).
○ 1st Quarter ○ 3rd Quarter	Enter your address.
○ 2nd Quarter ○ 4th Quarter	Enter your city, state, and ZIP code.

Privacy Act and Paperwork Reduction Act Notice.
We ask for the information on Form 941-SS to carry out the Internal Revenue laws of the United States. We need it to figure and collect the right amount of tax. Subtitle C, Employment Taxes, of the Internal Revenue Code imposes employment taxes on wages. This form is used to determine the amount of the taxes that you owe. Section 6011 requires you to provide the requested information if the tax is applicable to you. Section 6109 requires you to provide your identification number. If you fail to provide this information in a timely manner or provide false or fraudulent information, you may be subject to penalties and interest.

You are not required to provide the information requested on a form that is subject to the Paperwork Reduction Act unless the form displays a valid OMB control number. Books and records relating to a form or instructions must be retained as long as their contents may become material in the administration of any Internal Revenue law.

Generally, tax returns and return information are confidential, as required by section 6103. However, section 6103 allows or requires the IRS to disclose or give the information shown on your tax return to others as described in the Code. For example, we may disclose your tax information to the Department of Justice for civil and criminal litigation, and to cities, states, the District of Columbia, and U.S. commonwealths and possessions for use in administering their tax laws. We may also disclose this information to other countries under a tax treaty, to federal and state agencies to enforce federal nontax criminal laws, or to federal law enforcement and intelligence agencies to combat terrorism.

The time needed to complete and file Form 941-SS will vary depending on individual circumstances. The estimated average time is:

Recordkeeping . . . . 10 hrs., 31 min.

Learning about the law or the form . . . . 18 min.

Preparing, copying, assembling, and sending the form to the IRS . . . . 28 min.

If you have comments concerning the accuracy of these time estimates or suggestions for making Form 941-SS simpler, we would be happy to hear from you. You can write to: Internal Revenue Service, Tax Products Coordinating Committee, SE:W:CAR:MP:T:T:SP, 1111 Constitution Ave. NW, IR-6526, Washington, DC 20224. **Do not** send Form 941-SS to this address. Instead, see *Where Should You File?* in the Instructions for Form 941-SS.

Form **940 for 2010:** **Employer's Annual Federal Unemployment (FUTA) Tax Return**   850110

Department of the Treasury — Internal Revenue Service

OMB No. 1545-0028

(EIN)
Employer identification number [ ][ ] – [ ][ ][ ][ ][ ][ ][ ]

Name *(not your trade name)* [   ]

Trade name *(if any)* [   ]

Address [   ]
Number   Street   Suite or room number
[   ] [   ] [   ]
City   State   ZIP code

Type of Return
(Check all that apply.)

☐ **a.** Amended
☐ **b.** Successor employer
☐ **c.** No payments to employees in 2010
☐ **d.** Final: Business closed or stopped paying wages

Read the separate instructions before you fill out this form. Please type or print within the boxes.

Part 1: Tell us about your return. If any line does NOT apply, leave it blank.

1   If you were required to pay your state unemployment tax in ...

     1a **One state only,** write the state abbreviation . . . . . **1a** [ ][ ]
     - OR -
     1b **More than one state** (You are a multi-state employer) . . . . **1b** ☐ Check here. Fill out Schedule A.

2   If you paid wages in a state that is subject to CREDIT REDUCTION . . . . **2** ☐ Check here. Fill out Schedule A (Form 940), Part 2.

Part 2: Determine your FUTA tax before adjustments for 2010. If any line does NOT apply, leave it blank.

3   **Total payments to all employees** . . . . **3** [   ] .

4   **Payments exempt from FUTA tax** . . . . **4** [   ] .

     Check all that apply: **4a** ☐ Fringe benefits   **4c** ☐ Retirement/Pension **4e** ☐ Other
     4b ☐ Group-term life insurance **4d** ☐ Dependent care

5   **Total of payments made to each employee in excess of $7,000** . . . **5** [   ] .

6   **Subtotal** (line 4 + line 5 = line 6) . . . . **6** [   ] .

7   **Total taxable FUTA wages** (line 3 – line 6 = line 7) . . . . **7** [   ] .

8   **FUTA tax before adjustments** (line 7 × .008 = line 8) . . . . **8** [   ] .

Part 3: Determine your adjustments. If any line does NOT apply, leave it blank.

9   If ALL of the taxable FUTA wages you paid were excluded from state unemployment tax, **multiply line 7 by .054** (line 7 × .054 = line 9). Then go to line 12 . . . . **9** [   ] .

10 If SOME of the taxable FUTA wages you paid were excluded from state unemployment tax, **OR** you paid ANY state unemployment tax late (after the due date for filing Form 940), fill out the worksheet in the instructions. Enter the amount from line 7 of the worksheet . . . . . **10** [   ] .

11 If credit reduction applies, enter the amount from line 3 of Schedule A (Form 940) . . . . **11** [   ] .

Part 4: Determine your FUTA tax and balance due or overpayment for 2010. If any line does NOT apply, leave it blank.

12 **Total FUTA tax after adjustments** (lines 8 + 9 + 10 + 11 = line 12) . . . . **12** [   ] .

13 **FUTA tax deposited for the year, including any overpayment applied from a prior year** . **13** [   ] .

14 **Balance due** (If line 12 is more than line 13, enter the difference on line 14.)
     • If line 14 is more than $500, you must deposit your tax.
     • If line 14 is $500 or less, you may pay with this return. For more information on how to pay, see the separate instructions . . . . **14** [   ] .

15 **Overpayment** (If line 13 is more than line 12, enter the difference on line 15 and check a box below.) . . . . **15** [   ] .

Check one: ☐ Apply to next return.
                ☐ Send a refund.

▶ You **MUST** fill out both pages of this form and **SIGN** it.

Next ▶

For Privacy Act and Paperwork Reduction Act Notice, see the back of Form 940-V, Payment Voucher.   Cat. No. 11234O   Form **940** (2010)

850210

Name *(not your trade name)*	Employer identification number (EIN)

Part 5: Report your FUTA tax liability by quarter only if line 12 is more than $500. If not, go to Part 6.

16 Report the amount of your FUTA tax liability for each quarter; do NOT enter the amount you deposited. If you had no liability for a quarter, leave the line blank.

16a **1st quarter** (January 1 – March 31) . . . . **16a** [.]

16b **2nd quarter** (April 1 – June 30) . . . . **16b** [.]

16c **3rd quarter** (July 1 – September 30) . . . . **16c** [.]

16d **4th quarter** (October 1 – December 31) . . . . **16d** [.]

17 **Total tax liability for the year** (lines 16a + 16b + 16c + 16d = line 17) **17** [.] **Total must equal line 12.**

Part 6: May we speak with your third-party designee?

Do you want to allow an employee, a paid tax preparer, or another person to discuss this return with the IRS? See the instructions for details.

☐ **Yes.** Designee's name and phone number [   ] [   ]

Select a 5-digit Personal Identification Number (PIN) to use when talking to IRS [   ] [   ] [   ] [   ] [   ]

☐ **No.**

Part 7: Sign here. You MUST fill out both pages of this form and SIGN it.

Under penalties of perjury, I declare that I have examined this return, including accompanying schedules and statements, and to the best of my knowledge and belief, it is true, correct, and complete, and that no part of any payment made to a state unemployment fund claimed as a credit was, or is to be, deducted from the payments made to employees. Declaration of preparer (other than taxpayer) is based on all information of which preparer has any knowledge.

✗ **Sign your name here** [   ]

Print your name here [   ]

Print your title here [   ]

Date [/   /   ]

Best daytime phone [   ]

Paid preparer use only   Check if you are self-employed . . . ☐

Preparer's name	[ ]	PTIN [ ]
Preparer's signature	[ ]	Date [/ /]
Firm's name (or yours if self-employed)	[ ]	EIN [ ]
Address	[ ]	Phone [ ]
City	[ ] State [ ]	ZIP code [ ]

Page **2** Form **940** (2010)

Form 940-V, Payment Voucher

What Is Form 940-V?

Form 940-V is a transmittal form for your check or money order. Using Form 940-V allows us to process your payment more accurately and efficiently. If you have any balance due of $500 or less on your 2010 Form 940, fill out Form 940-V and send it with your check or money order.

Note. If your balance is more than $500, see *When Must You Deposit Your FUTA Tax?* in the Instructions for Form 940.

How Do You Fill Out Form 940-V?

Type or print clearly.

Box 1. Enter your employer identification number (EIN). Do not enter your social security number (SSN).

Box 2. Enter the amount of your payment. Be sure to put dollars and cents in the appropriate spaces.

Box 3. Enter your business name and complete address exactly as they appear on your Form 940.

How Should You Prepare Your Payment?

- Make your check or money order payable to the *United States Treasury*. Do not send cash.
- On the memo line of your check or money order, write:
  - your EIN,
  - Form 940, and
  - 2010.
- Carefully detach Form 940-V along the dotted line.
- Do not staple your payment to the voucher.
- Mail your 2010 Form 940, your payment, and Form 940-V in the envelope that came with your 2010 Form 940 instruction booklet. If you do not have that envelope, use the table in the Instructions for Form 940 to find the mailing address.

✂ ▼ **Detach Here and Mail With Your Payment and Form 940.** ▼ ✂

Form **940-V**	**Payment Voucher**	OMB No. 1545-0028
Department of the Treasury Internal Revenue Service	▶ Do not staple or attach this voucher to your payment.	20**10**

1 Enter your employer identification number (EIN).	2 Enter the amount of your payment. ▶	Dollars	Cents

3 Enter your business name (individual name if sole proprietor).

Enter your address.

Enter your city, state, and ZIP code.

Privacy Act and Paperwork Reduction Act Notice.
We ask for the information on this form to carry out the Internal Revenue laws of the United States. We need it to figure and collect the right amount of tax. Chapter 23, Federal Unemployment Tax Act, of Subtitle C, Employment Taxes, of the Internal Revenue Code imposes a tax on employers with respect to employees. This form is used to determine the amount of the tax that you owe. Section 6011 requires you to provide the requested information if you are liable for FUTA tax under section 3301. Section 6109 requires you to provide your identification number. If you fail to provide this information in a timely manner or provide a false or fraudulent form, you may be subject to penalties and interest.

You are not required to provide the information requested on a form that is subject to the Paperwork Reduction Act unless the form displays a valid OMB control number. Books and records relating to a form or instructions must be retained as long as their contents may become material in the administration of any Internal Revenue law.

Generally, tax returns and return information are confidential, as required by section 6103. However, section 6103 allows or requires the IRS to disclose or give the information shown on your tax return to others as described in the Code. For example, we may disclose your tax information to the Department of Justice for civil and criminal litigation, and to cities, states, the District of Columbia, and U.S. commonwealths and possessions to administer their tax laws. We may also disclose this information to other countries under a tax treaty, to federal and state agencies to enforce federal non-tax criminal laws, or to federal law enforcement and intelligence agencies to combat terrorism.

The time needed to complete and file this form will vary depending on individual circumstances. The estimated average time is:

Recordkeeping . . . . 9 hr., 19 min.

Learning about the law or the form . . . 1 hr., 23 min.

Preparing, copying, assembling, and sending form to the IRS . . . . 1 hr., 36 min.

If you have comments concerning the accuracy of these time estimates or suggestions for making Form 940 simpler, we would be happy to hear from you. You can write to: Internal Revenue Service, Tax Products Coordinating Committee, SE:W:CAR:MP:T:SP, 1111 Constitution Avenue, NW, IR-6526, Washington, DC 20224. **Do not** send Form 940 to this address. Instead, see *Where Do You File?* on page 2 of the Instructions for Form 940.

E

Sample Employment Agreement*

Employee Employment Agreement

This Employment Agreement ("Agreement") made as of January 1, 2012, by and between Physician, MD (hereinafter referred to as "Employee") and THE PRACTICE, a State for-profit corporation (herein referred to as the "Practice").

Recitals:

WHEREAS, Practice desires to employ the Employee and the Employee desires to accept such employment and to perform all Employee services pursuant to the terms and conditions hereof.

Note: The agreement included in this Appendix is an actual contract for a hospital recruiting a pediatrician and should be used as an example only. For more information on physician employment agreements for hospitals, medical groups, or affiliate organizations, the AMA offers physicians an Annotated Model Physician-Hospital Employment Agreement that can enhance physicians' understanding and negotiating position as they navigate employment contracts and opportunities in various practice settings. This valuable resource addresses the specific needs of physicians who are preparing to negotiate an employment contract with a hospital or related entity. AMA members may view the interactive Physician-Hospital Agreement online for free. Nonmembers may purchase access to the current edition through http://amascb.pdn.ipublishcentral.com/. For an overview and the Table of Contents of the agreement, go to www.ama-assn.org.

NOW, THEREFORE, for and in consideration of such employment of the Employee by Practice, the mutual covenants hereinafter set forth, and other good and valuable consideration, the receipt and legal sufficiency of which are hereby acknowledged, the parties hereto agree as follows:

1. Appointment

The Practice hereby employs Employee, and Employee accepts such employment, to provide professional medical services on behalf of the Practice, in accordance with the terms of this Agreement.

2. Duties, Responsibilities, and Qualifications of Employee

2.1 General.

Employee agrees to devote his/her professional efforts in the full-time practice of medicine exclusively in the interest of the Practice. See Addendum A for a summary of specialty services (not necessarily all-inclusive). Employee will not engage in the practice of medicine other than for the Practice. Full-time practice is defined as a minimum of 40 hours per week. Employee will maintain a reasonable schedule for the performance of professional medical services. In addition, Employee shall be responsible for the following:

(a) Performing the duties directed from time to time by the Practice, including but not limited to providing professional medical services for which the Employee is qualified.

(b) Providing professional medical services on a full-time basis during regular business hours.

(c) Providing assistance after regular business hours in coordination with the directives of the Practice, as previously agreed to in writing.

(d) Participating in managed care, Medicaid, or Medicare plans.

(e) Continually working to improve quality while maintaining reasonable costs for medical care rendered to patients.

(f) Participating for reasonable periods of time in functions within the Practice as deemed necessary.

(g) Keeping and maintaining or causing to be kept and maintained appropriate records, including without limitation patient charts on a timely basis. Also, being in accordance with the statutes and/or requirements of professional, governmental, third-party payers, and record keeping and reporting requirements.

(h) Preparing and attending to in connection with all such services all reports and correspondence necessary or appropriate under the circumstances.

(i) Performing functions reasonably necessary to maintain and improve professional skills, including seeking and maintaining applicable professional standards and/or designations.

(j) Providing professional medical services and conducting his/her professional duties in accordance with current health care and medical standards in the Anytown community, and with such ethical standards of professional conduct in practices may, from time to time during the term hereof, be required or recommended by the American Medical Association.

(k) Complying with any and all statutes, laws, rules, regulations, and ordinances of all governmental authorities. This also includes, but is not limited to, the rules and regulations of the [state] Medical Board and ethical standards of the American Medical Association, the [state] Medical Association and the [medical society] (or whichever specialty applies).

(l) Refraining from doing any act that will render Employee subject to any disciplinary order, sanction, or decree of any federal or state governmental agency having jurisdiction over the practice of medicine.

(m) Employee shall notify the Practice within 24 hours after the occurrence of any event which causes the Employee to fail to meet one or more of the qualifications set forth in Section 2.2.

(n) Employee shall carry out the duties required of him/her in this section on a full-time basis. Employee shall devote full time attention together with his/her best endeavors and skill for the interest, benefit, and best advantage of the Practice and its efforts to serve and treat patients with consistently high quality professional care.

(o) Employee shall observe and comply with all reasonable rules and regulations of the Practice now in force or as may hereafter be adopted from time to time by the Practice either written or oral as long as such rules and regulations are communicated to the Employee, and will act in a manner consistent with the best interest of the Practice.

(p) Employee shall provide the Practice with verification of license, board certification, or any other recognized professional status, if applicable, upon request by the Practice.

2.2 Employee Qualifications.

Employee must meet the following qualifications at all times during the term of this Agreement:

(a) Be duly licensed and authorized to practice medicine under the laws of the State of [state].

(b) Maintain all necessary narcotics and controlled substances registration numbers and licenses required for the performance of his/her duties.

(c) Never have been reprimanded, sanctioned, or disciplined by any licensing board, state, or medical society or any health care facility.

(d) Never have had his/her license to practice medicine suspended, curtailed, denied, or revoked by the Medical Board of [state] or any other state licensing board.

(e) Except as previously disclosed in writing and waived in writing by the Practice, never have been entered against Employee (or another practice in which Employee was employed) a final judgment in a malpractice action.

(f) Except as previously disclosed in writing and waived by the Practice in writing, never have been an action against Employee based on an allegation of malpractice by Employee (or another practice employing Employee) which has been settled by payment to the plaintiff.

(g) Never have been denied membership or reappointment of membership on the medical staff of any hospital, and no hospital medical staff membership or clinical privileges of the Employee have ever been curtailed, denied, or revoked.

(h) Be on the active medical staff of the Hospital with clinical privileges self-sufficient to perform all services required of him/her under this Agreement.

(i) Unless waived in writing by the Practice, be board certified in Employee's specialty or, if not so, use best efforts to become board certified in Employee's primary area of specialization.

(j) Not be subject to any disciplinary order, sanction, or decree of any federal or state governmental agency having jurisdiction over the payment for health care services or practice of medicine.

(k) Be a participating provider with, and agree to accept assignment from, [state's] medical assistance program (Medicaid) and any other third-party payers, including any Blue Cross/Blue Shield plan, health maintenance organization, and/or preferred provider organization with which the Practice determines that it is desirable for him/her to so participate.

(l) Not have been convicted of any crime (other than minor traffic violation) or been arrested for a crime involving immoral conduct tending to injure the reputation of the Practice.

(m) Not have been involved directly with an organization or health care provider that has been suspended from, or otherwise not permitted to continue as a participating provider in the Medicare or Medicaid programs or any other governmental payment program(s) for any reason.

(n) Not have been involved directly with an organization or health care provider that has been suspended from, or otherwise not permitted to continue as a participating provider in any managed care organization for reasons related to the quality of patient care or patient satisfaction.

2.3 Managed Care.
As directed by the Practice in its sole discretion, Employee shall be required to apply his/her best efforts to provide professional services commensurate with Employee's qualifications and/or experience to the Practice's patients in a thorough manner. Employee shall make a best effort to become and remain a participating provider in all health benefit plans and complete and sign all contracts and other documents with or for third-party payers which may be necessary to participate in such plans. Employee shall not contract individually with third-party payers for reimbursement of services provided during the term of this Agreement unless directed by the Practice to do so. If required by any plan, Employee agrees to be responsible for providing and coordinating the overall health care of patients assigned to Employee. Employee agrees not to close Employee's practice to new patients without the consent of the Practice.

2.4 Call Coverage.
It is herein agreed that Employee will participate in a call rotation with the Practice specialty group (i.e., [specialty]). Employee will take call on Employee's own patients during regular office hours Monday through Friday. Employee will arrange for and notify the Practice in advance if call is being shifted to another physician.

2.5 Hospital Privileges.
Employee shall maintain active medical staff privileges in the specialty of [specialty] at the Practice, Anytown, USA (the "Hospital"). Employee should actively participate in the activities of the Hospital with regard to employee recruitment, pertinent community events, and Hospital and medical staff meetings directed by the Practice from time to time.

2.6 Employee's Warranties.
Employee warrants that he/she shall not:

(a) Contract any debt on account of the Practice, or in any manner pledge the credit thereof, except as approved by the Practice and in accordance with the provisions of this Agreement; or

(b) This clause shall not restrict or prevent Employee from personally, on his/her own account, investing or trading in stocks, bonds, securities, commodities, real estate, or other forms of investment for his/her family, or to have other business interests which do not interfere with his/her full-time employment as a practicing physician employed by the Practice. However, Employee may not invest in companies that are currently clients of the Practice and also those that could become clients of the Practice in the future. This pertains but is not limited to technology vendors, hospital companies, medical practices, and other health care entities.

2.7 Clinical Performance.
Employee will participate and allow the Practice to establish appropriate medical committees to assure effective utilization and quality of care for patients. Such medical committees will assist the Practice in the development, implementation, and administration of utilization management and performance improvement programs.

3. Duties and Responsibilities of the Practice

3.1 Support Services.
The Practice, at its sole cost and expense, will provide appropriate office space, equipment, furnishings, and supplies as the Practice reasonably determines necessary for the proper operation and conduct of a physician practicing with Employee's specialty. Further the intent of this subsection is that the Practice shall furnish to the Employee at its expense as may be reasonably necessary and determined by the Practice for the performance for the Employee's professional medical service the following:

1. Adequate office space;

2. Equipment and furniture;

3. Utilities and supplies; and

4. Support personnel

3.1.1 The Practice will provide and the Employee will use the medical office only for the purpose of providing services pursuant to this Agreement. Nothing in this Agreement will be construed by either party to constitute a lease to the Employee of the medical office. Employee shall use the medical office in the capacity of a licensee only and the Practice shall at all times have free and full access to the medical office.

3.1.2 The Practice may require Employee to relocate his/her practice of medicine to other medical offices located in the Practice service area that the Practice owns, operates, and manages or which it shall establish from time to time. Employee hereby agrees to relocate to other medical offices during the term of this Agreement upon reasonable request by the Practice.

3.1.3 The Practice will bill and collect all fees for professional medical services rendered by the Employee under this Agreement, whether such professional medical services are provided to patients in the medical office, the Hospital, or any other location. The Practice will determine at its sole discretion the amounts of professional fees to be charged to patients for Employee professional medical services. The Practice or an agent of the Practice will collect all professional fees. In the event that the Employee receives any professional fees directly, he/she will promptly remit these to the Practice. Under no circumstances may Employee receive and retain any payments from any existing, previous or prospective Practice client or patient. Receipt of such is grounds for immediate termination of employment of Employee by the Practice.

3.1.4 The compensation payable to the Employee pursuant to the compensation subsection herein is for Employee's professional medical services and Employee's services to the Practice are and shall be during the term of the Agreement the Employee's sole compensation for all such services.

3.1.5 The Practice will maintain complete and accurate records of the time Employee spends providing services under this Agreement in accordance with the standard Practice procedures for maintenance of such records. These records will comply with all regulations and instructions issued under the Medicare program and shall separately identify the time spent on professional medical services, services to the Hospital and services that do not qualify for reimbursement under the Medicare program.

3.1.6 The Practice and Employee will comply with provisions of the law affecting the Practice's reimbursement. The Practice and Employee will do nothing that will adversely affect such reimbursement, or the Medicare provider status of the Practice.

3.1.7 The Practice will provide to the Employee quarterly unaudited financial statements and other applicable management reports related to the operation of the Employee's portion of the medical practice in which Employee operates. Employee may have such financial statements analyzed or audited at Employee's expense.

3.2 Professional Liability and Other Insurance.

During the term of this Agreement, the Practice shall, at its expense, obtain and maintain professional malpractice insurance to cover liabilities of both the Practice and Employee resulting from the practice of medicine by Employee on behalf of the Practice. Such coverage shall be for the same amount as provided in the Hospital's Medical Staff privileges bylaws. All tail insurance will be the responsibility of the employee.

3.2.1 The Practice and Employee acknowledge that it is a condition to his/her employment, pursuant to this Agreement, that the Employee must be insurable at standard rates established by the Practice's professional liability insurer.

Any increase in the Practice standard rates resulting from Employee's inclusion in the Practice's professional liability coverage shall be grounds for immediate termination of this Agreement unless the Practice Board, by unanimous consent, allows the Employee to personally reimburse at the difference between its standard rate and the increase resulting from its inclusion of Employee in the Practice's professional liability coverage.

3.2.2 If Employee resigns from employment with the Practice (other than as a result of death, disability, or retirement) or if Employee is terminated from employment pursuant to Section 4.2.1. or Section 4.6 of this Agreement, Employee shall provide, at Employee's own expenses, "tail" liability coverage for Employee (related to work performed before, during, or after Employee's employment by the Practice).

3.2.3 The Practice shall also maintain comprehensive general liability insurance with respect to the medical office and related facilities. Total coverage and premium shall be at the discretion of the Practice.

3.3 Compensation.

The Practice will pay Employee compensation pursuant to the provisions of this Section 3.3. Employee's compensation will be comprised of two major components. This includes base compensation and a component of incentive compensation. All payments made

under this Section 3.3 are subject to applicable income taxes and
other payroll withholding taxes and typical benefits that are also
withheld from gross compensation. These will be paid in accordance with the Practice's usual and customary payroll practices
and policies.

3.3.1 Base Compensation.   Base compensation will be established on a quarterly basis prior to the beginning of each
calendar quarter. This will be established relative to the
adjusted productivity (as herein defined in Section 3.3.2) of
the Employee for the previous four calendar quarters. The
base pay for that quarter will equal one-fourth of the base pay
set forth below corresponding to the Employee's Net Collections for the previous four calendar quarters:

I.	Net Collections	$100,000
	Base Pay	$40,000
II.	Net Collections	$130,000
	Base Pay	$50,000
III.	Net Collections	$160,000
	Base Pay	$60,000
IV.	Net Collections	$200,000
	Base Pay	$70,000
V.	Net Collections	$230,000
	Base Pay	$80,000
VI.	Net Collections	$260,000
	Base Pay	$90,000
VII.	Net Collections	$290,000
	Base Pay	$100,000
VIII.	Net Collections	$320,000
	Base Pay	$110,000

For the first quarter of this Agreement, the parties shall use
the Employee's Net Collections from Employee's services for
the previous four calendar quarters even though this Agreement was not in effect.

3.3.2 Productivity Defined.   For purposes of the interpretation
and designation of base compensation (and other forms of compensation as herein outlined in this Agreement) "productivity"
will be based upon net collections generated only from services
personally performed by Employee. Net collections are herein
defined as the net revenue (based upon the normal fee schedule as established by the Practice) that the Practice physically
receives in payment for employee professional fees generated.
However, should the ratio of net collections to net charges ever
become less than 85%, Employee's compensation and associated productivity will be calculated as if it were 85%.

3.3.3 Incentive Compensation, Excess Productivity. In addition to base pay, Employee may be entitled to a bonus at the end of each calendar quarter pursuant to this Subsection 3.3.3. In the event Employee's annualized productivity for any calendar quarter exceeds the previous year's pay band productivity, the Employee will be entitled to a bonus. This will be calculated and be paid by the end of the month subsequent to the end of the calendar quarter. The calculation of the bonus is as follows:

Employee's Net Collections for the quarter		$ xxxx
Times 4 (to annualize)	×	4
Equals annualized productivity	=	$ xxxxxx
Net Collections from previous 4 quarters minus pay band total		$ (xxxxxx)
Equals excess subject to bonus	=	$ xxxxx
Times employee share (see below)	×	0.45*
Equals annualized bonus	=	$ xxxx
Times 0.25 to convert to quarter	×	0.25
Equals quarterly bonus	=	$ xxxx

3.4 Vacation, Sick, and Personal Leave.

The Practice shall provide Employee with the following leaves of absence during the Term of this Agreement, during which Employee's fixed-base compensation shall continue to be paid in full:

---

*The Employee share will equal either forty-five percent (45%), fifty-five percent (55%), or sixty-five percent (65%). In the event the Employee's calendar quarter annualized Net Collections is less than his/her base pay multiplied by two, the Employee's share will equal forty-five percent (45%). In the event such annualized Net Collections is at least equal to his/her base pay multiplied by two, but less than his/her base pay multiplied by a factor of 2.5, the Employee's share will equal fifty-five percent (55%). In the event such annualized Net Collections is more than his/her base pay multiplied by a factor of 2.5, the Employee share will equal sixty-five percent (65%).

3.4.1 During each twelve- (12-) month period of the term of this Agreement, 25 work days are authorized to be used for vacation, sick leave, and/or for attendance at professional meetings. Employee and the Practice shall mutually agree upon the period or periods to be taken, in advance. Employee is required to complete the appropriate request forms and arrange for call coverage per established guidelines. However, it is understood by the Practice and Employee that not more than two (2) consecutive weeks for vacation and/or meeting time shall be taken at one time. Unused vacation, sick leave, and/or continuing medical education time can be carried over from one year to the next up to a maximum of two (2) weeks (or ten [10] work days). The maximum available Paid Time Off for vacation/continuing education is five (5) weeks (or 25 days) in any given year of the contract.

3.4.2 Holidays as established by the Practice.

3.5 Benefits.
The Practice shall provide Employee with the following benefits, all at the Practice's expense on the same basis as similarly situated employees:

3.5.1 Health insurance for Employee (during leaves of absence, except family medical leave, premiums become the responsibility of the Employee on leave).

3.5.2 Reimbursement of expenses incurred for attendance and/or participation in continuing medical education courses, to a maximum of One Thousand Five Hundred Dollars ($1,500.00) per twelve- (12-) month period of the term of this Agreement.

3.5.3 Reimbursement of all medical license fees and professional fees and dues (in one organization), in the same amount and under the same conditions as other employed physicians of the Practice.

3.5.4 Long-term disability insurance (per the Practice's policy).

3.6 The Practice Authority.
The Practice shall exercise direction over and give support to Employee in regard to standards, policies, record keeping, treatment procedures, and fees to be charged; but such direction and support shall not interfere with the usual physician/patient relationship nor be in violation of acceptable medical ethics.

3.7 Base Compensation Pay Band and Incentive Criteria Adjustments.
Each December during the term of this Agreement, the Practice may adjust in its sole discretion the Net Collections benchmarks and corresponding base pays (as well as the assumed contractual allowance/discount rate) set forth in Section 3.3 by written notice to Employee. Any such adjustment will become effective January 1 following the written notice. This would be completed in order to establish an appropriate base pay and productivity scale commensurate with current benchmarking standards and overall operation of the Practice network. In addition, the benefits set forth in Section 3.5 may be subject to adjustment by the Practice during December each year, with an effective date of January 1 following notice of such change.

4. Term and Termination

4.1 Term.
The Term ("term") of this Agreement shall commence January 1, 2012, and continue through and including the first anniversary of the Effective Date ("Initial Term") unless sooner terminated by the Practice or Employee as provided herein. This Agreement shall automatically renew for an additional one year period on each anniversary date of the Effective Term after the Initial Term has elapsed ("Renewal Term") unless sooner terminated by the Practice or Employee as provided herein. The Initial Term along with any Renewal Term shall be referred to in this Agreement as the "Term" of this agreement.

4.2 Termination.
This Agreement may be terminated as follows:

4.2.1 By the Practice. In the event that Employee materially fails to perform the duties or responsibilities required under this Agreement (including any noncompetition or confidentiality provisions), the Practice may give written notice to Employee of such material failure to perform and demand performance. If Employee fails to cure such material non-performance within 60 days of such written notice, the Practice may terminate this Agreement without waiver of any rights the Practice may have against Employee for such failure to perform. In addition, the Practice may terminate Employee immediately by written notice for patient safety reasons or in the event Employee fails to meet one or more of the qualifications set forth in Section 2.2.

4.2.2 By Employee.   In the event that the Practice materially fails to perform its duties as required under this Agreement, Employee may give written notice to the Practice of such material failure to perform and demand performance. If the Practice fails to cure such material non-performance within 60 days of such written notice, Employee may terminate this Agreement without waiver of any rights that Employee may have against the Practice for such failure to perform.

4.3 Termination for Death or Disability.
This Agreement shall be terminated effective immediately upon the death or permanent disability of Employee. For the purposes of this Agreement, the term "permanent disability" shall have the same meaning as set forth in the Practice's long-term disability insurance policy. In the event of a short-term disability, Employee shall receive benefits in accordance with the Practice's policy.

4.4 Violation of Code.
This Agreement may be terminated by Employee upon seven (7) days notice upon a finding by, or opinion of, an appropriate authority that Employee's continued employment with the Practice under this Agreement constitutes a violation of any appropriate code of conduct within the state of [state]. Such specific codes of conduct must be documented within the Practice's employee handbook and be consistent with the state's code of conduct.

4.5 Exclusion from Procurement Programs.
This employment Agreement shall immediately terminate, if for any reason the Employee is or shall become excluded from participating in Federal or State Payment Programs, including but not limited to any Federal or State health care programs.

4.6 Effect of Termination.
In the event of termination of this Agreement pursuant to this Section 4, all rights, duties, and obligations of both parties shall cease effective with the date of termination except as provided in this Section 4. Employee will be paid any base compensation and incentive-based compensation earned but not yet paid through the date of termination. Notwithstanding such termination, Employee shall continue to be bound by the restrictions set forth in Section 4.8 and it subsections. Also, any final interpretation of the status and eligibility of a bonus (productivity or nonproductivity based) at termination shall be at the sole discretion of the Practice.

With the exercise of the terms of this Section 4 in effect it does not release or discharge any party from any debt or liability that will have previously accrued or remains to be performed on or after the date of termination (as noted above, the interpretation of any out-standing bonuses due the Employee will rest with the Practice).

4.7 Rights and Obligations upon Termination.

The rights and obligations upon termination include access to books and records in compliance with applicable state and federal statutes. Upon termination of this Agreement, the Employee will remove his/her work items and materials from the medical office and turn over to the Practice all programs, records, patient and vendor lists, and material related to the services by the Employee under the terms and conditions of the Agreement. The Agreement at all times will be subject to state, local, and federal law. This includes but is not limited to the Social Security Act and the rules and regulations of the US Department of Health and Human Services. The parties further recognize that the Agreement shall be subject to the amendments to existing laws and new legislation such as the new federal/state economic stabilization program or health insurance program.

4.8 Covenant Not to Compete Non-Diversion and Non-Disclosure.

During the term of this Agreement, and for a period of one (1) year following expiration or termination of this Agreement, Employee shall not, directly or indirectly, on his/her own behalf or on behalf of any other person, organization, or entity, individually or collectively, in any fashion, form, or manner, in [Anytown, State] and within a five (5) mile radius of Anytown, engage in the practice of medicine, or provide any other services substantially similar to those required to be provided by Employee under this Agreement.

Notwithstanding the above, as long as Employee practices in totally private manner, independent of any affiliation with other health-care providers or any other corporate entity that might be a possible owner of the Practice, the restrictions of this Section shall not apply.

4.8.1 Non-diversion.
During the term of this Agreement and for one year after the termination of this Agreement, Employee shall not, directly or indirectly, on his/her behalf or on behalf of any other person, organization, or entity, contract in any manner for the services of, or induce or solicit the services of any of the Practice employees to work for Employee or any person, corporation, partnership, sole proprietorship, governmental agency, organization, joint venture, or other entity with whom or which Employee is associated, without the written consent of the owner of the Practice.

4.8.2 Non-disclosure.
Employee, during the course of his/her employment pursuant to this Agreement, will acquire

information concerning the Practice's finances, business practices, long-term and strategic plans, and similar matters (collectively, the "Confidential Information"). The Confidential Information is and shall remain the sole and exclusive property of the Practice. Employee may not at any time during the term of this Agreement or after the expiration or termination of this Agreement, for any reason whatsoever, with or without cause, directly or indirectly, use for any purpose or disclose or distribute to any person, corporation, partnership, sole proprietorship, governmental agency, organization, joint venture, or other entity any Confidential Information.

4.8.3 Establishment of Medical Practice.   Nothing in this Section 4 shall be construed to prohibit Employee, upon the expiration or termination for any reason whatsoever of this Agreement, from establishing a medical practice in a manner and location which does not conflict with any of the provisions of Section 4 of this Agreement.

4.8.4 Right to Injunctive Relief.   The parties hereto recognized that the Practice would suffer substantial and irreparable damages in the event of any breach of the terms of this Section by Employee, and also recognize that such damages would be difficult, if not impossible, to value in terms of monetary compensation, and accordingly, Employee agrees that in the event of any such further breach, such right to an injunction will be in addition to any other rights or remedies that may be available hereunder to the Practice.

4.8.5 Liquidated Damages.   If Employee violates any of the above provisions of Section 4.8, Employee will pay immediately to Employer the liquidated damages pursuant to the following schedule if:

(1) Employee leaves the Employer during the first month of employment hereunder: the sum of Ten Thousand Dollars ($10,000), as liquidated damages;

(2) Employee leaves the Employer after the first month of employment hereunder but before the end of the second month of employment hereunder: the sum of Fifteen Thousand Dollars ($15,000), as liquidated damages;

(3) Employee leaves the Employer on or after the end of the second month of employment hereunder but before the end of the third month of employment hereunder: the sum of Twenty-One Thousand Dollars ($21,000), as liquidated damages;

(4) Employee leaves the Employer on or after the third month of employment hereunder but before the end of the fourth month of employment hereunder: the sum of Twenty-Eight Thousand Dollars ($28,000), as liquidated damages;

(5) Employee leaves the Employer on or after the fourth month of employment hereunder but before the fifth month of employment hereunder: the sum of Thirty-Five Thousand Dollars ($35,000), as liquidated damages;

(6) Employee leaves the Employer on or after the fifth month of employment hereunder but before the end of the sixth month of employment hereunder: the sum of Forty-Two Thousand Dollars ($42,000), as liquidated damages;

(7) Employee leaves the Employer on or after the sixth month of employment hereunder: the sum of Eighty-Thousand Dollars ($80,000), as liquidated damages.

5. Miscellaneous

5.1 Patient Records.
For the purpose of this Agreement, all patient records shall be those of the Practice. Upon termination of this Agreement, patient records shall continue to be those of the Practice. If said patient(s) should continue their treatment with Employee, said records would then be copied and provided to the patient(s), after the appropriate signed release of the patient(s). Additionally, in the event a malpractice claim is filed or an investigation initiated against the Employee, a copy of pertinent patient records will be provided to the Employee.

5.2 Non-discrimination.
The Employee shall not discriminate on the basis of race, color, sex, age, religion, marital or health status, national origin, or handicap in providing services under this Agreement, provided that the Employee will be permitted to take sex or age into account in making reasonable clinical decisions. For example, the Employee can decline to treat a prospective patient on the basis of the prospective patient's _____ if the prospective patient is properly a _____ patient and if the Employee is not a _____.

5.3 Warranty of Authority.
The Practice represents and warrants to Employee that the Practice has the full power and authority to enter into this Agreement, and that upon execution of this Agreement by the Practice, this Agreement shall become a binding obligation of the Practice

enforceable against the Practice in accordance with its terms and applicable law.

5.4 Severability.

If any provision or portion of any provision of this Agreement is held to be unenforceable or invalid by a court of competent jurisdiction, the validity and enforceability of the remaining provisions of this Agreement will not be affected thereby.

5.5 Assignment.

Except as otherwise noted in this Agreement, the Employee shall not assign any of his/her rights or delegate any of his/her duties under this Agreement without the prior written consent of the Practice. This consent may be withheld at the sole discretion of the Practice. Any unauthorized attempted assignment by the Employee shall be null and void and have no force or effect.

5.6 Governing Law.

This Agreement has been executed and delivered in, and shall be interpreted, construed, and enforced pursuant to and in accordance with the laws of the State of [state].

5.7 Gender and Number.

Whenever the context hereof requires, the gender of all words shall include the masculine, feminine, and neuter, and the number of all words shall include the singular and plural.

5.8 Section and Other Headings.

The section and other headings contained in this Agreement are for reference purposes only and shall not affect, in any way, the meaning or interpretation of this Agreement.

5.9 Amendments and Agreement Execution.

This Agreement and amendments thereto shall be in writing and executed in multiple copies. Each multiple copy shall be deemed an original, but all multiple copies together shall constitute one and the same instrument.

5.10 Notices.

Any notice, demand, or communication required, permitted, or desired to be given hereunder shall be deemed effectively given when personally delivered or mailed by prepaid certified mail, return receipt requested, addressed as follows:

Employee	The Practice
Physician, MD	Owner, MD
400 Main Street	400 Main Street
Anytown, USA 55555	Anytown, USA 55555

or to any such other addresses, and to the attention of such other person(s) or officer(s) as either party may designate by written notice to the other party. Further, Employee shall at all times keep the Practice notified of his/her home address and home telephone number.

5.11 Waiver of Breach.

The waiver of either party of a breach or violation of any provision of this Agreement shall not operate as, or be construed to be, a waiver of any subsequent breach of the same or other provision hereof.

5.12 Additional Assurances.

The provisions of this Agreement shall be self-operative and shall not require further agreement by the parties except as may be specifically provided to the contrary; provided, however, each party shall, at the request of the other, execute such additional instruments and take such additional acts as may be necessary to effectuate this Agreement.

5.13 Violations of Law.

If, as a result of any development of law ("Development"), this Agreement or any part hereof may reasonably be interpreted to violate any state or federal laws, the parties shall meet and work with diligent speed to restructure this Agreement to bring it into compliance. If such restructuring is not completed within ninety (90) days after the parties' discovery of the Development, either party may terminate this Agreement upon one (1) day's notice.

5.14 Entire Agreement.

This Agreement supersedes all previous contracts and constitutes the entire Agreement between the parties. The Practice and Employee shall be entitled to no benefits other than those specified herein. No oral statements or prior written material not specifically incorporated herein shall be of any force and effect and no changes in or additions to this Agreement shall be recognized unless incorporated herein by amendments as provided herein, such amendment(s) to become effective on the day stipulated in such amendment(s). Both parties specifically acknowledge that in entering into and executing this Agreement, they rely solely upon the representation and agreements contained in this Agreement and no others.

5.15 Prior Employment Agreement.

The prior Employment Agreement between the parties is hereby terminated and shall have no further force or effect.

IN WITNESS WHEREOF, the parties have executed this Agreement in multiple originals as of the date above written.

FOR THE EMPLOYEE:

_____

Physician, MD

THE PRACTICE:

_____

Owner, MD

Addendum A
[Specialty] Employee Services

- Routine visits to a physician's office and the services thereby either the Employee or another health care provider. Typical service categories include evaluation, diagnosis, and treatment of an injury or illness. After-hours visits are included in this category.

- Periodic health assessments including all routine tests performed in the physician's office.

- Administration of injections, including the injectible.

- Visits and examinations during a stay in a hospital, emergency department, skilled nursing facility, or extended care facility. Consultation time is included.

- Physician home care when, in the opinion of the physician, the nature of the illness dictates such a need.

- Physician services related to routine diagnostic and laboratory services. Interpretation of results.

- Well care; sick care.

- Immunizations in accordance with accepted medical practice.

- Routine screening for hearing or vision correction.

- Preventative care and patient health education services.

- Minor surgical procedures, such as [specify], etc.

- Proper follow-up visits related to treatment in the physician's office.

- Telephone consultations.

- Usage of appropriate medical supplies, gauze, tape, bandages, and other routine medical supplies are examples, in the physician's office.

APPENDIX F

Pro Forma Income Statement

SCOPE OF THIS ASSIGNMENT

The Appraiser was retained to compile pro forma income statements on various purchase arrangements of John Doe, MD Family Practice (the "Practice"), a medical practice wholly owned by Dr. John Doe (the "Physician") and located in Anywhere, USA. Income statements from the Physician's personal tax returns (that portion pertaining to his medical practice) for the fiscal years ending December 31, 2007, through December 31, 2009, and estimated operating results for the year ended December 31, 2010, were reviewed and considered within the scope of work.

These pro forma income statements have been compiled to assist the Physician in evaluating the purchase scenarios employed in these pro formas. Prior historical financial information for these projections has been provided by the Practice. The purchasing organization has provided purchase prices, physician compensation arrangements, and expense parameters as noted. The Appraiser has made assumptions used in the computations as noted. We believe that the underlying assumptions provide a reasonable basis for the forecasts. However, there will be differences between the forecasted and actual results, because events and circumstances frequently do not occur as expected, and those differences may be material.

Terms and Conditions

The following are the terms and conditions used in completion of pro forma income statements:

1. All financial statements, tax returns, operating information, and other data concerning the Practice have been provided by management and have been accepted without further verification.

2. The forecasts compiled are for the sole purpose of this valuation, and such forecasts may not be relevant for any other purpose. No further use of the forecasts is authorized, anticipated, or intended.

3. All estimates of value are presented as an expression of the valuator's judgment based upon the facts and data obtained from all sources used in developing this valuation.

4. The values presented are stated before any taxes related to the transfer of any ownership interest.

5. There is no guarantee that the estimated values reported will be realized, in cash or otherwise, either now or at any future date.

6. The Appraiser has no financial interest in the practice of the Physician.

7. The fee for this compilation service is not contingent upon the values reported.

8. Current and future economic conditions, specifically as they relate to health care reform, which we have no control over or prediction of, may have an impact on the actual future performance of this Practice.

Definitions

Pro forma income statements are forecasts of estimated revenues, expenses, operating profits, and future cash flows.

Forecasts are estimates based on assumptions made by the Appraiser and/or the Practice's management.

The pro forma income statements prepared for this engagement do not consider the income tax effect upon operating results (both cash flow and net earnings). It is apparent that whatever effective corporate consolidated tax rate exists would be considered within the application of the Practice's contribution to the overall profits of the entire hospital system.

Pro Forma Considerations

In order to reach sound, reasonable conclusions as to the values being estimated, we analyzed and considered the following factors:

1. The going concern status of the Practice as of the compilation date.

2. The size of the Practice.

3. The history of the Practice, the specialty, and the management of the Practice.

4. The financial condition of the Practice from a historical perspective as of the compilation date.

5. Operating results of the Practice for a representative period with particular regard to the estimated earnings of the Practice before payment of Physician compensation, discretionary fringe benefits, and income taxes.

Pro Forma Assumptions

The following assumptions have been incorporated into the pro forma calculations.

- Eighty thousand dollars ($80,000) practice purchase price
- Physician compensation at a yearly base of $120,000
- Accelerated revenue growth during the first three (3) years followed by minimal percentage (3%) growth
- Additional expenses in the initial phase with a minimal percentage (2%) increase thereafter
- Physician bonus pay of fifty percent (50%) of collections in excess of $300,000

These separate amortization schedules were utilized: three (3), five (5), and seven (7) years.

A. Collections

Collections are projected to increase at an accelerated rate during 2011 (year 1), 2012 (year 2), and 2013 (year 3) at approximately fifteen percent (15%), ten percent (10%), and nine percent (9%), respectively.

During the remaining years of the pro forma, collections are projected at a minimal percentage growth rate of three percent (3%) annually.

B. Physician Compensation

Salary: The Physician's salary is proposed to be at a yearly base of $120,000 throughout the pro forma statements.

Bonus: Profit sharing is proposed to be fifty percent (50%) of collections in excess of $300,000.

C. Expenses

1. PAYROLL

   This expense includes the compensation paid to non-physician employees of the Practice. Baseline payroll is fiscal year 2010 (baseline year) employee salaries and wages. Annual increases of two percent (2%) are projected.

2. EMPLOYEE BENEFITS

   This expense includes payroll taxes, FICA, health and life insurance premiums, and retirement or profit sharing. An adjustment to actual 2010 employee benefits was performed to more closely simulate current industry standards. This adjusted figure was utilized as the working baseline. Benefits are projected to account for three percent (3%) of the Practice's collections during the initial year of the statement with a minimal decrease in subsequent years. The three percent (3%) rate was adjusted from 1.9 percent from the 2010 actual. However, this figure is still below the industry standard of 5.3 percent.

3. OFFICE SPACE (RENT)

   The Physician is currently in the final year of the lease, which does include a five-year option period that he has already exercised. The total space is approximately 1,100 sq. ft. The most recent fiscal year indicates a monthly rent expense of $2,157. The lease is fairly standard. It does call for an escalation of the percentage increase of the Consumer Pricing Index, with no more than a four percent (4%) increase per year.

4. OFFICE EXPENSE

   Fiscal year 2010 was utilized as a baseline with an escalated percentage increase of six percent (6%) during the first year of the pro forma (2011) to better correlate to projected collections. A two percent (2%) annual increase is projected during subsequent years.

5. OFFICE MAINTENANCE EXPENSE

   A reduction of fiscal year 2010 actual expenses in this area to 1.2% of projected collections was utilized to establish a baseline. This provides a suitable comparison to industry standards. A two percent (2%) annual increase is projected during subsequent years.

6. UTILITIES AND TELEPHONE EXPENSE

   Fiscal year 2010 actual expense was adjusted to reflect a proportional comparison to industry standards. A baseline of $3,000 was utilized for the baseline year. A two percent (2%)

annual increase is projected during the subsequent years of the pro forma.

7. MEDICAL SUPPLIES AND DRUGS
The percentage of this expense according to the Medical Group Management Association (MGMA) cost survey, based on the Practice's specialty, has a median value of 3.4% of collections. Actual 2010 expenses were 2.6% of collections. An adjustment was made to reflect a baseline figure more indicative with industry standard for this particular specialty. A baseline expense of $6,250 was utilized with future years reflecting a two percent (2%) projected increase.

8. LABORATORY
The projected laboratory expense increase would provide a reasonable correlation in respect to the 2011 collections expectations. Laboratory expense is expected to increase by two percent (2%) throughout the course of the pro forma.

9. MALPRACTICE INSURANCE
The percentage of this expense according to the MGMA Cost Survey, based on the Practice's specialty, has a median value of 1.9 percent of collections. Actual 2010 malpractice expense was 2.0 percent of collections. We have assumed that the Buyer will be able to obtain improved rates; thus, a $4,500 baseline was utilized providing a minimal percentage decrease from the industry average for year one (2011) of the pro forma. A two percent (2%) increase trend is seen throughout the remainder of the pro forma years.

10. ADVERTISING AND PUBLIC RELATIONS EXPENSE
The percentage of this expense according to the MGMA Cost Survey, based on the Practice's specialty, has a median value of 0.4% of collections. During 2010 the Practice did not incur any direct expense within this category. We have assumed an expense baseline within this area of $2,000 with two percent (2%) increases during subsequent years of the pro forma.

11. PROFESSIONAL SERVICES
This category includes accounting, attorney, consultants, and other professional advisors. There was no expense attributed to this category during fiscal year 2010. We have assumed a $3,000 baseline with subsequent two percent (2%) increases during the remaining years of the pro forma. MGMA standard for this expense associated with family practices is 0.8 percent of collection.

12. CONTINUING EDUCATION
This expense includes seminar fees, travel and lodging cost, dues, licenses, and subscriptions. A baseline of $2,000 was established with a two percent (2%) annual increase projection.

13. INTEREST EXPENSE

An imputed interest rate considering the repayment of the purchase investment over the amortized period has not been considered.

14. DEPRECIATION

Depreciation is considered in the computation of net earnings/
loss; however, it is not a factor in relation to cash flow.

15. TAX EFFECT UPON PRO FORMA INCOME STATEMENT

The income tax effect upon the operating results (both cash flow
and net earnings) is not officially considered within the guidelines of this analysis. Obviously, it is apparent that whatever
effective corporate consolidated tax rate exists would be considered within the application of the Practice's contribution to the
overall profits of the entire hospital system.

D. Purchase Price

A purchase price of $80,000 to be amortized over the terms of three (3),
five (5), and seven (7) years has been factored into this pro forma.

Interpretive Summary

The Physician operates a family practice in Anywhere, USA. He has
been practicing in the immediate area for more than 30 years and at the
present site for 15 years. Presently, the majority of the patients seen
within the Practice are from high-income professional backgrounds. A
significant volume of the patients are residents of the Metropolitan Area
and County, State service area.

Currently, the Practice has deliberately abstained from the acquisition of any managed care agreement. The Practice strictly practices under
fee-for-service engagements. This situation has caused the Practice to
experience fairly significant reductions in production and collections over
the past two to three years of operations. In as much as the Practice is
highly regarded with a solid patient base, the Physician has allowed the
Practice to age with little replacement of patients through time.

Utilizing 3- and 5-year amortization factors for the purchase price,
the pro forma for the Practice indicates profitability during year 3, positive cash flow commences during year 2, and the Practice repays capital
investment in year 4, assuming all excess cash is used to repay debt.

Assuming a seven (7) year amortization factor for the purchase
price, the Practice generates a profit and establishes positive cash flow
during year 2. Repayment of the capital investment occurs during year 4
of the projections.

Baseline expenses of $104,770 are forty-eight percent (48%) of the Practice's 2010 projected total collections. Expenses for 2011, the first year of the pro forma, are projected to be $107,645 or forty-three percent (43%) of the Practice's projected collections during this period. These percentages are below the industry overhead standards for a family practice of forty-three percent (43%) to forty-six percent (46%).

Income statements follow.

Dr. John Doe: Pro Forma Income Statement, 3-year Amortization of Purchase Price

Year	2011	2012	2013	2014	2015	2016	2017	2018	2019	2020	2021	2022	2023	2024	2025
Year Number	1	2	3	4	5	6	7	8	9	10	11	12	13	14	15
Collections	250,000	275,000	300,000	309,000	318,270	327,818	337,653	347,782	358,216	368,962	380,031	391,432	403,175	415,270	427,728
Physician Base Compensation	120,000	120,000	120,000	120,000	120,000	120,000	120,000	120,000	120,000	120,000	120,000	120,000	120,000	120,000	120,000
Physician Benefit Expense	24,000	24,000	24,000	24,000	24,000	24,000	24,000	24,000	24,000	24,000	24,000	24,000	24,000	24,000	24,000
Payroll, Office Staff	37,842	38,599	39,371	40,158	40,961	41,781	42,616	43,469	44,338	45,225	46,129	47,052	47,993	48,953	49,932
Employee Benefits	7,568	7,720	7,874	8,032	8,192	8,356	8,523	8,694	8,868	9,045	9,226	9,410	9,599	9,791	9,986
Office Rent	27,300	28,665	30,098	31,603	33,183	34,842	36,585	38,414	40,335	42,351	44,469	48,692	49,027	51,478	54,052
Office Expenses	8,160	8,323	8,490	8,659	8,833	9,009	9,189	9,373	9,561	9,752	9,947	10,146	10,349	10,556	10,767
Office Maintenance Expenses	3,060	3,121	3,184	3,247	3,312	3,378	3,446	3,515	3,585	3,657	3,730	3,805	3,881	3,958	4,038
Utilities/Telephone/Lease Equip.	3,060	3,121	3,184	3,247	3,312	3,378	3,446	3,515	3,585	3,657	3,730	3,805	3,881	3,958	4,038
Medical Supplies & Drugs	6,375	6,503	6,633	6,765	6,901	7,039	7,179	7,323	7,469	7,619	7,771	7,927	8,085	8,247	8,412
Laboratory	2,550	2,601	2,653	2,706	2,760	2,815	2,872	2,929	2,988	3,047	3,108	3,171	3,234	3,299	3,365
Malpractice Insurance	4,590	4,682	4,775	4,871	4,968	5,068	5,169	5,272	5,378	5,485	5,595	5,707	5,821	5,938	6,056
Advertising/Public Relations	2,040	2,081	2,122	2,165	2,208	2,252	2,297	2,343	2,390	2,438	2,487	2,536	2,587	2,639	2,692
Professional Services	3,060	3,121	3,184	3,247	3,312	3,378	3,446	3,515	3,585	3,657	3,730	3,805	3,881	3,958	4,038
Continuing Education	2,040	2,081	2,122	2,165	2,208	2,252	2,297	2,343	2,390	2,438	2,487	2,536	2,587	2,639	2,692
Subtotal, Non-physician Expenses	107,645	110,617	113,690	116,866	120,152	123,550	127,067	130,705	134,472	138,371	142,409	146,592	150,924	155,414	160,066
Total Direct Expenses	251,645	254,617	257,690	260,866	264,152	267,550	271,067	274,705	278,472	282,371	286,409	290,592	294,924	299,414	304,066
Collections Net of Direct Expenses	(1,645)	20,383	42,310	48,134	54,118	60,268	66,586	73,077	79,744	86,591	93,622	100,840	108,251	115,857	123,662
Physician Bonus (50% of collections in excess of 300,000)	0	0	0	4,500	9,135	13,909	18,826	23,891	29,108	34,481	40,016	45,716	51,587	57,635	63,864
Earnings Before Depreciation and Interest	(1,645)	20,383	42,310	43,634	44,983	46,359	47,760	49,186	50,636	52,110	53,606	55,124	56,663	58,222	59,798
Depreciation	5,000	5,000	5,000	5,000	5,000	0	0	0	0	0	0	0	0	0	0
Cash Flow	(1,645)	20,383	42,310	43,634	44,983	46,359	47,760	49,186	50,636	52,110	53,606	55,124	56,663	58,222	59,798
Amortization of Purchase Price	26,667	26,667	26,667	0	0	0	0	0	0	0	0	0	0	0	0
Net Earnings (Loss)	($33,312)	($11,284)	$10,644	$38,634	$39,983	$46,359	$47,760	$49,186	$50,636	$52,110	$53,606	$55,124	$56,663	$58,222	$59,798
Accumulated Earnings (Loss)	(33,312)	(44,596)	(33,952)	4,681	44,665	91,023	138,783	187,969	238,605	290,714	344,320	399,445	456,108	514,329	574,127
Excess Cash Flow Used To Repay Debt	(1,645)	20,383	42,310	18,952	0	0	0	0	0	0	0	0	0	0	0
Accumulated Excess Cash Flow	0	0	0	24,681	69,665	116,023	163,783	212,969	263,605	315,714	369,320	424,445	481,108	539,329	599,127

Highlights

- Practice has positive cash flow in year two (2).
- Practice repays capital investment in year four (4), assuming all excess cash is used to repay debt.
- Practice is profitable in year three (3).
- Inception-to-date profitability is achieved in year four (4).

Dr John Doe: Pro Forma Income Statement, 5-year Amortization of Purchase Price

Year	2011	2012	2013	2014	2015	2016	2017	2018	2019	2020	2021	2022	2023	2024	2025
Year Number	1	2	3	4	5	6	7	8	9	10	11	12	13	14	15
Collections	250,000	275,000	300,000	309,000	318,270	327,818	337,653	347,782	358,216	368,962	380,031	391,432	403,175	415,270	427,728
Physician Base Compensation	120,000	120,000	120,000	120,000	120,000	120,000	120,000	120,000	120,000	120,000	120,000	120,000	120,000	120,000	120,000
Physician Benefit Expense	24,000	24,000	24,000	24,000	24,000	24,000	24,000	24,000	24,000	24,000	24,000	24,000	24,000	24,000	24,000
Payroll, Office Staff	37,842	38,599	39,371	40,158	40,961	41,781	42,616	43,469	44,338	45,225	46,129	47,052	47,993	48,953	49,932
Employee Benefits	7,568	7,720	7,874	8,032	8,192	8,356	8,523	8,694	8,868	9,045	9,226	9,410	9,599	9,791	9,986
Office Rent	27,300	28,665	30,098	31,603	33,183	34,842	36,585	38,414	40,335	42,351	44,469	48,692	49,027	51,478	54,052
Office Expenses	8,160	8,323	8,490	8,659	8,833	9,009	9,189	9,373	9,561	9,752	9,947	10,146	10,349	10,556	10,767
Office Maintenance Expenses	3,060	3,121	3,184	3,247	3,312	3,378	3,446	3,515	3,585	3,657	3,730	3,805	3,881	3,958	4,038
Utilities/Telephone/Lease Equip.	3,060	3,121	3,184	3,247	3,312	3,378	3,446	3,515	3,585	3,657	3,730	3,805	3,881	3,958	4,038
Medical Supplies & Drugs	6,375	6,503	6,633	6,765	6,901	7,039	7,179	7,323	7,469	7,619	7,771	7,927	8,085	8,247	8,412
Laboratory	2,550	2,601	2,653	2,706	2,760	2,815	2,872	2,929	2,988	3,047	3,108	3,171	3,234	3,299	3,365
Malpractice Insurance	4,590	4,682	4,775	4,871	4,968	5,068	5,169	5,272	5,378	5,485	5,595	5,707	5,821	5,938	6,056
Advertising/Public Relations	2,040	2,081	2,122	2,165	2,208	2,252	2,297	2,343	2,390	2,438	2,487	2,536	2,587	2,639	2,692
Professional Services	3,060	3,121	3,184	3,247	3,312	3,378	3,446	3,515	3,585	3,657	3,730	3,805	3,881	3,958	4,038
Continuing Education	2,040	2,081	2,122	2,165	2,208	2,252	2,297	2,343	2,390	2,438	2,487	2,536	2,587	2,639	2,692
Subtotal, Non-physician Expenses	107,645	110,617	113,690	116,866	120,152	123,550	127,067	130,705	134,472	138,371	142,409	146,592	150,924	155,414	160,066
Total Direct Expenses	251,645	254,617	257,690	260,866	264,152	267,550	271,067	274,705	278,472	282,371	286,409	290,592	294,924	299,414	304,066
Collections Net of Direct Expenses	(1,645)	20,383	42,310	48,134	54,118	60,268	66,586	73,077	79,744	86,591	93,622	100,840	108,251	115,857	123,662
Physician Bonus (50% of collections in excess of 300,000)	0	0	0	4,500	9,135	13,909	18,826	23,891	29,108	34,481	40,016	45,716	51,587	57,635	63,864
Earnings Before Depreciation and Interest	(1,645)	20,383	42,310	43,634	44,983	46,359	47,760	49,186	50,636	52,110	53,606	55,124	56,663	58,222	59,798
Depreciation	5,000	5,000	5,000	5,000	5,000	0	0	0	0	0	0	0	0	0	0
Cash Flow	(1,645)	20,383	42,310	43,634	44,983	46,359	47,760	49,186	50,636	52,110	53,606	55,124	56,663	58,222	59,798
Amortization of Purchase Price	16,000	16,000	16,000	16,000	16,000	0	0	0	0	0	0	0	0	0	0
Net Earnings (Loss)	($22,645)	($617)	$21,310	$22,634	$23,983	$46,359	$47,760	$49,186	$50,636	$52,110	$53,606	$55,124	$56,663	$58,222	$59,798
Accumulated Earnings (Loss)	(22,645)	(23,263)	(1,952)	20,681	44,665	91,023	138,783	187,969	238,605	290,714	344,320	399,445	456,108	514,329	574,127
Excess Cash Flow Used To Repay Debt	(1,645)	20,383	42,310	18,952	0	0	0	0	0	0	0	0	0	0	0
Accumulated Excess Cash Flow	0	0	0	24,681	69,665	116,023	163,783	212,969	263,605	315,714	369,320	424,445	481,108	539,329	599,127

Highlights

- Practice has positive cash flow in year two (2).
- Practice repays capital investment in year four (4), assuming all excess cash is used to repay debt.
- Practice is profitable in year three (3).
- Inception-to-date profitability is achieved in year four (4).

Dr John Doe: Pro Forma Income Statement, 7-year Amortization of Purchase Price

Year	2011	2012	2013	2014	2015	2016	2017	2018	2019	2020	2021	2022	2023	2024	2025
Year Number	1	2	3	4	5	6	7	8	9	10	11	12	13	14	15
Collections	250,000	275,000	300,000	309,000	318,270	327,818	337,653	347,782	358,216	368,962	380,031	391,432	403,175	415,270	427,728
Physician Base Compensation	120,000	120,000	120,000	120,000	120,000	120,000	120,000	120,000	120,000	120,000	120,000	120,000	120,000	120,000	120,000
Physician Benefit Expense	24,000	24,000	24,000	24,000	24,000	24,000	24,000	24,000	24,000	24,000	24,000	24,000	24,000	24,000	24,000
Payroll, Office Staff	37,842	38,599	39,371	40,158	40,961	41,781	42,616	43,469	44,338	45,225	46,129	47,052	47,993	48,953	49,932
Employee Benefits	7,568	7,720	7,874	8,032	8,192	8,356	8,523	8,694	8,868	9,045	9,226	9,410	9,599	9,791	9,986
Office Rent	27,300	28,665	30,098	31,603	33,183	34,842	36,585	38,414	40,335	42,351	44,469	48,692	49,027	51,478	54,052
Office Expenses	8,160	8,323	8,490	8,659	8,833	9,009	9,189	9,373	9,561	9,752	9,947	10,146	10,349	10,556	10,767
Office Maintenance Expenses	3,060	3,121	3,184	3,247	3,312	3,378	3,446	3,515	3,585	3,657	3,730	3,805	3,881	3,958	4,038
Utilities/Telephone/Lease Equip.	3,060	3,121	3,184	3,247	3,312	3,378	3,446	3,515	3,585	3,657	3,730	3,805	3,881	3,958	4,038
Medical Supplies & Drugs	6,375	6,503	6,633	6,765	6,901	7,039	7,179	7,323	7,469	7,619	7,771	7,927	8,085	8,247	8,412
Laboratory 2,550	2,601	2,653	2,706	2,760	2,815	2,872	2,929	2,988	3,047	3,108	3,171	3,234	3,299	3,365	
Malpractice Insurance	4,590	4,682	4,775	4,871	4,968	5,068	5,169	5,272	5,378	5,485	5,595	5,707	5,821	5,938	6,056
Advertising/Public Relations	2,040	2,081	2,122	2,165	2,208	2,252	2,297	2,343	2,390	2,438	2,487	2,536	2,587	2,639	2,692
Professional Services	3,060	3,121	3,184	3,247	3,312	3,378	3,446	3,515	3,585	3,657	3,730	3,805	3,881	3,958	4,038
Continuing Education	2,040	2,081	2,122	2,165	2,208	2,252	2,297	2,343	2,390	2,438	2,487	2,536	2,587	2,639	2,692
Subtotal, Non-physician Expenses	107,645	110,617	113,690	116,866	120,152	123,550	127,067	130,705	134,472	138,371	142,409	146,592	150,924	155,414	160,066
Total Direct Expenses	251,645	254,617	257,690	260,866	264,152	267,550	271,067	274,705	278,472	282,371	286,409	290,592	294,924	299,414	304,066
Collections Net of Direct Expenses	(1,645)	20,383	42,310	48,134	54,118	60,268	66,586	73,077	79,744	86,591	93,622	100,840	108,251	115,857	123,662
Physician Bonus															
(50% of collections in excess of 300,000)	0	0	0	4,500	9,135	13,909	18,826	23,891	29,108	34,481	40,016	45,716	51,587	57,635	63,864
Earnings Before Depreciation and Interest	(1,645)	20,383	42,310	43,634	44,983	46,359	47,760	49,186	50,636	52,110	53,606	55,124	56,663	58,222	59,798
Depreciation	5,000	5,000	5,000	5,000	5,000	0	0	0	0	0	0	0	0	0	0
Cash Flow	(1,645)	20,383	42,310	43,634	44,983	46,359	47,760	49,186	50,636	52,110	53,606	55,124	56,663	58,222	59,798
Amortization of Purchase Price	11,429	11,429	11,429	11,429	11,429	11,429	11,429	0	0	0	0	0	0	0	0
Net Earnings (Loss)	($18,074)	$3,954	$25,882	$27,205	$28,555	$34,930	$36,331	$49,186	$50,636	$52,110	$53,606	$55,124	$56,663	$58,222	$59,798
Accumulated Earnings (Loss)	(18,074)	(14,120)	11,762	38,967	67,522	102,452	138,783	187,969	238,605	290,714	344,320	399,445	456,108	514,329	574,127
Excess Cash Flow Used To Repay Debt	(1,645)	20,383	42,310	18,952	0	0	0	0	0	0	0	0	0	0	0
Accumulated Excess Cash Flow	0	0	0	24,681	69,665	116,023	163,783	212,969	263,605	315,714	369,320	424,445	481,108	539,329	599,127

Highlights

- Practice has positive cash flow in year two (2).
- Practice repays capital investment in year four (4), assuming all excess cash is used to repay debt.
- Practice is profitable in year three (3).
- Inception-to-date profitability is achieved in year four (4).

GLOSSARY

This glossary serves as a reference relative to the terms and language associated with operations, reimbursement, and economic decision making within a medical practice. These terms help to standardize and clarify the business aspect of clinical medicine.

A

Account Payable   A debt owed to a creditor, often as a result of the purchase of merchandise, materials, supplies, or services. An account payable is normally a current liability resulting from day-to-day operations of the practice.

Account Receivable   A charge against a debtor, often from sales or services rendered. This receivable is not necessarily due or past due. An account receivable is the opposite of an *account payable* and is normally a current asset arising from standard business operations.

Accountable Care Organization (ACO)   A model of integrated care formulated to reduce costs and improve quality. ACOs are regulated by the Centers for Medicare and Medicaid. CMS formally defines ACO as an organization of health care providers that agrees to be accountable for the quality, cost, and overall care of Medicare beneficiaries who are enrolled in a traditional fee-for-service program.

Age Discrimination in Employment Act of 1967 (ADEA)   Act that prohibits discrimination in employment for persons age 40 and over.

Ambulatory Surgery Center (ASC)   An ASC is a health care facility that specializes in providing surgery, including certain pain management and diagnostic (eg, colonoscopy) services in an outpatient setting. ASC-qualified procedures can be considered more intensive than those done in the average doctor's office but not intensive enough to require a hospital stay. ASCs do not routinely provide emergency services to patients who have not been admitted to the ASC for another procedure. Also known as *outpatient surgery centers* or *same day surgery centers.*

Americans with Disabilities Act of 1990 (ADA)   An act that prohibits discrimination against a qualified individual with a disability because of his/her disability.

Application Service Provider (ASP)   A third-party entity that manages and distributes software-based services and solutions to customers across a wide area network from a central data center. ASPs are a way for companies to outsource some or almost all aspects of their information technology needs.

B

Bylaws   Written rules adopted by the shareholders of a corporation that govern its internal management and specify the procedures for carrying out the functions of the organization.

C

Capitated Plans   Under a capitated plan, health care service providers are paid a set amount for each enrolled person assigned to that physician or group of physicians, whether or not that person seeks care, per period of time. Providers who work under these plans focus on preventive health care as they will be financially rewarded more to keep a person from becoming ill than to treat them once they have become so.

Capitation   A method of reimbursement under managed care plans where professional providers receive a fixed fee per member per month for each of the plan's enrollees who have selected them as their primary care providers.

Certified Public Accountant (CPA)   An accountant certified by a state examining board as having fulfilled the requirements of state law to be a public accountant.

Chart of Accounts   A systematic list of all accounts in a general ledger, each accompanied by a reference number.

Clinical Laboratories Improvement Act (CLIA)   Federal law designed to set national quality standards for laboratory testing. The law covers all laboratories that engage in testing for assessment, diagnosis, prevention, or treatment purposes.

Commercial General Liability Coverage   Coverage for an insured when negligent acts and/or omissions result in bodily injury and/or property damage on the premises of a business, when someone is injured as the result of using the product manufactured or distributed by a business, or when someone is injured in the general operation of a business.

Consumer Price Index   A measure of inflation that measures the change in the cost of a fixed basket of products and services, including housing, electricity, food, and transportation. Also called *cost-of-living index.*

Controlled Substances Act of 1970   An act that regulates the prescribing and dispensing of psychoactive drugs, including narcotics, stimulants, depressants, and hallucinogens.

Corporation   Business organization authorized by a state (through a process called *incorporation*) to operate under the rules of the entity's charter.

Corporation C (C Corp) or S (S Corp)   The C corporation is the standard corporation, while the S corporation has elected a special tax status with the IRS. It gets its name because it is defined in Subchapter S of the Internal Revenue Code. To elect S corporation status when forming a corporation, Form 2553 must be filed with the IRS and all S corporation guidelines met.

D

Department of Health and Human Services (HHS)   A cabinet-level department of the US government with responsibility for the functions of various federal social welfare and health delivery agencies, such as the Food and Drug Administration. It also directs the US Office of Consumer Affairs, Office of Civil Rights, Administration on Aging, Public Health Service, Indian Health Service, Social Security Administration, and National Institutes of Health.

Department of Justice (DOJ)   The US federal department responsible for enforcing federal laws (including the enforcement of all civil rights legislation).

Department of Labor (DOL)   The US federal department responsible for promoting the working conditions of wage earners. The department's responsibilities include administering and enforcing federal labor laws guaranteeing workers' rights to safe and healthful working conditions, a minimum hourly wage and overtime pay, freedom from employment discrimination, unemployment insurance, and workers' compensation.

Drug Enforcement Agency (DEA) Federal agency responsible for enforcing laws and regulations governing narcotics and controlled substances; its goal is to immobilize drug trafficking organizations.

Due Diligence An investigation or audit of a potential investment. Due diligence serves to confirm all material facts in regard to a sale. Generally, due diligence refers to the care a reasonable person should take to obtain all the material facts before entering into an agreement or transaction with another party.

E

Employee Identification Number (EIN) A unique numerical identifier which is used to identify businesses, partnerships, or other entities. This number is used by the IRS for tax-related purposes.

Enterprise Value (EV) A measure of a company's value, often used as an alternative to straightforward market capitalization. Enterprise value is calculated as market cap plus debt, minority interest and preferred shares, minus total cash and cash equivalents.

Equal Employment Opportunity Commission (EEOC) The US Equal Employment Opportunity Commission (EEOC) is responsible for enforcing federal laws that make it illegal to discriminate against a job applicant or an employee because of the person's race, color, religion, sex (including pregnancy), national origin, age (40 or older), disability, or genetic information. Most employers with at least 15 employees are covered by EEOC laws (20 employees in age discrimination cases). Most labor unions and employment agencies are also covered. The laws apply to all types of work situations, including hiring, firing, promotions, harassment, training, wages, and benefits.

Equal Pay Act (EPA) Act that prohibits wage discrimination by requiring equal pay for equal work.

F

Fair Labor Standards Act (FLSA) An act that regulates employee status, overtime pay, child labor, minimum wage, record keeping, and other administrative concerns.

Fair Market Value Value (price) negotiated at arm's length between a willing buyer and a willing seller, each acting rationally in his or her own self-interest with knowledge of all relevant facts.

Family and Medical Leave Act (FMLA) An act that provides employees with up to 12 weeks of unpaid leave to care for family members or because of a serious health condition of the employee.

G

Generally Accepted Accounting Principles (GAAP) Standards, conventions, and rules accountants follow in recording and summarizing transactions, and in the preparation of financial statements. GAAP are a combination of authoritative standards (set by policy boards) and simply the commonly accepted ways of recording and reporting accounting information.

Genetic Information Information about an individual's genetic tests and the genetic tests of an individual's family members, as well as information about the manifestation of a disease or disorder in an individual's family members (ie, family medical history). Family medical history is included because it is often used to determine whether someone has an increased risk of getting a disease, disorder, or condition in the future.

Genetic Information Nondiscrimination Act (GINA)   An act that prohibits discrimination against individuals on the basis of their genetic information in both employment and health care.

Geographic Practice Cost Index (GPCI)   Numerical values that adjust each relative value unit (RVU) component to account for geographic differences, primarily in practice cost and malpractice risk.

Group Practice or Partnership   A group of persons licensed to practice medicine in the state, who, as their principal professional activity, and as a group responsibility, engage or undertake to engage in the coordinated practice of their profession primarily in one or more group practice facilities, and who (in their connection) share common overhead expenses (if such expenses are paid by the members of the group), medical and other records, and substantial portions of the equipment and the professional, technical, and administrative staffs.

H

Health Insurance Portability and Accountability Act (HIPAA)   Law designed to provide privacy standards to protect patients' medical records and other health information provided to health plans, doctors, hospitals and other health care providers. Developed by the Department of Health and Human Services, these standards provide patients with access to their medical records and more control over how their personal health information is used and disclosed.

Health Maintenance Organization (HMO)   An organization responsible for providing or arranging the provision of comprehensive health care services on a prepayment basis to voluntarily enrolled persons within a designated population. The providers are aligned and under contract with the plan for a fixed and periodic payment. When an HMO purchases an institution that delivers health care, this model is fully integrated because both financing and delivery of care are provided to the enrolled members.

I

Independent Physician Associations (IPA)   Entities formed by physicians, sometimes with another health care provider, such as a hospital. Generally, they are formed to provide a vehicle for effective contracting with managed care purchasers. IPAs contract with HMOs, PPOs, and other managed care companies to provide professional medical services. They differ from group practices in that IPA practices remain independent. Also known as *independent practice associations*.

Information Services Organization (ISO)   An organization formed to assist medical practices with their technology needs. Typically, practices outsource to an ISO to procure hardware and support.

J

Joint Commission on Accreditation of Healthcare Organizations (JCAHO)   A private, voluntary, not-for-profit group that provides accreditation to US hospitals and other health care facilities (long-term care, mental health, ambulatory care).

L

Limited Liability Corporation (LLC)   A business structure allowed by state statute. LLCs are popular because, similar to a corporation, owners have limited personal liability for the debts and actions of the LLC. Other features of LLCs are more like a partnership, providing management flexibility and the benefit of pass-through taxation.

M

Maldistribution   Faulty, unequal, or unfair distribution. For example, the attraction of urban and suburban areas creates a maldistribution of health care providers.

Malpractice Insurance   Insurance against the risk of suffering financial damage because of professional misconduct or lack of ordinary skill. Malpractice requires that the patient prove some injury and that the injury was the result of negligence on the part of the professional.

Management Service Organization (MSO)   An organization formed to provide a cross section of business functions, primarily for administrative management services for physician practices. However, sometimes the primary purpose is for managed care contracting. MSOs may also be structured to purchase physician practices and conduct administrative functions for other practices that may not be purchased. Services include accounting, billing, facility management, utilization review, consulting, computer software installation and support, professional fees, marketing, personnel services, etc. Financial arrangements of MSOs are varied. Ownership could include a combination of physicians, hospital, or each of them individually or even include a health care company and insurance company or private investors.

Meaningful Use (MU)   Meaningful use, in a health information technology (HIT) context, is a yet to be determined critical level for the use of electronic health records (EHR) and related technology within a health care organization. According to the provisions of the Healthcare Information Technology for Economic and Clinical Health Act (HITECH), health care organizations that have achieved meaningful use by 2011 will be eligible for incentive payments; those who have failed to achieve that standard by 2015 may be penalized.

Medicaid Provider Number   Refers to the number under which a beneficiary files Medicaid claims. It helps to identify the health care consumer.

Medicare Provider Number   Refers to the number that uniquely identifies a health care provider and is used on billing forms submitted to Medicare.

N

National Conversion Factor (CF)   A dollar amount multiplied by an RVU to calculate total payment for a unique CPT code: Total payment ($) = CF ($) × RVU. The 2011 National Conversion Factor is 33.9674.

Net Asset Value (NAV)   The value of an entity's assets less the value of its liabilities.

O

Occupational Safety and Health Administration (OSHA)   US government agency that administers the Occupational Safety and Health Act of 1970. This act established minimum health and safety standards for workers and provides for the inspection of places of employment and the penalizing of employers who do not provide conditions that meet the established standards.

Office of the Inspector General (OIG)   A division of the Department of Justice (DOJ) that conducts independent investigations, audits, inspections, and special reviews of US Department of Justice personnel and programs to detect and deter waste, fraud, abuse, and misconduct, and to promote integrity, economy, efficiency, and effectiveness in Department of Justice operations.

OHSA Guidelines for Bloodborne Pathogens   OSHA'S bloodborne pathogens guidelines protect employees who work in occupations where they are at risk of exposure to blood or other potentially infectious materials.

OSHA Hazard Communication Standard   Mandate states that companies producing and using hazardous materials must provide employees with information and training on the proper handling and use of these materials.

P

Partnership   Relationship between two or more people who share resources and operations in a jointly run organization. Partners (also called *owners*) share the profits and losses incurred for the business in which they have invested.

Personal Digital Assistant (PDA)   A term for any small mobile handheld device that provides computing and information storage and retrieval capabilities for personal or business use, often for keeping schedule calendars and address book information.

Physician Quality and Reporting System (PQRS)   The PQRS program provides a financial incentive to eligible professionals for voluntarily reporting data on specific quality measures applied to the Medicare population.

Point of Service Plans (POS)   A health care option that allows members to choose at the time medical services are needed whether they will go to a provider within the plan's network or seek medical care outside the network. Members are encouraged, but not required, to choose a primary care physician. Subscribers who choose not to use the primary care physician must pay higher deductibles and copayments than those using network physicians.

Preferred Provider Organization (PPO)   A plan or an organization that contracts with a specific and limited list of independent providers at a discounted fee for service in exchange for a channeled (or directed) patient base.

Pregnancy Discrimination Act of 1972   An amendment to Title VII of the Civil Rights Act of 1964 that prevents discrimination on the basis of pregnancy, childbirth, or related medical conditions, which constitute unlawful sex discrimination. The act states that women who are pregnant must be treated in the same manner as other applicants or employees with similar abilities or limitations.

Professional Liability Insurance   Since basic liability policies do not protect against situations arising out of business or professional pursuits, professional liability insurance is purchased by individuals who hold themselves out to the general public as having greater than average expertise in particular areas (ie, specialists in various professional fields).

Professional Limited Liability Corporation (PLLC)   Similar to a professional corporation in that both are organized for the purpose of providing professional services. Professionals—such as accountants, architects, lawyers, engineers, chiropractors, dentists, and doctors—are permitted in many states to form a standard LLC. However, some states require that these individuals form a PLLC, a similar but distinct entity from the limited liability company.

R

Railroad Retirement Board (RRB)   An independent agency in the executive branch of the US government created to administer a social insurance program providing retirement benefits to the country's railroad workers. The RRB serves US railroad workers and their families, and administers retirement, survivor, unemployment, and sickness benefits.

Relative Value Unit (RVU)   A numerical value that depicts the amount of physician effort, risk, and resources for one service relative to all others.

Resource-Based Relative Value System (RBRVS)   A system of valuing physician services developed by researchers at the Harvard School of Public Health and implemented by the Medicare program in 1992.

S

Services Employment and Reemployment Rights Act of 1994 (USERRA)   This act covers virtually every individual who serves in or has served in the uniformed services and applies to all employers in the public and private sectors, including federal employers. The law seeks to ensure that those who serve their country can retain their civilian employment and benefits and can seek employment free from discrimination because of their service. USERRA provides protection for disabled veterans, requiring employers to make reasonable efforts to accommodate the disability, and also provides employees with Department of Labor assistance in processing claims.

Sole Proprietorship   A business owned by a single individual.

Sub S Corporation   A corporation whose profits and losses are taxed to its owners on their individual income tax returns instead of being taxed as a corporation. Subchapter S status allows a corporation the limited liability benefits of a corporation with the tax benefits of taxation at the personal tax rate.

T

Tail Insurance   A malpractice insurance rider or supplement to a claims-made policy that provides coverage for an incident that occurred while the insurance was in effect but was not filed by the time the insurer-policyholder relationship terminated. (As an example, a physician is in private practice from 2000 to 2010 and then goes into hospital employment starting in 2011. At the onset of the new practice situation, the physician would procure a tail policy that covers any claims that could arise in the future that pertain to the 2000–2010 period when in private practice.)

Title VII of the Civil Rights Act of 1964   Act that prohibits discrimination by covered employers on the basis of race, color, religion, sex, or national origin. Title VII also prohibits discrimination against an individual because of his or her association with another individual of a particular race, color, religion, sex, or national origin.

W

Windows CE© Device   Windows CE is based on the Microsoft Windows operating system, but it is designed for including or embedding in mobile and other space-constrained devices. Although Microsoft does not explain the *CE,* it reportedly stood for "Consumer Electronics."

Workers' Compensation Insurance   A state-mandated insurance program that provides benefits for health care costs and lost wages to qualified employees and their dependants if an employee suffers a work-related injury or disease.

INDEX

Page numbers in italics indicate figures and tables. For information about individual medical specialties, see entries under "Societies, medical" and "Specialties, medical."